HIPAA in Practice

The Health Information Manager's Perspective

AHIMA HIM Products and Services Team

AHIMA

American Health Information
Management Association®

ISBN 1-58426-061-0
AHIMA Product No. AB104004
Production No. IPC 1000-504

AHIMA Staff:
  Harry Rhodes, MBA, RHIA,CHP, Director of HIM Products and Services
  Beth Hjort, RHIA, CHP, Professional Practice Manager
  Marcia Loellbach, MS, Project Editor
  Sarah Aho, College of St. Scholastica, Reviewer

AHIMA strives to recognize the value of people from every racial and ethnic background as well as all genders, age groups, and sexual orientations by building its membership and leadership resources to reflect the rich diversity of the American population. AHIMA encourages the celebration and promotion of human diversity through education, mentoring, recognition, leadership, and other programs.

American Health Information Management Association
233 North Michigan Avenue, Suite 2150
Chicago, Illinois 60601-5800

http://www.ahima.org

Contents

Part 3   **Facilitating and Controlling Patient Access**

Part 4   **Disclosing Health Record Information**

Part 5   **Copying, Printing, and Transmitting Health Information**

Acknowledgments

We acknowledge with thanks the work of those individuals who authored or contributed to the practice briefs, position statements, and journal articles contained in this book.

Margret Amatayakul, MBA, RHIA, CHPS, FHIMSS
Gordon Apple, JD
Holly Ballam, RHIA
Londa Bechert, RHIA
Sue Biedermann, MSHP, RHIA
Rita K. Bowen, MA, RHIA, CHP
Mary Brandt, MBA, RHIA, CHE, CHP
Jill Burrington-Brown, MS, RHIA
Jill Callahan Dennis, JD, RHIA
Michelle Dougherty, RHIA
Rose Dunn, RHIA, CPA, FACHE
Lorraine Fernandes, RHIA
Donna Fletcher, MPA, RHIA
Joseph Fodor
Sandra R. Fuller, MA, RHIA
Karen G. Grant, RHIA, CHP
Steven Greenberg, RHIA
Pamela T. Haines, RHIA
Joseph Harford, MS
Beth Hjort, RHIA, CHP
Gwen Hughes, RHIA, CHP
Simone Handler Hutchinson, Esq.
Merida L. Johns, PhD, RHIA
Tim Keough, MPA, RHIA
Claire Dixon Lee, PhD, RHIA
Michael R. Lee
Robbyn Lessig, RHIA, CIS
Chris Mansueti
Connie Matthews

Kelly McLendon, RHIA
Dale Miller, CISSP, CHP
Donald P. Mon, PhD
Gretchen Murphy, MEd, RHIA
Sandra Nutten
Carole Okamoto, MBA, RHIA, CPHQ
Brenda Olson, RHIA, CHP
Monica Pappas, RHIA
Carol Ann Quinsey, RHIA, CHPS
Harry B. Rhodes, MBA, RHIA, CHP
Lynn Richards, RHIA
Dan Rode, MBA, FHFMA
Julie A. Roth, MHSA, JD, RHIA
Ron Roth
Michael Ruano, CHS
Cheryl M. Smith, RHIT, CPHQ
David Sobel, PhD, CHP
Marsha Steele, RHIA
Mary Thomason, RHIA, CHP
Jonathan P. Tomes, JD
Shawn Trimble
Dorothy Grandolfi Wagg, JD, RHIA, CHP (In Memoriam)
Tom Walsh, CISSP
Pam Waymack
Abner E. Weintraub
Vicki Wheatley, RHIA, MS
William Woloszyn, RHIA

Introduction

Beth Hjort, RHIA, CHP

Since the mid-1990s, the American Health Information Management Association (AHIMA) has shepherded the health information management (HIM) profession through revolutionary changes in privacy and confidentiality law. With articles, practice briefs, and position statements over the past several years, AHIMA has helped clarify and anchor the Health Insurance Portability and Accountability Act of 1996 (HIPAA) for HIM professionals and their employers. *HIPAA in Practice: The Health Information Manager's Perspective* is a compilation of these guiding materials.

Every American, from the beginning to the end of life, enjoys a fundamental, but somewhat fragile, right to privacy that is rooted in both tradition and law. There is no arena in which this right is more cherished or more unsettled than in the confidentiality of personally identifiable health information. Lawmakers, judges, and healthcare professionals are constantly struggling to balance individual privacy interests with the interests of the larger society. The Hippocratic Oath, which dates from the fourth or fifth century B.C., requires physicians to protect all knowledge of individual patients "which ought not to be spread abroad." In the modern world, however, the reality is that health information is seen by more than just patient and physician.

Personal health information is maintained not only by physicians, but also in the records and databases of hospitals and clinics, laboratories, pharmacies, insurance companies, and managed care organizations. Personal health data are frequently shared with universities and pharmaceutical companies for medical and health-service research purposes. By law, certain medical information must be reported to state and local governments. This information is then disseminated by mandate from databases to public health agencies and law enforcement agencies.

Efficient availability of medical information has numerous benefits for both individuals and societies. The ability to access medical information has saved the lives of unconscious patients brought to hospital emergency departments. Pharmacists detect dangerous, sometimes potentially lethal, drug combinations. Public health authorities are able to promptly detect and take emergency action against infectious disease epidemics thanks to computerized records. Researchers use databases to analyze the causes of illness (AHIMA 1999).

Yet, these legitimate forms of health information dissemination create legitimate confidentiality concerns. Our current hybrid environment of paper-based and electronic media focuses HIM attention on the fact that individually-identifiable health information should be made available only for the right reasons, to the appropriate people, and to the extent necessary.

As we follow the continuum of United States privacy and security developments, the convergence of related and emerging issues is unmistakable.

Administrative Simplification

In the mid 1990s, complexities and inequities in the healthcare system gave rise on August 21, 1996, to Public Law 104-191, later to become known as HIPAA. The ensuing industry stir over the nation's first uniform privacy and security laws embedded in the new public law all but camouflaged the law's original mission. The multifaceted intentions to simplify claims processing, impact waste, address health insurance coverage, and combat fraud and abuse, among others, promulgated an "if-then" reaction to the Administrative Simplification portion of the law. If our claims are processed through electronic means, then standardization is needed and the issues of privacy and security inherent in electronic transmission must be dealt with along with efficiency and cost-effectiveness improvements.

Patient Rights

With the HIPAA privacy rule, a patient's right to privacy and the security of his or her health information, beyond claims, became a national focus for the first time in U.S. history. With the creation of HIPAA, all U.S. healthcare providers must comply no matter where they operate or what type of service they deliver. Patients now have broader rights and a say in how their protected health information (PHI) is used. Individuals who seek healthcare services in different states due to referral or relocation will no longer be party to such disparate privacy and security protections. Consumer attention has been aroused, while consumer involvement and interest have been enhanced.

Medical Errors

Healthcare industry and public concern were stirred with the publication of the high incidence of medical errors in our country. Perhaps more alarming than the numbers cited by the Institute of Medicine in separate reports over the past several years (IOM 1999, 2001, 2004) is the fact that many more medical errors go unreported. These atrocious findings, often due to systems problems and human error, are believed largely reversible by the use of available, advanced information technologies.

Patient Safety

Patient safety concerns are a significant impetus behind the current national push to develop the functionality and standardization necessary for industry adoption of the electronic health record (EHR) and the National Health Information Infrastructure (NHII). Federal and industry leaders are working together to expedite the development of both.

The potential breadth and depth of the uses of individual and aggregated electronic health data is both staggering and exciting when one considers the exponential strides that could be made in healthcare knowledge, disease management, and bioterrorism responsiveness when widespread electronic medical data become useable information.

The intertwined nature of these issues leads one to see the importance of moving toward a universally adopted electronic healthcare environment and to see that the commitment to privacy and security is one that will endure amidst a changing healthcare industry and world. Privacy and security issues are tightly woven with other critical issues on the healthcare horizon.

By asserting health information and privacy and security knowledge, health information managers have made, and will continue to make, a difference. AHIMA and its members are guided by the principle that confidentiality is essential in fostering trust between patients and healthcare providers. This principle will not change. Healthcare data, no matter how easily accessed, will only be complete and accurate if individuals feel safe enough to share private information openly with caregivers.

Questions of the confidentially of individually-identifiable patient information have been of primary concern for AHIMA since the association was founded in 1928. HIM professionals have guided healthcare organizations through the complexities and inconsistencies of disparate privacy "marching orders." They have been leaders in organizational policy development, helping to balance state directives with a number of impacting factors: federal laws and regulations, developing case law, accreditation standards, and the emergence of industry best practices. Policy customization has been necessary to ensure compliance on all fronts. HIM professionals have used patient confidentiality rights as a filter through which they have made decisions for as long as the HIM profession has been in existence.

HIPAA brought an opportunity to re-evaluate, renew and, in come cases, restructure privacy policies and procedures. But the ingrained knowledge of HIM practitioners remained the foundation on which those changes were launched. Despite the nuances in the new law and adaptations necessary for compliance, HIM professionals were no strangers to the interpretation confusion that it brought. They have been making sense of overlapping and conflictive messages throughout the ages. And they continue to lead the process, though now the gatekeeping challenges are changing with the increasing prevalence of the electronic medium.

Although anyone could launch a Web search to increase his or her HIM-related HIPAA knowledge, it would not have yielded a convenient compendium such as *HIPAA in Practice*. Interpretation of HIPAA regulations can be an art, even for those with decades of privacy and security background. Even though the Department of Health and Human Services has made it clear that the implications of HIPAA regulations will be carefully watched as they are put into practice, we are bound to them until further changes are announced. This includes the sticky situations of compromised care because of regulatory misinterpretation.

It can be seen from the following articles, practice briefs, and position statements that although there is now a federal floor, there remain myriad impacting factors that HIM professionals must balance as privacy leaders. These works represent the settling of the privacy and security rules to their current state of existence in conjunction with the other factors.

Although the privacy rule was launched a year prior to publication of this work, government sentiment is that "while the rule may settle, it *will* remain." The security rule, currently in its two-year preparation period and slated for implementation on April 21, 2005, has not shown the same level of volatility in its progression to a final stage as did the privacy law. These documents are expected to remain current, as they follow industry security best practices.

Our readers can think of these readings individually and collectively as research done for them by both AHIMA in its goal to serve member needs and by the authors, who set out to answer hard questions and present an adaptable interpretation. Readers will find various types of readings grouped by functional content areas.

This collection will be especially helpful for HIM students who are preparing to step into privacy and security leadership roles upon graduation. It will be a comforting and convenient shelf resource for seasoned HIM professionals as well. Beyond these two primary audiences, anyone who wants to dig deeper into the complexity of privacy and security will find a balanced representation of the issues to increase their HIM confidence and understanding. The more confident privacy and security leaders are, the more trust they will spread to bring health information dissemination to an optimal place for the greater good.

References

AHIMA. 1999. "Confidentiality of Medical Records: A Situation Analysis and AHIMA's Position." A white paper on the profession's and the association's position on the confidentiality issue prior to HIPAA. American Health Information Management Association.

Institute of Medicine. 1999. "To Err Is Human: Building a Safer Health System." Committee on Quality of Health Care in America. Washington, D.C.: Institute of Medicine.

_____. 2001. "Crossing the Quality Chasm: A New Health System for the 21st Century." Committee on Quality of Health Care in America. Washington, D.C.: Institute of Medicine.

_____.2004."Patient Safety: Achieving a New Standard for Care." Board on Health Care Services. Washington D.C.: Institute of Medicine

Part 1

Understanding HIPAA Fundamentals

Statement on the Privacy, Confidentiality, and Security of Health Records

AHIMA's Position

AHIMA calls upon the healthcare and information technology industries and the government to ensure that privacy, confidentiality, and security protections, and the use of technology to secure such protections, are afforded to all so that the electronic health record—no matter where it resides or how it is transferred—remains protected with integrity, and that the record's subject (the "individual") is assisted in understanding and using these technology tools in his or her transmission and maintenance of personal health information. With the advent of the electronic health record and the transfer of an individual's health information through electronic media, including the Internet, the need for privacy, confidentiality and security protection takes on new meanings and challenges.

AHIMA members believe privacy, confidentiality, and security are essential components of the health record and of fostering trust between healthcare consumers and providers. Trust is essential if the health information collected is to serve as a complete and accurate foundation not only for patient health information but also for clinical care, research, payment, and healthcare policymaking. Health information and data are now being developed on aspects of an individual's health and care that have not been considered by law or practice.

Privacy and confidentiality laws have not kept pace with these developments, and federal preemption under the Health Insurance Portability and Accountability Act of 1996 (HIPAA) has created a "floor" for privacy protection rather than raised the HIPAA requirement to a national ceiling. At the same time, HIPAA has not provided the necessary relief from inconsistent administration, a burden whose elimination was set as a goal of this legislation. In addition, health data, especially in areas such as genetics, could cause irreparable harm to an individual if accessed by an inappropriate party. AHIMA, therefore, calls upon the healthcare industry and government to ensure full, uniform protection, security, and administration of every individual's health information.

Current Situation

Educated and certified AHIMA members have been committed for 75 years to ensuring patient healthcare information is used to fulfill appropriate needs as provided by consent or law—a

Position statement approved by the AHIMA Board of Directors, July 10, 2003.

balancing act complicated by the lack of uniform national guidelines governing healthcare privacy and confidentiality. Health information management (HIM) professionals handle millions of pieces of health information each day, and HIM professionals have assumed the task of ensuring as much protection, security, and integrity of an individual's health information privacy and confidentiality as possible. The ability to effect such protection, however, has changed with time, technology, and legislation.

Today, the health record is not just a paper file. It includes documentation, data, records, and information that might reside, for a single individual, in a number of entities and locations. It might be in the individual's own possession, and it could be in paper or electronic media or a combination of both. The task of ensuring the privacy, confidentiality, and security of an individual's health information therefore becomes all the more challenging as the nation moves into an electronic healthcare world and the industry moves between paper and computer.

The history and breadth of the privacy issue is long and wide. This is only a glimpse of the issue, where it has been, and where it appears to be going:

- In the 1990s, the privacy issue was debated extensively by Congress, culminating in the passage of administrative simplification legislation in HIPAA. HIPAA was not the end of the debate, but to date Congress has passed no additional legislation.

- HIPAA mandated both privacy and security regulations. The privacy regulation was implemented by most of the healthcare industry on April 14, 2003. On April 21, 2003 the final security regulation—identified as a subset of privacy—became effective, with initial implementation for most healthcare-related entities required by April 21, 2005.

- HIPAA does not affect all entities (especially nonhealthcare entities) that might send, receive, or transmit an individual's health information; therefore, its protections are limited. Current laws do not adequately address the new technology, systems, and processes that affect health information, or the various ways institutions, professionals, and the individual might access or transmit information, especially today through the Internet, intranets, or other networks. New threats in the form of "identity theft" also require attention. Comprehensive and nonconflicting rules and regulations remain necessary to deal with health information in the total environment.

- A public need exists to share health information, including, at times, information that can identify a specific individual. Such needs include maintaining the public health, medical research, addressing medical error, bioterrorism monitoring, or preventing medical fraud. The balance between an individual's right to privacy and the public good, as well as the need for a national healthcare information infrastructure to move, collect, and store such information, must be resolved.

- Medical science and technology continue to mature, and new data is being created that, when accessed, could be used to discriminate against an individual. How this data should be used and protected is another example of the problems facing this nation as it attempts to protect an individual's privacy and confidentiality.

- Current HIPAA laws and regulations have not fully addressed myriad state and federal laws, which leave conflicts for those trying to comply with them. HIM professionals, whose function it is to protect privacy and confidentiality and maintain security, are faced with a conflict between advocating administrative uniformity and creating a high standard or "ceiling" for privacy and confidentiality protections across state boundaries. Privacy cannot be sacrificed for expediency. The need continues for a uniform federal law preempting all others, so that protection and administration are uniform.

Privacy, confidentiality, and security of health information will be achieved when:

- Privacy and confidentiality protections are uniform and set the high standard throughout the country through federal preemptive law(s) that establish fair, reasonable, and uniform health information practices, across all states, which understand and respect the rights of the individual and the public and apply to the medium in which such information is stored, transferred, or accessed.

- An individual will have the right to:

  —Access his or her health information in any setting (with minimal limits)

  —Have an understanding of his or her privacy rights and options

  —Be notified about all information practices concerning his or her information

  —Have the right to appropriately challenge the accuracy of his or her health information

  —Have the right, in certain electronic or Internet situations, to opt-in or authorize the collection or use of information beyond what is originally authorized by the individual or law

- The collection and use of health information will be permitted only for legitimate purposes, and only as provided by law, and will be uniform across all jurisdictions and entities and for all individuals.

- Credentialed HIM professionals, given their training and education in privacy and information release and HIM, are considered the primary custodians of health information and principal experts in maintaining the privacy, confidentiality, and security of information in the healthcare industry.

- Laws, practices, and technologies are put in place to provide protections required to maintain appropriate privacy, confidentiality, security, and integrity of health information.

Because the issue of health information privacy, confidentiality, and security is so broad, AHIMA fully expects to issue position statements regarding individual aspects of this issue. With almost 75 years of ensuring the management and protection of health records, AHIMA has a number of definitions and "best practices" related to privacy and confidentiality, including its "Definition for the Legal Medical Record." This information can be obtained at the AHIMA Web site.

Preemption of the HIPAA Privacy Rule

Gwen Hughes, RHIA, CHP

The HIPAA privacy rule includes numerous requirements for the use and disclosure of individually identifiable health information. In some cases, covered entities will be able to comply with both the privacy rule and their state's laws and regulations. In other cases, covered entities will have to make a choice between the privacy rule and state laws. How can covered entities ensure they are making the lawful choice?

This practice brief will explore what the privacy rule says about preemption. In addition, it will provide readers with a framework for making lawful preemption decisions.

Legal Requirements

Covered entities must comply with both federal and state privacy laws and regulations when they can. The privacy rule preempts state law when state law is contrary to the privacy rule. According to the rule, a state law is contrary when:

- A covered entity would find it impossible to comply with both state and federal requirements.

- Adhering to state law would stand as an obstacle to achieving the full purpose of the administrative simplification portions of HIPAA.

Exceptions to Federal Preemption

As is the case with many of the standards within the HIPAA privacy rule, there are exceptions. According to the privacy rule, state law prevails in the following four situations:

- The state law relates to the reporting of disease or injury, child abuse, birth, or death, or for the conduct of public health surveillance, investigation, or intervention.

- State law requires a health plan to report or provide access to information for the purpose of management audits, financial audits, program monitoring and evaluation, or the licensure or certification of facilities or individuals.

Source: Hughes, Gwen. "Preemption of the HIPAA Privacy Rule (AHIMA Practice Brief)." *Journal of AHIMA* 73, no. 2 (2002): 56A–C.

- A determination is made by the Secretary of Health and Human Services (HHS) under §160.204. This section allows a state's chief elected official or designee to petition for an exception from preemption when the state's law is necessary to prevent healthcare fraud and abuse, regulate insurance and health plans, collect healthcare delivery or cost information, ensure public health, safety, or welfare, or regulate controlled substances.

- State law relates to the privacy of health information and is more stringent than privacy rule requirements.

"More Stringent" Criteria

More stringent means state law meets one or more of the following six criteria:

- State law further prohibits or restricts a use or disclosure permitted in the privacy rule. This exception does not apply, however, when the disclosure is required by the secretary of HHS to determine compliance with the rule or to the individual who is the subject of the individually identifiable health information.

- State law permits greater rights of access to or amendment by the individual who is the subject of the individually identifiable health information. This exception, however, is not intended to preempt state law that authorizes or prohibits disclosure of protected health information about a minor to a parent, guardian, or person acting in loco parentis of such minor.

- State law permits greater rights of access to the individual who is the subject of the individually identifiable health information about its use, disclosure, or the individual's rights or remedies with regard to individual's health information.

- State law contains authorization or consent requirements that narrow the scope or duration, reduce the coercive effect, or increase the privacy protections (such as by expanding the criteria) afforded the individual.

- State law provides for more detailed record keeping or retention of information for a longer period.

- State law provides greater privacy protection for the individual who is the subject of the individually identifiable health information. (State and federal laws providing extra confidentiality protection for AIDS/HIV information, mental health, alcohol and drug abuse, other sexually transmitted and communicable diseases, and genetic information laws will almost certainly provide greater privacy protection and therefore not be preempted.)

Recommendations

Covered entities may find that the number of preemption decisions needed number in the tens or hundreds. Although they can certainly address preemption questions as the need arises, covered entities may find that decisions made by employees will vary. As a result, application of the privacy rule may be inconsistent. Referring such preemption decisions to legal counsel, however, can create difficulties meeting turnaround requirements and may prove costly.

As an alternative option, covered entities may find it advantageous to work together as an alliance. For example, they might want to work with the state health information management association, state hospital association, and legal counsel to assess variations between federal and state privacy rules. This alliance might determine whether covered entities can adhere to both federal and state requirements, or whether covered entities must apply the federal or state law.

This alliance might also determine whether an exception should be requested of the secretary or if changes in state law should be introduced. Should they decide to pursue either course, they could work together to achieve such an end.

The benefits of such an alliance would include:

- Generation of a preemption database containing considered preemption decisions

- More consistent practice in applying state and federal privacy provisions

- More effective efforts seeking changes in state law or exceptions through the secretary of HHS

In the absence of a preemption database, covered entities may want to create their own database using a preemption decision form as a starting point. (See Figure 1.1, Sample Preemption Decision Form.) This form could be completed and retained in a preemption database for reference by others in the organization when faced with similar questions of preemption. If the matter needs to be referred to legal counsel, the preemption decision form could be forwarded to legal counsel and a copy retained in the preemption database. On receipt of the attorney's reply, the reply could be matched to the copy of the preemption decision form in the preemption database. Covered entities may wish to summarize preemption decisions using an electronic table accessible throughout the organization. (See Figure 1.2, Sample Preemption Decision Summary Log).

Once you have made a preemption decision, incorporate that decision in your policies and procedures where appropriate. In addition, incorporate some type of ongoing monitoring process to make sure staff are aware of an adherence to preemption determinations.

References

Health Insurance Portability and Accountability Act of 1996. Public Law 104-191.

"Standards for the Privacy of Individually Identifiable Health Information; Final Rule." 45 CFR Part 160. *Federal Register* 65, no. 250 (December 28, 2000).

Tomes, Jonathan P. *The Compliance Guide to HIPAA and the HHS Regulations.* Overland Park, KS: Veterans Press, 2001.

Figure 1.1. Sample preemption decision form

1. **What is the issue you need to resolve?**

2. **What does the privacy rule say about the issue (include citation)?**

3. **What does the state law or regulation say (include citation)?**

4. **Can you comply with both the privacy rule and state law or regulation?**
   - ☐ Yes (Implement procedures that enable you to comply with both federal and state law.)
   - ☐ No (Go to question #5)

5. **In general, the privacy rule preempts state law. There are, however, four exceptions. Does your issue meet one or more of the following exceptions?**
   - ☐ Relates to the reporting of disease or injury, child abuse, birth, death, or the conduct of public health surveillance, investigation, or intervention
   - ☐ Relates to the requirement that a health plan report or provide access to information for the purpose of management audits, financial audits, program monitoring, and evaluation or the licensure or certification of facilities or individuals
   - ☐ The Secretary of Health and Human Services granted an exception under Section 160.204 of the HIPAA privacy rule.
   - ☐ State law or regulation is **more stringent** than the privacy rule. In other words, it meets one or more of the criteria below:
     - ☐ State law further prohibits a use or disclosure of information other than to the individual or secretary of HHS.
     - ☐ State law permits greater rights of access to the individual who is the subject of the protected health information. (Note: This is not intended to preempt other state law to the extent that it authorizes or prohibits disclosure of protected health information about a minor to a parent, guardian, or person acting *in loco parentis* of such minor.)
     - ☐ State law provides greater information about use, disclosure, rights, and remedies to the individual who is the subject of the individually identifiable health information.
     - ☐ State law requires a narrower scope or duration, increases the privacy protections afforded (such as by expanding the criteria for), or reduces the coercive effect of the consent or authorization.
     - ☐ State law provides for more detailed record keeping or retention of information for a longer period.
     - ☐ State law provides greater privacy protection for the individual who is the subject of the individually identifiable health information.
   - ☐ No, my issue does not meet one of the four exceptions above. (Apply federal law.)
   - ☐ Yes, I have checked one or more of the four exceptions. (Apply state law or regulation.)

6. Is the decision about whether to adhere to either or both federal and state law clear?
   - ☐ **Yes.** My organization must adhere to:
     - ☐ Both federal and state law or regulation
     - ☐ Federal law or regulation
     - ☐ State law or regulation
   - ☐ **No.** Refer to legal counsel.

Employee Name _____ Employee Title/Department _____

Extension _____ Date _____

Date Submitted to Legal Counsel _____

Subsequent Comments: (Please date and sign)

This sample form was developed by AHIMA for discussion purposes only. It should not be used without review by your organization's legal counsel to ensure compliance with local and state laws.

Figure 1.2.   Sample preemption decision summary log

Issue	HIPAA standard and citation	State standard and citation	Decision (Check appropriate box below)			Date	Preemption decision made by:
			Adhere to both federal and state laws	Adhere to federal law	Adhere to state law		

This sample form was developed by AHIMA for discussion purposes only. It should not be used without review by your organization's legal counsel to ensure compliance with local and state laws.

Patient Anonymity

Harry B. Rhodes, MBA, RHIA, CHP

Background

Section 2, Paragraph 4 of *The Privacy Act of 1974 (Public Law 93–579)* states, "The right to privacy is a personal and fundamental right protected by the Constitution of the United States."[1] Even though the words "right to privacy" do not specifically appear anywhere in the U.S. Constitution, a number of constitutional scholars concur that the right to privacy is implied in the document. Through the evolution of common law, the status of individual privacy has evolved from a privilege to a right.

This right to privacy continues to evolve. Each new advance in information technology heightens society's expectation that individual privacy should be actively protected. For example, not long ago, many local newspapers published the names of all patients admitted to local hospitals. Over time, society has changed its view of the practice of openly revealing patient admission information. This view, reinforced by numerous accounts of negative and damaging experiences involving breaches of patient privacy, has induced many facilities to subscribe to policies that strictly protect patient anonymity.

Today, many patients are seeking control of their personal health information. This change in public opinion is a response to the increasing number of entities seeking access to identifiable patient information, as well as the increasing speed and volume at which information can be transmitted.

The Impact of HIPAA's Privacy Rule

In the *Health Insurance Portability and Accountability Act, Final Privacy Rule* (45 CFR, parts 160 through 164), the federal government requires covered entities to provide individuals with a notice of information practices and to obtain a written consent from the individual for use and disclosure of the information for treatment, payment, and healthcare operations. Generally speaking, unless an information practice is addressed in the notice and consent obtained, use or disclosure would require a specific authorization. Of interest, however, are a few exceptions.

Source: Rhodes, Harry. "Patient Anonymity (Updated) (AHIMA Practice Brief)." *Journal of AHIMA* 72, no. 5 (2001): 64O–R.

Use and Disclosure for Directory Purposes

The final privacy rule allows a covered entity to use or disclose protected health information for directory purposes without the individual's written consent or authorization, provided the individual was informed of the intended use or disclosure in advance and had the opportunity to either agree to or prohibit the use or disclosure. Furthermore, the rule allows the covered entity the option to inform and obtain the individual's objection or agreement orally.

The covered entity may disclose for directory purposes the individual's name, location within the facility, and condition in general terms that do not communicate specific information. This information may be provided to clergy and persons who ask for the individual by name. Clergy may also be provided with the individual's religious affiliation.

Should a patient object to having his or her protected health information used or disclosed for directory purposes, a mechanism must exist to prevent placement of the information in the public directory and its subsequent disclosure.

If the opportunity to object cannot practicably be provided because of an individual's incapacity or an emergency treatment circumstance, a covered provider may use or disclose some or all of the directory information if such disclosure is consistent with a prior expressed preference and in the individual's best interest. The covered provider must inform the individual and provide an opportunity to object when it becomes practicable to do so.

Use and Disclosure to Family and Close Personal Friends

Similarly, covered entities may also disclose to an individual's family, close personal friends, or other persons identified by the individual protected health information without prior written consent or written authorization if the covered entity obtains the individual's agreement and provides the individual with the opportunity to object, or if the covered entity reasonably infers from the circumstances that the individual does not object to the disclosure.

If the individual is not present or does not have the opportunity to agree or object to the use or disclosure because of incapacity or an emergency circumstance, the covered entity may determine whether the disclosure is in the best interest of the individual and if so, disclose only the information that is directly relevant to the person's involvement with the individual's care.

Use and Disclosure for Notification Purposes

The covered entity may also use or disclose protected health information to notify or assist in the notification of a family member, a personal representative, or another person responsible for the care of the individual as to the individual's location, general condition, or death. This disclosure may take place if the covered entity obtains the individual's agreement and provides the individual with the opportunity to object to the disclosure (and the individual does not express an objection) or the covered entity reasonably infers from the circumstances that the individual does not object to the disclosure.

If the individual is not present or does not have the opportunity to agree or object to the use or disclosure for notification because of incapacity or an emergency circumstance, the covered entity may determine whether the disclosure is in the best interest of the individual and, if so, disclose only the protected information that is directly relevant to the person's involvement with the individual's care.

A covered entity may also use or disclose protected health information to a public or private entity authorized by law or by its charter to assist in disaster relief efforts for the purpose of coordinating notification.

Other Uses and Disclosures Required by Law

Covered entities may use or disclose protected health information to the extent that such use or disclosure is required by law and the disclosure complies with and is limited to the relevant requirements. Covered entities may make such disclosures to organizations such as:

- Public health authorities authorized by law to collect or receive such information for the purpose of preventing or controlling disease, injury, disability, or recording vital events such as birth or death

- Health oversight agencies for activities authorized by law

- Individuals exposed to a communicable disease or who may otherwise be at risk of contracting or spreading a disease or condition if the covered entity or public health authority is authorized by law to notify such person

- Employers responsible for workplace medical surveillance to record illness or injury or to carry out responsibilities for workplace medical surveillance (in order to comply with its obligations under 29 CFR parts 1904 through 1928 and 30 CFR parts 50 through 90 or under state law having a similar purpose.) In this case, however, the covered entity must provide the individual with a copy of the notice of information practices or have it posted in a prominent place where care is provided.

- Public health or government authorities for law enforcement purposes. (For example, information may be disclosed for use in reports of abuse, neglect, or domestic violence or as required by laws that require the reporting of certain types of wounds or other physical injuries. Furthermore, entities may disclose information in compliance with the requirements of a valid court order, warrant, subpoena, or summons, as well as in response to a law enforcement official's request for such information for the purpose of identifying or locating a suspect, fugitive, material witness, or missing person or about an individual who is or is suspected to be a victim of a crime.)

- Coroners, medical examiners, and funeral directors for the purpose of identifying a deceased person, determining a cause of death, or duties as authorized by law

- Organ procurement organizations or other entities engaged in the procurement, banking, or transplantation of cadaveric organs, eyes, or tissue for the purpose of facilitating donation and transplantation

State Laws

Many states have legislation or regulation about the use and disclosure of health information, including information that may be released without an individual's consent.

The HIPAA final privacy rule preempts state laws, except where state law is more stringent or where an exception is granted by the secretary of the Department of Health and Human Services.

Recommendations

Organizations will need to develop policies and mechanisms compliant with federal and state laws that allow the patient to control, to the extent possible, the amount and type of protected information released.

Because the process of determining the more stringent federal or state law is complex, seek the advice of legal counsel in originating or finalizing such policies and procedures.

Remember that the underlying axiom of a patient anonymity policy should be that, as one industry publication puts it, "the patient has the option to expressly state that he or she does not want any information, including confirmation of his/her presence in the facility, released."[2] This is true with the exception of disclosures required by law.

Designating a Spokesperson

Your facility policy should specify exactly who is authorized to assign patient anonymity. Establish a mechanism to immediately notify key staff involved in protecting patient anonymity (e.g., security, public relations, or administration) each time anonymity is provided to a patient.

The HIPAA final privacy rule requires a covered entity to designate a privacy official who is responsible for the development and implementation of the policies and procedures of the entity. This designated privacy official is one possible candidate for the responsibility of managing patient anonymity.

Designate a spokesperson to address any inquiries received from the media or other authorities. Weekend and evening coverage for the spokesperson should also be provided. An individual experienced in healthcare public relations would be a good choice for the spokesperson position. If such a person is unavailable, the chosen staff member should be someone with excellent public speaking ability and strong communication skills.

A spokesperson should never release information that would embarrass a patient. In situations where there is a known potential risk of danger to the patient should his/her location be revealed, the spokesperson should not release any information or confirmation of the patient's presence.

Procedures should ensure that any information approved for release is consistent and accurate. Once anonymity status has been assigned, no information regarding the patient's presence in the facility or condition should be released without the patient's authorization.

Expect that employees may be approached by individuals outside the organization seeking information on patients. The best defense to this type of tactic is regularly scheduled employee education coupled with strong, well-written policies that are widely distributed to all employees, volunteers, and contractors.

Only a patient's physician should make statements regarding diagnosis or prognosis. The spokesperson should use the following one-word condition descriptions when releasing information about the patient:

Undetermined: Patient is awaiting physician and assessment.

Good: Vital signs are stable and within normal limits. Patient is conscious and comfortable. Indicators are excellent.

Fair: Vital signs are stable and within normal limits. Patient is conscious, but may be uncomfortable. Indicators are favorable.

Serious: Vital signs may be unstable and not within normal limits. Patient is acutely ill. Indicators are questionable.

Critical: Vital signs are unstable and not within normal limits. Patient may be unconscious. Indicators are unfavorable.

"Stable" should not be used as a condition. Furthermore, this term should not be used in combination with other conditions, which by definition often indicate a patient is unstable.[3]

Following review and written approval by the patient, a more explicit statement could be released should the patient believe a detailed statement is appropriate under the circumstances.

In situations where the news media is seeking access to health information that the patient has refused to release, the burden of compelling the health provider to release information should be on the news media unless disclosure is otherwise required by law.

Protecting Against Threats to Patient Privacy

Special procedures for handling the patient records of individuals who request anonymity can be developed. Among the steps that can be taken to protect unauthorized disclosures are:

- Omitting the patient's name from the cover of the record.

- Using an alphanumeric code or alias name in place of the patient's real name. One format used is a combination of the patient's initials and business office account number. Use of an alias name such as John Doe for all patients can be confusing, especially if more than one John Doe is registered at a time.

- Replacing the patient's name with an alphanumeric code or alias name on all "bed boards," bulletin boards, and patient room signs.

- Restricting computer system access to those users who need to know the patient's identity to perform their jobs.

- Placing a warning message on the access screens of all patients that request anonymity. The warning should remind the user that they are about to access a restricted file and that security audits are performed at the facility.

- Designating one individual responsible for controlling access to the restricted medical record in facilities with paper record systems. The record should be maintained in a secure area when it is not being used by a healthcare provider.

- Employing a mechanism that will lock out a user that attempts to access information beyond his/her security clearance with repeated use of an improper code.

- Performing periodic audits to ensure that the organization's policies are being followed and are still effective.

- Employing mechanisms that will alert the facility security officer when a system user attempts to access information beyond his or her security clearance.

- Developing written policies outlining access to patient information.

- Providing employees, medical staff members, students, and volunteers with specific training about their responsibility to protect confidentiality of patient health information.

- Requiring that at the time of employment all staff members, students, and volunteers are required to sign a nondisclosure agreement. Organizational policy should require an annual review of confidentiality policies with acknowledgment.

- Upon discharge, limiting access to the record during the chart completion process to designated employees with a valid need to know.

- Once the chart is completed, placing it in a secure file that is accessible only to the director of health information management and other designated staff members. Charts should not be made available for research or reviews unless a special release is obtained first.

- At discharge, placing the patient's actual name in the master patient index with a cross-walk software application to the alias.

Prior to developing policies and procedures, the facility should carefully review all applicable state laws addressing the release of identifiable patient information.

Notes

1. The Privacy Protection Study Commission. *The Privacy Act of 1974: An Assessment.* Washington, DC: 1977, Appendix 4.

2. Society for Healthcare Strategy and Market Development. *General Guide for the Release of Information on the Condition of Patients.* Chicago, IL: 1997.

3. Ibid.

References

"Standards for Privacy of Individually Identifiable Health Information; Final Rule." 45 CFR Parts 160 and 164. *Federal Register* 65, no. 250 (December 28, 2000). Available at http://aspe.hhs.gov/admnsimp/.

Douglass, Kara. "Inside Track: Madonna Slept Here." *Hospitals and Health Networks* no.14 (1997): 61.

Goldman, Janlori, and Mulligan, Deirdre. *Privacy and Health Information Systems: A Guide to Protecting Patient Confidentiality.* Washington, DC: The Center for Democracy & Technology, 1996.

Health Law Center, Hospital Law Manual, Administrator's Volume. Aspen Publishers, Inc., Volume 1B, Section 3–19, 1995, 51–55.

Lewton, Kathleen L. *Public Relations in Health Care: A Guide for Professionals.* Chicago, IL: American Hospital Publishing, Inc., 1995.

Privacy Protection Study Commission. *The Privacy Act of 1974: An Assessment.* Washington, DC: Superintendent of Documents, U.S. Government Printing Office, 1977.

"Protecting the Privacy of the Rich and Famous." *Medical Record Briefing* 12, no. 7 (1997): 4–5.

Roach, William H. "Legal Review: Coping with Celebrity Patients." *Topics In Health Record Management* 12, no. 2 (1991): 67–72.

Roach, William H. *Medical Records and the Law.* Gaithersburg, MD: Aspen Publishers, 1994.

Rowland, Howard S., and Rowland, Beatrice L. *Hospital Legal Forms, Checklists, & Guidelines.* Volume 2. Gaithersburg, MD: Aspen Publishing Co., 1997.

Society for Healthcare Strategy and Market Development. *General Guide for the Release of Information on the Condition of Patients.* Chicago, IL: American Hospital Association, 1997.

Regulation of Health Information Processing in an Outsourcing Environment

A Joint Position Statement issued by:

American Health Information Management Association (AHIMA),
California Health Information Association (CHIA),
American Association for Medical Transcription (AAMT),
Medical Transcription Industry Alliance (MTIA)

Objective

To outline the factors that need to be considered to effectively address the issue of processing of personal health data and information irrespective of the location where it is processed.

Currently, a number of state legislators and members of Congress are examining this practice from the perspective of protecting the privacy rights and jobs of US citizens—both issues of great importance to the American public including the members of our respective associations.

This statement urges legislators to examine the issues surrounding off shore health information processing in their totality in order to avoid legislative actions that produce serious and unintended consequences for patients, healthcare organizations, workers, and the economy—now and in the future.

Workforce

Legislation prohibiting or encumbering outsourcing would have a direct and immediate adverse effect on patients and healthcare organizations. It would quickly overwhelm the current workforce preventing essential patient information from being transcribed timely and accurately, if at all. Possible implications include:

- Disruption and adverse impact to patient care. Without proper and timely transcribed histories and physical exams, for example, patients cannot go to surgery.

Source: Position Statement, approved by the Board of Directors, American Health Information Management Association, March 2004.

- Loss of JCAHO Accreditation. Unless operative reports are immediately available, hospitals can lose accreditation by the Joint Commission on Accreditation of Health Care Organizations, which in turn threatens the organization's eligibility to receive payments from Medicare and other third party payers.

- Disruption of payment. Without timely transcribed reports, qualified coders are impeded from assigning the necessary billing codes and providers and healthcare organizations cannot get reimbursed for services provided.

The demand for medical transcription and other health information processing in the US has increased sharply in recent years in response to an increasing volume of patient information, increased regulation and litigation, and the drive toward an electronic health record. However, there has not been a corresponding increase in the number of skilled workers needed to handle this workload.

According to the US Department of Labor, medical transcriptionists held 101,000 jobs in 2002, with 7 out of 10 working in hospitals and physician offices. Outsourcing transcription work and advancements in speech recognition technology are not expected to significantly reduce the need for well-trained medical transcriptionists domestically.[1] The Department of Labor also reports that 97,000 new health information technicians will be needed by the end of this decade to fill new jobs and replace those who are retiring.[2] The health information technician occupational category includes specially trained knowledge workers who process medical record data (by transcribing dictated reports), coding medical records for billing, and handling other specialized functions. There are simply not enough of these skilled workers in the US to fill the jobs available today nor are there any measures in place to remedy this shortage to meet forecasted demands.

To prohibit outsourcing without concurrently addressing workforce development would be counterproductive. Any law that restricts outsourcing must make provisions for workforce training. Training new health information technicians who have the requisite skills requires at least one year and is best done in an accredited community college program. However, expanding training programs at community colleges is a daunting fiscal challenge that would burden cash-strapped state budgets. So, while training is certainly a solution, it is not quick or inexpensive.

Information Processing Technology

New information and communication technology (ICT) makes it possible to outsource information with greater security than ever before. For example, in the UC San Francisco Medical Center case—where a foreign-based transcriptionist employed by an outsourcing firm threatened to expose identifiable patient information on the Internet—technology, in combination with strong policy, training and monitoring could have prevented the transcriptionist from knowing the identity of the individuals whose information she was processing.

An important public policy contribution that state legislators and Congress can make is to support full deployment of ICT to bring healthcare into the information age. Adoption of ICT has profound long-term benefits for quality, safety and cost effectiveness of care by enabling important advances in information security that are currently out of reach in today's "hybrid" environment that involves both paper and digital records.

Technology can enhance these processes and add efficiencies that can lessen the very real impact of this shortage of knowledge workers. Emerging technologies that will play significant roles in this process include:

- Voice recognition technology is becoming capable of producing text documents

- Artificial intelligence engines can scan text documents and assign billing codes

- Direct entry of data by clinicians via templates

Over time, these technologies will allow us to redeploy scarce knowledge workers to perform more sophisticated functions such as data quality control or data analytics. The workforce development and technology strategies must be carefully balanced to meet short and long-term needs. Taking shortcuts in training to supplement today's workforce will leave these workers without the skills needed to perform the jobs of tomorrow.

Cost

Health care costs are a national concern. Not only is the industry outsourcing information processing to address workforce shortages, it also is using outsourcing as a cost control strategy enabling health care organizations to redirect scarce staff resources. There are many models for outsourcing and within the US it is a common practice and has been for many years. Even so, it is estimated that less than 10% of medical transcription is currently being done outside the US. Some of the current proposed legislation intends to prohibit US health care providers, payers or outsourcing companies to send information overseas regardless of what measures are in place to ensure the privacy and security of the process.

Other proposed legislation would call for institutions to first explain the potential for outsourcing to the patient and allow them to opt-out. This solution would be extraordinarily difficult to administer and would increase administrative costs since there are no systems to automate this process and performing this function manually would be untenable. Entities will have to essentially turn off the automated data systems and dictation-to-transcription systems that process millions of such occurrences a day and "pick out" the data for individuals that do not want their information going overseas. As noted above, such requirements would also affect the timely delivery of patient care services and have enormous cost consequences.

Laws and Standards

AHIMA, AAMT, CHIA and MTIA are committed to strong privacy and security protections for personal health information. Our organizations advocated for a strong federal privacy and security standard and have been leaders in implementing the US Health Insurance Portability and Accountability Act of 1996 (HIPAA).

We have advocated full compliance by our members and have supported enactment of the provisions of HIPAA that impose penalties for violations. Outsourcing companies are considered business associates under HIPAA and our organizations have provided extensive education and advice on how to effectively manage outsourcing relationships. We believe that it is important to 1) continuously reinforce adherence to sound policies and procedures that comply with HIPAA, 2) improve the due diligence used in establishing and monitoring outsourcing contracts, 3) identify areas where the HIPAA regulations need to be improved, and 4) punish those who violate the rules.

It would be counter-productive and harmful to health care organizations if new state laws are established that make it impractical for national outsourcing companies to do business within a particular state. Further, many health care systems operate in a number of states.

Therefore, we urge legislators to think about national and global business structures when addressing issues relating to health information. This is no longer a local issue.

Summary

Policy makers must consider the workforce, technology, cost and legal implications of their legislative proposals. AHIMA, AAMT, CHIA and MTIA urge lawmakers to craft regulatory solutions that enforce HIPAA and support advancements in modern health information processing practices that improve the quality and cost of health care.

We also urge increased investment in health information workforce development and implementation of new technologies to advance critical healthcare outcomes—timely, accurate, accessible and secure information to support patient care. It is essential that state legislatures reinforce the importance of improving information processing solutions for healthcare and not take actions that will produce unintended and detrimental consequences.

Notes

1. Bureau of Labor Statistics, U.S. Department of Labor, *Occupational Outlook Handbook, 2004–05 Edition,* Medical Transcriptionists, on the Internet at http://www.bls.gov/oco/ocos271.htm (visited March 07, 2004).

2. Hecker, D. E. "Occupational employment projections to 2010." *Monthly Labor Review,* November 2001, p. 57–84.

Who's Covered by HIPAA?

Dan Rode, MBA, FHFMA

One of the mysteries of the administrative simplification section of the Health Insurance Portability and Accountability Act of 1996 (HIPAA) is determining who is covered or comes under the requirements of the act. This article will examine HIPAA to unravel some of the mystery of "who's covered?" To do so, we'll refer to HIPAA (PL 104-191) and the final rules for transactions and code sets and privacy.

To find the original text of the final and proposed rules, go to the Department of Health and Human Services (HHS) administrative simplification Web site at http://aspe.os.dhhs.gov/admnsimp/.

Defining HIPAA's Terms

The HIPAA legislation covered a vast array of healthcare issues. For this article, we'll focus on Subtitle F, the administrative simplification section.

To identify who is covered, let's first look at HIPAA's definitions, which include very legalistic descriptions of the terms:

- Health care clearinghouse: "A public or private entity that processes or facilitates the processing of nonstandard data elements of health information into standard data elements." (Obviously, you have to read the definitions of data elements to understand the meaning.)

- Health care provider: "Includes a provider of services [as defined under Social Security and Medicare statutes], a provider of medical or other health services [also defined elsewhere], and any other person furnishing health care services or supplies."

- Health plan: "An individual or group plan that provides or pays the cost of medical care." The section 1171 definition of health plan goes on to describe 13 subgroups that fit this definition and leaves room for additional groups. For example, Medicare Plus-Choice plans have been created since 1996.

Source: Rode, Dan. "HIPAA on the Job: Who's Covered by HIPAA." *Journal of AHIMA* 72, no. 3 (2001): 16A–16C.

Section 1172 of HIPAA sets general requirements for the standards and indicates that their applicability to "any standard adopted . . . shall apply, in whole or in part, to the following persons:

1. A health plan

2. A health care clearinghouse

3. A health care provider who transmits any health information in electronic form in connection with a transaction" named elsewhere in HIPAA

Section 1173 notes that "The Secretary shall adopt standards providing for a standard unique health identifier for each individual [patient], employer, health plan, and health care provider for use in the health care system." We are still waiting to see these final regulations for healthcare providers and employers and proposed regulations for health plans. Congress, in the years since HIPAA was enacted, has halted any development of an individual/patient identifier, indicating that such an identifier can only be developed after the passage of a comprehensive privacy bill.

Section 1175 states that "If a person desires to conduct a [electronic] transaction . . . with a health plan as a standard transaction:

(A)   The health plan may not refuse to conduct such transaction as a standard transaction;

(B)   The insurance plan may not delay such transaction, or otherwise adversely affect, or attempt to adversely affect, the person or the transaction on the ground that the transaction is a standard transaction; and

(C)   The information transmitted and received in connection with the transaction shall be in the form of standard data elements of health information."

Section 1175 also states that "a health plan may satisfy the requirements . . . by:

(A)   Directly transmitting and receiving standard data elements of health information; or

(B)   Submitting nonstandard data elements to a health care clearinghouse for processing into standard data elements and transmission by the health care clearinghouse, and receiving standard data elements through the health care clearinghouse."

Similar language is expressed in Section 1175 to allow a person (provider) to use clearinghouses as well.

As you can see, Congress placed significant responsibilities on healthcare plans, while clearinghouses and providers' roles are somewhat less significant. Recognizing that not all healthcare plans are the same, Congress further stipulated (Section 1174) that "in the case of a small health plan . . . [requirements] . . . shall be applied by substituting '36 months' for '24 months' . . . the Secretary [DHHS] shall determine the plans that qualify as small health plans."

"Person" generally describes an individual or entity that acts as one of the three covered entities (health plans, healthcare clearinghouses, or healthcare providers). In HIPAA's Section 1177, a person could also be one of these or any other individual who then would be subject to this section's prohibition against "wrongful disclosure of individually identifiable health information." Penalties in this section range from $50,000 to $250,000 in fines or up to 10 years of imprisonment.

The congressional authors of HIPAA left out a few specific entities, essentially for political purposes. Thus, while HIPAA calls for electronic standards for enrollment and premium payments, it does not call for employers to be covered entities and use such electronic transaction standards. HIPAA also exempts workers' compensation plans and liability insurers (e.g., property and casualty or auto) from using the HIPAA standards, although several of the national liability insurers will probably adopt the standards anyway.

Who Is Affected by the Transaction and Code Set Standards?

The regulations related to transaction and code set standards essentially maintain the applicability definitions as described in HIPAA—health plans, healthcare clearinghouses, and providers who transmit any health information in electronic form in connection with a covered transaction.

The regulations take a cue from HIPAA and extend coverage to "business associates," defined as "a person who performs a function or activity regulated by this . . . [regulation] . . . on behalf of a covered entity." The definition also indicates that some business associates could also be covered entities, depending on the function they are performing, such as a hospital-based business office that sells billing services to a physician.

The definition of group health plan is changed to mean "an employee welfare benefit plan . . . [as defined in ERISA] . . . , including insured and self-insured plans, to the extent that the plan provides medical care as defined in the . . . [Public Health Service Act] . . . , including items and services paid for as medical care to employees or their dependents directly or through insurance, reimbursement or otherwise that:

1. Has 50 or more participants . . . [as defined by ERISA . . .] or

2. Is administered by an entity other than the employer that established and maintains the plan."

The regulations set the definition of a small versus large health plan on the basis of a Small Business Administration definition that makes the cut between large and small at $5 million maximum in receipts or premiums. Plans that are designated small will receive an extra 12 months to implement the transaction and coding regulations (October 16, 2003, as opposed to October 16, 2002, for large plans).

The clearinghouse definition remains the same, but it has been changed to indicate functions that make an entity a clearinghouse. Similarly, the regulation spells out when a transaction fits the standards and therefore makes the healthcare provider a covered entity.

In these regulations, HHS also tends to use functions or transactions to define who is covered. For instance, the requirements for covered entities include:

(a) "General Rule. Except as otherwise provided . . . if a covered entity conducts with another covered entity (or within the same covered entity), using electronic media, a transaction for which the Secretary has adopted a standard under this . . . [regulation] . . . the covered entity must conduct the transaction as a standard transaction."

(b) "Exception for direct data entry transactions. A health care provider electing to use direct data entry offered by a health plan to conduct a transaction for which a standard has been adopted under this part must use the applicable data content and data condition requirements of the standard when conducting the transaction. The health care provider is not required to use the format requirements of the standard."

(c) "Use of a business associate. A covered entity may use a business associate, including a health care clearinghouse, to conduct a transaction covered by this part. If a covered entity chooses to use a business associate to conduct all or part of a transaction on behalf of the covered entity, the covered entity must require the business associate to do the following: (1) Comply with all applicable requirements of this part. (2) Require any agent or subcontractor to comply with all applicable requirements of this part."

In discussing its "coordination of benefits" transaction, HHS allows health plans some option as to whether they have to be involved in such a transaction. Health plans that choose to participate then must meet an additional set of regulations.

The transaction and code set regulations leave a healthcare provider free to use paper, a clearinghouse, or the standard transaction set. They do not allow a provider to use an electronic transaction that is not standard. It is important to note that while this HIPAA regulation does not require the use of electronic standards, health plans (payers) might make this a requirement, which immediately means that the provider would have to meet the standard for electronic transmissions or use a clearinghouse.

Additionally, while the claims and payment/remittance X12 transactions chosen by HHS are already widely in use, most of the remaining provider/plan transactions are not widely used. Here, providers and plans are free to use nonelectronic transactions in any way they wish. However, if they move to electronic transactions, they must move to the standard transaction, data set, and so on.

Who's Covered by the Privacy Regulations?

The HIPAA privacy standards essentially require adherence by the same entities as those covered under the transaction and code set standards. The privacy regulations, however, have been extended to cover all healthcare information, whether or not it is in electronic form.

For providers, the privacy rules appear to mean that provider entities that engage in any electronic transactions will be covered by these HIPAA requirements for all health information, whether or not the specific information in question is in an electronic format. In reality, this rule effectively covers all healthcare providers, in part because it will be difficult to avoid electronic transaction requirements from federal and state payers, and because it will be difficult to explain to patients why one provider can choose not to abide by the privacy regulations and most will.

While employers are exempted by the transaction regulation, they are indirectly covered under the privacy regulation in their role as sponsor (final payer). Here the regulation requires health plans, through their contracts with sponsors/employers, to keep private health information separate from other personnel data and private. Meanwhile, HIPAA legislation does not cover liability and workers' compensation plans under the privacy regulations and, as noted, does not require employers to use the HIPAA transactions. Any changes here require additional legislation.

What Else Do I Need to Know?

A few final thoughts about coverage under HIPAA:

- While HIPAA law exempts some entities from using the transactions standards and abiding with the privacy requirements, there is nothing to prevent such an entity from adopting these standards.

- While HIPAA law may exempt covered entities from the regulations, public opinion may not. Entities—especially those that have covered and noncovered units—must consider the public/customer's conception of HIPAA. Nonconformance could cost more in the long run.

- Some entities have been concerned that being "covered" by HIPAA means that they must collect and transmit all the data in a particular standard. While HIPAA requires that a health plan must accept a fully compliant standard, nothing prevents a provider and a plan from agreeing to transmit less than the total data set, as long as the transaction itself continues to follow other transaction requirements.

- The HIPAA rules that have currently been published are expected to be implemented in the next two to three years. An entity's status could quickly change in today's healthcare environment. It might be easier to accept standards and work with them than to avoid them and be caught short later.

- The HIPAA rules set up different (later) implementation dates for small health plans. However, there is no prohibition preventing plans from implementing sooner—say, at the same time as larger plans.

- The HIPAA rules set up an "implement by" date(s), but do not prevent plans, providers, or states from setting earlier dates.

The original concept behind HIPAA was for the healthcare industry to have one standard. Such a situation would generate a number of cost and administrative benefits. The first step toward realizing the potential benefits is to answer the question "Who's covered?"

Debate Surrounding Unique Health Identifier Continues

Vicki Wheatley, RHIA, MS

Whatever happened to the unique health identifier for individuals (UHI)? The UHI was one of four identifiers included in HIPAA. In July 1998 the Department of Health and Human Services (HHS) and the former Health Care Financing Administration (now the Centers for Medicare and Medicaid Services [CMS]) published a notice of intent to move forward on defining the UHI, also referred to as the unique patient identifier or universal patient identifier.

While work toward the adoption of a UHI has been suspended more or less indefinitely, debate continues regarding the relevance and format of the UHI.

Concerns and Resistance Reign

Initially, delays were recommended by the National Committee on Vital and Health Statistics (NCVHS) to allow time for Congress to pass legislation that would address privacy and confidentiality issues surrounding the use of the UHI. The standards for privacy of individually identifiable health information were published in December 2000 with an effective date of April 2001 and a compliance date of April 2003. Yet, even with the privacy laws in effect, consumer and trade groups and individuals continue to have legitimate concerns regarding the government's ability to administer the UHI program and adequately protect privacy.

Public resistance will be a significant factor in the adoption of any UHI program. Continued delays in research and development of proposed rules seem to be due to lack of financial support. In 1999 Congress denied funding to HHS for continued work on the unique identifier. Congress suspended work on the HIPAA requirement for a UHI in the fiscal year 2002 Budget Appropriations Act by barring HHS from using any of its funding to "promulgate or adopt any final standard . . . providing for, or providing for the assignment of, a unique health identifier for an individual . . . until legislation is enacted specifically approving the standard."[1]

Serious Obstacles

HIPAA defines the UHI as part of a comprehensive plan to achieve uniform standards for exchange of health data. The UHI is expected to have many benefits, including reductions in administrative costs and improvements in the quality of patient care.

Source: Wheatley, Vicki. "Debate Surrounding Unique Health Identifier Continues." *Journal of AHIMA* 75, no. 2 (February 2004): 58–59.

Opponents of the UHI are concerned about privacy and the risk that more facets of an individual's life would be vulnerable to unauthorized or inappropriate inspection. Many citizen groups and physician groups are outspoken in their opposition to the UHI. The controversy over adoption of UHI has centered on the privacy issue, with some believing that privacy is important but can be managed appropriately, and others believing privacy protection outweighs any clinical or administrative benefit. The Association of American Physicians and Surgeons has stated, "Administrative simplification is a euphemism for government control of your records."[2] The public's concern over privacy protections, fear of identity theft, and general mistrust of the government will continue to generate serious obstacles to adoption and widespread use of the UHI.

Functions of the UHI

The original HIPAA objectives directed that the UHI support four basic functions:

- Positive identification of the individual patient

- Identification of information relative to the patient

- Protection of privacy and confidentiality

- Reduction of healthcare operational cost

In order for the UHI to be successfully deployed, a technical and administrative infrastructure would be required. Six components are necessary for the UHI:

- Identifier scheme (numeric, alphanumeric, etc.)

- Identification information (name, fingerprint, etc.)

- Index

- Mechanism for hiding or encrypting the identifier

- Technology infrastructure

- Administrative infrastructure

Format of the UHI

Currently, patients are identified within a healthcare organization by a medical record number (MRN). Patients seen at multiple organizations receive multiple MRNs. These numbers provide unique identification only within the specific facility that issued the MRN. To provide unique patient identification across multiple organizations, a reliable unique patient identifier is required.

Several different formats for the UHI have been proposed. A detailed analysis of each of the identifier proposals is contained in a 1997 report to HHS titled "Analysis of Unique Patient Identifier Options."[3] The identifier proposals have been sorted into five broad categories:

1. Unique identifiers based on the Social Security Number (SSN)

2. Identifiers not based on the SSN

3. Proposals that do not require universal unique identifiers

4. Hybrid proposals

5. Cryptography methods that are not identifiers

The ideal UHI must meet critical functional requirements. Functional performance is independent of the numbering scheme itself. Any of the above categories of proposed identifiers can achieve the functional goals of a UHI as long as the other supporting components are present. Perhaps the most significant challenge to UHI implementation is the required infrastructure. The system for assigning numbers must be available around the clock with rapid response time. It must also be accurate, secure, user friendly, technologically up to date, scalable, flexible, and easy to maintain. That is a tall order and one not easily fulfilled.

What Now?

Since the notice of intent was published, there has been no further action and no proposed rules have been published. Without funding, work on developing the UHI has been halted. Until dollars are allocated to continue the work, it is unlikely that any significant action will be taken.

Continuing discussions will most likely focus on privacy concerns, developing the infrastructure, and addressing the issues surrounding implementation of any universal patient identification methodology. We must find realistic solutions for complex issues such as practicality, public support, cost effectiveness, and privacy. Along with funding, strong leadership is required to steer this process in the right direction. Waiting for options to materialize and succeed by themselves will not fulfill the need for accurate patient identification adequately or in a timely manner.

While we await decisions from Congress, regardless of the eventual outcome, each facility should take steps now to improve the quality of master patient index data. This data is the key to identifying patients within healthcare organizations today, and it could be the foundation for unique health identifiers in the future.

Notes

1. National Committee on Vital and Health Statistics. "Fifth Annual Report to Congress on the Implementation of the Administrative Simplification Provisions of the Health Insurance Portability and Accountability Act." August 24, 2002.

2. Vernon, Wes. "Medical Group: Regs Would Create National Database of Patient Records." March 28, 2001.

3. Appavu, Soloman. "Analysis of Unique Patient Identifier Options: Final Report." November 24, 1997. Prepared for the Department of Health and Human Services.

References

HIPAA Administrative Simplification Regulations are available at the Centers for Medicare and Medicaid Services Web site at www.cms.hhs.gov/hipaa.

Unique Patient Identifier/Universal Identifier Proposals are available at www.hipaanet.com/jhitaexecutive.htm and www.hipaanet.com/UHI-1.htm.

Getting "Hip" to Other Privacy Laws, Part 1

Julie A. Roth, MHSA, JD, RHIA

Although HIPAA currently enjoys the privacy spotlight, it is only one of several federal laws aimed at privacy protection. We have federal protections for everything from our medical and financial information to what videos we rent. When you add the various state privacy laws and accrediting body standards to the mix, privacy becomes an ever-evolving sea of statutes, rules, regulations, standards, and case decisions.

This article highlights and simplifies three of the federal privacy laws: one that protects our information in the hands of federal agencies, another that protects our education records, and a law that protects our financial information.

Privacy Act of 1974

If you work in healthcare, you've been following the HIPAA privacy standards for almost a year. But did you know that federal agencies have followed similar standards for nearly 30 years? The Privacy Act of 1974 requires federal agencies holding personally identifiable records to safeguard that information and provide individuals with certain privacy rights.

Federal agencies collect records about individuals for a variety of reasons. For example, an agency may collect medical records to determine an individual's eligibility for federal employment or participation in a federal benefit program. Agencies must describe what records are collected about individuals and how they are used, protected, and disclosed by publishing a notice in the Federal Register. Only information necessary to accomplish legitimate agency activities may be collected or used, and policies to safeguard the confidentiality of this information must be implemented.

Before disclosing records to a third party, an individual's written consent must be obtained. However, agencies may use individuals' records as necessary to carry out internal activities without consent. They may also make disclosures pursuant to certain law enforcement requests, court orders, health and safety issues, and to comply with specific laws and governmental needs.

Balancing out the consent exceptions, agencies must account for nonconsensual disclosures by documenting when, to whom, and why a particular disclosure was made. With limited exceptions, agencies must make this accounting available to an individual upon his or her request.

Source: Roth, Julie. "Getting 'Hip' to Other Privacy Laws." *Journal of AHIMA* 75, no. 2 (2004): 50–52.

In general, individuals may access their records, but each agency defines its own terms and appropriate limitations. If an individual discovers an inaccuracy in a record, he or she may request that the record be amended. An agency may decline to amend a record, but it must provide a review process and allow the individual to file a statement of disagreement. Any subsequent disclosures of the record must reference the dispute and include the statement.

Family Educational Rights

Under the HIPAA privacy rule, we now enjoy the right to access and control our medical information. We've had similar rights regarding our education records since 1974. The Family Educational Rights and Privacy Act (FERPA) provides students who attend or have attended a federally funded educational institution with certain rights regarding their records (for the purposes of this article, "students" includes adult students or parents of a minor student).

Education records contain personally identifiable information about students, such as social security numbers and other sensitive information like grades and enrollment history. In primary and secondary institutions, school health records of students under 18 are education records. Treatment records of students 18 and older, and those maintained by postsecondary institutions, become education records when they are disclosed to anyone (including students) other than treatment providers. When disclosed to treatment providers, these records are excluded from FERPA requirements.

To protect education records, FERPA requires institutions to obtain a student's written consent before disclosing student information to third parties. Several disclosures are excluded from this requirement, such as disclosures to appropriate staff, other schools to which a student seeks to enroll, and organizations connected with a student's financial aid. Records may also be disclosed as necessary for certain educational oversight activities, limited health and safety emergencies, or as required by law.

Directory information such as a student's name, address, and academic achievements may be disclosed without consent, but students must first be notified of this practice and be given an opportunity to opt out of the directory. Whenever an institution receives a request for student information or makes a disclosure without a student's written consent, it must document specific information in the student's record. Internal and directory requests and disclosures are exempt from this requirement.

In addition to providing consent rights, FERPA allows students to inspect their records. If factors such as distance make inspection impractical, students must be provided with copies or some other means of access. Letters of recommendation to which a student has voluntarily waived access and certain financial records are not available for inspection. Students may ask that inaccurate or misleading information in their records be amended and must be provided with a hearing if the institution denies the request. If the final decision is in favor of the institution, the student may place a statement of disagreement in the disputed record and have it included with any subsequent disclosures.

Gramm-Leach-Bliley Act

Have you ever wondered why you began receiving privacy notices from your financial institutions over the last few years? The Gramm-Leach-Bliley Act (GLBA) is responsible. This law requires financial institutions to protect your nonpublic information (NPI) by informing you about their privacy policies and allowing you to opt out of certain disclosures.

Although the GLBA mostly affects banks and other traditional financial institutions, a hospital may be covered if it conducts banking-related financial activities, such as routinely charging interest on patients' long-term payment plans. You have a right to a privacy and opt-out notice from a financial institution even if you are not a regular customer and only occasionally use its services as a "consumer" by doing something like withdrawing cash from a foreign ATM. A customer is entitled to the privacy and opt-out notices at the outset of the relationship and each year thereafter. A consumer should receive the notices before his or her NPI is shared.

The privacy notice describes what NPI the financial institution collects and discloses and the parties with whom it may share that information. Generally, NPI such as payment history and account numbers is collected from forms, applications, and transactions. This information may be shared inside the corporate family or sometimes with nonaffiliated third parties, such as retailers and marketers. The notice must also describe any disclosures required by law, how NPI is safeguarded, and how former-customer NPI is handled.

The opt-out notice must provide an opportunity to prevent disclosures to nonaffiliated third parties through some reasonable means, such as calling a toll-free number or mailing in a form. The opt-out right has several significant exceptions. Consumers do not have the right to opt out of disclosures necessary to administer authorized transactions, comply with various reporting laws, or carry out numerous other legally permitted activities. It is important to keep abreast of these privacy laws to uphold the integrity of privacy both within and outside the healthcare arena.

Figure 1.3, Privacy at a Glance, Part One, summarizes the various aspects of these three laws.

Figure 1.3. **Privacy at a glance, part one**

	The Privacy Act of 1974 (5 U.S.C. § 552a)	The Family Educational Rights and Privacy Act of 1974 (20 U.S.C. § 1232g)	The Gramm-Leach-Bliley Act, 1999 (15 U.S.C. § 6801 et. seq)
Applies to	• Federal agencies	• Educational agencies and institutions receiving certain federal funding	• Financial institutions
Protected Information	• Records—any grouping of information containing names, identifying numbers, symbols, or other identifiers	• Education records—records (any medium) containing personally identifiable information directly related to a student	• Nonpublic personal information (NPI)—personally identifiable financial information that is not publicly available
Protected Persons	• Individuals	• Students	• Consumers and customers
Notice	• Describes agency policies for collecting, maintaining, using, disclosing, and protecting records • Published in Federal Register • Referred to on agency forms	• Describes rights and procedures for access, amendment, consents, and complaints • Provided annually by any reasonable means	• Describes NPI collected, disclosed, and opt-out right • Delivered to consumers prior to disclosing NPI, to customers annually
Disclosures	• Written consent required –Numerous exceptions	• Written consent required –Numerous exceptions	• Opt-out right –Numerous exceptions
Accounting for Disclosures	• Tracks recipient, date, and purpose of most nonconsensual disclosures • Retained at least five years	• Record of most requests, disclosures, and their purposes • Permanently placed in education record	None
Amending Information	• Amend inaccurate, irrelevant, untimely, or incomplete records • Provide review process for disputes • Individual may submit statement of disagreement	• Amend inaccurate, misleading, or inappropriate records • Provide hearing for disputes • Student may submit statement of disagreement	None
Safeguarding Information	• Administrative, technical, and physical safeguards	• Limited disclosure	• Administrative, technical, and physical safeguards
Enforcement	• Civil action by individual • Criminal penalties	• Department of Education enforcement • Federal funding may be terminated	• Multiple federal agency enforcement

Getting "Hip" to Other Privacy Laws, Part 2

Julie A. Roth, MHSA, JD, RHIA

The HIPAA privacy rule is just one of several federal laws that protect the privacy of nonpublic information. But privacy is not a new concept in healthcare. Healthcare workers have long protected medical information under a variety of state and federal laws, accreditation standards, and rules of ethical conduct.

Generally, covered entities must continue to meet these standards when they provide greater privacy protections than HIPAA. This article highlights some federal healthcare laws that coexist with the HIPAA privacy rule to protect the confidentiality of patient information.

Protection of Human Subjects

The Federal Policy for the Protection of Human Subjects (common rule) protects the rights and privacy of human research subjects. With certain exceptions, it applies to entities conducting research supported or regulated by federal agencies. Human subjects research is conducted when a living individual's identifiable private information is used to contribute to generalizable knowledge.

An institutional review board (IRB) must approve human subjects research projects and clinical investigations. As part of this process, an IRB requires the existence of adequate protections for the privacy of subjects and the confidentiality of data, proportionate to the privacy risks. An informed consent describing how the confidentiality of identifiable records will be maintained must be sought from each subject. Under certain circumstances, such as when the only record linking the subject to the research would be the consent form itself, an IRB may waive the informed consent requirement. If research is being conducted by a covered entity under the HIPAA privacy rule, it must adhere to additional requirements for using and disclosing research subjects' protected health information.

A research institution may request a certificate of confidentiality (COC) from the National Institutes of Health whenever an IRB-approved research project involves the collection of personally identifiable sensitive information (such as genetic data). If granted, a COC allows an institution to refuse to make "involuntary disclosures" of identifying information about research subjects in response to subpoenas, court orders, and other legal mandates. Certain

Source: Roth, Julie A. "Getting 'Hip' to Other Privacy Laws, Part 2." *Journal of AHIMA* 75, no. 3 (March 2004): 48–50.

"voluntary" disclosures are permitted when necessary for maintaining public health, provided the informed consent contains a statement to this effect. Disclosures may also be made for program evaluations, audits, and in response to a subject's written consent.

Confidentiality of Alcohol and Drug Abuse Patient Records

The Confidentiality of Alcohol and Drug Abuse Patient Records rule has protected the privacy of patients treated in federally assisted alcohol and drug abuse programs since 1987. Programs are providers or facilities that provide alcohol or drug abuse care. Federal assistance is broadly defined and includes certification of provider status under the Medicare program or registration to dispense federally controlled substances.

At the time of admission, a program must inform a patient that his or her records are legally protected and give the patient a written summary of those protections. A program cannot acknowledge a patient's presence without written consent or a court order. Internal access to records must be appropriately limited, and a patient's written consent is required prior to disclosing records to third parties. Recipients must be notified in writing that they may not redisclose the records without the patient's written consent and that the law restricts use of the records in criminal matters. Whenever a request for patient information must be denied, the denial cannot affirmatively reveal that a patient is connected with drug or alcohol abuse.

In certain situations, a program may disclose patient information without written consent. Governmental agencies and private third-party payers may use patient records to conduct on-site audit and evaluation activities. If records are removed, the recipient must agree in writing to certain confidentiality protections.

Patient information may be used for research purposes provided that specific confidentiality protections are in place. The human subjects laws and the HIPAA privacy rule may apply as well. Patient information may also be disclosed in response to a valid subpoena accompanied by an authorizing court order.

Other Privacy Protections

To participate in the Medicare and Medicaid programs, providers must meet Conditions of Participation standards designed to ensure that program beneficiaries receive quality care. Numerous standards grant patients' control over their medical information and require providers to safeguard patient confidentiality. Hospitals must have procedures in place to protect clinical records from unauthorized access or alteration and may only release original records as permitted by law. Patients have a right of access to their own records within a reasonable time.

In hospice and home health settings, similar procedures for safeguarding the confidentiality of clinical records are required. Home health patients must be advised on how clinical records are disclosed and must consent in writing to disclosures not otherwise permitted by law. Nursing facility residents also have the right to the confidentiality of their clinical records and may generally approve or deny the release of records. However, records may be released to a healthcare institution where a resident is being transferred or as required by law.

The Clinical Laboratory Improvement laws govern the certification of laboratories conducting human specimen testing. Under these laws, laboratories may generally use patient information as necessary to carry out testing and quality improvement activities, provided confidentiality protections are in place. Specimens and reports must positively identify the patient throughout the testing process and be accessible in a timely manner.

Test results may be released to individuals authorized under state law to order or receive results, the laboratory requesting the test, and the individual responsible for using the test results. If an error occurs in the reporting process or test results indicate critical or "panic" values, the laboratory must immediately alert the individual or entity requesting the test or the individual using the test results.

Although the four privacy laws addressed in this article may not be as well known, their impact on patient care is significant. (See Figure 1.4, Privacy at a Glance, Part Two, for a summary of these laws.) By becoming more familiar with some of the lesser-known laws, we can all become more knowledgeable about privacy's important place in healthcare.

Figure 1.4.   Privacy at a glance, part two

	Protection of Human Subjects (45 CFR Part 46)	Confidentiality of Alcohol and Drug Abuse Patient Records (42 CFR Part 2)	Conditions of Participation (42 CFR Part 418, 482, 484) Standards & Certification (42 CFR Part 483)	Clinical Laboratory Improvements (42 CFR Part 493)
Applies to	• Institutions conducting federally supported human subjects research	• Federally assisted drug and alcohol abuse programs	• Medicare and Medicaid certified providers	• Laboratories performing testing on human specimens for diagnosis or treatment
Protected Information	• Identifiable private information	• Patient identifying information	• Personal and clinical records	• Not specified • Infer individually identifiable patient information
Protected Persons	• Human subjects	• Patients diagnosed, treated, or referred by federally assisted programs	• Medicare and Medicaid beneficiaries	• Persons whose specimens are submitted to laboratories
Privacy Notice	• Informed consent document	• Provide summary of protections at admission or patient's capacity • Sample notice in regulations	• Nursing facilities—notice of rights and services includes privacy information • Home health—must advise patient of policies and procedures regarding disclosure	None
Uses and Disclosures with Consent	• Informed consent required prior to using identifiable private information • Additional HIPAA privacy rule requirements may apply	• Disclosures not otherwise permitted require written consent • Include prohibition of redisclosure notice	• Hospitals—must release only to authorized individuals • Nursing facilities—residents may approve release of records • Home health—written consent required when disclosure not legally authorized	• Not specifically addressed • Disclosures limited to "authorized persons" or individual responsible for using test results
Uses and Disclosures without Consent	• IRB may waive informed consent requirement • Additional HIPAA privacy rule requirements may apply	• Medical emergencies • Research activities • Audits and evaluations • Subpoenas with authorizing court orders	• Hospitals—as permitted or required by law • Nursing facilities—as required by law to providers where patient is transferred	• Not specifically addressed • Must report panic values to individuals who ordered or use test results
Safeguarding Information	• IRB requires confidentiality protections	• Must keep records secure • Procedures regulating access	• Hospitals—access and alteration procedures • Hospice and home health—safeguard clinical records against loss, destruction, and unauthorized use	• Confidentiality must be protected in all phases of the testing process

Part 2
Administering HIPAA

Managing Individual Rights Requirements under HIPAA Privacy

Margret Amatayakul, MBA, RHIA, CHPS, FHIMSS

If your physicians' attitude toward patients requesting to amend their medical record is "I'd tell them to take a hike and then call my attorney," your environment is not unique. These words, in fact, are the verbatim response of a physician upon hearing the HIPAA privacy requirement that individuals have the right to request a covered entity to amend their health information. (This physician would be even more surprised to learn that although a provider may deny an individual's request for amendment, the request and denial must be appended or linked to the record if requested by the individual.)

This is just one example of the HIPAA privacy rule's provisions related to individual rights with respect to protected health information and the paradigm shift necessary to achieve compliance. This article offers suggestions for changing notions about individual rights to health information, defines terms associated with the privacy rights standards, and provides a table of documentation requirements.

Privacy Is Not New, But Rights Vary

The principle of privacy in healthcare dates back to Hippocrates, and all healthcare professionals adopt a form of the Hippocratic oath at the start of their professional life. For many reasons, however, the notion that individuals have rights to their health information has not typically been part of the privacy concept.

Privacy has always meant that health information must be kept confidential. It has generally been established by state statute or courts that a provider owns the physical records created by the provider in delivering care to individuals, subject to the individual's limited interest in the information. Caregivers recognize the need for patients to authorize release of information, but many believe patients have neither the right to access nor the knowledge to understand the content of their medical record.

In recent years, individuals have become much more educated on health issues and have had to play a much greater role in managing the flow of their information among multiple providers. As a result, individuals have demanded greater rights in their health information, and many states have adopted statutes providing for such rights in a variety of ways. Individuals

Source: Amatayakul, Margret. "Managing Individual Rights Requirements under HIPAA Privacy (HIPAA on the Job Series)." *Journal of AHIMA* 72, no. 6 (2001): 16A–D.

concerned about privacy rights had significant influence over inclusion of privacy standards in HIPAA.

The Privacy Paradigm and the Golden Rule

The very physician who expressed alarm over the idea that patients could amend their records took a step back when it was suggested that the privacy rule is essentially the Golden Rule. John Fanning, HHS' privacy officer, notes "we are all data subjects,"[1] and identifies citations from many of the great religions (Jewish scholar Hillel, the books of Matthew and Luke, and Confucius) that support the notion that "we should treat information about others as we would want others to treat information about us."

Presenting individuals' privacy rights to providers as yet another government regulation will only trigger consternation. While it is obviously necessary to follow the requirements in the regulations, approaching the issue from the perspective of patient care, quality, and communications as part of healthcare accessibility and portability under HIPAA goes a long way in turning around potentially negative attitudes.

Direct caregivers are primarily affected by the exercise of individuals' privacy rights. They need to understand why such rights are important to their patients and how to handle such requests. To do so, they should be involved in establishing privacy rights policies for the organization.

Although this is not a HIPAA mandate, caregivers may also want to review documentation policies and standards as a complement to establishing privacy policies. Many have developed comprehensive and tailored instructions for patients. Others provide encounter or discharge summaries to patients on a routine basis as part of patient education.

We all know it is not a good practice to write demeaning information about the patient or others in medical records—and HIPAA does not preclude use of abbreviations or medical terms. It is important, however, to bear in mind that a patient (or any individual the patient authorizes to receive a copy of the record) will be reading it, so ensuring accuracy, completeness, and appropriate language should remain a priority.

To What Do Individual Privacy Rights Apply?

The final privacy rule broadened the scope of privacy protection from solely individually identifiable health information in electronic form to such information in any form or medium, including paper and oral. Obviously, access can only be granted to information that is recorded in paper or electronic form. Hence, the privacy rule introduces the term "designated record set."

For a covered healthcare provider, this refers to medical records and billing records about individuals. For a health plan, it means the enrollment, payment, claims adjudication, and case or medical management record systems.

Some have suggested that the designated record set does not include "shadow records" or records maintained apart from the "official medical record." Sometimes these are created because a provider has difficulty getting access to records in a large, complex environment, for conducting research, or to achieve special protection such as for psychotherapy notes.

HIPAA, however, applies to any information retained for purposes of making decisions about individuals, although it has exceptions for psychotherapy notes and conditions for research. Any organization that suspects the existence of shadow records used for purposes of making decisions about individuals needs to be vigilant about identifying them and considering them as part of the designated record set for purposes of patients exercising their privacy rights. Most provider settings prefer to correct problems associated with access to records than to encourage maintenance of shadow records.

A careful review of the regulation's privacy rights reveals specific requirements related to informing patients of their rights, accepting and denying requests, and documenting actions. Figure 2.1, Patient Rights at a Glance, provides a summary of the key elements associated with each of the categories of individual privacy rights as they apply to providers. Some differences for health plans are not included.

Note

1. John Fanning, conversation with author, March 2, 2001.

Figure 2.1.   Patient rights at a glance

Right	Request	Acceptance	Termination	Timeliness	Fee	Denial	Review
Right to request restriction of uses and disclosures	Provider must permit request, but does not have to be in writing.	Provider not required to agree, but if accepted, must not violate restriction except for emergency care.	Provider may terminate if individual agrees or requests in writing, oral agreement is documented, or written notice for information created after.	There is no provision for addressing timeliness.	There is no provision for a fee.	There are no requirements associated with denying restriction.	Not applicable
Right to receive confidential communications	Provider may require written request for receiving communications by alternative means or locations.	Provider must accommodate reasonable requests and may condition on how payment will be handled, but may not require explanation.	There is no provision for termination.	There is no provision for addressing timeliness.	There is no provision for a fee.	Not applicable	Not applicable
Right of access to information	Provider must permit request for copying and inspection and may, upon notice, require requests in writing. Provider may supply a summary or explanation of information instead if individual agrees in advance.	Provider may deny access *without opportunity for review* if information is: psychotherapy notes, compiled for legal proceeding, subject to CLIA, about inmate and could cause harm, subject of research to which denial of access has been agreed, subject to Privacy Act, or obtained from someone else in confidence. Provider may deny access *with opportunity to review* if: licensed professional determines access may endanger life or safety, there is reference to another person and access could cause harm, or request made by personal representative who may cause harm.	Individuals have right of access for as long as information is maintained in designated record set.	Provider must act upon a request within 30 days. If information is not maintained on site, provider may extend by no more than 30 days if individual is notified of reasons for delay and given date for access.	Provider may impose reasonable, cost-based fee for copying, postage, and preparing an explanation or summary.	If access is denied, provider must provide timely written explanation in plain language, containing basis for denial, review rights if applicable, description of how to file a complaint, and source of information not maintained by provider if known. Provider must also give individual access to any part of information not covered under grounds for denial.	An individual may request a review of a denial by a different healthcare professional.

Figure 2.1. (Continued)

Right	Request	Acceptance	Termination	Timeliness	Fee	Denial	Review
Right to amend information	Provider must permit requests to amend a designated record set and may, upon notice, require request in writing and a reason.	If amendment is accepted, provider must append or link to record set and obtain and document identification and agreement to have provider notify relevant persons with which amendment needs to be shared. Provider may deny amendment if information: was not created by the provider unless individual provides reasonable basis that originator is no longer available to act on request, is not part of designated record set, would not be available for access, or is accurate and complete.	Amendment applies for as long as information is maintained in designated record set.	Provider must act upon a request within 60 days of receipt. If unable to act on request within 60 days, provider may extend time by no more than 30 days provided individual is notified of reasons for delay and given date to amend.	There is no provision for a fee.	If amendment is denied, provider must provide timely written explanation in plain language, containing basis for denial, right to submit written statement of disagreement, right to request provider include request and denial with any future disclosures of information that is subject of amendment, and description of how to file a complaint.	Provider must accept written statement of disagreement (of limited length). Provider may prepare written rebuttal and must copy individual. Provider must append or link request, denial, disagreement, and rebuttal to record and include such or accurate summary with any subsequent disclosure. If no written disagreement, provider must include request and denial, or summary, in subsequent disclosures only if individual has requested such action.
Right to accounting of disclosures	Provider must provide individual with written accounting including date of disclosure, name and address of recipient, description of information disclosed, purpose of disclosure or copy of individual's written authorization or other request for disclosure.	Provider must provide individual and retain documentation of written accounting of disclosures of protected health information made in six years prior to date of request, except for disclosures to carry out treatment, payment, and healthcare operations; individuals about themselves; facility's directory or persons involved in care; national security; and correctional institutions or certain law enforcement situations that occurred prior to compliance date.	Not applicable	Provider must act upon request within 60 days of receipt. If unable to provide accounting, provider may extend time by no more than 30 days provided individual is notified of reasons for delay.	First accounting in any 12-month period must be provided without charge. A reasonable, cost-based fee may be charged for subsequent accountings in 12-month period if individual is notified in advance.	Provider must temporarily suspend right to receive an accounting of disclosures to health oversight agency or law enforcement official if agency or official provides written statement that accounting would impede their activities.	There is no provision for review of temporary suspension.

Sorting Out Employee Sanctions

Jill Burrington-Brown, MS, RHIA

Has your organization addressed sanctions related to privacy and security issues? Both the final privacy rule and final security rule address this issue. The privacy rule states that the covered entity must "have and apply appropriate sanctions against members of its workforce who fail to comply with the privacy policies and procedures of the covered entity," and the security rule states relatively the same thing. Every covered entity must have policies and procedures that address:

- Appropriate employee behavior regarding privacy and security
- Typical sanctions for noncompliance of the policies and procedures
- Communication to and education of the work force
- The sanction application process (investigations and terminations)

The covered entity should develop privacy and security sanction policies with the involvement of all interested stakeholders such as privacy and security officers, executives, and the human resources, quality improvement, risk management, and HIM departments. Using their expertise and existing policies will ensure a more successful implementation of your program. This article will explain how to implement an employee compliance and sanction program.

Start with the Basics

What does the employee need to know about privacy and security? The best way to deliver the message is to explain it as simply as possible:

- Privacy is important.
- Medical information is confidential.
- There are specific times when you may share what you know.

Source: Burrington-Brown, Jill. "Sorting Out Employee Sanctions." *Journal of AHIMA* 74, no. 6 (June 2003): 53–54.

Certainly those of us in HIM already understand this, but the audience will be broad and include personnel who may not be familiar with basic HIM notions about security and privacy of patient health information. Explaining the above concepts through the use of scenarios (both real and fictional) will help explain the breadth and depth of the issue.

Spell Out Sanctions

Employees must be informed of the disciplinary actions the covered entity will take in the event of a privacy or security incident. This must also include giving notice of the possible civil and criminal penalties for misuse or misappropriation of health information.

Sanctions might include verbal warnings, removal of system privileges, and termination of employment. Organizations will want to consider the range of disciplinary actions, from verbal or written warnings to termination of employment, and match them to the types of infractions. For example, violations that are inadvertent, of low severity, and indicate a need for training may only require verbal correction and retraining. Such violations might be clinician conversations in semipublic areas or delivery of health records to the wrong clinical area.

Deliberate, intentional infractions should trigger a disciplinary process that results in termination of employment. These types of infractions might include the sale of confidential information or the unauthorized access of health information out of curiosity. Whatever the infractions, covered entities must make every effort to apply the sanctions evenly across all job classes in order to avoid actions that might lead to employment discrimination charges.

Make Time for Training

Educating staff is the next step in building a reasonable compliance and sanction program. The covered entity should provide and document privacy training to all staff as is appropriate to their job duties. The organization should include not only the policies regarding protected health information (PHI) but also the consequences of both inadvertent and deliberate violations of PHI policies.

The covered entity should document that staff training was provided. It should also have each member sign a confidentiality agreement indicating understanding of the policies and the possible repercussions of any type of security or privacy incident.

Investigating Violations

Organizations must address the process of investigation. While the privacy rule specifies that a privacy officer must be appointed and be responsible about the development and implementation of policies and procedures, this does not mean the privacy officer is responsible for the roles traditionally fulfilled by human resources. In fact, the privacy officer must work through the complaint, investigation, and employee sanction process with human resources to make sure all other applicable employment laws and union regulations are followed.

It is also important to note that the privacy officer may not need to be involved in all employee actions if the policies and procedures are detailed and thorough. Finally, if sanctions are applied in any disciplinary process, they must be documented.

Many healthcare organizations include volunteers and credentialed healthcare staff in their work force. Because this part of the work force is not controlled by employment, the sanction process must be carefully considered in order to be appropriately and fairly applied.

The sanctions for minor, inadvertent infractions can be quite similar to those for the employed work force. However, job suspensions and terminations are more difficult with volunteers and physicians who are not hired. Asking the volunteer not to return does not seem as severe a consequence as job termination, but it may be what the organization decides is appropriate.

A physician who has gone through an extensive credentialing process will likely have the medical staff bylaws to follow. These bylaws should be reviewed for compliance with the rules and to establish a process for physician infractions requiring more severe consequences than retraining.

Members of an organization's work force will better understand the need for privacy and security policies when they understand that the civil and criminal penalties for violations of the rules are stiff. Civil fines can amount to $25,000 for repeated violations in the same year, and the deliberate misuse of PHI can incur a $250,000 fine along with 10 years imprisonment.

References

Arnall Golden Gregory LLP. "Privacy Rule Takes Effect April 14, 2001: The Clock is Ticking." *HIPAA Bulletin.* May 2001.

Opus Communications. "Develop Employee Sanctions for Privacy Violations." *Briefings on HIPAA* 2, no. 7 (2002): 1–3.

"Standards for Privacy of Individually Identifiable Health Information; Final Rule." 45 CFR Parts 160 and 164. *Federal Register* 67, no. 157 (August 14, 2002). Available at http://aspe.hhs.gov/ admnsimp/.

Documenting Your Compliance with HIPAA's Privacy Rule

Margret Amatayakul, MBA, RHIA, CHPS, FHIMSS

While possibly not granting every wish on a HIM professional's privacy wish list, the final rule on privacy, issued in December 2000, comes close to addressing most of the principles we espouse. Now—perhaps—we may see more precautions, both to limit use and disclosure to healthcare purposes and to afford individuals rights to their health information.

The qualifying "perhaps" recognizes that today, more than ever before, information flows through our organizations at lightning speed. More people within an organization can easily print healthcare documents, automatically send a fax, and e-mail attachments. The risk of even well-intentioned and permitted—but not documented—disclosure is greater than ever before. And while new compliance and enforcement provisions in the final privacy rule provide the Department of Health and Human Services (HHS) broad compliance powers, the actual level of enforcement further qualifies the impact the rule may have.

Regulation vs. Legislation— What's the Difference?

Another qualification is the fact that the privacy rule is regulation, not legislation. HIPAA required the privacy issue to be handled, by default, by regulation if Congress did not pass legislation on it.

As a result, the rule only applies to information held by covered entities (a health plan, clearinghouse, or provider who transmits any health information in electronic form in connection with a transaction included in HIPAA). The final rule expands protected health information to include not only information in electronic form, but information in oral and paper form, but only when held by a covered entity. This includes providers who send paper claims to a clearinghouse or billing service that converts them to electronic form to send to a health plan. It is unknown how many providers rely solely on paper transactions and are therefore excluded from compliance.

All other organizations that have access to health information, such as employers, banks, and schools, are not covered entities. In an attempt to protect information in such organizations, the covered entity must have a business associate contract requiring the business associate to

Source: Amatayakul, Margret. "Documenting Your Compliance with HIPAA's Privacy Rule (HIPAA on the Job series)." *Journal of AHIMA* 72, no. 4 (2001): 16A–D.

protect the health information, but putting the burden on the covered entity to see that the contract is enforced.

The final privacy rule also does not preempt more stringent state laws. Many states are passing more stringent laws to fill perceived gaps created by HIPAA. As a result, everyone will need to monitor state law, determine which is more stringent, and act accordingly.

Finally, the scope of HIPAA does not include private right of action, meaning that individuals cannot use it as a basis for a lawsuit when an egregious act occurs as a result of wrongful disclosure.

The Privacy Balancing Act

The fundamental premise upon which the privacy rule is based is that it should be easy to use health information for healthcare purposes and very difficult to use it for any other purpose. To carry out such a premise, HHS has had to strike a balance between individuals who want total restrictions on health information and covered entities and others who need the information to care for patients and carry out their work.

There is also a balance between too much and too little in terms of compliance activities. A word search of the final rule and its preamble reveals that the term "reasonable" is used 256 times. "Reasonable" relates to the manner in which the rule is implemented by various sizes and types of covered entities. For example, a single practitioner is unlikely to perform sophisticated statistical calculations to deidentify information. Alternatively, a large health plan or academic medical center may be expected to apply a statistical process to ensure that information shared with employers or data for research is completely deidentified.

Perhaps the most important role an HIM professional can play with respect to HIPAA's privacy rule is that of reconciler—making sense out of the rule, interpreting it for others, and overseeing the myriad of documentation required to demonstrate compliance.

How Can I Document Compliance?

The key to compliance with the privacy rule lies in documentation. Our mantra has always been "if it's not documented, it wasn't done." To apply the rule to actual practice, it is helpful to categorize three major types of documentation that will contribute to providers' compliance. The sample checklists in this article offer guidance on what you should document to support your compliance decisions. (This analysis does not focus on specific requirements for health plans, nor should it be a substitute for careful reading of the rule itself.)

HIPAA does not require a specific privacy compliance plan. It does require creation of policies and procedures that are reasonably designed, taking into account size and type of activities. It also describes compliance reports that must be submitted to the secretary of HHS if compliance must be ascertained.

While such reports are not required on a routine basis, it is advisable to prepare them for internal use and in the event they are required. Documentation of all policies, procedures, communications, and actions must be retained for six years from date of creation or when last in effect, and must be kept up to date with any changes in the law. Therefore, it may be useful to develop an internal privacy compliance plan and compile a file of or index to all relevant documents, their creation and revision dates, authority for use, etc.

Although auditing is not required, it may be a good idea to periodically audit practices associated with some of this documentation to ensure compliance. (See Figure 2.2, A General Policy Checklist.)

Figure 2.2.   Documenting your compliance

A General Policy Checklist

☐ **Personnel designations** (privacy officer/office responsible for receiving complaints): Job description, with authority commensurate with responsibility. It is strongly recommended that this person be knowledgeable about the content and flow of health information and able to serve in a patient advocacy role.

☐ **Minimum necessary *use:*** Classification of persons, categorization of information, applicable conditions. This may be manifested in access control list technology for electronic information and assignment of access authorization for paper information. It is recommended that this be periodically audited.

☐ **Minimum necessary *disclosures:***

    ☐ Routine/recurring: Policy and procedure required; recommend periodic audits

    ☐ Other nonroutine/recurring disclosures: Criteria to limit disclosure, procedure for reviewing requests

☐ **Minimum necessary *requests* by public officials, professional members of the work force or business associate, or researchers:** Requests for information made by a covered entity when requesting information from other covered entities must be kept to the minimum necessary. It will be interesting to see how this applies to health plans when they must provide justification for disclosure of an entire medical record.

☐ **Deidentification:** Policy and procedure for deidentification and reidentification (code for reidentification may not be derived from information about the individual); periodic audit recommended.

☐ **Personal representative:** Documentation of name and relationship recommended

☐ **Confidential communications:** Policy and procedure for documentation and conditions (although provider may not require an explanation for the request). Such communications are fairly commonplace today for laboratory test reporting. It is suggested that the request for communications to be sent to an alternative location be retained as a record of compliance.

☐ **Uses and disclosures consistent with notice:** Wording of notice will require attention to completeness with respect to the standard, and it should be informative without potentially inviting an avalanche of requests. It is suggested that a periodic audit be used to ensure that uses and disclosures are, indeed, consistent with the notice.

☐ **Whistleblower protections:** Whistleblowers may disclose protected health information in the course of filing a complaint. Human resource policies should include provisions for such activity without retaliation.

Documents Ensuring Individuals' Rights

Documents required to comply with individuals' rights include the following:

☐ **Consent:** Form should comply with the specific requirements in the rule and signed consents should be retained.

☐ **Authorization:** There are specific requirements for general authorizations as well as those for specific types of disclosures.

☐ **Verification** of identity and documentation of permitted disclosures where authorization is required: There should be policy and procedure for the verification process; it is suggested that documentation associated with the verification process be retained.

☐ **Use and disclosure without authorization** for facility directories and involvement in care: Individuals must be informed that they will be included in facility directories, such as current census, and that a disclosure may be made to clergy or others who ask for the individual by name. Family members or others may also be provided information during the care process. Neither of these disclosures requires authorization, but individuals must be explicitly informed and given the opportunity to object, or the provider must reasonably infer that there is no objection. While documentation is not required, if there is any doubt about the right of opportunity, it would be wise to at least document the communication. If there is a request for restriction or objection, it is recommended that this be documented. It may also be a good practice to have a standard procedure for informing individuals.

(Continued on next page)

Figure 2.2.   (Continued)

☐ **Uses and disclosures for which consent, authorization, or opportunity to agree or object is not required:** Document use or disclosure for purposes of accounting for disclosure.

☐ **Research** where institutional review board or privacy board has approved alteration or waiver of authorization: Document alternation or waiver criteria.

☐ **Marketing and fund-raising communications** without authorization: Review communications to ensure they meet requirements.

☐ **Notice of privacy practices:** Notice includes specific content requirements. Document provision of notice and all revisions.

☐ **Rights to request restrictions** on disclosure, access, amendment, and accounting for disclosures: Establish policy with respect to what will be accepted and what will be denied. Develop procedures and documentation processes for carrying out these requests, denials, and adjudication of denials.

☐ **Training:** Retain copy of content and attendance records. Although certification of work force member attending the training and abiding by the procedures and recertification every three years are no longer required, these are solid business practices an organization may wish to consider adopting anyway.

☐ **Safeguard:** The requirement to adopt administrative, technical, and physical safeguards to protect privacy essentially refers to the security proposed rule.

☐ **Complaints:** Policy, procedures, and office for receipt and disposition should be established. Retain complaint and documentation of action.

☐ **Sanctions:** Most providers have confidentiality agreements that indicate that breaches of confidentiality may lead to termination. It is advisable to establish more detail concerning escalation of actions and sanctions.

Documentation to Protect Contractual Obligations

Documentation required to protect **contractual obligations** is the third category that a provider should ensure exists. These include:

☐ **Business associate contract:** Contract must establish permitted and required uses and disclosures and safeguard information. Providers will have many associates, from contract transcription services that clearly have access to protected health information, to information, systems vendors who may have dial-in access for troubleshooting and providing updates. A data flow diagram may help identify all direct business associates. Although separate contracts are not required for downstream recipients of protected health information, identifying these can help ensure that the associates' agents are addressed in the contracts.

☐ **Healthcare component of hybrid entity:** Document relationship and responsibilities of covered entity. Ensure that plan agreement is updated to incorporate new restrictions on disclosure, including use of summary information.

☐ **Affiliated covered entities:** Many providers have business ventures. If these are other providers (such as a retail pharmacy or home health agency), document designation of affiliation and responsibilities with respect to joint notices and other documents.

☐ **Multiple covered functions:** Many providers also operate health plans. Document relationships and responsibilities.

☐ **Mitigation of harmful effect of a use or disclosure:** Establish a tracking mechanism and procedure for action.

Catching Up with HIPAA: Managing Noncompliance

Abner E. Weintraub

With the April 14 HIPAA privacy deadline behind us, many covered entities are still struggling to become compliant. Limited budgets and staff, conflicting advice, and unforeseen delays have all conspired to keep many covered entities from meeting the deadline.

What do you tell patients and other constituents when you're behind with compliance? How do you manage media inquiries, legal challenges, and business associates when you're not quite ready to do HIPAA right? This article provides practical guidance to minimize the damage that being out of compliance could cause while you put the final pieces of your HIPAA compliance program in place.

What Went Wrong?

You planned, you intended, you tried, but somehow the HIPAA privacy deadline passed and your organization is still not ready. Many factors may have hindered your efforts, but now is not the time to analyze what went wrong. You have more important things to do.

HIPAA presents a unique problem. Unlike most other federal healthcare laws, patients and consumers actually know about HIPAA and their new HIPAA rights. The public is learning about HIPAA through media reports in television, radio, and print. We are also telling patients about HIPAA with our notice of privacy practices and getting signatures affirming its receipt. There is no hiding HIPAA. It's time to manage your organization's compliance.

Should You Be Concerned?

Absolutely. Lack of compliance with or violations of HIPAA's privacy rule could result in many problems, such as:

- Fines and other sanctions under HIPAA law

- Legal actions from patients under state and (non-HIPAA) federal law

Source: Weintraub, Abner E. "Catching Up with HIPAA: Managing Noncompliance." *Journal of AHIMA* 74, no. 5 (May 2003): 67–68.

- Problems with the Joint Commission, National Committee for Quality Assurance, and other accrediting bodies

- Media exposure resulting in loss of reputation, credibility, and patients

- Higher insurance premiums

HIPAA's privacy rule is enforced by the Office for Civil Rights (OCR) of the US Department of Health and Human Services. OCR's enforcement will be primarily "complaint driven," meaning few, if any, surprise inspections for privacy compliance. But these inspections should be the least of your worries.

While patients do not have a clear right to a private "cause of action" under HIPAA, plaintiffs may sue under state tort laws such as "right to privacy." The federal statutes will allege to be the standard of care that the covered entity fell below. And if a breach of the rules and subsequent damages result, all the elements for a tort claim (action brought about when one party believes another has caused harm through wrongful conduct and the party bringing action is seeking compensation for that harm) will be met. To be safe, you must understand the difference between noncompliance and actual violations of HIPAA's privacy rule.

Noncompliance versus Violations

Just being out of compliance with the privacy rule could be seen as a violation itself. But noncompliance and rule violations are not the same. HIPAA's privacy rule is all about protecting confidential patient information known as protected health information (PHI). A quick look at HIPAA's fines and sanctions reveals a little recognized, but very important fact: the smaller penalties are for "failure to comply," while the serious penalties are for "wrongful disclosures" of PHI.

Your organization's biggest risk as you complete compliance is not what could happen if your noncompliance is discovered. Rather, it is that you or your employees might accidentally or willfully cause serious privacy violations and suffer serious consequences.

What to Do Now

If you are still working on privacy compliance, the following suggestions can help you minimize problems:

Make elements that are visible to patients and outsiders your top priority. Your notice of privacy practices, privacy complaint form, and patients' rights request forms are the most visible symbols of HIPAA compliance. Be certain these are done first, along with the systems and processes to support them.

Train yourself and your employees properly. HIPAA requires training for all employees but does not specify the type of training or how it should be delivered. Because behavior can create the most serious HIPAA violations, employees are your greatest vulnerability, and effective training is your best insurance against HIPAA violations.

Create clear policies and procedures. These are essential to understanding daily life under HIPAA for employees. Consider saving time by purchasing and customizing model policies.

Remind patients their health privacy is paramount. Create privacy awareness by frequently reminding patients that your organization is very careful about protecting their privacy. Show this in the careful way that doctors or staff discuss confidential matters with patients, lower their voices, or move to more private areas (HIPAA's "reasonable precautions") to show they are serious about protecting patient privacy.

Be ready to document your compliance status. If challenged by patients, business associates, the courts, or the media before you're fully compliant, be ready to clearly state why you're behind and what you're doing about it. It's more difficult to argue with a latecomer who is working overtime to finish than with one who appears to be complacent.

Continue your compliance efforts aggressively. If your temporary noncompliance is discovered, you may have to prepare an explanatory statement or pay a small fine. But if you or your employees commit serious violations of the privacy rule, even accidentally, the consequences could be catastrophic.

Understanding the Minimum Necessary Standard

Beth Hjort, RHIT, CHP

HIM professionals have long made it a practice to limit information disclosed to that information required to fulfill the stated purpose. For example, an HIM professional would not disclose information about a woman's breast removal on a workers' compensation claim for a lacerated finger. Instead, the HIM professional would limit information disclosed to that related only to the injured finger. In other words, the HIM professional would disclose only that information the recipient needs to know.

The Standards for Privacy of Individually Identifiable Health Information, more commonly called the Health Insurance Portability and Accountability Act (HIPAA) final privacy rule, formalize and expand the need-to-know principle. The revised principle is known as the minimum necessary standard. It is important that HIM professionals understand the minimum necessary standard, as most covered entities (CEs) [were required to comply] no later than April 14, 2003.[1]

HIPAA Final Privacy Rule

Minimum Necessary Standard Applicability

The August 14, 2002, version of the HIPAA final privacy rule states that the minimum necessary standard applies when using or disclosing protected health information (PHI), or when requesting PHI from another CE.[2] It goes on to say that CEs must make reasonable efforts to limit PHI to the minimum necessary to accomplish the intended purpose of the use, disclosure, or request.

The rule, however, provides some exceptions. It says that the minimum necessary standard does not apply to:

- Disclosures to or requests by healthcare providers for treatment

- Disclosures to the individual who is the subject of the information

- Uses or disclosures made pursuant to an authorization

Source: Hjort, Beth. "Understanding the Minimum Necessary Standard (AHIMA Practice Brief)" (Updated March 2003).

- Uses or disclosures required for compliance with the standardized HIPAA transactions

- Disclosures to the Department of Health and Human Services when disclosure of information is required under the rule for enforcement purposes

- Uses or disclosures required by law

Applying the Standard When Disclosing Information

The implementation specifications for the minimum necessary standard require that:[3]

- CEs identify the persons or classes of persons in their work force who need access to PHI.

- CEs identify the category or categories of PHI for which access is needed for the person or classes of persons and any conditions appropriate to such access.

- CEs make reasonable efforts to limit the work force's access to PHI to that which is needed to carry out their duties.

- For any type of disclosure that occurs on a routine and recurring basis, CEs implement policies and procedures that limit the PHI disclosed to the amount reasonably necessary to achieve the purpose of the disclosure.

- For all other disclosures, CEs develop criteria designed to limit the PHI disclosed to the information reasonably necessary to accomplish the purpose for which disclosure is sought, and review requests for disclosure on an individual basis in accordance with such criteria.

The rule states that CEs may rely on the judgment of the party requesting the disclosure as to the minimum amount of information needed when the request is made by:

- A public official or agency for a disclosure permitted under 45 CFR 164.512 (uses and disclosures for which consent, an authorization, or opportunity to agree or object is not required)

- Another CE

- A professional who is a work force member or business associate of the CE holding the information

- A researcher with appropriate documentation from an institutional review board or privacy board

The rule does not require that the CE rely on the judgment of the requester, however. The CE retains the right to make its own minimum necessary determination for disclosures to which the minimum necessary standard applies.

Incidental Uses and Disclosures

While the privacy rule holds CEs responsible for making reasonable efforts to limit information use and disclosure to the minimum necessary and to guard against inappropriate intentional or unintentional releases, it recognizes the likelihood that inadvertent releases may occur as a by-product of normal healthcare practices. As such, an additional provision was included in the August 14, 2002, privacy rule modifications making incidental disclosure permissible "to the extent that the CE has applied reasonable safeguards as required by 164.530(c) and implemented the minimum necessary standard, where applicable, as required by 164.502(b) and 164.514(d)" (page 53193). Without conscientious compliance to the minimum necessary standards, incidental disclosures would be considered a violation of the privacy rule.

Requesting Protected Information

Further, the implementation specifications for the minimum necessary standard state that:

- When requesting PHI from other covered entities, a CE must limit any request for PHI to that which is reasonably necessary to accomplish the purpose for which the request is made.

- For a request that is made on a routine and recurring basis, a CE must implement policies and procedures that limit the PHI requested to the amount reasonably necessary to accomplish the purpose for which the request is made.

- For all other requests, a CE must review the request on an individual basis to determine that the PHI sought is limited to the information reasonably necessary to accomplish the purpose for which the request is made.

A CE may not use, disclose, or request an entire medical record, except when the entire medical record is specifically justified as the amount of information that is reasonably necessary to accomplish the purpose of the use, disclosure, or request.

Recommendations

- Study the minimum necessary standard and the December 4, 2002, HIPAA Privacy Guidance.

- Evaluate where, when, and how PHI is requested.

- Evaluate when, where, and how PHI is disclosed.

- Develop policies and procedures to ensure that the information requested and disclosed is the minimum necessary to fulfill the stated purpose:

    —Develop policies and procedures for fulfilling routine requests for information on a consistent basis.

    —Develop policies and procedures to determine which requests must be scrutinized for compliance with the minimum necessary requirements.

    —Develop policies and procedures to ensure that the information requested and disclosed for nonroutine requests is the minimum necessary to fulfill the stated purpose.

- Educate and train staff about appropriate application of the standards when requesting, using, or disclosing health information.

- Evaluate work force access needs to PHI. Identify the information the individuals or categories of individuals need to know to do their jobs. Maintain documentation of such determinations.

- Develop policies and procedures that limit access by the work force to only the PHI they need to know to do their jobs.

- Develop policies and procedures that ensure that the minimum necessary standard is applied to the request when appropriate. For example, develop a system for periodically auditing disclosures made to ensure that the minimum necessary requirements were met where appropriate. Take corrective action when indicated.

Notes

1. Health plans, healthcare clearinghouses, and healthcare providers who submit certain transactions electronically.

2. 42 CFR, Section 164.502 (b).

3. 42 CFR, Section 164.514 (d).

References

Office for Civil Rights. Guidance explaining significant aspects of the privacy rule. December 4, 2002. Available at www.hhs.gov/ocr/hipaa/privacy.html.

"Standards for Privacy of Individually Identifiable Health Information; Final Rule." 45 CFR Parts 160 through 164. *Federal Register* 67, no. 157 (August 14, 2002).

Implementing the Minimum Necessary Standard

Margret Amatayakul, MBA, RHIA, CHPS, FHIMSS
Mary D. Brandt, RHIA, CHE, CHP
Jill Callahan Dennis, JD, RHIA

The minimum necessary standard in HIPAA's privacy rule requires covered entities to make reasonable efforts to limit protected health information (PHI) to the minimum necessary to accomplish the intended purpose of the use, disclosure, or request.

The challenge with implementing the minimum necessary standard is defining what is "reasonably necessary" and determining how minimum necessary uses, disclosures, and requests will be managed in the nonautomated and automated worlds.

Regulatory Requirements

The minimum necessary standard does not apply to disclosures to or requests by a healthcare provider for treatment, uses, or disclosures made to the individual or as authorized by the individual or to the secretary of the Department of Health and Human Services (HHS) for compliance enforcement.[1]

For the minimum necessary standard, the privacy rule requires that the covered entity identify persons or classes of persons in its work force who need access to PHI and the category or categories of PHI to which access is needed and any conditions appropriate to such access.[2] This constitutes the requirements for ensuring minimum necessary use. For routine and recurring disclosures, the rule requires the covered entity to implement standard protocols that limit the disclosures to the amount reasonably necessary to achieve the purpose of the disclosures.[3] For all other disclosures, the covered entity must develop criteria designed to limit the PHI disclosed to the minimum necessary. Covered entities must also limit any request they make for PHI to that which is reasonably necessary.

This practice brief addresses a perspective for handling minimum necessary use and for offering tools to address both routine and nonroutine minimum necessary disclosures and requests.

Achieving and Monitoring Adherence

Once policies and procedures to ensure minimum necessary uses and disclosures have been established, the covered entity must make reasonable efforts to limit the use of PHI in accordance

Source: Amatayakul, Margret; Mary D. Brandt, and Jill Callahan Dennis. "Implementing the Minimum Necessary Standard (AHIMA Practice Brief)." *Journal of AHIMA* 73, no. 9 (2002): 96A–F.

with those policies and procedures. This ongoing monitoring of compliance will require culture change, training, and regular compliance monitoring.

The culture change may be the most difficult task to accomplish. In many provider settings, clinicians are used to having total access to any patient's medical record. While the minimum necessary standard does not apply to use and disclosure for treatment, the provider has a responsibility to verify that uses and disclosures are indeed for treatment purposes.

In any instance in which the identity or authority of a requestor is not known to the covered entity, section 164.514(h) of the privacy rule requires that the covered entity obtain applicable documentation, statements, or representations in support of the purpose of the request and/or identity of the requestor.

Discussing with the covered entity's own clinicians the underlying purpose of the minimum necessary standard, assuring them that they will always have appropriate access to information for patient care, and recognizing the value of accountability relative to uses and disclosures should help alleviate their concerns.

Notes

1. The minimum necessary standard is also distinguished from the confidential communication standard, which permits patients to ask that confidential communications be handled in alternative locations or by alternative means. Confidential communications pertain to discussions and other communications with patients or other members of the work force about treatment and is designed to keep legitimate communications from being overheard or seen by those without authority to have such information.

2. When responding to questions on access controls, HHS refers visitors to its Web site to the National Institute of Standards and Technology (NIST) publication NIST SP 800-12, *An Introduction to Computer Security: The NIST Handbook,* Chapter 17, "Logical Access Control."

3. According to HHS, "This is not a strict standard and covered entities need not limit information uses or disclosures to those that are absolutely needed to serve the purpose. Rather, this is a reasonableness standard that calls for an approach consistent with the best practices and guidelines already used by many providers today to limit the unnecessary sharing of medical information."

What's Your Designated Record Set?

Margret Amatayakul, MBA, RHIA, CHPS, FHIMSS
Pam Waymack

The HIPAA privacy rule provides individuals the right to request access to and amendment of their protected health information maintained in a designated record set (DRS). To ensure that the DRS is completely identified but excludes information that does not pertain, covered entities should adopt a definition that clearly identifies what is included and what is excluded.

Many providers may take for granted that the DRS is what is between the covers of the patient chart. However, what constitutes the chart varies by provider, setting, and health plan, and the notion of the DRS will vary as well. The privacy rule's definition is somewhat fluid: "A group of records maintained by or for a covered entity that is: [for a provider] the medical records and billing records about individuals; [for a health plan] the enrollment, payment, claims adjudication, and case or medical management record systems; or [for any covered entity] used, in whole or in part, by or for the covered entity to make decisions about individuals."

It is important to recognize that the DRS definition does not address the means or location of storage of the information. The DRS, therefore, is not necessarily information contained solely in a single repository, but very likely information located in multiple places and from multiple sources. Some of the information may even be in an outsourced location for health plans that use a disease management company, a pharmacy benefits management company, or other structures for part of their information processing.

Start with the Legal Medical Record . . .

There are several approaches providers can take in defining their designated record set. A good place to start is AHIMA's definition of the legal medical record.[1] Key principles in this definition are:

- The inclusion of official business record of provider

- The exclusion of source data (e.g., films, videos) unless interpretations, summarizations, or transcriptions are not available

---

Source: Amatayakul, Margret, and Pam Waymack. "What's Your Designated Record Set?" (HIPAA on the Job series) *Journal of AHIMA* 73, no. 6 (2002): 16A–C.

- The exclusion of administrative data, such as authorization for release of information, vital certificate worksheets, audit trails, copies of claims, etc.

- The exclusion of derived data for purposes of accreditation and other aggregate data

The DRS shares many features with the legal medical record. First, the DRS should not include information used for operational purposes of the organization, such as quality improvement data. The definition of operations provided in the privacy rule is a good source of identifying what is considered operational and therefore not what constitutes treatment (or medical records) and payment (or billing records).

Another similarity the legal medical record shares with the DRS is that guidance imposed by more stringent state laws and other regulations must be observed. Examples of situations in which more stringent laws must be observed would include HIPAA's requirements with respect to excluding psychotherapy notes, instances in which information was created as part of a research study to which the patient has temporarily waived right to access, or instances in which information was created in anticipation of a legal action.

Like the legal medical record, the DRS should not include copies of records from other providers. While information from these records may have been used in making decisions about care, patients should be directed to request access to or amendment of such information from the originating provider. In fact, the provider may deny access to such information on the grounds that the information was not created by the provider. Ideally, clinicians using such information should document such use in, for example, a progress note summarizing the information reviewed.

Finally, the content of the DRS may be in multiple locations and media, including paper and electronic forms.

. . . Then Go Beyond It

Despite the similarities between the two, the legal medical record does not meet the requirements of the DRS in a few key areas.

First, the DRS must include both medical and billing records, thus, some of the administrative data in a provider setting, such as a claim, would be included in the DRS. For a health plan, much of the DRS will be related to billing information. Consider using the privacy rule's definitions of treatment and payment as sources for defining what is included in medical and billing records.

Second, many covered entities would prefer not to include source data that are not interpreted, summarized, or transcribed. While it would not be wrong to include such data, they are not likely to be retained for a long period of time nor directly accessible in a format that is easy to copy or permit a patient to review. Indeed, some of this information may be on scraps of paper, in the comment fields of claims adjudication systems, or in voice form. Keep in mind that access and amendment do not entitle an individual to alter the information. Even in the case of an amendment, much like any correction a provider or health plan makes today, an amendment should be linked to or referenced as something added but never substituted for an existing part of the business records of the covered entity.

Third, whereas the legal medical record substantiates the business function of the provider (which is the care provided to the patient), the DRS is created to respond to patients' requests concerning the information used in making decisions about them. While these are not mutually exclusive purposes, they are somewhat different.

Keep the Purpose in Mind

Once the DRS has been defined in terms of what it includes and excludes, the next step is to identify where the included information can be obtained (such as from the HIM department, business office, clinic, or medical management department) and in what format it may be supplied to the patient (for example, viewing from a monitor or reviewing a printout only). (See Figure 2.3, Sample Designated Record Set Definition.)

Another key consideration is when and where the DRS will be available. Many providers are concerned about giving the patient access to the DRS during the patient care encounter because it may be incomplete or it could be difficult to maintain its integrity. Indeed, the original copy of the DRS is a legal document and patients cannot remove any of its content or write in it.

The privacy rule does not specify when or where the record should be available, therefore providers should establish specific policies. However, because the purpose of the DRS is to provide access and amendment, the most important time for a patient to have such access or to make an amendment may be during an admission or other patient care encounter and while it may be incomplete.

Figure 2.3.   Sample designated record set definition

Excluded Items	Included Items	Form Supplied to Patient	Source
Source data, including photographs, films, monitoring strips, videotapes, slides, and worksheets	Legal medical record, including photographs, strips, and other source data incorporated into progress notes	Copy of paper chart, printout, or summarization, view computer screen or original record with attendant only	Physician, head nurse, HIM department
Administrative data, such as audit trails, appointment schedules, and practice guidelines that do not imbed patient data	Patient-specific claim, remittance, eligibility response, and claim status response, charge screen, statement of account balance, and payment agreement	Copy of paper document or printout only	Business office
	Consent and authorization forms, Medicare ABN letter, Medicare Life Time Reserve Letter, Medicare Notice of Noncoverage Letter, and copy of insurance card	Copy of paper document only	Business office, HIM department
Other provider records	Patient-submitted documentation and referral letters	Copy of paper chart or printout, computer screen or original record with attendant only	HIM department, physician office
Derived data	Minimum data set specific to patient	View with attendant only	HIM department

Note: When photographs are mounted within the paper medical record or embedded as an image within an electronic file, they are part of the designated record set. When photographs are maintained separately, they are not part of the designated record set.

Customer Service Is Key

Defining the DRS is not the same as preparing a medical record in response to a subpoena. Its scope should be carefully considered in advance of its use. Further, the definition should be documented so that it is known to all within the organization and can be applied consistently. The underlying purpose in defining the DRS is key to determining inclusions and exclusions, and mode of access and the definition should not be created in isolation.

Understanding its purposes and the access this purpose demands must be considered. For example, providing access to an incomplete record during an admission might be discouraged, so instead, the provider could offer to review a page or portion of the record with the patient using this as an educational opportunity or even offer a summary of the record in lieu of a copy of the entire record. Likewise, it is during the claim adjudication process that an individual may be most interested in access to information retained by the health plan.

It is important to maintain a customer service attitude: the right of the patient to access information on which care or payment decisions are being based is the underlying purpose of defining the DRS. If the patient has reason to believe the DRS contains erroneous information, it is better to permit access and amendment than for the information to go uncorrected with a harmful effect on the patient. While some requests for access and amendment may seem inappropriate, attempting to hide information can have a negative effect on the provider–patient or health plan–customer relationship.

Note

1. Amatayakul, Margret A. "Practice Brief: Definition of the Health Record for Legal Purposes." *Journal of AHIMA* 72, no. 9 (2001): 88A–H.

Defining the Designated Record Set

Gwen Hughes, RHIA, CHP

On December 28, 2000, the federal government published the Standards for Privacy of Individually Identifiable Health Information, more commonly referred to as the HIPAA privacy rule. The privacy rule was amended on August 14, 2002. The rule establishes the right of individuals to inspect, obtain a copy of, and request amendments to information about them in a designated record set. But what is a designated record set?

HIPAA Privacy Rule

Privacy Rule Standards

Section 164.524 of the privacy rule states that individuals generally have a right to inspect and obtain a copy of protected health information (PHI) about them in a designated record set.

In addition, section 164.526 of the rule states that individuals generally have a right to have a covered entity amend PHI about them in a designated record set.

Privacy Rule Definitions

The privacy rule (section 164.501) provides the following definitions for designated record set and PHI in order to clarify the access and amendment standards summarized in the previous paragraphs.

Designated record set is defined as a group of records maintained by or for a covered entity that is:

- The medical and billing records about individuals maintained by or for a covered healthcare provider

- The enrollment, payment, claims adjudication, and case or medical management record systems maintained by or for a health plan, or

- Information used in whole or in part by or for the covered entity to make decisions about individuals

Source: Hughes, Gwen. "Defining the Designated Record Set (AHIMA Practice Brief)." *Journal of AHIMA* 74, no. 1 (2003): 64A–D.

Protected health information is defined as individually identifiable health information maintained in or transmitted by electronic media (Internet, extranet, leased lines, dial-up lines, private networks, magnetic tape, disks, or compact disk media). The definition specifically excludes education and employment records.

Privacy Rule Preamble

In addition to the definition of designated record set, the December 28, 2000, privacy rule preamble provides some additional guidelines.

The preamble states that for covered healthcare providers, designated record sets include, at a minimum, the medical and billing records about individuals maintained by or for the provider. The preamble also says that the minimum designated record set for health plans includes the enrollment, payment, claims adjudication, and case or medical management record systems of the plan.

Additionally, the preamble states that designated record sets include any other group of records used in whole or in part, by or for a covered entity, to make decisions about individuals.

According to the preamble, records held by a business associate that meet the definition of designated record set are part of the covered entity's designated record set. However, the individual's rights to access, amend, and receive an accounting of disclosures does not attach to the business associate's records if the business associate's information is the same as information maintained by the covered entity.

Although the privacy rule does not mention a clearinghouse's minimum designated record set specifically, the preamble notes that where clearinghouses are business associates of covered entities or maintain records that are used in whole or part to make decisions about individuals, clearinghouses may indeed have designated record sets.

The preamble emphasizes that individuals have a right to access and request amendments only to PHI in a designated record set. Therefore, information obtained during a phone conversation, for example, is subject to access only to the extent that it is recorded in the designated record set. The rule does not require a covered entity to provide access to all individually identifiable health information, because the benefits of access to information not used to make decisions about individuals is limited and is outweighed by the burdens of locating, retrieving, and providing access to such information.

The preamble also underscores the fact that covered entities often incorporate the same PHI in a variety of different data systems, not all of which will be used to make decisions about individuals. The preamble provides an example in which information systems used for quality control or peer review analyses may not be used to make decisions about individuals. In this example, the preamble says the information systems would not fall within the definition of designated record set. Furthermore, the preamble states that it does not require entities to grant an individual access to PHI maintained in these types of information systems.

The privacy rule and discussions in the preamble also make it clear that individuals do not have a right of access to:

- Psychotherapy notes

- Information compiled in reasonable anticipation of, or for use in, a civil, criminal, or administrative action or proceeding

- PHI held by clinical laboratories if the Clinical Laboratory Improvements Amendments of 1988 (CLIA) prohibit such access

- PHI held by certain research laboratories that are exempt from the CLIA regulations (164.524)

CLIA regulations state that clinical laboratories may provide clinical laboratory test records and reports only to "authorized persons," as defined primarily by state law. When, according to state law, an individual is not an authorized person, this restriction effectively prohibits the clinical laboratory from providing an individual direct access to this information.

Individuals do not have access to PHI held by certain research laboratories that are exempt from the CLIA regulations. The CLIA regulations specifically exempt the components or functions of research laboratories that test human specimens but do not report patient-specific results for the diagnosis, prevention, or treatment of any disease, impairment, or assessment of the health of individual patients.

Section 164.524 of the preamble states that a general principle is that a covered entity is to provide access to PHI in accordance with the rule regardless of whether the covered entity created the information. The rule defines, however, rare circumstances in which access to information contained within the designated record set can be denied. For example, access can be denied when, in the exercise of professional judgment, it is likely to endanger the life or physical safety of the individual or another person.

Other Federal Laws/Regulations

Other federal laws and regulations also give individuals the right to access their health information.

The Privacy Act of 1974, like the HIPAA privacy rule, gives individuals the right to access and request amendments to their records.[1] The act defines record as "any item, collection, or grouping of information about an individual that is maintained by an agency, including, but not limited to, his education, financial transactions, medical history, and criminal or employment history and that contains his name, or the identifying number, symbol, or other identifying particular assigned to the individual, such as a finger or voice print or a photograph."

The Medicare Conditions of Participation for State Long-term Care Facilities state that the resident or his or her legal representative has the right to access "all records pertaining to himself or herself" including current clinical records.[2] All records is not defined, however.

The Confidentiality of Alcohol and Drug Abuse Patient Records regulation allows federally subsidized alcohol and drug abuse programs to give patients access to their own records, including the opportunity to inspect and copy any records that the program maintains about the patient.[3] The regulation defines records as "any information, whether recorded or not, relating to a patient received or acquired by a federally assisted alcohol or drug program."

The Occupational Safety and Health Administration (OSHA) requires that employers document certain employee injuries, including medical care provided in relation to those injuries. Employees and their designated representatives generally have access to such reports of injuries and related health records.[4]

The HIPAA privacy rule makes it clear that it is not intended to preempt other existing federal laws and regulations. Therefore, if an individual's rights of access are greater under another applicable federal law, the individual should be afforded the greater access.

State Laws

Many states have laws or regulations that give individuals the right to their health information. Some state laws may define health information more broadly than the privacy rule. Some states may not limit access and amendment to PHI in a designated record set. When state laws or regulations afford individuals greater rights of access, the covered entity must adhere to state law (section 45 CFR 160.201-160.205).

Discussion

The authors of the HIPAA privacy rule attempted to balance the difficulties faced by covered entities in providing individuals with all the information maintained about them with an individual's right to information. By using the term designated record set, the privacy rule attempts to relieve organizations of the need to retrieve information from telephone message pads, surgery schedules, appointment logs, and other databases in which individual health information might appear but that is not used to make care or payment decisions about the individual.

Yet, despite the definitions and discussions about the designated record set in the privacy rule, organizations struggle to decide what should and should not be considered their designated record set.

Notes

1. Privacy Act of 1974. 5 USC, Section 552A.

2. Health Care Financing Administration, Department of Health and Human Services. "Conditions of Participation for State Long-term Care Facilities." *Code of Federal Regulations,* 2000. 42 CFR, Chapter IV, Part 483.

3. "Confidentiality of Alcohol and Drug Abuse Patient Records." 42 CFR, Part 2.

4. Occupational Safety and Health Administration, Department of Labor. "Recording and Reporting Occupational Injuries and Illnesses." *Code of Federal Regulations,* 2002. 29 CFR, Chapter 17, Part 1904.35, Section 657.

5. Amatayakul, Margret et al. "Practice Brief: Definition of the Health Record for Legal Purposes." *Journal of AHIMA* 72, no. 9 (2001): 88A–H.

References

NCHICA Designated Record Sets Work Group and Privacy and Confidentialty Focus Group. "Guidance for Identifying Designated Record Sets under HIPAA." August 16, 2002.

"Standards for Privacy of Individually Identifiable Health Information; Final Rule." 45 CFR Parts 160 and 164. *Federal Register* 65, no. 250 (December 28, 2000).

"Standards for Privacy of Individually Identifiable Health Information; Final Rule." 45 CFR Parts 160 and 164. *Federal Register* 67, no. 157 (August 14, 2002).

Handling Complaints and Mitigation

Jill Burrington-Brown, MS, RHIA

Many HIM professionals are experienced at managing various types of complaints that arise in day-to-day health information operations. HIM professionals consult with physicians about chart completion, lost records, and missing dictation. They also work with patients and their families who sometimes have differing expectations of what services should be provided to them and at what cost.

The HIM professional is uniquely qualified to perform the function of handling privacy complaints due to privacy knowledge and experience. However, effective conflict and dispute resolution may not always exist in our professional skill set and therefore must be learned.[1]

Accreditation and Legal Requirements

Joint Commission

The Elements of Performance for standard RI.1.2.120 address the resolution of complaints by patients. The standards require a complaint resolution process and that individuals are informed about the process. The standards also require response by the organization and that the organization informs patients about their right to file complaints with the state authority.[2]

HIPAA: General Administrative Requirements

HIPAA addresses complaints made to the secretary of the Department of Health and Human Services in Section 160.306. Additionally, the Office for Civil Rights (OCR) Web site gives instructions to individuals who wish to make a complaint. The covered entity is required to cooperate with any investigation OCR makes on receipt of a complaint and must permit OCR access to any of the information it deems necessary. While OCR states its purpose is to provide assistance and guidance toward resolution, the covered entity should try to resolve patient and individual complaints before they become complaints to OCR.

Source: Burrington-Brown, Jill. "Handling Complaints and Mitigation (AHIMA Practice Brief)." *Journal of AHIMA* 74, no. 10 (November 2003): 64A–C.

HIPAA Privacy Rule

Section 164.530 (d) requires a covered entity provide a process for individuals to make complaints concerning the covered entity's privacy policies or its compliance with them. A covered entity must document all complaints, their disposition, and the application of appropriate sanctions to members of the work force when noncompliance of privacy policies and procedures is indicated.[3]

State Laws

Covered entities should examine applicable state laws, if any, for additional guidance.

Philosophy

What is the philosophy your organization demonstrates regarding complaints? It is realistic to expect that complaints will occur. The organization should be prepared to respond in a constructive manner and consider that the complaint will offer an opportunity for improvement.[4]

Your organization should be aware that OCR has an online complaint process accessible by mail, fax, and e-mail, and offers assistance to the public via telephone.[5] It is important to consider that receiving and responding to complaints should be as convenient for the individual at your facility as it is for them through OCR.

If HIM professionals understand that much patient frustration stems from misunderstanding and misinformation rather than the actual denial of rights, we can be more proactive about how we communicate and welcome chances to improve our organizations' communication.[6]

Guidelines for Administering, Resolving Patient Complaints

Make it easy for individuals to voice a concern. Your organization must make sure the process is delineated in your notice of privacy practices. It should also state to whom and where a concern or complaint should be addressed.

If an individual arrives in person to complain, consider talking with him or her about his or her complaint rather than asking the individual to fill out a form. If your organization has a form, you might consider filling it out yourself. There are advantages of asking the individual to fill out the form, including getting the complaint in his or her own words, obtaining the individual's signature, and making sure all the information you would like to have is completed.

The biggest disadvantage with requesting that individuals fill out a complaint form is that it depersonalizes the process and may appear as though you are asking the individual to "jump through hoops." Whatever method you choose to capture the complaint, be sure to make the individual feel welcome to express his or her unhappiness.

When you receive a written complaint, call and make an appointment with the individual to discuss the complaint. It would be best to see the individual in person if it is a complaint you cannot manage over the telephone.

The Interview

Begin the interview with an open-ended request such as, "Tell me what happened." In your notes, capture the words the individual is using. Be open to the possibility that his or her issue is valid and worth complaining about. If you are not welcoming and open, the individual will not believe you are there to assist him or her in the resolution of the complaint. This may escalate an individual's decision to report his or her complaint to the OCR or other reporting authority.

During this process, listen for two things: the reason the individual is making the complaint (which may not be the reason initially stated) and what the individual wants out of the process (an apology may be all that is needed). Toward the end of the interview, ask the individual what he or she hopes to gain from the complaint process. You may ask the individual, "What do you think will make this right?" if it seems appropriate.

At the end of your interview, thank the individual for coming in to talk about the issue and promise a response within a reasonable time frame. One week might be reasonable for some issues, where two or three weeks might be more reasonable, depending on what needs to be investigated. Whatever you decide, make a commitment to get back to the individual within a certain time frame and keep this promise.

Quickly follow up with a letter thanking the individual and reiterating the complaint he or she made, along with what you have promised to do in follow-up. Be sure to document the commitment to get back to the individual by a certain time or date.

Investigate the complaint after your conference is concluded. Interview the people involved and review the medical record if it is relevant to the complaint. Note the information that supports the complaint and the information that refutes the complaint.

Reporting to Risk Manager, Insurance Representative, Attorney

You may be required to report the complaint to your organization's malpractice insurance carrier. Some carriers require all complaints to be reported at the time of the complaint, while others only require notice if there will be an insurance claim. If this is the case, you will need to work closely with your organization's risk manager and insurance claims representative to make sure the organization's process is set up correctly.

You may also need to determine if the complaint will require assistance from your attorney. Again, some malpractice insurance carriers require notification before attorneys are contacted. If this is the case, you should involve your organization's risk manager. If the individual with the complaint has already obtained an attorney, then it is best to notify the proper individuals and get legal advice before proceeding.

Resolution, Mitigation

At this point, you may want to determine what the cost to your organization will be, from both a financial and public relations standpoint, if you do not resolve the conflict in a mutually satisfactory manner. What will it cost to meet the expectations of the individual? Compare that to the cost of a possible OCR or other authority's investigation. Also compare the costs of possible litigation and using an attorney should the complaint go that far. Your organization will need to determine, perhaps on a case-by-case basis, when it is important to be "right" and when it is important to resolve a matter quickly by negotiating with the individual even if you do not believe you have made an error.

When your organization has made an error or a breach, consider the damages to the individual. What has happened to the individual and what is the seriousness of the damage? Look at the HIPAA regulations and compare the seriousness of the complaint to the types of issues stated in PL 104-191, sections 1176–1177 regarding sanctions. What can you do to mitigate the results of the error or breach? Much will depend on what the individual wants. Consider the following options:

- An apology for the situation

- Disciplinary action against employees (This requires your organization's human resource department's involvement and the involvement of the employee's supervisory staff. It should be noted that you will not be able to explain this process to the individual filing the complaint, as these procedures are generally considered private within an organization.)

- Repair of whatever system or process caused the complaint or breach (requires policy changes and education of staff)

- Some part of the bill paid by the facility

- A cash amount based on work loss, expenses incurred, or another actual financial loss

Also consider the following gestures of goodwill and good public relations for more minor issues:

- Gift certificates for dinner

- Movie or theater tickets

- Flowers

Anything more than this type of mitigation will require either facility insurance company or attorney involvement. Again, understanding the boundaries and processes used by either is very important.

Proactive Mitigation

An organization may discover an error or breach of privacy that the patient is unaware of. The organization must then consider how it will inform the patient and determine the necessary mitigation. Joint Commission standards require that patients and, when appropriate, their family members be informed about the outcomes of care, including unanticipated outcomes.[7] Organizations must determine:

- In what circumstances notification should occur

- How they will notify an individual of an error or breach

- How mitigation will be carried out

Documentation

Set up your documentation at the beginning of the process. Make detailed notes of every conversation and record any decisions or promises made by any person participating in the process. Record dates of any action taken and any mitigation offered and accepted.

If the complaint is privacy related, your organization must keep this documentation for at least six years, according to the HIPAA privacy rule. You will need to compare that law with your state retention laws, which may be more restrictive.

Organizations should consider using any existing incident reporting system to track and follow individual complaints. There are a number of advantages to using such a system, such as protection in some states from this information being discovered in the legal process. Covered entities should remember that the object of the complaint process is resolution and the avoidance of escalation to an OCR complaint or litigation, if possible.

Notes

1. Odidison, Joyce. "How Can We Assist Clients in Becoming More Successful at Conflict Resolution?" November 2002.

2. Joint Commission on Accreditation of Healthcare Organizations. *2004 Comprehensive Accreditation Manual for Hospitals.* Prepublication Edition. Oakbrook Terrace, IL: Joint Commission, 2003.

3. 45 CFR, Subtitle A, Subchapter C, Parts 160, 162, and 164, Section 530(d). Available online at http://aspe.hhs.gov/admnsimp/bannerps.htm.

4. McCleave, Spencer H. "How to Respond to a Formal Patient Complaint." *Seminars in Medical Practice 4,* no. 2 (2001).

5. U.S. Department of Health and Human Services, Office for Civil Rights. "How to File a Health Information Privacy Complaint with the Office for Civil Rights." June 2000. Available online at www.hhs.gov/ocr/privacy howtofile.htm.

6. Cerminara, Kathy L. "Deal with Patient Complaints before Arrival of Subpoenas." *Managed Care Magazine,* June 9, 2003.

7. Joint Commission on Accreditation of Healthcare Organizations. *2004 Comprehensive Accreditation Manual for Hospitals.* Prepublication Edition. Oak Brook Terrace, IL: Joint Commission, 2003.

Reference

Hjort, Beth. "Handling Complaints." Presentation at the AHIMA "Getting Practical with Privacy and Security" seminars (2003).

The First Line of Defense against Privacy Complaints

Margret Amatayakul, MBA, RHIA, CHPS, FHIMSS

Every healthcare provider has experienced managing patient complaints, whether they are about cold food, unresponsive staff, or missed medication. However, when it comes to privacy and confidentiality, complaints need to be handled a bit differently. In this article, we'll explore how to handle privacy complaints under HIPAA.

The notice of privacy practices given to individuals must include information about filing complaints with both the covered entity and the secretary of the U.S. Department of Health and Human Services (HHS). In addition to the notice, any denial of access or amendment must be accompanied by information on how to file a complaint with the covered entity and the secretary. The privacy rule does not limit the opportunity to file complaints to patients or health plan enrollees, therefore permitting members of the work force, oversight bodies such as state health departments or the Joint Commission, and the public to file a complaint.

A Careful Response Is Key

A covered entity should make every effort to encourage potential complainants to first address their complaints to the entity itself. The covered entity should make it easy to file a complaint and be highly responsive. For example, the employee responsible for receiving privacy complaints should have a pleasant demeanor and proper training in how to respond to such complaints. Further, forms on which to record complaints should be designed to promote goodwill and invite ideas for improvement. Regardless of how the complaint is received, the organization should stress the importance it places on privacy and its receptivity to learning about privacy concerns. To demonstrate HIPAA compliance, ask for the complaint in writing or document the complaint when it is received.

Every identifiable complaint should generate an investigation and a response. The investigation should focus on both the specific complaint and any patterns of similar complaints. It is helpful to coordinate privacy complaints with security incidents to determine potential causal relationships. If after an investigation it is determined that no actual violation occurred, the covered entity should recognize that perception of a violation is as important as an actual violation and may need to take corrective action steps to overcome erroneous perceptions.

Source: Amatayakul, Margret. "The First Line of Defense against Privacy Complaints (HIPAA on the Job series)." *Journal of AHIMA* 73, no. 9 (2002): 24A–C.

The organization should respond to every identifiable complaint received. If the complaint was filed in person or on the phone, it should be documented and followed with a phone call or letter. The response should include a statement of appreciation for the individual's value as a patient/customer and a recognition of the time and interest taken in advising the covered entity of the privacy concern.

The privacy response should be made promptly and include information about measures being taken to continuously improve privacy practices. Exercise care in acknowledging an actual privacy violation and in describing any new procedures implemented. Privacy is a very personal matter and can therefore be a very ambiguous area to address. What one individual may consider an invasion of privacy or violation of privacy rights may not be a violation to another individual. Keep in mind that the passage of time may change perceptions as well.

Finally, if an investigation reveals an actual violation, it is best to involve risk management and legal counsel in drafting the response that best suits the situation, including any offer of mitigation.

Complaints Can Yield HHS Investigations

The greatest potential impact of the privacy complaint requirement is that a complaint filed with HHS may result in an investigation of the covered entity. An investigation requires the covered entity to supply a compliance report and documentation of its privacy practices. It must demonstrate that it has privacy policies and procedures and members of its work force have been trained. The contents of the compliance report are not specified, but covered entities would be advised to ensure they monitor compliance and document findings and corrective action.

A simple spreadsheet or database can be used as an index to policies and procedures as they relate to the HIPAA privacy standards and to catalog training. This same tool can be used to tally privacy complaints against standards and to record the organization's own assessment. (See Figure 2.4, Privacy and Security Event Log.)

An Opportunity for Consolidation

Planning the provision of the notice on filing a privacy complaint and how to provide an appropriate response also presents an opportunity to coordinate a process that has become fragmented and resource-intensive in many organizations. As a result of many different regulations

Figure 2.4.   Privacy and security event log

Standard	Related Policies and Procedures	Training		Number and Description of Events	Owner	Resolution	Follow Up
		All	Target				
Notice of privacy practices	Policy and procedure for provision of notice & acknowledgment of receipt	Annual	Admitting/ registration	3—Lack of understanding 1—Non-receipt	Corporate compliance Admitting/ registration	Added summary to acknowledgment form Retrained admitting/ registration staff	Patient satisfaction survey

and accreditation initiatives, healthcare providers have added measures like corporate compliance hotlines, sentinel event reporting, patient satisfaction surveys, and patient relations/ customer service activities to their existing incident reporting mechanisms, risk management, and quality improvement activities. HIPAA adds privacy complaint collection and security incident reporting.

Many providers are recognizing this situation as an opportunity to revamp and potentially consolidate these activities. Multiple independent reporting mechanisms can be confusing and may result in lack of appropriate reporting simply because it is not clear to whom an event should be reported. Further, detecting violation patterns may be more difficult if complaints are captured through different systems.

Consider the following options for collecting and tracking privacy complaints:

- Centralize reporting, with respective areas analyzing the events for appropriate action. Software used in the information technology department's help desk could be used for receiving and tracking all issues and their resolution, while the actual investigation and corrective action is taking place in the separate departments of risk management, compliance, etc.

- Set up individual reporting mechanisms and "first line of defense" in the respective departments, but consolidating results at the back end for quality improvement.

- Centralize all functions with a single point of contact, resolution, and reporting.

HIPAA has become the driving force behind consolidating privacy policies and procedures because privacy cuts across all disciplines and organizational boundaries. In fact, it may be the catalyst needed to address many other areas needing greater coordination. A good way to begin an organizational assessment is by creating a flowchart of all potential points of complaint contact and how each follows through to resolution and reporting. If the organization chooses to retain multiple points of collection, the flowchart may be useful in explaining to the work force what issues are addressed where and how they get resolved.

Letters of Agreement/Contracts

Harry B. Rhodes, MBA, RHIA
Gwen Hughes, RHIA, CHP

Healthcare organizations enter into written contracts every day. Typically, the HIM professional secures contracts for transcription, record copying, imaging, record storage, coding, other outsourcing, or consulting services. Although contracts can prevent confusion and conflict, they can also bind the inattentive signer to conditions that are difficult or impossible to meet. The purpose of this brief is to empower HIM professionals to draft, review, and secure sound, discerning contracts.

The Department of Health and Human Services proposes model business associate contract language in the appendix to the final privacy rule published on August 14, 2002. Further, in its model compliance plans, the Office of the Inspector General advises against entering into a contract that may induce a vendor to commit a fraudulent practice, such as upcoding.

Legal and Regulatory Requirements

A contract is a legally binding and legally enforceable promise or set of promises between two or more competent parties. The requirements for a contract include:

- An offer

- Acceptance of the offer

- Consent

- Consideration (the value, usually monetary)

- Competent parties' legality (the activities described therein are not contrary to law, public policy, or the peace, health, or morals of a community)

- A requirement that some contracts be in writing

The standards for privacy of individually identifiable health information, also known as the HIPAA privacy rule (42 CFR Part 160–164), state that contracts between a HIPAA-covered

---

Source: Rhodes, Harry, and Gwen Hughes. "Letters of Agreement/Contracts (AHIMA Practice Brief)" (Updated April 2003).

entity (healthcare providers who submit health information electronically, health plans, and healthcare clearinghouses) and any business associate to whom protected patient health information is disclosed must establish the permitted and required uses and disclosures of information by the business associate. The contract may not authorize the business associate to use or further disclose protected health information (PHI) in a manner that would violate the requirements if done by the covered entity (CE), except that:

- The contract may permit the business associate to use and disclose PHI for the proper management and administration of the business associate to carry out the legal responsibilities of the business associate.

- The contract may permit the business associate to provide data aggregation services relating to the healthcare operations of the CE.

The contract must also provide that the business associate will:

- Not use or further disclose the information other than as permitted or required by the contract or as required by law

- Use appropriate safeguards to prevent use or disclosure of information other than as provided for by its contract

- Report to the CE any use or disclosure of the information not provided for by its contract of which it becomes aware

- Ensure that any agents, including a subcontractor to whom it provides PHI received from or created or received by the business associate on behalf of the CE, agree to the same restrictions and conditions that apply to the business partner with respect to such information

- Make available PHI in accordance with section 164.526

- Make available PHI for amendment and incorporate any amendments to PHI in accordance with 164.526

- Make available the information required to provide an accounting of disclosures in accordance with 164.528

- Make its internal practices, books, and records related to the use and disclosure of PHI received from or created or received by the business associate on behalf of the CE available to the secretary of HHS for the purpose of determining the CE's compliance with this subpart

- At termination of the contract, if feasible, return or destroy all PHI received from or created or received by the business associate on behalf of the CE that the business partner still maintains in any form and retain no copies of such information; or, if such return or destruction is not feasible, extend the protections of the contract to the information and limit further uses and disclosures to those purposes that make the return or destruction of the information unfeasible

- Use PHI to report violations of law to appropriate federal and state authorities, consistent with 164.502(j)(1)

The contract must also provide that:

- The business associate shall be notified by the CE of any limitation(s) in its notice of privacy practices in accordance with 45 CFR 164.520 to the extent that such limitations may affect the business associate's use or disclosure of PHI.

- The business associate shall be notified by the CE of any changes in or revocation of permission by individual to use or disclose PHI to the extent that such changes may affect business associate's use or disclosure of PHI.

- The business associate shall be notified by the CE of any restriction to the use or disclosure of PHI that the CE has agreed to in accordance with 45 CFR 164.522, to the extent that such restriction may affect the business associate's use or disclosure of PHI.

The contract must authorize the CE to terminate the contract, if the CE determines that the business associate has violated a material term of the contract.

Accreditation Requirements

The Joint Commission on Accreditation of Healthcare Organizations evaluates all healthcare services provided by the organization for which the Joint Commission has standards. This could include any service provided under contract. HIM-related contractors must not only comply with applicable HIM standards, but with performance improvement, human resources, and other applicable standards as well.

Contracts in General

Typically, contracts or letters of agreement with healthcare organizations include:

- The date the agreement was entered into

- A clause describing the relationship between the parties, such as independent contractor

- A description of the services to be provided

- Any expectations relative to completion, accuracy, or turnaround

- What the services will cost and when payment is due

- How or when the contract will terminate

- The contractor's obligation to secure and safeguard confidential patient health and proprietary information

- The contractor's obligations to meet or exceed applicable accreditation standards

- A "hold harmless" clause in which the contractor accepts responsibility for his or her actions and agrees to indemnify or compensate the healthcare facility for any claims against it that are the result of the contractor's actions or inaction

- When appropriate, a clause that neither organization will solicit an employee of the other party for a specified period without prior written approval of the other party

- When appropriate, a statement addressing the retention of intellectual property rights of tools, methodologies, and techniques in possession of the contractor or healthcare facility prior to the effective date of the contract

- A clause relative to dispute resolution

- Authorized signatures

Most vendors develop standard agreements/contracts for the products and services they provide but are generally willing to negotiate changes to those agreements to meet specific needs. HIM professionals who are independent contractors usually meet with an attorney once and obtain a contract that can be enforced in court. With minor revision, the same contract can be used for future clients.

Recommendations

Prior to entering into any written contract, the HIM professional should:

- Make sure the contract addresses the legal and accreditation elements described above.

- Ensure the contract addresses applicable contract elements described above.

- Conduct a literature, Web, and listserv search specific to the type of agreement being negotiated.

- Make sure the terms offered by a vendor are acceptable and appropriate to the situation.

- Include pertinent safeguards or clauses gleaned from searches of literature, the Web, and listservs.

- Discuss the contract, safeguards, and clauses that need to be included with risk management (if applicable) and legal counsel.

- Make sure the terms in the agreement require the contractor to originate, maintain, and make available on request documents showing compliance with various accreditation standards, such as copies of documentation showing employee competence.

- Secure two signed copies of the original contract once approved by the vendor, appropriate manager(s), risk manager (if applicable), and legal counsel; distribute one signed contract to the vendor and the other to the healthcare organization.

- Maintain a master inventory of contracts, including the location of the master copies and any renewal or termination dates.

HIM professionals who are independent contractors and must generate contracts frequently may find it useful to purchase legal document software. Those who choose to do so should compose a contract as they would for the typical client and have legal counsel review it.

The termination clause should require written notice if either party plans to terminate the contract. The number of days written notice required should take into account the length of time it will take the healthcare organization to procure alternative services.

For a sample consulting agreement contract, see Figure 2.5.

In addition to addressing the general legal, accreditation, and standard contract items discussed above, HIM professionals should make sure items specific to certain types of common HIM contracts are addressed as outlined in Figure 2.6, Additional Elements Appropriate to Specific Contract Types.

Figure 2.5.   Sample consulting agreement contract

This agreement is made effective as of [date], by and between [client and client address] and [contractor and contractor address]. In this Agreement, the party who is contracting to receive services shall be referred to as [client acronym], and the party who will be providing the services shall be referred to as [contractor acronym].

The parties agree as follows:

Description of Services: Commencing [date], [contractor] will provide the following services (collectively, the "Services"):

(Spell out specific services, any required due dates, and any required outcome measures. For example:

1. Review policies, procedures, and systems relative to health information privacy and security for compliance with federal and state law and regulation and standards of practice

2. Review policies, procedures, and systems relative to electronic signatures for compliance with federal and state law and regulation and standards of practice

3. Provide a written assessment identifying any shortcomings or opportunities for improvement and suggested methodologies for bringing existing practice into compliance with federal and state law or existing standards of practice)

Performance of Services: The manner in which the Services are to be performed and the specific hours to be worked by [contractor] shall be determined by [contractor]. [Client] will rely on [contractor] to work as many hours as may be reasonably necessary to fulfill [contractor's] obligations under this agreement.

Price and Payment Terms: [Client] will pay a fee to [contractor] for the Services in the amount of [dollar amount]. This fee shall be payable [method of payment, i.e., in a lump sum upon completion of the service, based on an hourly rate billed at the end of the month and payable within 30 days, etc.]. Upon termination of this Agreement, payments under this paragraph shall cease, however, [contractor] shall be entitled to payments for periods or partial periods that accrued prior to the date of termination and for which [contractor] has not yet been paid.

Term/Termination: This Agreement shall terminate automatically upon completion by [contractor] of the Services required by this Agreement. Either party may terminate this agreement with or without cause by submitting a 30-day written notice.

Relationship of Parties: It is understood by the parties that [contractor] is an independent contractor and not an employee of [client]. [Client] will not provide fringe benefits, including health insurance, holidays, paid vacation, or any other employee benefit, for the benefit of [contractor].

Confidentiality: [Contractor] recognizes that [client] has patient health information and other proprietary information (collectively, "Information") which are valuable, special, and unique assets of [client]. [Contractor] will not divulge, disclose, or communicate in any manner any Information to any third party without prior written consent. [Contractor] will protect the Information and treat it as strictly confidential. [Contractor] will abide by the requirements of 42 CFR, Part 164.506, Standards for Privacy of Individually Identifiable Health Information: Proposed Rule. A violation of this paragraph shall be a material violation of this agreement.

Legal Fees and Court Costs: In the event any legal action is taken to enforce this agreement or any portion thereof, the party that prevails in that suit shall be entitled to recover from the other, reasonable attorney fees plus the cost of said suit.

Notices: All notices required or permitted under this Agreement shall be in writing and shall be deemed delivered when delivered in person or deposited in the United States mail, postage prepaid, addressed as follows:

[Client Contact Name and Address]
[Contractor Contact Name and Address]

Such address may be changed from time to time by either party by providing written notice to the other in the manner set forth above.

Entire Agreement: This Agreement contains the entire agreement of the parties and there are no other promises or conditions in any other agreement whether oral or written. This Agreement supersedes any prior written or oral agreements between the parties.

Amendment: This Agreement may be modified or amended if the amendment is made in writing and is signed by both parties.

Severability: If any provision of this Agreement shall be held to be invalid or unenforceable for any reason, the remaining provisions shall continue to be valid and enforceable. If a court finds that any provision of this Agreement is invalid or unenforceable, but that by limiting such provision, it would become valid and enforceable, then such provision shall be deemed to be written, construed, and enforced as so limited.

Waiver of Contractual Right: The failure of either party to enforce any provision of this Agreement shall not be construed as a waiver or limitation of that party's right to subsequently enforce and compel strict compliance with every provision of this Agreement.

Applicable Law: This Agreement shall be governed by the laws of the State of [state].

Signature Party Receiving Service _____

Signature Party Providing Service _____

Figure 2.6.   Additional elements appropriate to specific contract types

Contracts for transcription services should also address:
- How and when physician demographic information will be supplied
- How and when patient demographic information will be provided
- The formats in which documents will be transcribed
- Who will provide dictation and transcription equipment
- Who will pay for dictation and transcription-related supplies and service contracts required to maintain equipment and supplies
- Who will pay local and long-distance telecommunication expenses
- How dictated health information will be secured during transport to the transcription service
- How turnaround time will be defined and measured, that is, from dictation to transmission of typed report
- Expected turnaround time for various report types and correcting errors
- How the chargeable unit will be defined and computed (such as lines, words, or characters)
- Cost per chargeable unit
- Additional charges (such as stat or changes to the original document made at the request of the dictator)
- How the charges will be adjusted when the transcription service fails to turn around documents in the time frames specified
- How many errors per unit will be considered acceptable
- How transcript errors will be corrected
- How the transcription service will ensure and measure quality
- How often reports of quality improvement (QI) activities will be provided by the transcription service
- How and in what medium transcribed documents will be returned to the healthcare organization
- How information will be transported to and from the healthcare facility
- How long information dictated and transcribed will reside on any transcription service database
- How information retained on transcription service database will be destroyed to ensure confidentiality

Contracts for record photocopy/disclosure services should also include:
- A statement that the copy service will comply with facility policy as well as state and federal law in evaluating and disclosing health information
- A specific number of hours or days that turnaround time will not exceed and how turnaround will be defined
- The types of requesters who will incur charges and the fees they will be required to pay
- Mechanism that will be used to ensure that turnaround standards are met
- The QI mechanism that will be used to assure the healthcare organization that the copy service is adhering to facility policy and state and federal law and frequency of QI reports
- The mechanism for reporting incidents (such as a record released with improper signatures or records mailed to the wrong person)
- The manner in which requests will be tracked and disclosures documented
- The process for handling disclosures when records cannot be located
- Identification of the party that will perform the various activities associated with processing requests for information
- Provisions that each party will be provided access to and any training needed to use specific systems owned or leased by the other party needed to carry out disclosure activities
- Standard document sets that will be included in response to specific types of requests
- A clause that specifies how, on termination of the contract, the parties will assure the healthcare facility has complete and accurate information regarding all requests and disclosures made during the contract

Figure 2.6.   (Continued)

Contracts for imaging services should also include:

- The manner in which imaging will be performed

- A definition and standard for turnaround

- The media to be used and method of labeling

- Identification of the party that will perform the various activities required to facilitate imaging

- The manner in which progress will be tracked and the frequency or means by which it will be communicated to the healthcare facility

- The mechanism that will be used to ensure quality and when and how those activities will be communicated

- All charges, including those associated with returning a file to the healthcare facility

- A requirement that the imaging vendor provide the healthcare facility with electronic indexing information in a format that can be merged with the master patient index

- A clause that addresses disposition of the record after imaging

Contracts for record storage providers should also include:

- The provisions the record storage company will employ to safeguard patient records

- The precautions employed by the record storage company to ensure information is disclosed only to authorized requesters

- The definition of turnaround standards and fees for various types of requested information

- Retrieval procedures for stat, after hour, weekend, and routine provision of health information

- How record locations will be tracked and the process and fees associated with searches for misplaced records

- Any adjustments in charges when records are not provided to the healthcare facility within agreed-on time frames

Contracts for coding providers should also include:

- Provisions that allow the healthcare facility to review assigned coders' resumes, contact previous healthcare facilities, and reject any coders believed to be a poor fit for the facility

- The type of coding to be done and any facility-provided encoding technology the coder is expected to use

- A statement as to acceptable standards of coding accuracy and how performance will be measured and that contract coders will adhere to specific coding guidelines

- Standards for terminating the use of a particular coder (i.e., seven days after verbal notice) when acceptable standards of accuracy are not maintained

- Standards for productivity and the method for determining whether adequate levels of productivity are maintained

---

References

Abdelhak, Mervat et al. *Health Information: Management of a Strategic Resource.* Philadelphia: W.B. Saunders, 1996.

Department of Health and Human Services. 42 CFR, Parts 160–164 "Standards for Privacy of Individually Identifiable Health Information"; Proposed Rule, November 3, 1999, part 164.506.

Joint Commission on Accreditation of Healthcare Organizations. *Comprehensive Accreditation Manual for Hospitals.* Oakbrook Terrace, IL: Joint Commission on Accreditation of Healthcare Organizations, 2000.

"Standards for the Privacy of Individually Identifiable Health Information; Final Rule." 45 CFR Parts 160–164. *Federal Register* 65, no. 250 (December 28, 2000).

"Standards for the Privacy of Individually Identifiable Health Information; Final Rule." 45 CFR Parts 160–164. *Federal Register* 67, No. 157 (August 14, 2002).

Tepper, Ron. *The Consultant's Proposal, Fee and Contract Problem Solver.* New York: John Wiley and Sons, 1993.

United under HIPAA: A Comparison of Arrangements and Agreements

Margret Amatayakul, MBA, RHIA, CHPS, FHIMSS

The HIPAA transactions, security, and privacy regulations identify five agreements and relationships that can be established between healthcare entities to achieve economies of scale and lessen HIPAA's administrative burden. They are:

- Affiliated covered entity (ACE)
- Business associate contract
- Chain of trust agreement
- Data use agreement
- Organized healthcare arrangement (OHCA)
- Trading partner agreement

What are the differences between these agreements and arrangements? What are the similarities? In this article, we'll review each type of arrangement and their accompanying requirements. See Figure 2.7, Comparison of HIPAA Agreements and Arrangements, for a summary of key characteristics.

Organizational Relationships

In an attempt to remove some of the administrative burden of complying with the HIPAA privacy rule, the rule permits two forms of organizational relationships to be identified and used to achieve economies of scale: the ACE designation and the OHCA.

Affiliated Covered Entity

Legally separate covered entities that are affiliated may designate themselves as a single covered entity for purposes of the HIPAA privacy rule. Under this affiliation, the organizations need only develop and disseminate one notice of privacy practices, comply with one set of policies and procedures, appoint one privacy official, administer common training programs, use one business associate contract, etc.

Source: Amatayakul, Margret. "United under HIPAA: A Comparison of Arrangements and Agreements (HIPAA on the Job series)." *Journal of AHIMA* 73, no. 8 (2002): 24A–D.

Figure 2.7.   Comparison of HIPAA arrangements and agreements

	Affiliated Covered Entity	Business Associate Contract	Chain of Trust Agreement	Data Use Agreement	Organized Health Care Arrangement	Trading Partner Agreement
Applicable rule	Privacy	Privacy	Security	Privacy	Privacy	Transactions
Required?	No	Yes	To be determined in final rule	Yes	No	No
Purpose	Economies of scale	Protection	Protection	Protect limited data set	Economies of scale	Communication
Originated by	Covered entities	Covered entity	Covered entity	Covered entity	Covered providers	Health plan or clearinghouse (typically)
With whom	Commonly owned covered entities	Business associates	Organizations receiving data	Recipient of limited data set	Nonowned providers	Provider (typically)

To be an ACE, the separate covered entities must be under common ownership or control. For example, an integrated delivery network that owns several hospitals, medical groups, and long-term care facilities may designate these entities as one ACE for HIPAA. The designation must be formally documented.

If the ACE combines the functions of a health plan, healthcare provider, and/or healthcare clearinghouse, it must comply with the standards applicable to each separate covered entity. For example, providers only need to provide the notice of privacy practices once, but health plans must do so every three years. Furthermore, a covered entity that performs multiple covered functions may use or disclose the protected health information of individuals who receive the covered entity's services only for purposes related to the appropriate function being performed.

Organized Health Care Arrangement (OHCA)

Because many healthcare settings are clinically integrated but not commonly owned or controlled, the HIPAA privacy rule also permits providers that typically provide healthcare to a common set of patients to designate themselves as an OHCA for purposes of HIPAA. For example, an academic medical center often includes university-affiliated physicians and a hospital or health system. Typically, the university is a separate legal entity, but the patients are treated by the faculty within the hospital or health system.

In addition to some of the economies of scale provided by the ACE, the OHCA assures a seamless approach to HIPAA for the patients being treated by the same providers. The notice of privacy practices, however, must clearly indicate which organizations are included.

The OHCA is a helpful designation because it permits the use of a joint notice of privacy practices and provides the ability to share protected health information throughout the OHCA for treatment, payment, and healthcare operations.

There are specific requirements for designation as an OHCA. For providers, the organizations must hold themselves out to the public as participating in a joint arrangement and they must jointly perform utilization review, quality assessment and improvement activities, or payment activities. (Health plans may also designate themselves as an OHCA if they meet certain specified criteria.) Interestingly, HIPAA does not require documentation of the OHCA designation, although it would be a good practice to do so. All components of an OHCA must agree on and comply with the content of the notice of privacy practices.

One potential disadvantage of the OHCA is that if provider components of one OHCA also belong to another OHCA, complying with the notice of privacy practices of each OHCA may become complicated. Medical groups that are not owned by a health system and enter into an OHCA with the system must create their own separate notice of privacy practices for patients they treat outside the umbrella of the health system. They must also comply with the separate, different notice of any other OHCA to which they belong (e.g., if they have admitting privileges at more than one hospital).

It is extremely important to emphasize that the purpose of the OHCA is solely for compliance with HIPAA. Each component continues to be responsible for its own actions. In other words, separate entities, separate risk.

Agreements and Contracts

Each of the HIPAA transactions, privacy, and security rules also references agreements or contracts among organizational entities—some of which are covered entities and some of which are organizations providing services to covered entities.

Trading Partner Agreement

The transaction rule describes the use of a trading partner agreement, which is a contract between two parties—generally each covered entities—that exchange the financial and administrative transactions (i.e., claims, eligibility verification, remittances, etc.), such as between a provider and a clearinghouse or a provider and a health plan.

The trading partner agreement would specify various technical requirements for communications protocols, such as how the transactions are to be addressed, what character set must be used, whether receipt will be acknowledged, and more. The transaction rule does not require a trading partner agreement, but if one is used, the rule specifies what may not be included in such an agreement.

Specifically, the trading partner agreement cannot:

- Change any definition, data condition, or use of a data element

- Add any data elements or segments to the maximum defined data set

- Require use of any codes or data elements that are marked "not used" or not in the implementation guide

- Change the meaning or intent of the standard's implementation specification

Business Associate Contract

The business associate contract is the most well known of the agreements and contracts identified in HIPAA. It is required by the privacy rule for use between covered entities and business associates, some of whom may be other covered entities.

A business associate is an individual or organization that performs a function involving use or disclosure of individually identifiable health information for a covered entity or OHCA. One covered entity may be a business associate of another covered entity if it performs such services for the other covered entity.

The covered entity or OHCA requesting the services must have a contract with the business associate to establish the permitted and required uses and disclosures of individually identifiable health information by the business associate.

There are several requirements with respect to the content of the business associate contract. They are:

- The business associate must have appropriate safeguards to prevent use or disclosure of information other than as provided for by its contract.

- The business associate must report to the covered entity any use or disclosure of the information not provided for by its contract of which it becomes aware.

- The business associate must ensure that any agents or subcontractors agree to the same restrictions and conditions that apply to the business associate with respect to the individually identifiable health information being processed.

- The business associate must also make available protected health information for patient access and amendment, must make any amendment provided to it from the covered entity, and provide an accounting of disclosures.

- The business associate must make its internal practices, books, and records relating to the use and disclosure of protected health information available to HHS for purposes of determining the covered entity's compliance.

- At termination of the contract, the business associate must return or destroy all protected health information. The contract must also authorize termination of the contract if the business associate is in material violation.

Sample contract provisions for the business associate contract are provided in the appendix to the preamble to the final privacy rule modification.

Data Use Agreement

New to the privacy rule modification is also the requirement for a data use agreement if the covered entity discloses a limited data set of protected health information to another entity. The limited data set is protected health information from which many, but not all of the data elements for deidentifying data have been removed. The data use agreement is very similar to the business associate contract, in which the recipient of the data set would agree to limit the use of the data for the purposes for which it was given to ensure the security of the data and not to identify the information or use it to contact any individual.

Chain of Trust Agreement

The chain of trust agreement was identified in HIPAA's proposed security rule. If individually identifiable health information is processed through a third party, the security rule would require that the parties enter into a chain of trust agreement.

The chain of trust agreement was described as a contract in which the parties agree to electronically exchange data and to protect the transmitted data. (The security rule did not specify the nature of these transactions.) The sender and receiver are required to and depend on each other to maintain the integrity and confidentiality of the transmitted information. Multiple two-party contracts may be involved in moving information from the originating party to the ultimate receiving party. For example, a provider may contract with a clearinghouse to transmit claims to the clearinghouse. The clearinghouse, in turn, may contract with another clearinghouse or with a payer for the further transmittal of those claims. The agreements provide for the same level of security to be maintained at all links in the chain when information moves from one organization to another.

It remains to be seen whether the final security rule will require a chain of trust agreement separate from the business associate contract. If it does, the contractual language could potentially become a part of a trading partner agreement.

A Common Goal

HIPAA's transactions, privacy, and security rules call for contractual obligations to afford confidentiality, data integrity, and availability to protected health information among both covered entities and otherwise. After examining each relationship, consider which ones would be appropriate for your healthcare organization to simplify the transition to HIPAA compliance.

Special Considerations for Business Associate Agreements: Substance Abuse Treatment, Federal Law Present Challenges

Pamela T. Haines, RHIA

If you are writing business associate agreements for a healthcare provider these days, you have probably discovered there are often no magic words or formulas that will produce an agreement. Although sample forms available from various sources may be helpful, generally no two business associates are alike.

If you treat patients whose information is subject to more stringent privacy protections under federal law (such as the drug and alcohol confidentiality law), you can plan to throw a qualified service organization agreement into the mix. Then there are the noncovered entities who may want to write your business associate agreement for you. These noncovered entities may have hundreds or thousands of other covered entity customers that also need an agreement.

Whatever the case, if you are the covered entity who is asking another person or company to perform a service for you or on your behalf, and they need protected health information to perform that service, you will need to ensure that no matter who writes the agreement, it conforms with your legal responsibilities.

First Things First—Defining Business Associate Agreements

The first step is determining whether the person or company that the covered entity wants to enter into a business associate agreement with does in fact meet the criteria of the privacy rule for a business associate agreement. Is the person or entity not a member of your work force? Is the person or entity going to perform or assist in performing legal, actuarial, accounting, consulting, data processing, accreditation, or other financial, management, or administrative services for your organization? Do any of these services involve the use or disclosure of protected health information?

Source: Haines, Pamela T. "Special Considerations for Business Associate Agreements: Substance Abuse Treatment, Federal Law Present Challenges." *Journal of AHIMA* 75, no. 4 (April 2004): 50–53.

Can this person or other entity provide you with satisfactory assurances that they will appropriately safeguard your company's protected health information? If not, then you cannot enter into a business associate agreement with that person or other entity. Keep in mind that a business associate agreement cannot be applied to another healthcare provider concerning the treatment of an individual, nor to a health plan as delineated in 164.504 of the rule. (See the text of the privacy rule, 45 CFR, Part 160.103, 164.502, and 164.504, for additional important details.)

The Privacy Rule and the Business Associate Agreement

Once you are sure a business associate agreement is appropriate, it may be helpful to start out with a sample business associate agreement form that generally addresses your needs, such as the one available on the Office for Civil Rights (OCR) Web page at www.hhs.gov/ocr/hipaa. If you do not have patients who are protected by other federal or state laws that are more stringent in protecting their privacy rights, you may be able to follow the OCR agreement and fill in the blanks.

The OCR sample business associate agreement consists of:

- Definitions

- Obligations and activities of the business associate

- Permitted uses and disclosures by the business associate (general and specific uses)

- Obligations of the covered entity

- Permissible requests by the covered entity

- Term and termination of the agreement with the business associate

Regarding permissible requests, the covered entity is prohibited from asking the business associate to do anything that would not be permissible under the privacy rule if likewise performed by the covered entity. An exception may be permitted if the business associate will use or disclose protected health information for (and the agreement includes provision for) data aggregation or management and administrative activities of the business associate. Sections 164.502(e) and 164.504(e) of the privacy rule should be read along with the sample agreement.

The Federal Drug and Alcohol Confidentiality Law and State Law

If you work for a covered entity that is federally assisted in some way and renders substance abuse services that meet the criteria of a program under the drug and alcohol confidentiality law—in other words, the covered entity "holds itself out as providing, and provides, alcohol or drug abuse diagnosis, treatment or referral for treatment (42 CFR, Part 2, 2.11)"[1]—then you must take this federal law into account as you write your business associate agreements. This can be done by inserting the qualified service organization agreement into the business associate agreement and ensuring that the business associate agreement aspects do not contradict the terms of the qualified service organization agreement. This agreement is very brief but comprehensive and reads as follows:

1. [The qualified service organization] acknowledges that in receiving, storing, processing, or otherwise dealing with any patient records [note: "records" refers to any information whether recorded or not] from the program, it is fully bound by these regulations; and

2. if necessary, will resist in judicial proceedings any efforts to obtain access to patient records except as permitted by these regulations.[2]

If you are familiar with the federal drug and alcohol confidentiality law, you will immediately realize the complexity of combining a qualified service organization and a business associate agreement. Aside from carrying out the services that they are providing to the program that has engaged them in the agreement, a qualified service organization/business associate is prohibited from redisclosing protected health information.

A qualified service organization agreement excludes disclosure of protected health information by the qualified service organization/business associate for the proper management and administration of the qualified service organization/business associate or to carry out its legal responsibilities because "any redisclosure of patient identifying information, even to an agent or subcontractor of the qualified service organization/business associate, remains strictly prohibited by 42 CFR, Part 2, unless the qualified service organization/business associate obtains written patient consent."[3]

All potential agreements must be reviewed to determine whether a qualified service organization/business associate agreement is permitted by 42 CFR, Part 2. For example, agreements cannot be signed with law enforcement departments or with other drug or alcohol treatment programs that provide the same services to patients as the drug and alcohol treatment program initiating the agreement. Business associate agreements for treatment, payment, and operation purposes are unnecessary under the privacy rule.

However, since substance abuse treatment programs cannot disclose protected health information for treatment, payment, and operation purposes without authorization, a qualified service organization agreement may only be permissible with a mental health provider as an alternative to patient authorization. On the other hand, the privacy rule permits a business associate agreement with accrediting organizations as an alternative to an authorization, while a qualified service organization agreement is not required to perform audit and evaluation activities—although the activities are strictly regulated by the law (2.53) and must be reflected in this business associate agreement.

In some instances state law may be more protective of the privacy rights of drug and alcohol, mental health, and other patients (e.g., HIV and AIDS patients) than the HIPAA privacy rule and 42 CFR, Part 2. If this is the case, the more restrictive law will generally take precedence and will need to be reflected in decisions related to engaging in business associate and qualified service organization agreements.

This article has illustrated just a few of the complications HIM professionals face in writing business associate agreements and qualified service organization/business associate agreements in compliance with the applicable laws that govern the protected health information of patients. There will be times when the HIM professional will need to consult an attorney familiar with both state and federal laws to clarify issues and concerns. At the same time, a wealth of professional expertise is also available for AHIMA members online in the AHIMA HIPAA-related Communities of Practice at www.ahima.org.

Although there is no magic bullet, careful planning and research can help you navigate this complicated process.

Notes

1. Public Health Service, Department of Health and Human Services. "Confidentiality of Alcohol and Drug Abuse Patient Records." *Code of Federal Regulations,* 2002. 42 CFR, Part 2. Available online at www.access.gpo.gov/nara/cfr/waisidx_02/42cfr2_02.html.

2. Ibid., 2.11.

3. The Legal Action Center specializes in legal and policy issues concerning people in treatment and recovery from alcohol and drug problems, people with HIV and AIDS, and people with histories of criminal justice system involvement. Its 2003 revision of *Confidentiality and Communication, A Guide to the Federal Drug and Alcohol Confidentiality Law and HIPAA* includes a sample qualified service organization/business associate agreement.

Another Layer of Regulations: Research under HIPAA

Margret Amatayakul, MBA, RHIA, CHPS, FHIMSS

HIPAA presents special challenges to providers who perform research. According to the Institute of Medicine, approximately 80,000 biomedical research studies using about 23 million volunteers are conducted per year. Most have some federal funding either through National Institutes of Health or Food and Drug Administration (FDA) processes.

Some of the challenges imposed by HIPAA directly relate to formal research studies, while others are more indirect consequences of the highly regulated nature of research on human subjects in general. In this article, we'll take a closer look at the actions required for use of protected health information (PHI) in research.

What Are the Regulations?

Research on human subjects is primarily regulated by the Department of Health and Human Services, which requires a researcher to have institutional review board (IRB) approval to conduct federally funded biomedical research.[1] The FDA, the Public Health Service, and various state statutes also impose regulations on such research.[2,3] While not very common, privately funded research does not fall under the IRB requirements. HIPAA, however, requires the creation and use of a privacy board to administer the privacy requirements.

Key to understanding how HIPAA plays such an important role in research is the IRB regulations' definition of human subject: it is a "living individual about whom an investigator conducting research obtains either data through intervention or interaction with the individual, or identifiable private information." An example of private information is cited in IRB regulations as a medical record. Therefore, a research study that is based solely on a review of medical records is as much research on human subjects as a study in which physical procedures are performed on a person or a person's environment is manipulated to collect data.

Figure 2.8, Actions Required for Use of PHI in Research, provides a summary of the various actions required by HIPAA for use and disclosure of PHI in research studies.

When Is an Authorization Required?

HIPAA's primary research requirement governs when an authorization for use and disclosure of PHI is required from a patient and what form the authorization may take. In other words,

Source: Amatayakul, Margret. "Another Layer of Regulations: Research under HIPAA." *Journal of AHIMA* 74, no. 1 (2003): 16A–D.

Figure 2.8.   Actions required for use of PHI in research

Type of Information	IRB	Researcher	Research Subject (patient or decedent)
PHI preparatory to research	None*	Representation that use is solely and necessary for research and will not be removed from covered entity	None
Deidentified health information	None*	Removal of safe-harbor data or statistical assurance of deidentification	None
Limited data set	None*	Removal of direct identifiers and data use agreement	None
Individually identifiable on health information on decedents	None*	Representation that use is solely and necessary for research on decedents and documentation of death upon request of covered entity	None
PHI of human subjects (whether research is interventional or record review)	Waive authorization requirement if determined that risk to privacy is minimal	Representation that: 1. Privacy risk is minimal based on: • plan to protect identifiers • plan to destroy identifiers unless there is a health or research reason to retain • written assurance that PHI will not be reused or redisclosed 2. Research requires use of specifically described PHI 3. Justify the waiver 4. Obtain IRB approval under normal or expedited review procedures	None
	Approve alteration of authorization (e.g., to restrict patient's access during study) if determined that risk to privacy is minimal	Same as above	Sign altered authorization form
	Approve research protocol ensuring that there is an authorization for use either combined with consent for and disclosure of PHI research or separate		Sign authorization combined with consent for research or sign standard authorization for use and disclosure of PHI for research as described in authorization

* There may be requirements imposed by the IRB, but there are none imposed by HIPAA.
©2002, Margret\A Consulting, LLC.

the authorization can be stand-alone, altered, or waived, or it can be combined with informed consent for research.

The decision about whether to use a compound authorization (one combined with the consent for research) or stand-alone authorization is complex.

The compound authorization option was included in HIPAA to reduce the burden of administering a separate document. However, the informed consent for research is so important that some researchers fear that adding the authorization for use and disclosure of PHI could result in an item being overlooked in the process of obtaining the informed consent.

Alternatively, protecting the confidentiality of identifiable private information is already one element of the consent for research, and other researchers see the HIPAA requirements as a natural extension.

If a stand-alone authorization is selected, the next decision may be whether to use the standard authorization typically employed for release of information or to create a special authorization. HIPAA does not specify which authorization must be used, only that it includes the core elements of a valid authorization. HIPAA even accommodates an expiration date like "end of research study" or "none" if an exact date is not known or the purpose is the creation and maintenance of a research database.

Core Elements

The core elements of a valid stand-alone authorization for release of information under HIPAA include:

- A description of the information to be used or disclosed that identifies the information in a specific and meaningful fashion

- The name or other specific identification of the person or class of persons authorized to make the requested use or disclosure

- The name or other specific identification of the person or class of persons to whom the covered entity may make the requested use or disclosure

- An expiration date or an expiration event (such as "end of research study") that relates to the individual or the purpose of the use or disclosure

- A statement of the individual's right to revoke the authorization in writing and the exceptions to the right to revoke, together with a description of how the individual may revoke the authorization

- A statement that information used or disclosed pursuant to the authorization may be subject to redisclosure by the recipient and no longer be protected by the privacy rule

- Signature of the individual and date

- If the authorization is signed by a personal representative of the individual, a description of such representative's authority to act for the individual

In addition to the form of authorization used, HIPAA permits the authorization to be altered or waived by the IRB or privacy board based on the researcher's assessment of privacy risk and justification. Some research studies may be blinded studies in which the participants should not have access to their medical records during the course of the study. With IRB or privacy board approval, the authorization may specify that patients waive their right to access and amend the medical record until the end of the research study.

Further, an IRB or privacy board may waive the requirement to obtain authorization for use and disclosure of information where there is justification of minimal risk to the patients' privacy. This might occur in a situation where the research is conducted using medical record review only. Some states, however, have stricter laws and require that patients be contacted for an authorization or, at minimum, be given notice that their records may be used in a research study unless they opt out.

A related issue is whether an organization's IRB should take on the task of monitoring authorizations for use and disclosure of PHI, or whether a separate privacy board should be created for this purpose. HIPAA does not require both an IRB and a privacy board, but it does not prevent an organization from having both entities.

Because of the volume of research and intensity of review that is required to ensure that research on human subjects meets all the regulatory safety requirements, the decision to create a separate privacy board is complex. In an informal survey of providers conducting a heavy volume of research, one-third indicated they would not create such a privacy board, one-third indicated they were strongly considering it or planned to create such a privacy board, and one-third had not made a decision at the time the survey was conducted.

When Is an Authorization Not Required?

There are several situations in which an authorization for use and disclosure of information is not required for research or certain aspects of research. For example, an authorization is not required when PHI has been deidentified and is no longer protected.

HIPAA identifies 19 safe-harbor data elements to be removed to create deidentified information. As an alternative, the rule also permits a statistical algorithm to be used to deidentify information. The August 14, 2002, final modification to the privacy rule also permits a limited data set of PHI to be used, without patient authorization, but with a data use agreement with the recipient of the limited data set. If either deidentified information or a limited data set are used for research, no accounting for disclosure is required if the patient requests such an accounting.

An authorization is not required for use and disclosure of PHI preparatory to research, as long as the researcher represents that the use of the information is solely for research preparation and will not be removed from the covered entity. Similarly, information about decedents is also exempt from requiring an authorization (by the next of kin or executor) for use in research if the researcher represents that use of the information is solely and necessary for research. Documentation of death may be required by the provider prior to disclosure.

Use and disclosure of PHI both on decedents and preparatory to research are subject to potential state law preemption. Where state law permits such disclosures without authorization, however, there is concern on the part of many organizations that "preparatory research" may be abused and used as an excuse to gain access to PHI for other than treatment, payment, or operations purposes. HIPAA requires researcher representation of the purpose, and some organizations are taking this a step further to require that the representation be in writing and authorized by a department chairperson or other person of authority. This provides an opportunity to verify the authority and identity of the requestor and to remind such users of their obligations to safeguard the information. A representation may have the components described in Figure 2.8.

How to Account for Research Disclosures

When an authorization is obtained for use and disclosure of PHI in a research study, an accounting for disclosures is not required. Likewise, information that has been deidentified or reduced to a limited data set does not require an accounting. However, for reviews preparatory to research or where an IRB or privacy board has waived the requirement for research, an accounting for disclosure is required. The August 14, 2002, final modification provides an option to simplify this task. If a research study has included more than 50 people, an accounting for disclosures may state that "protected health information of the individual may or may not have been disclosed for a particular protocol or other research activity." The accounting would be required to:

- Name the protocol

- Provide a plain language description of the protocol and criteria for selecting particular records

- Describe the type of PHI that was disclosed

- Give the date or period of time during which such disclosures occurred or may have occurred including the date of the last such disclosure during the accounting period

- Supply the name, address, and telephone number of the sponsoring entity and researcher to whom the information was disclosed

In addition, the organization is obligated to assist any person requesting an accounting to contact the entity that sponsored the research and researcher.

If an organization conducts many large studies over a long period of time, this process may simplify accounting for disclosures. In this way, the provider does not have to track every single patient whose record may have been included in a large study. However, the task of determining whether a person was reasonably likely to have been included in a study and assisting them in contacting the research sponsor and researcher could be more effort than simply accounting for every such disclosure in a log.

Research is a vital activity in healthcare, and it is not HIPAA's intent to stifle it. But individuals are concerned that their health information may not be fully protected in such studies and they want to know when and by whom their information is being used. Most research studies do an excellent job of protecting health information. In fact, it may be the requests for preparatory review and the databases created for use of information in the future that pose the greatest risk to breaches of confidentiality. These requests and repositories must have the same due diligence applied for privacy and security as any other system of medical records or health information.

Notes

1. Public Welfare, Department of Health and Human Services. "Protection of Human Subjects." *Code of Federal Regulations,* 2001. 45 CFR 46.

2. Food and Drug Administration, Department of Health and Human Services. "Protection of Human Subjects." *Code of Federal Regulations,* 2002. 21 CFR 50.

3. Food and Drug Administration, Department of Health and Human Services. "Institutional Review Boards." *Code of Federal Regulations,* 2002. 21 CFR 56.

Regulations Governing Research

Jill Burrington-Brown, MS, RHIA
Dorothy G. Wagg, JD, RHIA, CHP

The US Department of Health and Human Services (HHS) and several other federal agencies and departments including the Department of Education, the National Science Foundation, and the Consumer Product Safety Commission jointly promulgated regulations that have come to be known as the "common rule" regarding the protection of human subjects involved in research.[1]

These regulations establish a common federal policy for the protection of human subjects involved in research. For purposes of these regulations "research" is defined as "a systematic investigation including research development, testing, and evaluation designed to develop or contribute to generalizable knowledge."[2]

Federal Requirements

Research is not merely a study performed for quality improvement or other purposes, which would more accurately fall under the definition of healthcare operations, set forth in the standards for privacy of individually identifiable health information.[3] The common rule requires, among other things, that an institutional review board (IRB) review all research protocols under its purview even if informed consent to participate in the research study or protocol is to be obtained from individual participants.

Certain research activities are exempt from HHS and common rule oversight, including "research involving the collection or study of existing data, documents, records, pathological specimens, or diagnostic specimens, if these sources are publicly available or if the information is recorded by the investigator in such a manner that subjects cannot be identified, directly or through identifiers linked to the subjects."

However, research involving human subjects is generally regulated under the common rule. According to HHS regulations, "human subjects" are defined as "living individuals about whom an investigator conducting research obtains either data throughout intervention or interaction with the individual or identifiable private information." Research involving existing databases or abstract data from medical records falls under the same rules relating to access of protected health information (PHI).[4]

Source: Burrington-Brown, Jill, and Dorothy G. Wagg. "Regulations Governing Research (AHIMA Practice Brief)." *Journal of AHIMA* 74, no. 3 (2003): 56A–D.

The Food and Drug Administration (FDA) also imposes similar regulations on research involving human subjects.[5] For FDA purposes, "human subject" means "an individual who is or becomes a participant in research, either as a recipient of the test article or as a control. A subject may be either a healthy individual or a patient."[6]

Each institution engaged in research covered by the common rule and conducted or supported by a federal department or agency must provide written assurance satisfactory to the department or agency head that it will comply with the common rule's requirements. While completely private funding for research may exist, it is not common, nor is it under federal control, and the common rule requirements do not apply. If an organization meets the definition of covered entity (CE) for purposes of HIPAA and does not otherwise participate in federally funded research, only HIPAA's research rules would apply. If, however, an organization meets the CE definition under HIPAA, conducts federally funded research, and has given written assurances of compliance with the common rule, it must adhere to both sets of regulations.

Minimum Provisions

The common rule requires that research be reviewed and approved by an IRB and subject to continuing review by the IRB. At a minimum, the organization conducting research must provide:

- A statement of principles governing the institution in the discharge of its responsibilities for protecting the rights and welfare of human subjects of research conducted at or sponsored by the institution

- Designation of an IRB, including ensuring sufficient staff to support the IRB's review and record-keeping duties

- A list of IRB members identified by name, earned degrees, representative capacity, indications of experience such as board certifications and licenses sufficient to describe each member's chief anticipated contributions to IRB deliberations

- Written procedures that the IRB will follow for conducting review of research and for reporting its findings and actions to the investigator and the institution; for determining which projects require review more often than annually and which projects need verification from sources other than the investigators that no material changes have occurred since previous IRB review; and for ensuring prompt reporting to the IRB of proposed changes in a research activity

- Written procedures for ensuring prompt reporting to the IRB, appropriate institutional officials, and the federal authority of any unanticipated problems involving risks to subjects or others, any serious or continuing noncompliance, or any suspension or termination of IRB approval

IRB Membership

The composition of the IRB is also dictated by regulation. Each IRB must have at least five members with varying backgrounds to promote complete and adequate review of research activities commonly conducted by the organization. The IRB shall be sufficiently qualified through the experience, expertise, and diversity of the members, including consideration of race, gender, and cultural backgrounds and sensitivity to issues such as community attitudes, to promote respect for its advice and counsel in safeguarding the rights and welfare of human subjects.

In addition to possessing the professional competence necessary to review specific research activities, the IRB must be able to ascertain the acceptability of proposed research in terms of institutional commitments and regulations, applicable law, and standards of professional conduct and practice. IRB membership must be diverse, with members from the scientific and non-scientific community represented. At least one member must not be affiliated with the organization and the IRB may invite individuals with competence in special areas to assist in the review of issues that require expertise in addition to that available on the IRB.

Expedited Review

Not all areas of research must undergo scrutiny of the full IRB membership. A process known as "expedited review" has been established for research activities that present no more than minimal risk to human subjects and that involve procedures listed in the categories below. The IRB chairperson may request expedited review by one or more experienced reviewers designated by the chairperson from among members of the IRB. Each IRB that uses an expedited review procedure must ensure that all members are advised of research proposals that have been approved under the expedited review procedure.

It is important to note that expedited review may not be used where identification of the subjects or their responses would reasonably place them at risk of criminal or civil liability or be damaging to their financial standing, employability, insurability, or reputation. Nor should it be used when identification could be stigmatizing, unless reasonable and appropriate protections are implemented so that risks related to invasion of privacy and breach of confidentiality are no greater than minimal. Requirements for informed consent (or its waiver, alteration, or exception) apply regardless of the type of review (expedited or full IRB review):

1. Clinical studies of drugs and medical devices only when an investigational new drug application is not required or research on medical devices for which an investigational device exemption application is not required

2. Collection of blood samples by finger stick, heel stick, ear stick, or venipuncture from certain classes of persons

3. Prospective collection of biological specimens for research purposes by noninvasive means such as hair or sputum samples

4. Collection of data through noninvasive procedures such as physical sensors that are applied to the surface of the body

5. Research involving materials (data, documents, records, or specimens) that have been collected, or will be collected, solely for nonresearch purposes (such as medical treatment or diagnosis)

6. Collection of data from voice, video, digital, or image recordings made for research purposes

7. Research on individual or group characteristics or behavior, or research employing survey, interview, oral history, focus group, program evaluation, human factors evaluation, or quality assurance methodologies

8. Continuing review of research previously approved by the convened IRB

9. Continuing review of research, not conducted under an investigational new drug application or investigational device exemption, where categories two through eight do not apply but the IRB has determined and documented at a convened meeting that the research involves no greater than minimal risk and no additional risks have been identified

Informed Consent

A research investigator may not involve a human being as a subject in research unless the investigator has obtained a legally effective informed consent from the research subject. The information that is given to the research subject must be in plain language and contain at least the following:

- A statement that the study involves research, an explanation of the purposes of the research, and the expected duration of the subject's participation, a description of the procedures to be followed, and identification of any procedures that are experimental

- A description of any reasonably foreseeable risks or discomforts to the subject

- A description of any benefits to the subject or to others, which may reasonably be expected from the research

- A disclosure of appropriate alternative procedures or courses of treatment, if any, that might be advantageous to the subject

- A statement describing the extent, if any, to which confidentiality of records identifying the subject will be maintained

- For research involving more than minimal risk, an explanation as to whether any compensation and an explanation as to whether any medical treatments are available if injury occurs and, if so, what they consist of or where further information may be obtained

- Contact information for answers to pertinent questions about the research and research subjects' rights and in the event of a research-related injury to the subject

- A statement that participation is voluntary, refusal to participate will involve no penalty or loss of benefits to which the subject is otherwise entitled, and the subject may discontinue participation at any time without penalty or loss of benefits to which the subject is otherwise entitled

If appropriate and necessary, one or more of the following elements of information may also be provided to the research subject:

- A statement that the particular treatment or procedure may involve risks to the subject (or to the embryo or fetus, if the subject is or may become pregnant), which are currently unforeseeable

- Anticipated circumstances under which the subject's participation may be terminated by the investigator without regard to the subject's consent

- Any additional costs to the subject that may result from participation in the research

- The consequences of a subject's decision to withdraw from the research and procedures for orderly termination of participation by the subject

- A statement that significant new findings developed during the course of the research that may relate to the subject's willingness to continue participation will be provided to the subject

- The approximate number of subjects involved in the study

Waiver of Informed Consent

An IRB has the power to dispense with the need for written consent from the research subject. The IRB may approve a process that does not include, or which alters, some or all of the elements of informed consent set forth above, or waive the requirement to obtain informed consent provided the IRB finds and documents that:

- The research is to be conducted by or subject to the approval of state or local government officials and is designed to study, evaluate, or otherwise examine: public benefit or service programs, procedures for obtaining benefits or services under those programs, possible changes in or alternatives to those programs or procedures, or possible changes in methods or levels of payment for benefits or services under those programs.

- The research could not practicably be carried out without the waiver or alteration.

An IRB may also approve a consent procedure that does not include, or which alters, some or all of the elements of informed consent or waive the requirement to obtain informed consent if the IRB has documented evidence presented to it that:

- The research involves no more than minimal risk to the subjects.

- The waiver or alteration will not adversely affect the rights and welfare of the subjects.

- The research could not practicably be carried out without the waiver or alteration.

- Whenever appropriate, the subjects will be provided with additional pertinent information after participation.

An IRB may also waive the requirement for the investigator to obtain a signed consent form for some or all subjects if it finds either:

- That the only record linking the subject and the research would be the consent document and the principal risk would be potential harm resulting from a breach of confidentiality. Each subject will be asked whether the subject wants documentation linking the subject with the research, and the subject's wishes will govern.

- That the research presents no more than minimal risk of harm to subjects and involves no procedures for which written consent is normally required outside of the research context.

While waiver or alteration of consent or authorization may be allowed, these threshold determinations by and through an IRB must take place. For example, even when an investigator wants to use an existing database to create a mailing list to send out letters to recruit participants into a study, IRB review to ensure that the minimal risk determinations are appropriately made will be required. And in cases in which the written documentation of informed consent or authorization requirement is waived, the IRB may still require the investigator to provide research subjects with a written statement regarding the research.

HIPAA and Research

The HIPAA privacy rule builds on the existing federal protections.[7] When research is performed without individual authorization, the CE must obtain one of the following:

- IRB or privacy board approval in accordance with provisions above

- Representations from the researcher that the use or disclosure of the PHI is solely to prepare a research protocol for similar purposes preparatory to research

- Representations from the researcher that use or disclosure is solely for research on the PHI of decedents

- Limited data set use agreement entered into by both the CE and researcher

IRB/Privacy Board Approval

HIPAA allows for research without individual authorization, as follows (45 CFR 164.512 (i)(1)(i)):

- An IRB, established in accordance with relevant CFRs, has approved the waiver or alteration of the individual authorization required by Section 164.508 for use or disclosure of PHI

- A privacy board that:

   —Has a varied membership with appropriate professional competency to adequately review the research request and evaluate the effect of the research on an individual's privacy rights

   —Includes at least one member who is not associated with the CE, the researcher, or sponsor of research, and not related to anyone associated with the CE, researcher, or sponsor of research

   —Have no members who participate in the review of any project while having a conflict of interest

The IRB or privacy board must upon the approval of the research:

- Document the date the alteration or waiver of authorization was approved

- State that the alteration or waiver of authorization satisfies the three criteria in the rule

- Briefly describe the PHI to be used or accessed

- Document that the alteration or waiver of authorization has been reviewed and approved under normal or expedited review procedures

- Record the signature of the chair or acting chair of the IRB or privacy board, as applicable

For an IRB or privacy board to approve a waiver of authorization, three criteria must be met:

- There is no more than a minimal risk to the privacy of individuals included in the research.

- The research could not be conducted without the waiver of authorization or alteration.

- The research could not be conducted without access to and use of the PHI.[8]

Preparatory to Research

Under HIPAA's requirements, a CE does not need to obtain an authorization for use and disclosure of PHI when the use is preparatory to research and the researcher documents that:

- The use of PHI is to prepare a research protocol or another similar purpose.

- No PHI will be removed from the CE by the researcher.

- The PHI is necessary for research purposes.

Decedent Information

A CE does not need to obtain an authorization for use and disclosure of PHI when the use is regarding a decedent. The researcher must document the use of PHI is for research, the PHI is necessary for the research purpose, and the death of the individuals if the CE requests it.

Limited Data Sets

A CE and a researcher may enter into an agreement for use of a limited data set (Section 164.514(e)) only for the purposes of research, public health, or healthcare operations. A limited data set is data with the following 16 direct identifiers of the individual, or of relatives, employers, or household members of the individual excluded or removed:

> Name; address; telephone number; fax number; e-mail address; social security number; medical record number; health plan beneficiary number; account numbers; certificate/ license numbers; vehicle identification numbers and license plate numbers; device identifiers and serial numbers; Web universal resource locators (URLs); Internet protocol (IP) address numbers; biometric identifiers, including finger and voice prints; full face photographic images and any comparable images.

The limited data use agreement must document the permitted uses and disclosures of the information, who is permitted to use or receive the limited data set, and that the researcher agrees to:

- Not use or further disclose the information according to the terms of the agreement

- Use appropriate safeguards to prevent misuse or inappropriate disclosure

- Report to the CE any misuse or inappropriate disclosure

- Ensure that any agents, including a subcontractor, agree to the terms and conditions of the limited data use agreement

- Not identify the information or contact the individuals

Recommendations

The following are recommendations for handling PHI and research in your organization:

- Review existing mechanisms for review of requests for access to PHI within your organization.

  —Does your organization have an established IRB? Will the IRB also make decisions regarding access to PHI research-related PHI? Will your organization also establish a privacy board to deal with privacy issues in lieu of the IRB?

  —If your organization does not have an IRB, will you need to establish a privacy board to make determinations about access to PHI for research beyond healthcare operations?

- Determine who will make decisions about allowing access to PHI for requests preparatory to research or for access to PHI of decedents.

- Consider establishing standard operating procedures or criteria to assist with ensuring requests to access PHI prefatory to research or access to PHI of decedents are made in a consistent fashion.

- Consider whether your organization will accept approval from an outside IRB and, if so, the minimum necessary criteria that must be met to do so.

- Devise existing IRB or privacy board policies and procedures.

- Educate any IRB or privacy board members on existing and revised policies and procedures.

Notes

1. US Department of Health and Human Services. "Protection of Human Subjects." *Code of Federal Regulations,* 2002. 45 CFR, Part 46.

2. Ibid., section 102.

3. "Standards for Privacy of Individually Identifiable Health Information; Final Rule." 45 CFR, Parts 160 and 164. *Federal Register* 67, no. 157 (August 14, 2002).

4. "Protection of Human Subjects," Section 102.

5. US Department of Health and Human Services. "Food and Drugs." *Code of Federal Regulations,* 2002. 21 CFR, Part 56, Section 102.

6. Ibid.

7. Office for Civil Rights. "Medical Privacy-National Standards to Protect the Privacy of Personal Health Information." Section "Research."

8. Ibid., pp. 2–3.

Reference

Amatayakul, Margret. "Another Layer of Regulations: Research under HIPAA." *Journal of AHIMA* 74, no. 1 (2003): 16A–16D.

Think You're Ready? Don't Forget the Self-Insured Health Plan

Margret Amatayakul, MBA, RHIA, CHPS, FHIMSS

Many providers are putting the finishing touches on their HIPAA privacy compliance activities—but may have overlooked their self-insured health plan or assumed that their third-party administrator (TPA) was taking care of HIPAA compliance. Now is the time to take a closer look at your self-insured health plan.

What Is a Self-Insured Health Plan?

Many large employers (including hospitals, long-term care facilities, large physician practices, automotive and other manufacturers, and airline carriers) have found they can save money by self-insuring their employee health plans rather than purchasing coverage from private insurers. This self-insured health plan program is permitted under the Employee Retirement Income Security Act (ERISA) and may be known as an "ERISA plan." Self-insured health plans are considered group health plans (GHPs) and are subject to HIPAA regulations.

A group health plan, as defined by HIPAA (p. 82,799), is:

(A)n employee welfare benefit plan (as defined in . . . ERISA), including insured and self-insured plans, to the extent that the plan provides medical care . . . , including items and services paid for as medical care, to employees or their dependents directly or through insurance, reimbursement, or otherwise that:

1. Has 50 or more participants (as defined in . . . ERISA); or

2. Is administered by an entity other than the employer that established and maintains the plan.

As a practical matter, virtually all self-insured health plans are subject to HIPAA. Actuarial and cost considerations preclude employers with fewer than 50 participants (that is, employees or former employees eligible for benefits) from self-insuring. The Department of Health and Human Services (HHS) has stated that a health plan that uses a TPA is administered by another entity.

Note, however, that the privacy compliance date for a "small health plan" with receipts of $5 million or less has been extended by one year. HHS says that ERISA health plans should use proxy measures such as premiums or claims paid to calculate "receipts."

Source: Amatayakul, Margret. "Think You're Ready? Don't Forget the Self-Insured Health Plan." *Journal of AHIMA* 74, no. 3 (2003): 16A–D.

Employer versus GHP Responsibilities

Employers must grasp several crucial concepts and definitions to understand their HIPAA obligations. First, many GHPs are really only a piece of paper and most have no staff. The operations of the GHP are either contracted to a TPA, carried out by the employer's staff, or performed by the insurance issuer or health maintenance organization (HMO) from which the employer—through its GHP on paper—purchases benefits.

HHS, like ERISA, recognizes a distinction between the employer as plan sponsor and the insured or self-insured GHP maintained by the plan sponsor. The regulations do not directly regulate the employer. However, unless the employer complies with requirements outlined in the regulations, HIPAA restricts the GHP from disclosing protected health information (PHI) except for summary health information (SHI) to the employer or plan sponsor.

HIPAA appears to impose different obligations on insured and self-insured group health plans. An employer may provide health benefits through a GHP, health insurance issuer, or HMO. The preamble to the August 14, 2002 (p. 53,207), modification to the privacy regulations clarified that "an employer is not a hybrid entity simply because it is the plan sponsor of a group health plan. The employer/plan sponsor and group health plan are separate legal entities and, therefore, do not qualify as a hybrid entity." The GHP, however, will have plan documents with the plan sponsor that establishes how the plan will be administered.

A self-insured health plan may—and usually does—delegate claims processing and other plan administration functions to a TPA or administrative services only (ASO) vendor. However, the TPA is not a covered entity; rather, it is a business associate of the GHP.

What Are GHPs' Responsibilities?

A GHP is subject to all HIPAA regulations (that is, transactions and code sets, identifiers, privacy, and security), although sometimes in unique ways. With respect to privacy, there are several specific requirements and exceptions for GHPs. For the transactions, the GHP must be able to accept and send standard transactions if any entity requests that the plan conduct standard transactions.

What Are the Specific Privacy Requirements?

Figure 2.9, Compliance Responsibilities, summarizes the various scenarios in which insured and self-insured plans may operate and how their privacy rule compliance requirements vary.

Key to understanding the privacy requirements is first understanding who administers the plan and whether the plan receives PHI or only SHI. A GHP that is fully insured and receives only SHI and enrollment/disenrollment information avoids most of the responsibility for HIPAA compliance. However, if the insurer, HMO, or GHP provides PHI to the sponsor, the sponsor is required to certify that plan documents have been amended to incorporate privacy provisions. These certification requirements are summarized in Figure 2.10, Amending Plan Administration Documents. In some respects, they are similar to provisions of a business associate agreement and include organizational separation requirements.

If the plan sponsor is self-insured and administers the plan in-house or retains final adjudication responsibility for claims, it is obviously handling claims and, therefore, PHI. It is critical that the plan be identified and separated organizationally from all other employment-related functions. These GHPs must amend their plan documents to make the necessary organizational

Figure 2.9.   Compliance responsibilities

	Plan Sponsor of Insured Plan		Fully Insured GHP (Insurance Issuer or HMO)		Self-insured GHP, Administered by Self	Self-insured GHP, Administered by TPA	
Sponsor receives	SHI	PHI	SHI	PHI	PHI	SHI	PHI
Plan amendment	No	Yes	No	Yes	Yes	No	Yes
Certification	No	Yes	No	Yes	Yes	No	Yes
Organizational separation	No	Yes	No	Yes	Yes	No	Yes
Notice of privacy practices	No	No	No	See "Notice of Privacy Practices Requirements"	See "Notice"	See "Notice"	See "Notice"
Administrative requirements	No	No	Some*	All	All	All	All

* The GHP that is fully insured and has only SHI is subject only to the administrative requirements of privacy that it must not retaliate against any individual for participating in any privacy process, must not require individuals to waive their privacy rights, and must maintain plan administration documents.

Figure 2.10.   Amending plan administration documents

For a GHP to disclose PHI to the plan sponsor or to permit the disclosure of such information to the plan sponsor by a health insurance issuer or HMO, the plan documents of the GHP must be amended to:

- Establish permitted and required uses of PHI by the plan sponsor

- Require a certification by the plan sponsor to:

    —Not use or further disclose information other than as permitted or required

    —Ensure that any agents or subcontractors agree to the same conditions

    —Not use or disclose the information for employment-related actions

    —Report to the GHP any use or disclosure of which it is aware that is inconsistent with the permitted and required uses and disclosures

    —Make available PHI to individuals who request access

    —Make available PHI for amendment

    —Make available the information required to provide an accounting of disclosures

    —Make its internal practices, books, and records relating to the use and disclosure of PHI received from the GHP available to the secretary of HHS for determining compliance

    —When no longer needed, return or destroy PHI

    —Ensure adequate separation between the GHP and the plan sponsor, including:

      –Describing persons who may be given access to PHI

      –Restricting access to plan administration functions

      –Providing a mechanism for resolving issues of noncompliance

separation. They must also ensure compliance with the other privacy requirements, including providing a notice of privacy practices, and with all administrative requirements, such as having an information privacy official, employing safeguards, having privacy policies and procedures, and more.

If the self-insured plan uses a TPA, the type of information the plan receives must be established. If the TPA does not supply PHI to the plan sponsor, there is no need for plan documents to be amended to require organizational separation and certification.

Exercise caution here, however, because while the TPA may not directly supply PHI, some TPAs have made PHI available to the sponsor in the past. For example, a plan sponsor may have had access to claim information to assist employees with managing their claims. Many of these plan sponsors are now requesting that this access be discontinued and are referring their employees directly to the TPA for such assistance. When an employee voluntarily brings claim information to an employer or plan sponsor, the employee's authorization is implied. However, if the TPA supplies the plan sponsor with the information for the employee, the TPA should obtain an employee authorization.

For self-insured plans, because there is no insurance issuer or HMO, the plan sponsor is the GHP and must supply a notice of privacy practices and adhere to the administrative requirements. The TPA could draw up the notice, make the provision, provide the policies and procedures, and receive complaints, but it is the plan sponsor's responsibility to ensure the notice is accurate and has been provided and other requirements are met.

What Are the Transactions Requirements?

A GHP, as a covered health plan, must be able to accept ASC X12N and NCPDP (National Council on Prescription Drug Programs) standard transactions (for example, 837 claims or 270 eligibility inquiries) and return standard transactions (835 remittance advice or 271 eligibility response) if any entity requests the plan to conduct standard transactions.

Self-insured plans, whether self-administered or administered through a TPA, need to assess their capabilities to conduct the HIPAA transactions, and may need to analyze the costs and benefits of obtaining in-house translator software or using a clearinghouse. If a clearinghouse is chosen as the means to accept or return standard transactions, the plan may not pass the cost of the clearinghouse on to the provider. Plans also may not enter into any unilateral agreements with providers where they agree to use nonstandard electronic transactions.

What Is the Bottom Line?

The regulations are complicated with respect to self-insured plans and careful consideration of exact relationships is needed. It is essential that providers and other employers understand their relationship to their GHP and determine what their TPA is doing on their behalf, that plan documents are amended appropriately, and that they will be compliant by the respective deadlines.

Part 3

Facilitating and Controlling Patient Access

Patient Access and Amendment to Health Records

Gwen Hughes, RHIA, CHP

Background

Generally, consumers should be able to view, copy, and amend information collected and maintained about them. Until recently, however, the legal right to access and amend health records was afforded only to patients at healthcare organizations operated by the federal government or patients in states that had passed specific legislation affording them that right.

The Privacy Act of 1974

The Privacy Act of 1974 was designed to give citizens some control over the information collected about them by the federal government. It grants people the right to find out what information has been collected about them, to see and have a copy of that information, and to correct or amend the information. Healthcare organizations operated by the federal government, such as Veteran Administration and Indian Health Services, are bound by the act's provision.

Standards for Privacy of Individually Identifiable Health Information

More recently, the Standards for Privacy of Individually Identifiable Health Information (also known as the HIPAA privacy rule), which applies to healthcare plans, healthcare clearinghouses, and healthcare providers who transmit specific transactions electronically, established an individual's right to access and amend their information in all but a limited number of situations. Essentially, these regulations state that:

An individual has the right to inspect and obtain a copy of the individual's protected health information in a designated record set except for:[1]

- Psychotherapy notes

- Information compiled in anticipation or use in a civil, criminal, or administration action or proceeding

- Protected health information subject to the Clinical Laboratory Improvements Amendments (CLIA) of 1988 (CLIA, 42 USC 263a, is the federal law that spells out the requirements for the certification of clinical laboratories)

Source: Hughes, Gwen. "Patient Access and Amendment to Health Records (AHIMA Practice Brief)." *Journal of AHIMA* 72, no. 5 (2001): 64S–V.

- Protected health information exempt from CLIA, pursuant to 42 CFR 493.3(a)(2).

  In other words, protected health information generated by:

  —Facilities or facility components that perform testing for forensic purposes

  —Research laboratories that test human specimens but do not report patient-specific results for diagnosis, prevention, treatment, or the assessment of the health of individual patients

  —Laboratories certified by the National Institutes on Drug Abuse (NIDA) in which drug testing is performed that meets NIDA guidelines and regulations; however, other testing conducted by a NIDA-certified laboratory is not exempt

In the cases above, the covered entity may deny the individual access without providing an opportunity for review.

A covered entity may also deny an individual access without providing an opportunity for review when:

- The covered entity is a correctional institution or a healthcare provider acting under the direction of the correctional institution and an inmate's request to obtain a copy of protected health information would jeopardize the individual, other inmates, or the safety of any officer, employee, or other person at the correctional institution, or a person responsible for transporting the inmate.

- The individual agreed to temporary denial of access when consenting to participate in research that includes treatment, and the research is not yet complete.

- The records are subject to the Privacy Act of 1974 and the denial of access meets the requirements of that law.

- The protected health information was obtained from someone other than a healthcare provider under a promise of confidentiality and access would likely reveal the source of the information.

A covered entity may also deny an individual access for other reasons, provided that the individual is given a right to have such denials reviewed under the following circumstances:

- A licensed healthcare provider has determined that the access is likely to endanger the life or physical safety of the individual or another person.

- The protected health information makes reference to another person who is not a healthcare provider, and a licensed healthcare professional has determined that the access requested is likely to cause substantial harm to such other person.

- The request for access is made by the individual's personal representative and a licensed healthcare professional has determined that access is likely to cause substantial harm to the individual or another person.

Detailed requirements for denial review are outlined in section 45 CFR, section 164.524.

An individual has the right to request a covered entity amend his or her health information. Covered entities may require individuals to make such requests in writing and to provide a reason to support the amendment, provided that it informs individuals in advance of such requirements.

The covered entity may deny the request if the health information that is the subject of the request:

- Was not created by the covered entity, unless the originator is no longer available to act on the request

- Is not part of the individual's health record

- Would not be accessible to the individual for the reasons stated above

- Is accurate and complete

The covered entity must act on the individual's request for amendment no later than 60 days after receipt of the amendment. Provided the covered entity gives the individual a written statement of the reason for the delay, and the date by which the amendment will be processed, the covered entity may have a one-time extension of up to 30 days for an amendment request.

If the request is granted, the covered entity must:

- Insert the amendment or provide a link to the amendment at the site of the information that is the subject of the request for amendment

- Inform the individual that the amendment is accepted

- Obtain the individual's identification of and agreement to have the covered entity notify the relevant persons with whom the amendment needs to be shared

- Within a reasonable time frame, make reasonable efforts to provide the amendment to persons identified by the individual, and persons, including business associates, that the covered entity knows have the protected health information that is the subject of the amendment and that may have relied on or could foreseeably rely on the information to the detriment of the individual

If the covered entity denies the requested amendment, it must provide the individual with a timely, written denial written in plain language that contains:

- The basis for the denial

- The individual's right to submit a written statement disagreeing with the denial and how the individual may file such a statement

- A statement that if the individual does not submit a statement of disagreement, the individual may request that the covered entity provide the individual's request for amendment and the denial with any future disclosures of protected health information

- A description of how the individual may complain to the covered entity or the secretary of Health and Human Services

- The name or title and telephone number of the designated contact person who handles complaints for the covered entity

The covered entity must permit the individual to submit to the covered entity a written statement disagreeing with the denial of all or part of a requested amendment and the basis of such disagreement. The covered entity may reasonably limit the length of a statement of disagreement.

The covered entity may prepare a written rebuttal to the individual's statement of disagreement. Whenever such a rebuttal is prepared, the covered entity must provide a copy to the individual who submitted the statement of disagreement.

The covered entity must, as appropriate, identify the record of protected health information that is the subject of the disputed amendment and append or otherwise link the individual's request for an amendment, the covered entity's denial of the request, the individual's statement of disagreement, if any, and the covered entity's rebuttal, if any.

If a statement of disagreement has been submitted by the individual, the covered entity must include the material appended or an accurate summary of such information with any subsequent disclosure of the protected health information to which the disagreement relates.

If the individual has not submitted a written statement of disagreement, the covered entity must include the individual's request for amendment and its denial, or an accurate summary of such information, with any subsequent disclosure of protected health information only if the individual has requested such action.

When a subsequent disclosure is made using a standard transaction that does not permit the additional material to be included, the covered entity may separately transmit the material required.

A covered entity that is informed by another covered entity of an amendment to an individual's protected health information must amend the protected health information in written or electronic form.

A covered entity must document the titles for the persons or offices responsible for receiving and processing requests for amendments.

State Law

Individual states may also have laws or regulations that address how amendments should be processed, and healthcare organizations must comply with these requirements if they are more stringent than those outlined under the federal standards.

Recommendations

In order to comply with the standards for privacy of individually identifiable health information, it is necessary to:

1. Study federal and state requirements for patient access and amendments.

2. Draft an amendment form, policy, and procedure that complies with applicable provisions of federal and state law and regulation.

    A sample amendment policy and procedure is provided in Figure 3.1.

3. To simplify processing and maintain positive patient–provider relationships, consider a protocol in which amendments are generally accepted. The form below could serve as a vehicle wherein the individual could submit an amendment and the amendment could be accepted, even when the author disagrees with the amendment. The author of the disputed entry could note why he or she disagrees with the individual on the amendment form.

4. Educate staff as to the new policy, procedure, and forms.

5. Implement the new policy, procedure, and forms.

6. Monitor compliance and implement corrective action where indicated.

Figure 3.1.   Sample health record correction/amendment form

Request for Correction/Amendment of Health Information

Patient Name:_____ Birth date: _____

Patient Number: _____

Patient Address:_____

Date of Entry to be amended: _____

Type of entry to be amended: _____

Please explain how the entry is incorrect or incomplete. What should the entry say to be more accurate or complete?

_____

_____

_____

Would you like this amendment sent to anyone to whom we may have disclosed the information in the past? If so, please specify the name and address of the organization or individual.

_____   _____

           Name   Address

_____   _____

   Signature of Patient or Legal Representative   Date

For Healthcare Organization Use Only:

Date Received _____   Amendment has been: ☐ Accepted   ☐ Denied

If denied, check reason for denial:

☐ PHI was not created by this organization   ☐ PHI is not part of patient's designated record set

☐ PHI is not available to the patient   ☐ PHI is accurate and complete
   for inspection as required by federal law
   (e.g., psychotherapy notes)

Comments of Healthcare Practitioner:

_____

_____

_____   _____

         Name of Staff Member   Title

_____   _____

    Signature of Healthcare Practitioner   Date

Note: This sample form was developed by AHIMA for discussion purposes only. It should not be used without review by your organization's legal counsel to ensure compliance with local and state laws.

Managing Exceptions to HIPAA's Patient Access Rule

Gwen Hughes, RHIA, CHP

The HIPAA final privacy rule requires that covered entities allow individuals to access the medical and billing records maintained about them. However, the rule describes 10 exceptions. Accordingly, healthcare providers must establish a way to identify the medical and billing records to which these exceptions to access apply.

Exceptions to Remember

The HIPAA privacy rule grants individuals the right to information about them in a designated record set. The rule goes on to define designated record set as medical and billing records maintained by or for the covered entity to make decisions about these individuals. If information is not part of the designated record set, then according to HIPAA, an individual's request for such information can be denied.

The rule specifically addresses two types of such information:

1. Psychotherapy notes: Recorded by a mental health professional and maintained separately from the rest of the medical record, psychotherapy notes document or analyze conversation during a private or group counseling session. By definition, psychotherapy notes do not include medication records, counseling start and stop times, treatment records, results of clinical tests, diagnoses, functional status, symptoms, prognosis and progress, and psychotherapy notes maintained within the individual's regular health record.

2. Information compiled in anticipation of or for use in a civil, criminal, or administrative action or proceeding: In many organizations, for example, incident reports are generated when a patient falls or a medication is given in error. These reports are used to identify problems, implement corrective action, and to respond to civil, criminal, or administrative action. Although pieces of the information in the incident report such as the patient's condition are recorded in the patient's health record, incident reports are filed in separate administrative or legal files.

    The HIPAA privacy rule describes a third access exception that applies to information originated and maintained in laboratories:

Source: Hughes, Gwen. "Managing Exceptions to HIPAA's Patient Access Rule." *Journal of AHIMA* 72, no. 9 (2001): 90–92.

3. Information subject to the Clinical Laboratory Improvement Amendments of 1988 (CLIA).[1] Labs that are subject to CLIA must not grant patients access to test results if CLIA bans them from doing so. Research labs that are exempt from CLIA may also deny patients access to health information.[2]

If HIPAA limited exceptions only to psychotherapy notes, reports made in anticipation of legal action, and the release of test results by laboratories, covered entities would find it unnecessary to flag exceptions. Such exceptions would be relatively easy to manage. However, the next seven HIPAA exceptions describe specific scenarios that are more difficult to handle:

4. The patient is an inmate and obtaining a copy of his health information would jeopardize the health, safety, security, custody, or rehabilitation of the individual or other inmates, the safety of an officer, employee, other person at the correctional institution, or individual responsible for transporting the inmate.

5. The individual previously agreed to a temporary denial of access while part of a research project that includes treatment. The temporary denial of access applies as long as the research is in progress.

6. The individual's access to protected health information is subject to and may be denied under the Privacy Act of 1974.[3] The act applies to record systems operated by the federal government or pursuant to a contract with a government agency. The act therefore applies to information maintained in military hospitals and veterans administration and Indian health services.

7. The protected health information was obtained from someone other than a healthcare provider under a promise of confidentiality, and access would likely reveal the source of the information.

8. A licensed healthcare professional has determined that the access requested is likely to endanger the life or physical safety of the individual or another person.

9. The protected health information makes reference to another person (unless the other person is a healthcare provider) and a licensed healthcare professional has determined that access is likely to cause substantial harm to the other person.

10. The request for access is made by the individual's personal representative and a licensed healthcare professional has determined access is likely to cause substantial harm to the individual or another person.

Identifying the Exceptions

Identifying records to which the psychotherapy, legal proceeding, and laboratory exceptions apply is relatively simple. Identifying information or records to which the seven case-specific exceptions apply is more complex. So how can providers best flag these exceptions?

There are a number of possibilities:

1. Providers from whom access is requested can contact the attending physician whenever an individual requests access. In many settings, however, this is not a practical solution. There are numerous requests, the physician is busy, and recollection of information about the individual can be vague.

2. The individual or office charged with disclosure can read through every record entry looking for exceptions prior to disclosure. Again, this is not a practical solution in many settings. There are numerous requests, the ability to read the records is limited, and there are little or no human resources available to take on this responsibility.

3. Providers can use a color-coded label applied in a standard location on the chart or at the site of specific entries to highlight particularly sensitive information of which release to the individual or his legal representative may be inappropriate. This solution is fairly easy to implement, but not 100 percent accurate. Should sites decide to use this type of flagging solution, HIM professionals should anticipate questions by individuals about the meaning of the color-coded labels and train staff to give the appropriate response.

4. Providers can designate a location on the face sheet, problem list, or file folder on which the date of any sensitive entry can be recorded. The advantage of this particular method is that it can be done in a way that is more discrete than some other methods of flagging exceptions.

5. Providers can generate a disclosure restriction form such as that in Figure 3.2. Such a form might contain the patient's name, record number, entries to which access should be denied, the individual or personal representative to whom access should be denied, the duration the denial should be in place, and the signature and date of the individual generating the form. The form can be sent to the HIM department to be maintained in a paper or electronic database. While the individual is an inpatient, requests for access can be routed through the attending physician. Thereafter, staff charged with the responsibility of processing disclosures can check requests against disclosure restrictions forms maintained in a notebook, other paper file, or computer database.

HIM professionals can find it challenging to identify health record entries or circumstances in which it may be inappropriate to disclose information to the individual or the individual's legal representative. While there is a myriad of information, there are often just a few cases in which access needs to be denied. Nevertheless, it's important to develop a system for identifying entries that should not be disclosed. The disclosure restriction form or one of the other tools identified above may be the right solution for your organization.

Notes

1. *Clinical Laboratory Improvement Amendments of 1998,* 42 USC 263a.

2. "Laboratory Requirements." 42 CFR 493(a)(2)

3. *Privacy Act of 1974,* 5USC 522a.

References

Abdelhak, Mervat et al. *Health Information: Management of a Strategic Resource.* Philadelphia: W.B. Saunders, 1996.

"Standards for Privacy of Individually Identifiable Health Information; Final Rule." 45 CFR Parts 160 and 164. *Federal Register* 65, no. 250 (December 28, 2000).

Figure 3.2.   Sample disclosure restriction form

Patient Name _____

Health Record Number _____

Please check the box explaining why disclosure of specified information may not be appropriate.

☐ The patient is an inmate and obtaining such copy would jeopardize the health, safety, security, custody, or rehabilitation of the individual or other inmates, or the safety of an officer, employee, or other person at the correctional institution or responsible for transporting the inmate.

☐ The individual previously agreed to a temporary denial of access while the patient is part of a research project that includes treatment for as long as the research is in progress.

☐ The individual s access to protected health is subject to and may be denied under the Privacy Act, 5 USC 552a.

☐ The protected health information was obtained from someone other than a healthcare provider under a promise of confidentiality and access to the requested information would likely reveal the source of the information

Access with the right of review

☐ A licensed healthcare professional has determined that the access requested is likely to endanger the life or physical safety of the individual or another person.

☐ The protected health information makes reference to another person (unless the other person is a healthcare provider) and a licensed healthcare professional has determined that the access requested is likely to cause substantial harm to another person

☐ The request for access is made by the individual s personal representative and a licensed healthcare professional has determined that the provision of access to such personal representative is likely to cause substantial harm to the individual or another person

Please indicate which entries may not be appropriate for release:

Date of Entry	Entry Type (H&P, Progress Note, etc.)

Please indicate the individual or any legal representative to whom access should be denied:

Individual s Name	Relationship to Patient

Condition Upon Which Denial will Expire:

☐ Termination of research, anticipated on or about (date) _____

☐ Minor patient reaches age of majority

☐ Other_____

_____   _____   _____
Signature of Individual Submitting Form   Position/Title   Date

---

Notice of Privacy Practices

Gwen Hughes, RHIA, CHP

Timely, accurate and complete health information must be collected, maintained and made available to members of an individual's healthcare team so that members of the team can accurately diagnose and care for that individual. Most consumers understand and have no objections to this use of their information.

On the other hand, consumers may not be aware of the fact that their health information may also be used as:

- A legal document describing the care rendered
- Verification of services for which the individual or a third-party payer is billed
- A tool in evaluating the adequacy and appropriateness of care
- A tool in educating heath professionals
- A source of data for research
- A source of information for tracking disease so that public health officials can manage and improve the health of the nation
- A source of data for facility planning and marketing

Although consumers trust their caregivers to maintain the privacy of their health information, they are often skeptical about the security of their information when it is placed on computers or disclosed to others. Increasingly, consumers want to be informed about what information is collected and to have some control over how their information is used.

With this in mind, some states and, more recently, the federal government passed legislation requiring that health plans, healthcare clearinghouses, and healthcare providers furnish individuals with a notice of information practices.

Federal Requirements

Standards for Privacy of Individually Identifiable Health Information

In general, the federal Standards for Privacy of Individually Identifiable Health Information, also known as the HIPAA privacy rule (45 CFR Part 160–164) requires that:

Source: Hughes, Gwen. "Notice of Information Practices (AHIMA Practice Brief)" (Updated November 2002).

Except for certain variations or exceptions for health plans and correctional facilities, an individual has a right to notice as to the uses and disclosures of protected health information that may be made by the covered entity, as well as the individual's rights, and the covered entity's legal duties with respect to protected health information.

In general, the content of the notice must contain:

1. A header "THIS NOTICE DESCRIBES HOW INFORMATION ABOUT YOU MAY BE USED AND DISCLOSED AND HOW YOU CAN GET ACCESS TO THIS INFORMATION. PLEASE REVIEW IT CAREFULLY."

2. A description, including at least one example of the types of uses and disclosures that the covered entity is permitted to make for treatment, payment, and healthcare operations.

3. A description of each of the other purposes for which the covered entity is permitted or required to use or disclose protected health information without the individual's written consent or authorization.

4. A statement that other uses and disclosures will be made only with the individual's written authorization and that the individual may revoke such authorization.

5. When applicable, separate statements that the covered entity may contact the individual to provide appointment reminders or information about treatment alternatives or other health-related benefits and services that may be of interest to the individual; that the covered entity may contact the individual for fund-raising purposes on behalf of the covered entity; that the group health plan or health insurance issuer or HMO may disclose protected health information to the sponsor of the plan.

6. A statement of the individual's rights with respect to protected health information and a brief description of how the individual may exercise these rights including:

   • The right to request restrictions on certain uses and disclosures as provided by 45 CFR 164.522(a), including a statement that the covered entity is not required to agree to a requested restriction

   • The right to receive confidential communications of protected health information as provided by 164.522(b), as applicable

   • The right to inspect and copy protected health information as provided by 164.524

   • The right to amend protected health information as provided in 164.526

   • The right to receive an accounting of disclosures as provided in 164.528

   • The right to obtain a paper copy of the notice upon request as provided in 164.520

7. A statement that the covered entity is required by law to maintain the privacy of protected health information and to provide individuals with a notice of its legal duties and privacy practices with respect to protected health information.

8. A statement that the covered entity is required to abide by the terms of the notice currently in effect.

9. A statement that the covered entity reserves the right to change the terms of its notice and to make the new notice provisions effective for all protected health information that it maintains.

10. A statement describing how it will provide individuals with a revised notice.

11. A statement that individuals may complain to the covered entity and to the Secretary of Health and Human Services if they believe their privacy rights have been violated; a brief description as to how one files a complaint with the covered entity; and a statement that the individual will not be retaliated against for filing a complaint.

12. The name or title, and telephone number of a person or office to contact for further information.

13. An effective date, which may not be earlier than the date on which the notice is printed or otherwise published.

In the preamble to the August 14, 2002, final rule, the government encourages the use of a "layered notice." A layered notice consists of a short notice that briefly summarizes the individual's rights and other information, followed by a longer notice layered beneath that explains all the required notice elements.

A covered entity that is required to have a notice may not use or disclose protected health information in a manner inconsistent with such notice.

A covered healthcare provider with a direct treatment relationship with an individual must:

- Provide the notice no later than the date of the first service delivery, including service delivered electronically, or in an emergency treatment situation, as soon as reasonably practicable after the emergency situation.

- Have the notice available at the service delivery site for individuals to request and take with them.

- Post the notice in a clear and prominent location where it is reasonable to expect individuals seeking service from the covered healthcare provider to be able to read the notice.

A covered entity that maintains a Web site that provides information about the covered entity's customer services or benefits must prominently post its notice on its Web site.

A covered healthcare provider that provides care to its work force related to medical surveillance, work-related illness, or injury must provide a written notice to individuals seeking such care at the time healthcare is provided, or by posting a notice in a prominent place at the location where healthcare is provided.

The covered entity may provide the notice by e-mail if the individual agrees and agreement has not been withdrawn. If the covered entity knows that the e-mail transmission has failed, a paper copy of the notice must be provided to the individual.

Except in an emergency situation, the covered entity must make a good faith effort to obtain written acknowledgment of receipt of the notice. If it is not obtained, the covered entity must document the good faith effort and the reason why the acknowledgment was not obtained. If the notice is mailed, along with an acknowledgment form, the covered entity is not required to follow up to ensure the individual returns the acknowledgment form.

According to the August 14, 2002, final rule preamble, the Department of Health and Human Services believes that providers who provide notices electronically should be capable of capturing the individual's acknowledgment of receipt electronically in response to that transmission. The covered entity must promptly revise and distribute its notice whenever there is a material change to the uses or disclosures, the individual's rights, the covered entity's legal duties, or other privacy practices stated in the notice. Except when required by law, a material change to any term of the notice may not be implemented prior to the effective date of the notice in which such material change is reflected.

A covered entity must document compliance with the notice requirements by retaining copies of the notices issued and acknowledgments received.

Privacy Act of 1974 and Related Laws

The Privacy Act of 1974 (as amended) requires that federal agencies or organizations that collect and maintain information on behalf of the federal government provide individuals with a notice of privacy practices. This notice must identify:

- The statute or order that authorizes the government to solicit the information and whether either provision of the information is mandatory or voluntary

- The principal purposes for which the information is intended to be used

- The routine uses of the information

- The effects, if any, of not providing all or any part of the requested information

The notice may be written on the form on which the information is solicited or a separate form that can be kept by the individual.

The Gramm-Leach-Bliley Act requires financial institutions to provide customers with a notice of privacy policies and procedures and to satisfy various disclosure and consumer opt-out requirements.

The Privacy of Consumer Financial Information final rule implements the requirements outlined in the Act. Among its standards are procedural and content requirements for a notice of privacy practices.

Confidentiality of Drug and Alcohol Abuse Patient Records

The Confidentiality of Alcohol and Drug Abuse Patient Records rules (42 CFR, Chapter 1, Part 2) establish the following notice provisions for patients of federally assisted drug or alcohol abuse programs:

At the time of admission or as soon thereafter as the patient is capable of rational communication, each substance abuse program shall communicate to the patient that federal law and regulations protect the confidentiality of alcohol and drug abuse patient records. The program must also provide the patient with a written summary of the federal law and regulations.

The written summary of the federal law and regulations must include:

- A general description of the limited circumstances under which a program may acknowledge that an individual is present at a facility or disclose outside the program information identifying a patient as an alcohol or drug abuser

- A statement that violation of the federal law and regulations by a program is a crime and that suspected violations may be reported to appropriate authorities in accordance with these regulations

- A statement that information related to a patient's commission of a crime on the premises of the program or against personnel of the program is not protected

- A statement that reports of suspected child abuse and neglect made under State law to appropriate State or local authorities are not protected

- A citation to the federal law and regulations

The program may devise its own notice or use the sample provided by the federal government illustrated below. In addition, the program may include in the written summary information concerning State law and any program policy not inconsistent with State and federal law on the subject of confidentiality of alcohol and drug abuse patient records.

State Requirements

Some states have laws or regulations and provide specific requirements for a notice of health information practices.

Recommendations

1. Identify applicable notice requirements in both federal and state law.

2. Collect sample notices from associations and other organizations.

3. Identify the way information is used and disclosed in your organization.

4. Decide whether your organization will participate in an organized healthcare arrangement.

5. Assign an individual or department to serve as an initial point of contact for individuals requesting additional information or who would like to file a complaint relative to information privacy practices.

6. Decide how material changes in the notice will be communicated.

7. Although not a required element, consider providing space on the notice to allow an individual to request a restriction to the uses and disclosures of his or her health information.

8. Decide whether your organization will provide space for the acknowledgment on the notice or on a separate form.

9. Draft a notice that complies with federal and state law and regulations and accurately describes your organization's health information practices. (Although models are helpful, they cannot be used without adapting them to reflect actual practices in your organization.)

10. Decide whether to place a copy of the current notice in the individual's record with the individual's acknowledgment, or simply to maintain a copy of each version of the notice with the dates it was in effect in a separate file.

11. Ask legal counsel to help develop or review the notice.

12. Generate policies and procedures relative to the notice.

13. Educate and train staff.

14. Post the notice and make copies available for distribution where notice acknowledgments are obtained.

15. Implement and monitor compliance.

16. Prior to making material changes in information practices, generate a new notice and provide that new notice to individuals about whom protected health information is maintained.

(See Figure 3.3, Sample Notice of Health Information Practices, and Figure 3.4, Acknowledgment of Receipt of Notice.)

References

Privacy Act of 1974. 5 USC, Section 552A.

"Privacy of Consumer Financial Information; Final Rule." 16 CFR Part 313. *Federal Register* 65, No. 101.

Public Health Service, Department of Health and Human Services. "Confidentiality of Alcohol and Drug Abuse Patient Records." *Code of Federal Regulations, 2000.* 42 CFR, Chapter I, Part 2.

"Standards for Privacy of Individually Identifiable Health Information: Final Rule." 45 CFR Parts 160 and 164. *Federal Register* 67. No. 157 (August 14, 2002).

Figure 3.3.   Sample notice of health information practices

THIS NOTICE DESCRIBES HOW INFORMATION ABOUT YOU MAY BE USED AND DISCLOSED AND HOW YOU CAN GET ACCESS TO THIS INFORMATION. PLEASE REVIEW IT CAREFULLY.

Understanding Your Health Record/Information

Each time you visit a hospital, physician, or other healthcare provider, a record of your visit is made. Typically, this record contains your symptoms, examination and test results, diagnoses, treatment, and a plan for future care or treatment.

This information, often referred to as your health or medical record, serves as a:

- Basis for planning your care and treatment
- Means of communication among the many health professionals who contribute to your care
- Legal document describing the care you received
- Means by which you or a third party payer can verify that services billed were actually provided
- Tool in educating heath professionals
- Source of data for medical research
- Source of information for public health officials charged with improving the health of the nation
- Source of data for facility planning and marketing and
- Tool with which we can assess and continually work to improve the care we render and the outcomes we achieve.

Understanding what is in your record and how your health information is used helps you to:

- Ensure its accuracy
- Better understand who, what, when, where and why others may access your health information
- Make more informed decisions when authorizing disclosure to others.

Your Health Information Rights:

Although your health record is the physical property of the healthcare practitioner or facility that compiled it, the information belongs to you. You have the right to:

- Request a restriction on certain uses and disclosures of your information as provided by 45 CFR 164.522
- Obtain a paper copy of the notice of information practices upon request
- Inspect and copy your health record as provided for in 45 CFR 164.524
- Amend your health record as provided in 45 CFR 164.528
- Obtain an accounting of disclosures of your health information as provided in 45 CFR 164.528
- Request communications of your health information by alternative means or at alternative locations
- Revoke your authorization to use or disclose health information except to the extent that action has already been taken.

Our Responsibilities:

This organization is required to:

- Maintain the privacy of your health information
- Provide you with a notice as to our legal duties and privacy practices with respect to information we collect and maintain about you
- Abide by the terms of this notice

(Continued on next page)

Figure 3.3.   (Continued)

- Notify you if we are unable to agree to a requested restriction

- Accommodate reasonable requests you may have to communicate health information by alternative means or at alternative locations.

We reserve the right to change our practices and to make the new provisions effective for all protected health information we maintain. Should our information practices change, we will mail a revised notice to the address you've supplied us.

We will not use or disclose your health information without your authorization, except as described in this notice.

For More Information or to Report a Problem

If you have questions and would like additional information, you may contact the Director of Health Information Management at (444) 111-1111.

If you believe your privacy rights have been violated, you can file a complaint with the Director of Health Information Management or with the Secretary of Health and Human Services. There will be no retaliation for filing a complaint.

Examples of Disclosures for Treatment, Payment and Health Operations

We will use your health information for treatment. For example: Information obtained by a nurse, physician or other member of your healthcare team will be recorded in your record and used to determine the course of treatment that should work best for you. Your physician will document in your record his expectations of the members of your healthcare team. Members of your healthcare team will then record the actions they took and their observations. In that way the physician will know how you are responding to treatment.

We will also provide your physician or a subsequent healthcare provider with copies of various reports that should assist him/her in treating you once you're discharged from this hospital.

We will use your health information for payment. For example: A bill may be sent to you or a third party payer. The information on or accompanying the bill may include information that identifies you, as well as your diagnosis, procedures and supplies used.

We will use your health information for regular health operations. For example: Members of the medical staff, the risk or quality improvement manager, or members of the quality improvement team may use information in your health record to assess the care and outcomes in your case and others like it. This information will then be used in an effort to continually improve the quality and effectiveness of the healthcare and service we provide.

Other Uses or Disclosures

Business Associates: There are some services provided in our organization through contacts with business associates. Examples include physician services in the Emergency Department and Radiology, certain laboratory tests, and a copy service we use when making copies of your health record. When these services are contracted, we may disclose your health information to our business associate so that they can perform the job we've asked them to do and bill you or your third party payer for services rendered. So that your health information is protected, however, we require the business associate to appropriately safeguard your information.

Directory: Unless you notify us that you object, we will use your name, location in the facility, general condition, and religious affiliation for directory purposes. This information may be provided to members of the clergy and, except for religious affiliation to other people who ask for you by name.

Notification: We may use or disclose information to notify or assist in notifying a family member, personal representative, or another person responsible for your care, your location, and general condition.

Communication with Family: Health professionals, using their best judgment, may disclose to a family member, other relative, close personal friend or any other person you identify, health information relevant to that person's involvement in your care or payment related to your care.

Figure 3.3.   **(Continued)**

Research: We may disclose information to researchers when their research has been approved by an Institutional Review Board that has reviewed the research proposal and established protocols to ensure the privacy of your health information.

Funeral Directors: We may disclose health information to funeral directors consistent with applicable law to carry out their duties.

Organ Procurement Organizations: Consistent with applicable law, we may disclose health information to organ procurement organizations or other entities engaged in the procurement, banking, or transplantation of organs for the purpose of tissue donation and transplant.

Marketing: We may contact you to provide appointment reminders or information about treatment alternatives or other health related benefits and services that may be of interest to you.

Fund Raising: We may contact you as part of a fund-raising effort.

Food and Drug Administration (FDA): We may disclose to the FDA health information relative to adverse events with respect to food, supplements, product and product defects or post marketing surveillance information to enable product recalls, repairs or replacement.

Workers Compensation: We may disclose health information to the extent authorized by and to the extent necessary to comply with laws relating to workers compensation or other similar programs established by law.

Public Health: As required by law, we may disclose your health information to public health or legal authorities charged with preventing or controlling disease, injury or disability.

Correctional Institution: Should you be an inmate of a correctional institution, we may disclose to the institution or agents thereof, health information necessary for your health, and the health and safety of other individuals.

Law Enforcement: We may disclose health information for law enforcement purposes as required by law, or in response to a valid subpoena.

Federal law makes provision for your health information to be released to an appropriate health oversight agency, public health authority or attorney, provided that a workforce member or business associate believes in good faith that we have engaged in unlawful conduct or have otherwise violated professional or clinical standards and are potentially endangering one or more patients, workers or the public.

My signature below indicates that I have been provided with a copy of the notice of privacy practices.

_____   _____
                Signature of Patient or Legal Representative   Date

If signed by legal representative, relationship to patient _____

Effective Date:

Distribution: Original to provider; copy to patient

The above form is not meant to encompass all the various ways in which any particular facility may use health information. For example, those who use protected health information for fundraising or marketing will want to add those types of disclosures. It is intended to get the reader started insofar as developing their own notice. As with any form of this nature, the document should be reviewed and approved by legal counsel prior to implementation.

Figure 3.4.   Acknowledgment of Receipt of Notice

I understand that Company ABC is part of an organized healthcare arrangement that includes (list companies) and that these providers may share my health information for treatment, billing and healthcare operations. I have been given a copy of the organization's notice of privacy practices that describes how my health information is used and shared. I understand the organized healthcare arrangement has the right to change this notice at any time. I may obtain a current copy by contacting the hospital registration office, the doctors office or by visiting the Web site at www.xxx.com.

My signature below constitutes my acknowledgment that I have been provided with a copy of the notice of privacy practices.

_____   _____
                Signature of Patient or Legal Representative   Date

If signed by legal representative, relationship to patient :_____

The above form is provided for discussion purposes only. As with any form of this nature, the document should be reviewed and approved by legal counsel prior to implementation.

Source: AHIMA Practice Brief, "Notice of Information Practices" (Updated November 2002).

Is Your NPP Your Best Defense?

Michael R. Lee

In the event of a privacy-related legal challenge, the content of your organization's notice of privacy practices (NPP) will be a focal point for both plaintiff and defense arguments with respect to the protected health information (PHI) disclosure activities of your organization. Is your organization's NPP ready to come to your defense?

When the final privacy rule revisions were introduced in August 2002, two changes dramatically affected information exchanges: individual consent is no longer required and covered entities are granted wide latitude in sharing PHI without authorization under the umbrella of treatment, payment, and operations (TPO). Both these changes elevate the legal significance of your notice of privacy practices (NPP), making the document the basis for defending all your organization's PHI disclosure activities.

This article will discuss specific design and content requirements for the uses and disclosures section of your NPP to defend your organization's actions in the event of a privacy-related civil action.

A "Model Notice"

In the final privacy rule, the Department of Health and Human Services (HHS) states, "Adequate notice of privacy practices is a fundamental right afforded individuals . . . the Department believes that the elements required by §164.520(b) are important to fully inform the individual of the covered entity's (CE's) privacy practices, as well as his or her rights."

In response to public comments regarding a "model notice," HHS replied, "A covered entity's notice must reflect in sufficient detail the particular uses and disclosures that the entity may make. . . . Such uses and disclosures will likely be very different for each type of covered entity."

Here, HHS is suggesting that the NPP is the principal vehicle for informing an individual of all of his or her privacy rights. Further, there is no single solution to defining the specific content for the uses and disclosures section of an NPP.

In practice, one can envision a scenario in which each "disclosure encounter" could require a unique explanation that "fully informs" an individual of his or her "fundamental privacy rights" in that particular situation or context.

Source: Lee, Michael R. "Is Your NPP Your Best Defense?" *Journal of AHIMA* 74, no. 4 (April 2003): 56–57.

Partial Preemption, Adequate Notice

The difficulty with HHS' requirement for the NPP is that the content must satisfy the "adequate notice" and "fully inform" requirements by creating an NPP that describes "in sufficient detail the particular uses and disclosures that the CE may make."

The privacy rule is considered "partially preemptive" because the legislative intent is to provide additional privacy protections without preempting more protective privacy protections existing under other federal, state, and local jurisdictions. As a result, the "adequate notice" and "fully inform" objectives require a CE to provide an individual with a context-specific NPP that includes all relevant privacy protections provided by empowered jurisdictions. In situations in which the CE's uses or disclosures under the privacy rule are "prohibited or materially limited," the NPP "must reflect the more stringent applicable law."

NPP as a Contract

When a breach of contract occurs, the law considers it a duty to remedy the situation. Under this definition, one must conclude that an NPP is actually a contract under which an individual can hold a CE accountable for any uses or disclosures of PHI that are inconsistent with the entity's NPP.

The privacy rule grants CEs flexibility in sharing PHI under the umbrella of treatment, payment, and healthcare operations (TPO). However, it should be noted that by removing the requirement for "consent" in the final rule, HHS has fundamentally shifted the burden of proof to the CE in the event of privacy-related legal action. Without a signed consent or authorization, the NPP is the only means by which a CE can assert that in a given situation it was "permitted" to disclose the PHI in question.

Authorized, Permitted, Required Disclosures

The NPP must contain descriptions in sufficient detail to place the individual on notice of the uses and disclosures that are permitted or required. Within the scope of the NPP, there are three categories.

Authorized Disclosures

In general, authorized disclosures should be less problematic because each authorization must explicitly state what PHI is involved, the purpose, duration, and to whom it is released. It must also be signed by the individual.

NPP content must fully inform the individual of the CE's obligations under law to release PHI without authorization. In situations in which "other applicable law" provides superior privacy protections, the NPP must include these "fundamental rights" to satisfy the adequate notice requirement.

Permitted Disclosures

The NPP must contain a description and at least one example of the types of use and disclosure permitted for each TPO function.

Required Disclosures

The NPP must contain a description of each of the other non-TPO purposes for which the CE is permitted or required to use or disclose PHI without the individual's written authorization. In addition to federal, state, and local regulations, established case law should also be considered.

Develop a Layered Notice

To compound the NPP content challenge, the privacy rule imposes a duty on CEs to develop the NPP in plain language and in a clear, concise, easy-to-understand manner that is written for the "average reader," while fulfilling the NPP "adequate notice" and "fully inform" requirements. This is a significant challenge because the NPP is a contract that will be interpreted by attorneys related to legal contract performance. A possible solution is to develop a layered notice. This is encouraged but not required by HHS.

The layered notice requires three parts: short notice, long notice, and acknowledgment. All three must be presented to the individual. The short notice provides individuals with a brief summary of their rights. The long notice contains all the elements required under section 164.520. Acknowledgment of receipt satisfies the requirement to document a CE's good faith effort to obtain the individual's written acknowledgment of receipt of the entire notice (all three parts).

With all of the above considered, the importance and purpose of the notice of privacy practices is clear. Make sure your NPP is thorough—it could be your best defense.

References

Hjort, Beth. "Practice Brief: HIPAA Privacy and Security Training." *Journal of AHIMA* 73, no. 4 (2002): 60A–G.

Hughes, Gwen. "Practice Brief: Laws and Regulations Governing the Disclosure of Health Information." Updated November 2002.

Hughes, Gwen. "Practice Brief: Notice of Information Practices." Updated November 2002.

Hughes, Gwen. "Practice Brief: Preemption of the HIPAA Privacy Rule." *Journal of AHIMA* 73, no. 2 (2002): 56A–C.

"Standards for Privacy of Individually Identifiable Health Information; Final Rule." 45 CFR Parts 160 and 164. *Federal Register* 67, no. 157 (August 14, 2002).

Restriction Requests Pose New Challenges: HIM Departments Should Prepare Now for Patient Queries

Rita K. Bowen, MA, RHIA, CHP

Creating a process to handle patients' requests for restrictions on the use or disclosure of their health information may be one of the last items on your HIPAA checklist. Here's how to take care of it.

One of the benefits extended to patients under the HIPAA privacy rule is their right to restrict the use or disclosure of their protected health information (PHI). Accordingly, HIPAA requires covered entities to provide individuals with this right to restrict disclosures, though the covered entity is not required to agree to these restrictions (164.502). In this article, we'll explore ways to address this patient right and the policies that will need to be in place.

Putting Policies and Procedures in Place

To begin, let's review the groundwork for developing restriction policies and procedures:

- Defining the contents of the designated record set.

- Mapping the flow of PHI within your organization to determine if it can be restricted.

- Determining the required reporting items from your state. Although Congress intended the HIPAA legislation to protect state privacy laws that are more protective of privacy than federal regulations, the federal preemption in each state is difficult to predict and requires a thorough legal analysis.[1]

- Preparing the patient privacy notice. The privacy notice should describe the use and disclosure of patient information and provide an opportunity to agree or object to such disclosures.

Once the above elements are in place, your organization can draft policies and procedures that explain that covered entities must permit individuals the right to request that uses

Source: Bowen, Rita K. "Restriction Requests Pose New Challenges: HIM Departments Should Prepare Now for Patient Queries." *Journal of AHIMA* 74, no. 2 (2003): 32ff.

or disclosures of PHI be restricted for treatment, payment, or healthcare operations, and for release to other individuals who may be involved in the patient's care.[2] Additionally, the policies should include information on:

- How the patient can request to restrict information

- Designation of an appropriate person to accept and respond to requests

- The response documentation process

- How to ensure that an accepted restriction is honored

- The restriction termination process

Providers are not required to agree to any requested restriction, especially if it can be proved that such a restriction would interfere with legitimate treatment, payment, or operational processes of the organization. A designated individual may respond to requests for restriction, provided case scenarios have already been developed and tested as to the reasonableness of the patient's request. A team will need to evaluate undocumented request scenarios so that the patient's request receives thorough evaluation for compliance purposes. Further, the entity must be able to support each decision made to deny patients' requests for restriction of their information.

Healthcare providers must also accommodate reasonable requests for alternative means of communications and may not condition the accommodation on the basis of an explanation from the individual (164.522(b)(1)(I) and (2) (iii)). Health plans, in turn, must accommodate reasonable requests if the individual clearly states that the disclosures of all or part of the information could endanger the individual, and the plan may condition the accommodation on the receipt of such a statement in writing.

Responding to Requests

Every request to restrict information will require an easily understood written response that provides the basis for the approval or denial of the request. Covered entities must maintain an electronic or written record of the restriction decision for a minimum of six years from the date of its creation or the last date for which the restriction remains in effect, whichever is later.

If the patient's request is denied, the organization must provide direction to the patient on how to submit a written disagreement with the decision and how the requestor may file a complaint with the Department of Health and Human Services (HHS). When an organization responds negatively to a patient's request for a restriction, it may be best to meet with him or her in person. Patients may not understand why it is important that their health information be shared, but once they understand the need for information flow and their right to an accounting of disclosures, they often are amenable to the organization's use of their information.

If an organization agrees to a patient's request for restriction of PHI, it will need to ensure that the restriction is honored. Because the restriction process may be new to the organization, make sure that the system works, that staff members know who the contact person is, and that they are following the proscribed procedures. Develop checklists to ensure that the components needed to implement the process are in place. Components of your monitoring plan could include:

- Staff education on the rights behind the restriction process

- Availability of needed forms and educational materials

- Routing process for each request

- Documentation processes for request receipt, review, and response

- Thorough testing of critical processes, especially in high-risk, high-volume, problem-prone areas

- HIPAA "sentinel" events

Every member of your work force needs education about recognizing when a patient has been granted a request to restrict information. For example, you might have a special flag applied at the enterprise access level that indicates that a restriction of some type has been requested by the patient. Then, requests for such information could be routed to a central location for authorization or exception approval and notification processes. If your organization uses this method, it's critical that all members of the work force use the enterprise access level query process as their first step in accessing patient information. If the staff often bypass this step and move directly into independent systems such as their own department databases (such as radiology, laboratory, etc.), your facility risks violating the restriction.

Exceptions to the Rule

When a covered entity agrees to a restriction, it must do so in writing and ensure that it follows the restriction requirements. Similarly, the covered entity's business associates must also comply with the restrictions. HHS, in its commentary preceding the privacy rule, encourages covered entities to inform others of restrictions, as long as the communication does not disclose the restricted information itself. If your organization has considered scenarios in which a patient can restrict PHI, the time to test the feasibility of these restrictions is now.

Once the restriction is accepted, it is legally binding and covered entities are bound to those restrictions for as long as the individual requests except when superseded by mandatory or permitted disclosures for public purpose (164.512).

Additional exceptions include:

- Emergencies

- Public health authority (such as collection of information for controlling disease, injury or disability, exposure to communicable disease, report of abuse or neglect)

- Food and Drug Administration (to track products or conduct postmarketing surveillance or to report adverse events associated with product defects)

- Treating the employee as part of workplace surveillance

- Work-related illness or injury or workplace-related medical surveillance

- OSHA compliance

When restricted information has been released due to emergency need or other allowable exception, the covered entity is responsible for requesting that the information not be further disclosed. Consider creating a form letter for this purpose and keeping a copy in the patient's file. Part of your testing should ensure that the emergency exceptions for the release of restricted information are appropriately reported and documented.

If information is not handled appropriately, consider using the Joint Commission's sentinel event process.[3] When applied in the HIPAA privacy context, a sentinel event might be defined as an unexpected occurrence involving restricted information. These events are sentinel because they signal the need for immediate investigation and response. HHS recognized this when it included the requirement to take action to mitigate harmful effects of use or disclosure in violation of the policy (164.530(f)). The analysis should focus on systems and processes that require improvement. Try asking the following questions:

- What: Which steps of the process were not followed?

- Where: Is this a problem at one site or in all sites?

- When: Is the problem related to time of day or day of the week?

- Who: Is the problem related to positions or persons?

- Why: Are there factors that impede staff members from carrying out their responsibilities in the program?

Are You Ready for Requests for Restrictions?

Consider using the following implementation plan:

- Define your designated record sets.

- Map PHI within and outside of your organization.

- Define the use of PHI within your notice of privacy practice.

- Consider adding a provision to the consent-to-treat form that briefly describes the use of PHI and refers the patient to the privacy notice for more detailed information.

- Develop restriction request forms.

- Establish a centralized process for routing restriction requests.

- Establish a response process for restriction requests and assigning appropriate personnel to administer the process.

- Develop a workgroup that anticipates the types of restrictions requested, develops scenarios to determine "reasonableness," and has scenario responses ready.

- Determine workflow for response to restriction requests to ensure review and decision within the rule's time frame.

- Develop information materials that will inform the individual of the internal process and time frames for response.

- Develop a standard communication format to inform the individual of the decision and any recourse he or she may have.

- Ensure the personnel who handle patient information are aware that restrictions exist.

- Educate personnel on how to respond when the restriction flag is applied to the patient's information.

- Ensure that requests and documented response regarding restrictions on use and disclosure are retained for six years.

Terminating the Agreement

A provider or covered entity may terminate its agreement to a restriction of PHI if one of the following three conditions is met:

- The individual agrees to or requests the termination in writing.

- The individual orally agrees to the termination and the oral agreement is witnessed and documented.

- The covered entity informs the individual of the termination, indicating that the termination is effective only in respect to PHI created or received after the individual has been informed.

According to the rule's preamble (65 FR 82462, App. V), a note in the patient's medical record is sufficient documentation regarding the termination of patient restrictions. As the patient's request was legally binding, consider requiring that documentation to discontinue any restriction of PHI be witnessed or notarized.[4]

Consistency will be vital to ensuring patients' rights are upheld and facilities' needs are met when your organization responds to requests for restrictions. The more thoroughly you document your plan of action now, the more successful your organization will be.

Have You Held a Privacy Drill Lately?

Wondering if your policies and procedures are effective? Public health licensing agencies require fire and disaster drills, so consider holding a privacy drill. For example, you could use the "secret shopper" concept to determine if employees understand privacy policies and how to respond to a customer's request. When you conduct these drills, don't forget to test a variety of sites on different shifts and days. All your resources might be available Monday through Friday, but what would happen at midnight on Saturday? Drills can be monitored through direct observation or by asking staff members to document the steps they would take. The goal of the drills is to raise staff awareness. If you can make this fun for staff members they will be more likely to retain the knowledge.

Notes

1. Consider using legal counsel to assist with the preemption analysis. Additional legal resources include the Health Privacy Project Web site at www.healthprivacy.org/info-url_nocat2304/info-url_nocat.htm or AllLaw.com state resources at www.alllaw.com/state_resources/.

2. Gue, D'Arcy Guerin, and Steven J. Fox. *Guide to Medical Privacy and HIPAA*. Washington, DC: Thompson Publishing Group, 2002.

3. For more information, go to the Joint Commission Web site at www.jcaho.org.

4. *Guide to Medical Privacy and HIPAA*.

References

Amatayakul, Margret. *HIPAA Made Simple: A Practical Guide to Compliance.* Marblehead, MD: Opus Communications, 2001.

Boyle, Lisa, and Paul Knag. *HIPAA: A Guide to Healthcare Privacy and Security Law.* New York: Aspen Publishers, 2002.

Fernald, Frances R., ed. *HIPAA Patient Privacy Compliance Guide.* Washington, DC: Atlantic Information Services, 2002.

The Health Privacy Project Web site at www.healthprivacy.org.

"Standards for Privacy of Individually Identifiable Health Information; Final Rule." 45 CFR Parts 160 and 164. *Federal Register* 67, no. 157 (August 14, 2002).

Part 4

Disclosing Health Record Information

Laws and Regulations Governing the Disclosure of Health Information

Gwen Hughes, RHIA, CHP

Patients must be assured that the health information they share with healthcare professionals will remain confidential. Without such assurance, patients may withhold critical information that could affect the quality and outcome of care.

To date, the privacy and confidentiality of patient health information has been protected by a patchwork of federal and state laws and regulations, facility policy, professional standards of practice, and codes of ethics. The recently passed Standards for Privacy of Individually Identifiable Health Information (45 CFR, parts 160 and 164) under HIPAA establishes requirements for the protection of health information maintained by health plans, healthcare clearinghouses, and healthcare providers who transmit certain transactions electronically. These covered entities will likely need to establish or modify existing policies and procedures to comply with this new legislation.

Legal Requirements

There are a number of laws and regulations at both the federal and state level that govern the confidentiality of health information, as outlined below.

Standards for the Privacy of Individually Identifiable Health Information

The privacy rule:

- Preempts state law contrary to the privacy rule except when one of the following conditions is met:

    —An exception is made by the secretary of Health and Human Services.

    —A provision in state law is more stringent than the rule.

    —The state law relates to public health surveillance and reporting.

Source: Hughes, Gwen. "Laws and Regulations Governing the Disclosure of Health Information (AHIMA Practice Brief)" (Updated November 2002).

—The state law relates to reporting for the purpose of management or financial audits, program monitoring and evaluation, and licensure or certification of facilities or individuals.

- Establishes requirements for notice and acknowledgment:

  —Requires covered health providers and certain health plans to provide a notice of privacy practices

  —Requires covered healthcare providers to obtain from individuals an acknowledgment that they received the notice of privacy practices

- Establishes an individual's right to:

  —Opt out of the facility directory, or to request restrictions to other uses of his or her health information

  —Ask that communications be sent by alternative means or to an alternate address (for example, that correspondence be sent by e-mail or to a post office box)

  —Access his health information and limited situations wherein access may be denied

  —Request amendment of his health information

  —Obtain an accounting of disclosures of his or her health information

- Establishes requirements for use and disclosure:

  —Identifies uses and disclosures for which an authorization is required

  —Specifies who may authorize disclosure on behalf of an individual

  —Provides special protections for psychotherapy notes

  —Establishes a standard to limit the amount of information used or disclosed to the "minimum necessary" to accomplish the intended purpose

  —Requires that the covered entity identify members or classes of persons within its work force who need access to protected health information (PHI), the categories of information to which access is needed, and the conditions appropriate to such access

  —Establishes limitations on the use of PHI for fund raising and procedures wherein individuals must be allowed to opt out

  —Establishes requirements for deidentification of health information that can be disclosed without authorization

- Establishes certain administrative requirements:

  —Requires that the covered entity designate a privacy official

  —Requires that the covered entity designate a contact person who can provide additional information and receive complaints

  —Requires that the covered entity train all members of its work force on policies and procedures with respect to PHI

  —Requires that covered entities establish appropriate administrative, technical, and physical safeguards to protect health information

  —Establishes content or documentation requirements for policies and procedures, notices, authorizations, amendments, accounting of disclosures, complaints, and compliance

—Addresses fees that may be charged for disclosure

—Requires compliance by Apr. 14, 2003, for most covered entities (small health plans have until Apr. 14, 2004 to comply)

The Privacy Act of 1974

The Privacy Act of 1974 (5 USC, section 552A) was designed to give citizens some control over the information collected about them by the federal government and its agencies. It grants people the following rights:

- To find out what information was collected about them

- To see and have a copy of that information

- To correct or amend that information

- To exercise limited control of the disclosure of that information to other parties

Healthcare organizations operated by the federal government, such as Veterans Administration and Indian Health Services, are bound by the act's provisions. The act also applies to record systems operated pursuant to a contract with a federal government agency.

Confidentiality of Alcohol and Drug Abuse Patient Records

This rule (42 CFR, part 2) establishes additional privacy provisions for records of the identity, diagnosis, prognosis, or treatment of patients maintained in connection with a federally assisted drug or alcohol abuse program. When these regulations are less stringent than those of the final privacy rule, the final privacy rule would prevail. In general, the rule:

- Describes the written summary and communication that must occur at the time of admission or as soon as the patient is capable of rational communication, relative to the confidentiality of alcohol and drug abuse patient records under federal law

- Defines circumstances in which an individual's health information can be used and disclosed without patient authorization

- Requires that each disclosure of health information be accompanied by specific language prohibiting redisclosure

- Does not prohibit patient access

- Defines the requirements of a written consent

- Addresses who may consent on behalf of the patient

The Medicare Conditions of Participation

The Conditions for Coverage of Specialized Services Furnished by Suppliers (42 CFR, 486.161(a)) require that "clinical record information is recognized as confidential and is safeguarded against loss, destruction, or unauthorized use. Written procedures govern use and removal of records and include conditions for release of information. A patient's written consent is required for release of information not authorized by law."

The Conditions of Participation for Hospitals (42 CFR, 482.24(b)(3)) state, "The hospital must have a procedure for ensuring the confidentiality of patient records. Information from or copies of records may be released only to authorized individuals, and the hospital must ensure that unauthorized individuals cannot gain access to or alter patient records. Original medical records must be released by the hospital only in accordance with federal or state laws, court orders, or subpoenas."

The Conditions of Participation for Home Health Agencies (42 CFR, 484.48(b)) require that "clinical record information is safeguarded against loss or unauthorized use. Written procedures govern use and removal of records and the conditions for release of information. Patient's written consent is required for release of information not authorized by law."

The Requirements for States and Long-term Care Facilities (42 CFR, Part 483, section 483.10(b)(2)) state, "The resident or his or her legal representative has the right upon an oral or written request to access all records pertaining to himself or herself including current clinical records within 24 hours (excluding weekends and holidays) and after receipt of his or her records for inspection, to purchase at a cost not to exceed the community standard, photocopies of the records or any portions of them upon request and two working days advance notice to the facility." In section 483.10 (e), the regulation states, "The resident has the right to personal privacy and confidentiality of his or her personal and clinical records."

Institutional Review Boards

Within the provisions of the Institutional Review Board (IRB) rules (21 CFR, part 56) are requirements that the IRB ensure informed consent is sought from each research subject or his legally authorized representative, that the consent be appropriately documented, and that where appropriate, there are adequate provisions to protect the privacy of subjects and to maintain the confidentiality of data.

State Laws and Regulations

With the exception of Montana and Washington, which passed a version of the Uniform Health Information Act, state laws relative to the privacy and confidentiality of patient health information vary widely.

States may have special privacy requirements for patients tested, diagnosed, or treated for alcohol and drug abuse, sexually transmitted diseases, or mental health disorders. There may also be privacy and confidentiality requirements within state legislation or regulation related to insurance, workers compensation, public health, or research.

Accreditation Standards

In standard IM2, the Joint Commission on Accreditation of Healthcare Organizations requires that the confidentiality, security, and integrity of data and information be maintained.

Standards of Practice

Except where a consent or authorization clearly indicates otherwise, disclosures of information made pursuant to a valid authorization will be for information originated on or before the authorization was signed.

Except as otherwise required by federal or state law or regulation, or specified in the authorization itself, an authorization will expire no later than six months after it is signed.

Recommendations

To ensure compliance with federal and state laws and regulations that protect the confidentiality of health information and govern its disclosure, HIM professionals should:

1. Study the HIPAA standards for the privacy of individually identifiable health information.

2. Identify policies, procedures, and processes that must be developed or revised to comply with these standards.

3. Become knowledgeable about other applicable federal laws and regulations relative to privacy, confidentiality, and disclosure of patient health information.

4. Become knowledgeable about state laws and regulations relative to privacy, confidentiality, and disclosure of health information. To this end, links to state laws and regulations provided on state health information management association Web sites may prove helpful. State privacy law summaries maintained on the Health Privacy Project Web site (www.healthprivacy.org) may also prove of assistance. Consider performing a key word search of state laws by accessing AllLaw.com (www.alllaw.com/state_resources) or a similar state law Web site. Other resources worth consulting include component state health information management associations' confidentiality or release of information manuals, legal counsel, and the organization's malpractice insurer.

5. Develop an understanding about which rule prevails or how various requirements can be combined procedurally. For example, how can a health information manager combine the requirements for the notice of information practices in the privacy rule with those in the Confidentiality of Alcohol and Drug Abuse Patient Records rule and any requirements in state law. As another example, consider the necessary modifications to the release of information fee schedule to comply with both federal and state regulations insofar as reasonable charges.

6. Establish policies and procedures that comply with federal and state laws and regulations.

7. Ask legal counsel to ensure that new and revised policies and procedures comply with both federal and state laws and regulations.

8. Train members of the work force on policies and procedures with respect to protected health information.

9. Maintain appropriate documentation to demonstrate compliance with federal and state privacy law and regulation.

10. Review contracts with any business associates to whom information is disclosed and make sure the language contained therein is in compliance with the privacy rule.

11. Monitor compliance and implement corrective action where indicated.

12. Noncovered entities who maintain individually identifiable health information are encouraged to construct policies and procedures in which information obtained or disclosed is the minimum necessary, the work force is trained about the importance of privacy and confidentiality, and consumers are:

    - Informed about the organizations' information practices

- Provided access to health information about them

- Provided a mechanism to make amendments

- Asked for an authorization for disclosures not otherwise allowed by law

- Allowed access to and copies of disclosure logs

References

Food and Drug Administration, Department of Health and Human Services. "Institutional Review Board." *Code of Federal Regulations,* 2002. 21 CFR, Chapter I, Part 56.

Health Care Financing Administration, Department of Health and Human Services. "Conditions for Coverage of Specialized Services Furnished by Suppliers." *Code of Federal Regulations,* 2001. 42 CFR, Chapter IV, Part 486.

Health Care Financing Administration, Department of Health and Human Services. "Conditions of Participation for Home Health Agencies." *Code of Federal Regulations,* 2001. 42 CFR, Chapter IV, Part 484.

Health Care Financing Administration, Department of Health and Human Services. "Conditions of Participation for Hospitals." *Code of Federal Regulations,* 2001. 42 CFR, Chapter IV, Part 482.

Health Care Financing Administration, Department of Health and Human Services. "Requirements for States and Long-term Care Facilities." *Code of Federal Regulations,* 2001. 42 CFR, Chapter IV, Part 483.

Joint Commission on Accreditation of Healthcare Organizations. *Comprehensive Accreditation Manual for Hospitals.* Oakbrook Terrace, IL: Joint Commission on Accreditation of Healthcare Organizations, 2002.

The Privacy Act of 1974. 5 USC, Section 552A.

Public Health Service, Department of Health and Human Services. "Confidentiality of Alcohol and Drug Abuse Patient Records." *Code of Federal Regulations,* 2001. 42 CFR, Chapter I, Part 2.

"Standards for Privacy of Individually Identifiable Health Information; Final Rule." 45 CFR, Parts 160 and 164. *Federal Register* 67, no. 157 (August 14, 2002).

Rediscosure of Patient Health Information

Harry B. Rhodes, MBA, RHIA
Gwen Hughes, RHIA, CHP

A healthcare provider's records may contain patient information originated by another healthcare provider. For example, copies of selected reports are often sent by an attending physician to the hospital where a patient is admitted. Similarly, reports compiled during the patient's hospitalization are sent to the attending physician to assist in continued patient care. Information received from another or previous provider is then incorporated in the patient's health record at the receiving facility.

Although rediscosure of protected health information (PHI) is necessary for patient care across the healthcare continuum, the practice of rediscosure leads to questions about the appropriateness of disclosing information contained in one's record but originated at another healthcare facility.

Guidelines for the proper rediscosure of health information created by another or previous provider and made apart from one's designated record set exist at both the federal and state level. These rediscosure guidelines are applicable regardless of the form or medium of the health information.

Keep in mind that the transition to the electronic storage and management of PHI allows for the ready transfer of specific information as opposed to an entire report or record. The practice of disclosing specific information or "cutting and pasting" specific information can make identification of the author and origin of health information difficult to track, especially in electronic health record systems with weak audit trail functionality.

Federal Laws

Substance Abuse Patient Records

The Confidentiality of Alcohol and Drug Abuse Patient Records rules, which apply to records of the identity, diagnosis, prognosis, or treatment of patients maintained in connection with the performance of drug abuse prevention functions conducted, regulated, or directly or indirectly assisted by any department or agency of the US government, generally prohibit rediscosure of

Source: Rhodes, Harry, and Gwen Hughes. "Rediscosure of Patient Health Information (AHIMA Practice Brief)." *Journal of AHIMA* 74, no. 4 (April 2003): 56A–C.

health information. In fact, these rules require that a notice accompany each disclosure made with a patient's written consent. The notice must state:

> The information has been disclosed to you from records protected by federal confidentiality rules (42 CFR Part 2). The federal rules prohibit you from making any further disclosure of this information unless further disclosure is expressly permitted by the written consent of the person to whom it pertains or as otherwise permitted by 42 CFR Part 2. A general authorization for the release of medical or other information is not sufficient for this purpose. The federal rules restrict any use of the information to criminally investigate or prosecute any alcohol or drug abuse patient.

The rules do not prohibit redisclosure:

- To medical personnel to the extent necessary to address a genuine medical emergency

- If authorized by an appropriate court order of competent jurisdiction granted after an application showing good cause. However, the court is expected to impose appropriate safeguards against unauthorized disclosure.

HIPAA Final Privacy Rule

The HIPAA final privacy rule as published on December 28, 2000, defines health information as any information, whether oral or recorded, in any form or medium, that:

- Is created or received by a healthcare provider, health plan, public health authority, employer, life insurer, school or university, or healthcare clearinghouse; and,

- Relates to the past, present, or future physical or mental health or condition of an individual; the provision of healthcare to an individual; or the past, present, or future payment for the provision of healthcare to an individual

The final rule goes on to state that a valid authorization must include a statement that information used or disclosed pursuant to an authorization may be subject to redisclosure by the recipient and may no longer be protected by the rule.

The privacy rule generally requires covered entities to take reasonable steps to limit the use and disclosure of and requests for PHI to the minimum necessary to accomplish the intended purpose. The minimum necessary standard is addressed in section 164.502 of the rule. However, the minimum necessary standard does not apply to:

- The individual when requested and required under 164.524

- Disclosures required by the secretary of Health and Human Services (HHS) to investigate or determine the covered entities' compliance

- Disclosures to or requests by a healthcare provider for treatment uses

- Disclosures made to the secretary in accordance with subpart C of 160 (page 82805) for enforcement purposes

- Uses or disclosures made pursuant to an individual's authorization

- Disclosures and uses that are required by other state or federal laws

- Uses or disclosures required to comply with the HIPAA administrative simplification rules

OCR HIPAA Privacy Guidance

The following Office for Civil Rights (OCR) HIPAA privacy guidance was published on December 3, 2002, and addresses redisclosure of patient information:

Q: A provider might have a patient's medical record that contains older portions of a medical record that were created by another or previous provider. Will the HIPAA privacy rule permit a provider who is a covered entity to disclose a complete medical record even though portions of the record were created by other providers?

A: Yes, the privacy rule permits a provider who is a covered entity to disclose a complete medical record, including portions that were created by another provider, assuming that the disclosure is for a purpose permitted by the privacy rule, such as treatment.[1]

State Laws

Individual states may have their own laws or regulations relative to redisclosure for all or some particularly sensitive types of health information. State laws are not preempted where they give more confidentiality protection than the HIPAA final privacy regulations except where state laws make it more difficult for patients to access their own health information.

Recommendations

1. Unless otherwise required by state law, incorporate in your own facility's designated record set the health information generated by other healthcare providers needed for patient diagnosis and treatment.

2. Become knowledgeable about and implement organizational compliance with federal and state laws and regulations that address redisclosure. Any redisclosure must comply with federal and state laws and regulations.

3. Consult with legal counsel when federal and state redisclosure requirements differ and it's unclear which should prevail.

4. Develop facility policies and procedures that address redisclosure. Be sure to include the requirement that prior to disclosure, the disclosing staff member verify the authority of the person to receive the information.

5. Modify existing authorization forms to incorporate required language in the HIPAA final privacy rule.

6. In general, healthcare providers should:

   - Rediscle to other healthcare providers PHI when it is necessary to ensure the health and safety of the patient

   - Rediscle requested health information to patients when necessary, but after first encouraging the patient to obtain the most complete and accurate copies from the originating healthcare provider

   - Rediscle PHI when necessary to comply with a valid authorization

   - Rediscle PHI when necessary to comply with a legal process. Only rediscle PHI located within your legal health record (the designated record set). Note that you may be compelled by the legal discovery process to release additional individually identifiable health information if access to the information is deemed necessary for the stated purpose[2]

7. Ask legal counsel to review draft policies and procedures prior to implementation.

8. Educate staff on new or revised policies and procedures relative to redisclosure.

9. Implement policies and procedures and monitor compliance.

10. When in doubt about a potential redisclosure, consult legal counsel.

11. When asked to certify or testify about the authenticity of redisclosed health information, state that the information was received from another healthcare facility's medical record through normal business practices, your facility received the information in good faith, and that you cannot knowledgeably speak about the record-keeping practices of the originating organization.

12. Modify existing certification forms when indicated.

Notes

1. Office for Civil Rights, Department of Health and Human Services. "OCR Guidance Explaining Significant Aspects of the Privacy Rule." December 4, 2002. Available at http://www.hipaadvisory.com/regs/finalprivacy mod/guidance.htm.

2. Hughes, Gwen. "Practice Brief: Defining the Designated Record Set." *Journal of AHIMA* 74, no. 1 (2003): 64A–D.

References

Public Health Service, Department of Health and Human Services. "Confidentiality of Alcohol and Drug Abuse Patient Records." *Code of Federal Regulations,* 2000. 42 CFR, Chapter I, Part 2.

"Standards for the Privacy of Individually Identifiable Health Information; Final Rule." 45 CFR Parts 160 through 164. *Federal Register* 65, no. 250 (December 28, 2000).

"Standards for the Privacy of Individually Identifiable Health Information; Final Rule." 45 CFR Parts 160 through 164. *Federal Register* 67, no. 157 (August 14, 2002).

Tomes, Jonathan P. *The Compliance Guide to HIPAA and the HHS Regulations.* Overland Park, KS: Veterans Press, 2001.

Required Content for Authorizations to Disclose

Gwen Hughes, RHIA, CHP

In the past, healthcare providers disclosed individually identifiable health information to comply with valid authorizations, laws and regulations, professional ethics, and accreditation standards. The federal government had not yet established standards regulating the disclosure of most individually identifiable health information or what constituted a valid authorization, except in the case of substance abuse records. State laws or regulations relative to authorization content varied or were nonexistent.

The HIPAA final privacy rule, published in the December 28, 2000, *Federal Register,* establishes standards for information disclosure including what constitutes a valid authorization. The rule was amended on August 14, 2002. It applies to covered entities, which are health plans, healthcare clearinghouses, and healthcare providers that transmit specific information electronically. Most covered entities must comply with the amended rule by April 14, 2003.

This practice brief will explore the portion of the rule that addresses authorization content. It will also provide an overview of other federal and state laws and regulations regarding authorization content.

Legal Requirements

HIPAA

Section 164.508 of the final privacy rule states that covered entities may not use or disclose protected health information without a valid authorization, except as otherwise permitted or required in the privacy rule.

General Authorization Content

The rule states that a valid authorization must be in plain language and contain at least the following core elements:

- A specific and meaningful description of the information to be used or disclosed

- The name or other specific identification of the person(s) or class of persons authorized to use or disclose the information

---

Source: Hughes, Gwen. "Required Content for Authorizations to Disclose (AHIMA Practice Brief)" (Updated October 2002).

- The name or other specific identification of the person(s) or class of persons to whom the covered entity may make the use or disclosure

- A description of each purpose of the requested use or disclosure. The statement "at the request of the individual" is sufficient when an individual initiates the authorization and does not provide a statement of the purpose

- An expiration date or event that relates to the individual or the purpose of the use or disclosure. The statement "end of the research study," "none," or similar language is sufficient if the authorization is for a use or disclosure for research, including for the creation and maintenance of a research database or repository

- Signature of the individual and date. If the authorization is signed by a personal representative of the individual, a description of the representative's authority to act for the individual

In addition to the core elements, the rule states that a valid authorization must include:

1. A statement of the individual's right to revoke the authorization in writing and either:

   - A reference to the revocation right and procedures described in the notice; or,

   - A statement about the exceptions to the right to revoke and a description of how the individual may revoke the authorization

   Exceptions to the right to revoke include situations in which the covered entity has already taken action in reliance on the authorization or the authorization was obtained as a condition of obtaining insurance coverage.

2. A statement about the ability or inability of the covered entity to condition treatment, payment, enrollment, or eligibility for benefits on the authorization:

   - The covered entity must state that it will not condition treatment, payment, enrollment, or eligibility for benefits on whether the individual signs the authorization; or,

   - The covered entity must describe the consequences of a refusal to sign an authorization when the covered entity conditions research-related treatment, enrollment or eligibility for benefits, or the provision of healthcare solely for the purpose of creating protected health information for a third party on obtaining an authorization.

3. A statement that information used or disclosed pursuant to the authorization may be subject to redisclosure by the recipient and may no longer be protected by the rule.

Marketing content: The authorization must also include a statement about any direct or indirect remuneration it has or will receive from a third party when the authorization sought is for marketing purposes.

Content when authorization is requested by a covered entity: The covered entity must provide the individual with a copy of the signed authorization when the covered entity seeks the authorization. Therefore, covered entities may want to consider printing their authorization form on multiple-part paper (carbon or carbonless) and listing the distribution of the various copies on the front page. For example, text on the authorization form might indicate that the top copy is to be maintained by the covered entity, the second copy is to be given to the individual, and the third copy is to accompany any disclosure of protected health information.

Compound Authorizations

An authorization may be combined with another document to create a compound authorization only as described below:

Research: An authorization for the use or disclosure of protected health information for a research study may be combined with any other type of written permission for the same research, including a consent to participate in the research or another authorization to disclose protected health information from the research.

Psychotherapy notes: An authorization for the use or disclosure of psychotherapy notes may be combined with another authorization for the use or disclosure of psychotherapy notes. For example, an individual can complete an authorization that requests his psychotherapy notes be sent to his attorney and a second mental health professional. An authorization for psychotherapy notes may not be combined, however, with an authorization for disclosure of general health information or research.

General: An authorization for the disclosure of general health information may be combined with another authorization for the disclosure of general health information. However, a general authorization that conditions treatment, payment, enrollment, or eligibility for benefits on completion may not be combined with another authorization. For example, an insurance company may not combine an authorization they require as a condition of enrolling in their plan with another authorization.

Defective Authorizations

The privacy rule declares invalid any authorization with the following defects:

- The expiration date or event has passed or occurred.

- The authorization is missing one or more items of content described above.

- The authorization is known to have been revoked.

- The authorization violates a privacy rule standard on conditioning or compound authorizations.

- Material information in the authorization is known to be false.

Discussion

Perhaps one of the unintended consequences of the privacy rule is that handwritten, patient-generated authorizations may often be invalid under the rule, as most do not contain an expiration date or a statement about the individual's right to revoke the authorization. To minimize the number of invalid authorizations received, the covered entity may want to post its authorization form on its Web site and encourage individuals to use it. Covered entities may also want to provide instructions for obtaining the authorization form on appropriate automated telephone messages. In addition, covered entities may find it beneficial to distribute new authorization forms to organizations that routinely request patient health information, such as local law firms, insurance companies, and law enforcement agencies.

Substance Abuse

The Confidentiality of Alcohol and Drug Abuse Patient Records Rule applies to federally assisted alcohol and drug abuse programs. The rule establishes the following content requirements for authorizations to disclose individually identifiable patient health information generated by alcohol or drug abuse programs:

- The specific name or general designation of the program or person permitted to make the disclosure

- The name or title of the individual or the name of the organization to which disclosure is to be made

- Patient name

- Purpose of disclosure

- How much and what kind of information is to be disclosed

- The signature of the patient or legal representative

- The date on which the authorization is signed

- A statement that the authorization is subject to revocation at any time except to the extent that the program or person who is to make the disclosure has already acted in reliance on it. Acting in reliance includes the provision of services in reliance on a valid authorization or consent to disclose information to a third-party payer.

- The date, event, or condition upon which the authorization will expire if not revoked. This date, event, or condition must ensure that the authorization will last no longer than reasonably necessary to serve the purpose for which it is given.

State

Individual states may have laws or regulations defining authorization content. For example, some state laws require that authorizations to disclose HIV are separate and apart from any other authorizations an individual may sign for release of protected health information. When such laws or regulations exist, consult section 160 of the HIPAA privacy rule to determine how to apply the preemption requirements.

Recommendations

- Study both federal and state requirements for authorizations.
- Draft a sample authorization form that complies with federal and state laws and regulations. (See Figure 4.1, Sample Authorization to Use or Disclose Health Information.)
- Ask the risk manager and legal counsel to review your draft authorization form.
- Update or generate new policies and procedures relative to the new authorization.
- Order appropriate quantities of the approved authorization form.
- Educate and train staff.

Figure 4.1.   Sample authorization to use or disclose health information

Patient Name: _____ Health Record Number: _____ Date of Birth: _____

1. I authorize the use or disclosure of the above named individual's health information as described below.

2. The following individual(s) or organization(s) are authorized to make the disclosure:

    _____

    _____

3. The type of information to be used or disclosed is as follows (check the appropriate boxes and include other information where indicated)

    ☐ Problem list   ☐ X-ray and imaging reports (please describe the dates or types
    ☐ Medication list   of X rays or images you would like disclosed):
    ☐ List of allergies
    ☐ Immunization records   _____
    ☐ Most recent history   _____
    ☐ Most recent discharge summary   ☐ Consultation reports from (please supply doctors' names):
    ☐ Lab results (please describe the   _____
        dates or types of lab tests you   _____
        would like disclosed):   ☐ Entire record
                                           ☐ Other (please describe):

    _____   _____

    _____   _____

4. I understand that the information in my health record may include information relating to sexually transmitted disease, acquired immunodeficiency syndrome (AIDS), or human immunodeficiency virus (HIV). It may also include information about behavioral or mental health services, and treatment for alcohol and drug abuse.

5. The information identified above may be used by or disclosed to the following individuals or organization(s):

    Name: _____   Name: _____

    Address: _____   Address: _____

6. This information for which I'm authorizing disclosure will be used for the following purpose:

    ☐ My personal records   ☐ Other (please describe): _____
    ☐ Sharing with other health care providers as needed   _____

7. I understand that I have a right to revoke this authorization at any time. I understand that if I revoke this authorization, I must do so in writing and present my written revocation to the health information management department. I understand that the revocation will not apply to information that has already been released in response to this authorization. I understand that the revocation will not apply to my insurance company when the law provides my insurer with the right to contest a claim under my policy.

8. This authorization will expire (insert date or event): _____

    If I fail to specify an expiration date or event, this authorization will expire six months from the date on which it was signed.

9. I understand that once the above information is disclosed, it may be redisclosed by the recipient and the information may not be protected by federal privacy laws or regulations.

10. I understand authorizing the use or disclosure of the information identified above is voluntary. I need not sign this form to ensure healthcare treatment.

_____   _____
        Signature of patient or legal representative   Date

If signed by legal representative, relationship to patient _____

_____   _____
        Signature of witness   Date

Distribution of copies: Original to provider; copy to patient; copy to accompany use or disclosure

Note: The types of documents listed on the authorization form may need to be modified depending on the particular healthcare setting. Authorizations for marketing need to disclose whether remuneration was received by the covered entity. This form was developed by AHIMA for discussion purposes only. It should not be used without review by your organization's legal counsel to ensure compliance with other federal and state laws and regulations.

- Replace all supplies of the old authorization forms with new ones.

- Post the approved authorization form on the organization's Web site.

- Distribute new authorization forms to frequent requesters.

References

Brandt, Mary D. *Release and Disclosure: Guidelines Regarding Maintenance and Disclosure of Health Information.* Chicago: American Health Information Management Association, 1997.

Public Health Service, Department of Health and Human Services. "Confidentiality of Alcohol and Drug Abuse Patient Records." *Code of Federal Regulations,* 2000. 42 CFR, Chapter I, Part 2.

"Standards for Privacy of Individually Identifiable Health Information: Final Rule." 45 CFR Parts 160 and 164. *Federal Register* 67, no. 157 (August 14, 2002).

Consent for Uses and Disclosures of Information

In the past, the terms "consent" and "authorization" have been used somewhat interchangeably in reference to written legal permission to disclose health information. As a standard of practice, healthcare providers obtained an individual's permission to disclose health information to entities outside the organization, but as a rule did not obtain the individual's permission to use or disclose health information for treatment, healthcare operations, or disclosures otherwise mandated or authorized by law.

New federal standards for privacy of individually identifiable health information (also known as the HIPAA final privacy rule) were published December 28, 2000, and introduced the concept of consents for treatment, payment, and healthcare operations, which made it necessary to distinguish between the two terms. These consents were intended to grant individuals seeking healthcare services the right to give permission to the covered entity to use their individually identifiable healthcare information for treatment, payment, and healthcare operations prior to the occurrence.

However, members of the healthcare industry expressed significant operational concerns, which triggered reconsideration and withdrawal of the consent requirement. They called attention to the potential for interruptions in efficient delivery of healthcare services and operations while permission to use protected health information was being sought. In addition, opposing opinions challenging the compromise of individual privacy rights with relaxation of the consent requirements were also heard.

Legal Requirements

Not wanting to impede or block efficient healthcare operations and privacy protections, the Department of Health and Human Services released amendments to section 164.506 of the

---

Note: In 2002, the Department of Health and Human Services changed the Standards for Privacy of Individually Identifiable Health Information (the "Privacy Rule") to eliminate entirely any required HIPAA consent for the use or disclosure of patient health information for purposes of treatment, payment, or operations (TPO). The information in this article pertains to healthcare providers who opt to obtain consents for TPO purposes or when state law requires a consent.

Source: "Consent for Uses and Disclosures of Information (AHIMA Practice Brief)" (Updated October 2002).

privacy rule on August 14, 2002, and eliminated the requirement for the consent, leaving covered entities the option to use it. Nothing in the preamble or the amended rule discourages a covered entity from implementing the optional consent when determined prudent and desirable. No particular design requirements are directed. Those choosing to implement the consent have complete freedom in structure, process, and format. This provides individual states flexibility in exercising regulatory directives. Further, a covered entity may, at its own discretion, choose to apply the original December 28, 2000, consent requirements.

Along with this change, other sections of the rule were strengthened and reinforced. Section 164.520 now requires written acknowledgment of receipt of the notice of privacy practices by the individual or documentation by the covered entity of reasonable effort to obtain written acknowledgment.[1] Additionally, the rule states that the consent is not to be used as a substitute for compliance with the authorization requirements addressed in section 164.508. In the absence of a consent requirement, implementation guidelines state:

- "A covered entity may use or disclose protected health information for its own treatment, payment, or healthcare operations.

- A covered entity may disclose protected health information for treatment activities of a healthcare provider.

- A covered entity may disclose protected health information to another covered entity or a healthcare provider for the payment activities of the entity that receives the information.

- A covered entity may disclose protected health information to another covered entity for healthcare operations activities of the entity that receives the information if each entity either has or had a relationship with the individual who is the subject of the protected health information being requested, the protected health information pertains to such relationship, and the disclosure is:

  —For a purpose listed in paragraph (1) or (2) of the definition of healthcare operations,[2] or

  —For the purpose of healthcare fraud and abuse detection or compliance

- A covered entity that participates in an organized healthcare arrangement may disclose protected health information about an individual to another covered entity that participates in the organized healthcare arrangement for any healthcare operations activities of the organized healthcare arrangement."

- The modified rule further clarifies the optional consent as differing from informed consent for treatment within state laws by renaming it "consent for uses and disclosures of information."

Recommendations

While providing a healthcare organization guidance on best choice for a consent option, HIM professionals should consider the following:

- Involve key organizational leaders in evaluating philosophy and suitability to implement the consent to use and disclose PHI prior to treatment, payment, and healthcare operations.

- Consider any state requirements for the use and disclosure of health information.

- If implementing a consent policy and practice:

  —Know that covered entities are not forbidden to adopt the details of the original regulations as a blueprint for their implementation processes.

  —Ensure policy and procedure clarity in the coordination of the consent process with the notice of privacy practices acknowledgment mandate.

- Whether or not your organization is implementing the consent option, ensure reliable policies and procedures for obtaining written acknowledgment of receipt of the notice of privacy practices and handling of restrictions to privacy practices.[3]

Notes

1. For more information on notice of privacy practices, see the "Notice of Information Practices (Updated)" Practice Brief available on the AHIMA Web site at www.ahima.org.

2. The definition of healthcare operations includes operations such as quality assessment and improvement activities; reviewing the competence or qualifications of healthcare professionals; underwriting premium rating, etc., for health insurance or benefits; medical review/legal services/auditing functions including fraud and abuse detection; business planning and development; business management; and general administrative activities.

3. See the "Notice of Information Practices (Updated)" Practice Brief.

Reference

"Standards for Privacy of Individually Identifiable Health Information; Final Rule." 45 CFR Parts 160 and 164. *Federal Register* 67, no. 157 (August 14, 2002).

Obtaining Satisfactory Assurance for PHI Disclosure

Carol Ann Quinsey, RHIA, CHPS

Obtaining "satisfactory assurance" in the privacy rule may sound like something new, but the concept has been around for a long time. Do you know what it means and how it affects your HIM department? This article will explain what obtaining satisfactory assurance means and how it can be implemented in your organization's HIM department.

Keeping Patients Informed

Those who have acted as records custodians in HIM departments have long had to comply with subpoenas and other discovery processes. If subpoenas do not come with clear authority of a court of the proper jurisdiction, some HIM department staff are required to contact patients or legal representatives to be sure they understand that their protected health information (PHI) has been requested as part of a legal process.

When contacting patients, there is an opportunity to inform them of their rights with regard to the subpoena. This process ensures that the patient has had an opportunity to raise an objection to the release of their PHI. Patients are generally very appreciative of this type of outreach from HIM staff. While they may choose not to object to the subpoena or other lawful process, they still view the covered entity as taking steps to protect their health information.

The HIPAA final rule refers to this same concept in Section 164.512 (e) (1) (ii). The final rule states that a covered entity may respond to a subpoena, discovery request, or other lawful process requesting the disclosure of PHI that is not accompanied by a court order if the covered entity has received satisfactory assurance that the party seeking the information has made reasonable efforts to notify the subject (patient) of the request.

Obtaining Assurance

A covered entity can receive satisfactory assurance in three ways. If a subpoena is accompanied by a court order by a court of the proper jurisdiction, the covered entity is deemed to have received satisfactory assurance. Absent a court order, these are the steps a covered entity can take to determine if it has received satisfactory assurance:

Source: Quinsey, Carol Ann. "Obtaining Satisfactory Assurance for PHI Disclosure." *Journal of AHIMA* 74, no. 6 (June 2003): 54–55.

- The party requesting the PHI may send a written statement to the covered entity with accompanying documentation demonstrating that it has made a good faith effort to contact the subject of the requested PHI. (A good faith effort is described in the rule as contacting the individual at his or her current or last known address.)

- The notice to the individual must have contained sufficient information about the legal proceedings to permit the individual to raise an objection to the release of his or her medical information.

- Enough time must have elapsed from the delivery of the notice to the individual for any objections to be raised. Or, if the individual filed objections to the release of his or her PHI, such objections must have been resolved by the appropriate court or administrative tribunal.

- The disclosures being sought in the subpoena, discovery request, or other lawful process are consistent with such resolution by the appropriate court or administrative tribunal.

The third option that may be used to provide "satisfactory assurance" to the covered entity is to obtain a qualified protective order. In the rule, a "qualified protective order" means that the parties are prohibited from using or disclosing the PHI for any purpose other than the litigation or proceeding for which it was requested. It also requires the return of the PHI to the covered entity or the destruction of the PHI (including all copies made) at the end of the litigation or proceeding.

A qualified protective order may be used to provide satisfactory assurance to the covered entity if:

- Both parties of the dispute have agreed to a qualified protective order that has been presented to the court with jurisdiction over the dispute.

- The party seeking the PHI has requested a qualified protective order from such a court.

Review State Laws

Individual state laws must be reviewed to determine if there are details about how notice to the individual must be delivered or the length of time an individual has to raise an objection to the proceeding. Some states may have rules about the content of notices delivered to patients.

Covered entities should be aware of these laws when determining whether satisfactory assurance has been obtained. All these details must be incorporated into the policies and procedures for the HIM department staff charged with the disclosure of the PHI.

Proceed with Disclosure

A covered entity is deemed to have received satisfactory assurance if the requirements for one of the three options above have been met. Once satisfactory assurance has been documented, the covered entity may proceed with disclosure of the requested PHI in accordance with its standard procedures.

If the covered entity has not received documented satisfactory assurance, disclosure pursuant to the subpoena should not be made. A decision not to disclose should be made in conjunction with legal counsel. Covered entities should develop form letters to inform all parties involved of a decision not to release PHI.

Reference

"Standards for Privacy of Individually Identifiable Health Information; Final Rule." 45 CFR Part 164.512 *Federal Register* 67, no. 157 (August 14, 2002).

Simple Steps to Tracking Disclosures

Gwen Hughes, RHIA, CHP

The many exceptions to the HIPAA privacy rule's accounting of disclosures standard make it difficult to determine what must be tracked. Although the rule gives patients the right to receive an accounting of disclosures of their health information, it lists several exceptions. This article offers a process that will help your organization determine what needs to be tracked.

Make a List

Perhaps the easiest way to determine what must be tracked is to list the types of disclosures made in your organization. When compiling the list, include all types of disclosures from the designated record set. Remember that the designated record set includes both billing and clinical information. It is also important to list disclosures made by departments other than HIM—for example, radiology, social services, and nursing.

Next, check each disclosure against the privacy rule's list of exceptions. These exceptions are:

- To carry out treatment, payment, and healthcare operations

- To the individual

- For directory or notification purposes

- To federal officials for the conduct of national security

- To a correctional institution or law enforcement official having lawful custody of an individual

- Pursuant to a valid authorization (if the proposed amendment becomes final)

For example, as shown in Figure 4.2, Sample Disclosure List, the first disclosure is to a third-party payer for the purpose of obtaining preauthorization. The privacy rule does not require that this disclosure be tracked. It defines payment to include preauthorization and accepts disclosures for payment from the tracking requirement. Therefore, according to the privacy rule, the provider need not track disclosures for preauthorization.

Source: Hughes, Gwen. "Simple Steps to Tracking Disclosures." *Journal of AHIMA* 73, no. 7 (2002): 68–70.

Figure 4.2.   **Sample disclosure list**

Disclosures	Tracking Required by HIPAA?	Tracking Required by State?	Rationale for HIPAA Tracking Exception	Rationale for State Tracking Exception
Preadmission Clinic				
Obtaining preauthorization	no	no	payment	third-party payer
Providing limited demographic information to contract lab for admission lab work	no	no	treatment	healthcare
Volunteers				
Providing directory information to individuals who ask for the patient by name	no	no	directory	directory
Nursing				
Reporting infectious diseases to public health authority as required by law	no	yes	healthcare operations—population based	
Reporting potential child abuse to appropriate government authority as required by law	yes	yes		
Reporting gunshot wounds to appropriate government authority as required by law	yes	yes		
Communicating needed information to secure needed services for patient from contracted dietary, lab, and therapy departments	no	no	treatment	healthcare
Communicating information to patients' physicians	no	no	treatment	healthcare
Communicating the patient's status to the patient's family appropriate to their involvement in the patient's care	no	no	treatment	oral information

Figure 4.2.   (Continued)

Disclosures	Tracking Required by HIPAA?	Tracking Required by State?	Rationale for HIPAA Tracking Exception	Rationale for State Tracking Exception
Nursing *(continued)*				
Producing a surgery schedule for coordination of services; used by numerous departments within the organization	no	no	treatment	healthcare
Lab				
Sending physician copies of lab results to physicians' offices	no	no	treatment	healthcare
Radiology				
Patients picking up original copies of X rays	no	yes	individual	
Sending original copies of X rays to other physicians	no	no	treatment	healthcare
Sending copies of X-ray reports to physicians' offices	no	no	treatment	healthcare
Health Information Management				
Disclosing information to individuals identified by the patient in a valid authorization	decision pending	yes	depends on whether proposed privacy rule amendment becomes final	
Allowing patients access to or copies of their health information	no	yes	individual	
Sending copies of dictated reports to the patient's physician (and other physicians as directed by the dictating physician)	no	no	treatment	
Reporting births and deaths to Vital Statistics	yes	no		doesn't meet definition of disclosure

(Continued on next page)

Figure 4.2. (Continued)

Disclosures	Tracking Required by HIPAA?	Tracking Required by State?	Rationale for HIPAA Tracking Exception	Rationale for State Tracking Exception
Health Information Management (*continued*)				
Allowing third-party payers who contract with the organization to conduct audits of record	no	no	payment	third-party payer
Allowing risk management insurer to audit the records as part of their premium setting	no	no	healthcare operations	actuarial
Allowing financial auditors to access the records to see if documentation supports bills	no	no	payment	third-party payer
Providing third-party payers with copies of reports in health records to substantiate charges and facilitate payment	no	no	payment	third-party payer
Providing access to record to legal department at malpractice insurer in anticipation of legal action	no	no	healthcare operations	legal
Providing attorneys with copies of a record in anticipation of legal action	no	no	healthcare operations	legal
Allowing researchers with appropriate institutional review board approval to access records	see note in rationale column	see note in rationale column	doesn't require tracking if information is deidentified or if for improving health, reducing costs, or protocol development	will need to evaluate specific studies against the requirements
The provision of records or data to committees charged with credentialing or performance improvement activities	no	no	healthcare operations	quality assurance peer review
Allowing the Joint Commission access to health information for accreditation purposes	no	no	quality assessment and improvement	administrative

Figure 4.2.   (Continued)

Disclosures	Tracking Required by HIPAA?	Tracking Required by State?	Rationale for HIPAA Tracking Exception	Rationale for State Tracking Exception
Utilization Management				
Obtaining certification for continued stay	no	no	payment	third-party payer
Discharge Planning or Social Services				
Sending information to another healthcare provider for potential transfer	no	no	treatment	healthcare
Information Services				
Sending cost report information to the state	see note in rationale column	no	depending on purpose may fall under definition of healthcare operations	doesn't meet the definition of a disclosure of the patient's record
Generation of fund-raising letters using patient demographic information	no	no	healthcare operations	not considered health information
Patient Accounts				
Sending copies of the itemized bill to the patient's attorney on receipt of a valid authorization	decision pending	no	depends on whether proposed privacy rule amendment becomes final	disclosures of billing information do not have to be tracked
Sending copies of the itemized bill upon request to the patient or guarantor when concerns are expressed about the charges	no	no	payment	disclosures of billing information do not have to be tracked

This sample form was developed by AHIMA for discussion purposes only. It should not be used without review by your organization's legal counsel to ensure compliance with local and state laws.

After checking the disclosure against the privacy rule's exceptions, place a notation to the right of the disclosure indicating whether tracking is necessary, and, if not, why not. Such records will be helpful if the Department of Health and Human Services ever questions the organization's decision not to track a certain type of disclosure.

Check It Twice

Repeat this process for each disclosure on the list. After evaluating each disclosure listed against the exceptions in the privacy rule, use a similar process to evaluate each disclosure against state laws or regulations.

In the sample list provided, the state requires that disclosures to the individual be tracked. The privacy rule does not. When state tracking requirements are more stringent than those of the privacy rule, the organization must track the disclosure.

Organizations will find that the privacy rule requires that very few disclosures be tracked. They must, however, comply with state law when it requires tracking that the privacy rule does not. Organizations may find that many disclosures that must be tracked are not made from the HIM department, but rather by departments such as information services or nursing. Sometimes it can be difficult to determine whether some disclosures must be tracked. In such situations, organizations may want to seek legal counsel.

Replicating the process above will help organizations design an effective disclosure tracking system that captures all required disclosures.

Release of Information Reimbursement Laws and Regulations

Beth Hjort, RHIA, CHP

Background

Releasing health information to other healthcare providers and authorized users is a basic function when managing health information. To the untrained eye, the distribution (or release) of health information may appear to be a simple task. Closer analysis of the process reveals that many forces and factors must be addressed to ensure that the release of information (ROI) is prompt, accurate, complete, and confidential.

Factors that affect the cost of release of information include:[1,2,3]

- Labor costs involved with ensuring authorization appropriateness

- Labor costs and software associated with logging requests in a database

- Labor costs and expenses involved in physically retrieving health information from on-site and off-site storage facilities

- Capital costs associated with copying equipment (copy machines, microfilm, and microfiche readers/printers)

- Expense costs for paper, toner, and equipment maintenance involved in copying

- Labor costs associated with the physical copying of health information

- Labor costs associated with re-filing retrieved health information

- Supplies and handling expense involved in preparing a document for mailing

- Postal expense

- Expense associated with invoicing for copies

- Collections and bad debt expense

- Real estate costs: work space and storage space for the ROI and copying functions

---

Source: Hjort, Beth. "Practice Brief: Release of Information Reimbursement Laws and Regulations" (Updated) 2004. This information supplants information contained in the January 1999 "Release of Information Laws and Regulations" practice brief.

Typically, the HIM unit of a healthcare organization faces the challenge of providing the ROI function with limited budget allocations. Departments that cannot commit resources to this function must choose between operating with a constant backlog of requests or outsourcing all or part of the ROI function. In addition, "non-billable" requests may become an overhead expense to healthcare providers that outsource the ROI function. HIM professionals working in states that have established release of health information laws or regulations face the additional challenge of providing the ROI service within the constraints of the state laws or regulations.

Federal Requirements

HIPAA's final privacy rule section 164.524(c)(4), access of individuals to protected health information, states:

> **Fees.** If the individual requests a copy of the protected health information or agrees to a summary or explanation of such information, the covered entity may impose a reasonable, cost-based fee, provided that the fee includes only the cost of:
> (i) Copying, including the cost of supplies for and labor of copying the protected health information requested by the individual
> (ii) Postage, when the individual has requested that the copy or the summary or explanation be mailed
> (iii) Preparing an explanation or summary of the protected health information, if agreed to by the individual as required by paragraph (c)(2)(ii) of this section
>
> (c) Implementation specifications: provision of access (2)(ii) The covered entity may provide the individual with a summary of the protected health information or may provide an explanation of the protected health information to which access has been provided, if:
> (A) The individual agrees in advance to such a summary or explanation; and
> (B) The individual agrees in advance to the fees imposed, if any, by the covered entity for such summary or explanation.

The December 28, 2000, final privacy rule was clarified by the August 14, 2002, *Federal Register* update to say that section "164.24(c)(4) limits only the fees that may be charged to the individuals, or to their personal representatives in accordance with 164.502(g) . . . The fee limitations . . . do not apply to any other permissible disclosures . . ." Distinguishing the requestor is an issue for providers. For example, attorney requests are sometimes disguised as patient requests.

It can be noted that retrieval and processing labor are not specifically stated in the rule's criteria for calculating reasonable, cost-based fees. When taken literally, copying is the only labor cost allowed. The preamble states, "Covered entities may not charge any fees for retrieving or handling the information or for processing the request." It should also be noted that HIPAA's reference to record copy fees is positioned within the sections covering patient rights. Because many healthcare organizations waive patient fees for personal use, the impact may be minimal.

HIPAA further allows for charging of patient requests for accountings of disclosures. Section164.528 states:

> (2) the covered entity must provide the first accounting to an individual in any 12-month period without charge. The covered entity may impose a reasonable, cost-based fee for each subsequent request for an accounting by the same individual within the 12-month period, provided that the covered entity informs the individual in advance of the fee and provides the individual

with an opportunity to withdraw or modify the request for a subsequent accounting in order to avoid or reduce the fee.

HIPAA is designed to work with other federal laws and regulations, not to preempt them. Specific federal programs may have regulations referencing copy fee guidelines that should be considered when arriving at a 'reasonable' definition. For example:

- Effective January 5, 2004, the Centers for Medicare and Medicaid Services raised release of health information cost reimbursement for quality improvement organizations (QIOs, formerly known as PROs) requests for health information on Medicare patients to $.12 per page.

- The State Operations Manual for Long Term Care Facilities, regulation F153 (2)(ii), directs LTC facilities to allow an individual to purchase copies of his/her own records "at a cost not to exceed the community standard." The correspondent interpretive guideline §483.10(b)(2) further instructs an organization to follow the state standard if existing or if not the rate used by the public library, the post office, or a commercial copy center.

- In 29CFR1910.1020(e), the Occupational Safety and Health Administration (OSHA) provides for related records requested by an employee or designated representative to be supplied without cost the first time and allows reasonable charges for additional copies of the same information. "Reasonable" is defined as "non-discriminatory administrative costs (i.e., search and copying expenses but not including overhead expenses).

State Regulations

Because HIPAA's requirements do not address charging for record copy requests other than from patients, state regulations continue to provide the most specific guidelines. The preamble of the privacy rule leads us to believe that reliance on more specific state laws can be presumed acceptable. However, since it's not part of the rule, it could be legally tested. The Department of Health and Human Services Office for Civil Rights, the governmental enforcing arm for HIPAA's privacy rule, clarified for AHIMA that covered entities (CE) should use state laws as guidance in fee setting.

The most recently passed state statutes represent a compromise between the parties and are representative of the costs involved in the ROI process. The majority of states have specific laws and regulations that should be used in establishing facility release of information copy cost fee schedules. These state ROI cost laws and regulations tend to vary depending on the requesting entity, i.e., workers' comp, state disability, or attorney/patient. State laws and regulations should be verified to ensure compliance with ROI cost guidelines that vary with the requesting entity.

While HIM managers recognize the potential for specific state laws to preempt HIPAA under a more stringent status and where greater privacy rights would prevail, copy costs represent one of several areas within HIPAA, not necessarily pertaining to privacy issues, where federal law differs from state laws. Because many states have case law addressing the reasonableness definition, interpretation against HIPAA's description will be determined over time. The OCR clarified for AHIMA that each CE should determine reasonable cost-based fees for its own operations. If a complaint is received, OCR would look at the fee structure defined as "reasonable" by the organization and how it was determined and consider state law in evaluating unique organizational circumstances. OCR reminds us of its intention to work supportively with CEs, applying "good faith effort" to HIPAA compliance practices.

Recommendations

- Work with your organization's cost accountant to determine copy costs. The accountant will be knowledgeable of Medicare cost report requirements related to non-revenue generating departments, such as square footage, teaching services, and capital. Together, HIM and accounting staff have information needed to complete the project accurately. (See Figure 4.3, Cost Items for Release of Information Services.)

- While developing or updating your organization's policies and procedures, investigate and become knowledgeable about the HIPAA privacy law and any other federal and state laws and regulations addressing the patient's right to access and acquire copies of his or her health records.

- Ensure policies and procedures address the use of an external copy service, if applicable.

- Each healthcare provider should develop a ROI policy and reasonable copy cost fee schedule representing the needs of its patients, physicians, researchers, third party payers, and other legitimate requesters. The policy should comply with legal and regulatory requirements.

- Policies and procedures should ensure reasonable responsiveness. Release of patient health information should be respectful of the needs of continued patient care, legal requirements, research, education, and other legitimate uses and should meet HIPAA's timeliness requirements.

- While fees may differ for different types of requests, they should be consistently applied for each type of request unless otherwise mandated. Organizations may use copy service vendors yet handle some ROI requests internally, both within the same department or within the organization. Consistency throughout the organization is essential.

- If charging a fee for accounting of disclosure listings, include the fees in the ROI policy.

- If charging for medical record copies related to research requests, such as flat or per case fees, include this factor in the ROI policy.

- Cost calculation records used to determine copy charge policy should be retained to demonstrate how "reasonable" charges were determined.

- Periodically recalculate copy costs. Actual costs and a definition of "reasonable" may vary as operations change, such as when releasing information from an electronic system with expedited retrieval, no re-filing requirements, and potential electronic transmission.

- Consider federal regulations other than HIPAA if your organization receives reimbursement from federal programs for patient services.

- In the absence of specific state or federal regulatory requirements for ROI cost, providers should establish fees that are appropriate and legitimately cover the reasonable costs of the organization. Comparing ROI fee schedules with other local facilities could be interpreted as price-fixing and could lead to antitrust implications.

- HIM professionals should be involved in the negotiation of managed care contracts to ensure adequate reimbursement for copies.

- A healthcare provider would be wise to include a clause in the managed care contract that reserves the right to renegotiate the copy fee portion of the contract should ROI laws change.

- When dealing with out-of-state requests for health information, the ROI cost law/regulation of the state where the healthcare provider is located normally prevails.

Figure 4.3.   Cost items for release of information services

Item	Labor-Time/Cost	Product Cost	Other
Pick up mail			
Sort mail			
Open mail		Letter opener	Desk, workspace Chair
Read request to verify it qualifies			
Look up medical record number			MPI system Application maintenance fees Computer, network access
Enter information on search form		Form	
Determine encounters, dates and types			MPI system
Enter information on search form		Form (same as above)	

Enter request in log (paper or automated)		Application maintenance fees	Correspondence system or
			    paper log
			Application maintenance fees
			Computer (may be same one
			    as above)
			Maintenance on computer

Determine location(s) of record(s) in the department			Record tracking system Application maintenance fees Computer (may be same as above)
Go to locations and find record			
Prepare outguide or enter into record tracking system		Outguide slip	Record tracking system
Take record to ROI location			Space Visitor chairs Visitor table or writing surface Lighting AC/heat Carpet/paint Parking area

(Continued on next page)

Figure 4.3.   (Continued)

Item	Labor-Time/Cost	Product Cost	Other
Review record for items required			
If not there, prepare rejection letter			Staple remover
Print letter		Paper Printer toner	Printer Maintenance on printer
Review documents to determine if there are any restricted items			
Copy or scan items required		Paper (8.5 × 11, 11 × 14, ledger sizes) Copier toner Copier developer Copier drum Microfilm printer toner Microfilm printer paper	Copy machine/scanner Copy machine/scanner maintenance Microfilm reader printer Microfilm reader printer maintenance
Staple copies together		Stapler Staples	
Replace originals back in chart			Restaple or fasten on clip or clamp together
Replace chart where found			
Update record tracking system			Record tracking system
Count copies prepared			
Prepare invoice			Correspondence system or calculator
Print invoice		Paper	Printer
Prepare cover letter to accompany copies and invoice		Form letter	Correspondence system
Print cover letter		Paper	Printer
Prepare envelope		Envelopes (9 × 12″, 10 × 13″, and other sizes)	
Calculate postage			Calculator Postage machine

Figure 4.3. **(Continued)**

Item	Labor-Time/Cost	Product Cost	Other
Postage		Stamps or prepaid postage	
Take envelope to mailroom/mailbox		Mail basket	
Exception: Delay processing request because document is incomplete			May occur multiple times for same request Percent of time it occurs
Exception: Reject request for inadequate information or out of date		Form letter Envelope (#10)	Correspondence system Percent of time it occurs
Exception: Reject request because item not in chart		Form letter Envelope (#10)	Percent of time it occurs
Exception: Send invoice without copies (pre-pay)		Paper Envelope (#10)	Correspondence system Percent of time it occurs
Exception: Set aside record or copies and hold for payment			Shelving Percent of time it occurs
Receive payment			
Exception: Follow up on payments not received			Bad debt expense Percent of time it occurs
Log payment			Correspondence system
Prepare deposit slip of monies		Deposit slip	
Deliver monies to cashier		Money bag	
Exception: Receive subpoena			Percent of time it occurs
Exception: Establish appointment on schedule		Calendar	Percent of time it occurs
Exception: Determine if court order is required			Percent of time it occurs
Supplies		Pencils, pens, paper clips, tape, scissors, mailing labels	
Authorization forms for individuals requesting		Forms	
Envelopes to mail out forms		Envelopes (#10)	

(Continued on next page)

Figure 4.3. (Continued)

Item	Labor-Time/Cost	Product Cost	Other
Telephone(s)		Monthly charges Long distance charges	Telephone Voice mail
Other equipment		Fax cover sheets Telephone line Telephone line charges	Fax machine
Other expense—overhead and indirect expenses	Mailroom Payroll Cashier Accounting Materials Dept. management Legal counsel Telecommuni- cations Is Print shop Cafeteria HR Administration Benefits and taxes Plant operations		Reference materials Education and training Depreciation Interest expense
Free copies			
Total free copies			
Partial pay copies			
Total partial pay copies			
PRO/QIO copies			
Total PRO/QIO copies			
Bad debt			
Off-site storage return fees or processing fees			
Total pages copied			

Useful resources may include the American Hospital Association's *Estimated Useful Lives of Depreciable Hospital Assets* and hospital cost report/accounting records.

Reprinted with permission from Rose T. Dunn, CPA, RHIA, FACHE, First Class Solutions, Inc., 2003.

Accessing State Laws on Copy Fees

State health authorities are the most dependable resource for current state copy costs, because state laws change periodically. Other Web resources are also helpful:

- Contact information for public health officials is available at http://www.health.gov/hpcomments/Guide/state_PH.htm

- Many states have government Web sites that may post laws related to healthcare. These sites typically have URLs like http://www.statename.gov

- All state laws for all 50 states are accessible at http://www.alllaw.com/state_resources/. This site is most useful if you know the citations

- Facilitators for AHIMA's geographic Communities of Practice (CoP) have been asked to post and maintain current state copy fees within respective state CoP "Resources" sections for easy member reference. Community members aware of changes in state law are encouraged to initiate updates for this important reference

- The law offices of Thomas J. Lamb, P.A., have compiled an online state-by-state reference to copy fees at http://www.lamblawoffice.com/medical-records-copying-charges .html#Pennsylvania

Notes

1. Dunn, Rose. "Copying Records: The Saga Continues." *For the Record* 9, no. 7 (1997): 18–25.

2. Dunn, Rose. "Copying Costs: Help Is as Close as Your 1040." *For the Record* 10, no. 7 (1998): 22–23.

3. Dunn, Rose. "Cost Items for Release of Information Services (ROI)."

References

Dunn, Rose. "Calculating Costs for Accounting of Disclosures." *Journal of AHIMA* 74, no. 5 (May 2003): 65–66.

Dunn, Rose. "Copying Records." *For the Record* 4, no. 18 (1992).

Dunn, Rose. "HIPAA Copy Charges for Medical Records." *Healthcare Financial Management* 57, no. 12 (2003): 36–38.

"Medicare Program; Photocopying Reimbursement Methodology." 42 CFR Parts 412, 413, 476, and 484. *Federal Register* Volume 68, no. 234 (December 5, 2003).

Occupational Safety and Health Administration, Department of Labor. "Occupational Safety and Health Standards, Toxic and Hazardous Substances, Access to employee exposure and medical records. 29 CFR 1910.1020(e) *Code of Federal Regulations* Title 29, Volume 6 (revised as of July 1, 2003).

"Standards for Privacy of Individually Identifiable Health Information; Final Rule." 45 CFR Part 164. *Federal Register* 65, no. 250 (December 28, 2000).

"Standards for Privacy of Individually Identifiable Health Information; Final Rule." 45 CFR Parts 160 and 164. *Federal Register* 67, no. 157 (August 14, 2002).

State Operations Manual for Long Term Care Facilities, regulation F153 (2)(ii) p 84. Available online at http://www.cms.gov/manuals/pub07pdf/AP-P-PP.pdf.

Thompson, Ann L. "Medical Records Copying Services: Are They Worth the Cost?" *For the Record* 9, no. 25 (1997): 4.

Preparing for Suspension of Disclosure Accounting

Carol Ann Quinsey, RHIA, CHPS

Are the rules for the suspension of disclosure accounting keeping your organization in suspense?

Section 164.528 of the privacy rule outlines the requirements for accounting of disclosures for individuals. Section 164.528 (a)(2)(i) calls for suspension of disclosure accounting if requested by a health oversight or law enforcement agency. This article will explain suspension of disclosure accounting so your organization is prepared to handle these requests.

Written versus Oral Requests

There are two ways a covered entity may be asked to suspend disclosure of accounting—written or oral. First, the rule states that accounting of disclosures must be suspended if the health oversight or law enforcement agency has made a written request to the covered entity and states that such an accounting to the individual would be reasonably likely to impede the agency's activities. The statement must specify the time period covered by the suspension of accounting. The rule goes on to state that if an oral request is made to a covered entity by a health oversight or law enforcement agency, the covered entity must:

- Document the statement (request), including the identity of the person making the statement.

- Temporarily suspend the individual's right to an accounting of disclosures subject to the statement.

- Limit a temporary suspension to 30 days unless a written statement is submitted to the covered entity during the 30-day period.

Determining Policies, Procedures

Can your organization respond if a patient asks for an accounting of disclosures during a time when a suspension of disclosure accounting is in effect? As you consider your options, it may be helpful to imagine what the circumstances might be when a patient asks for an accounting of disclosures.

Source: Quinsey, Carol. "Preparing for Suspension of Disclosure Accounting." *Journal of AHIMA* 74, no. 7 (July/August 2003): 61.

Consider the following questions: Is it likely that a patient is just curious about disclosures of his or her medical information, and the request is only coincidental with the suspension? Or does the patient suspect something is being investigated and is looking for proof? Should your organization let the time allowed by the privacy rule elapse before producing the accounting if it would allow you to pass through the suspension period? Or should you respond to the individual as soon as it is practical to do so?

Each covered entity should determine how to proceed. The rule does not clearly state what disclosure accounting is suspended. Your organization will need to address questions like: Is all disclosure accounting suspended during the time period of the request? Or does the suspension of accounting only cover disclosures made to the specific agency that requested the suspension? Executive management and legal counsel should be involved in making the decision of how to interpret this before writing policies and procedures.

Turnaround Time

Covered entities are allowed 60 to 90 days to provide an accounting of disclosures to individuals. However, a copy of a patient's medical record must be produced in 30 to 60 days and even more quickly in some states. Patients could perceive that they are being "put off" if they are told that it will take 60 to 90 days to produce an accounting of disclosures.

If a patient requests an accounting during a time of suspension, it seems reasonable to contact the agency requesting the suspension of accounting to determine if the suspension still needs to be in place. If the suspension can be terminated, disclosure accounting could take place following routine procedures. If the suspension is still required, each covered entity needs procedures for how to respond.

Reporting What You Can

If the covered entity chooses to respond to the patient with an accounting of disclosures that are not subject to the suspension, your organization could accompany the accounting with a cover letter stating, "This is a list of disclosures that can be reported at this time" or similar language. If there are no disclosures other than those subject to the suspension, language in the letter to the patient could state, "We have no disclosures to report at the present time."

What happens if the patient requests a later accounting of disclosures and realizes that there are disclosures listed that were not reported in a previous accounting? The covered entity can explain that it was bound by the privacy rule to honor a request not to report disclosures to the specific agency at the time of the patient's previous request and that the time period for such suspension has expired, allowing you to provide a complete list.

There are positives and negatives to reporting or not reporting in the event of a suspension of disclosure accounting. It is important to consider all facets of the procedure before you are faced with a request from a patient or his or her representative for an accounting of disclosures. Policies that allow staff flexibility in responding while ensuring that the organization has carefully considered and endorsed a policy and procedure to handle suspensions of disclosure accounting will allow staff to respond confidently.

Reference

"Standards for Privacy of Individually Identifiable Health Information; Final Rule." 45 CFR Parts 160 and 164. *Federal Register* 67, no. 157 (August 14, 2002).

Due Diligence in Moderation: Disclosing PHI

Margret Amatayakul, MBA, RHIA, CHPS, FHIMSS

Direct caregivers have long been concerned about balancing patient protections with "customer" relations: Who do you talk to and how much do you tell? This was an issue long before HIPAA, and has only become more complex with HIPAA. And while HIPAA provides guidance, there are still no easy answers about disclosure.

HIPAA's many standards and possible interpretations have led to some unintended consequences. In the past, facilities may have tended toward disclosing patient information when a judgment call was needed. Today, however, facilities are overly cautious about disclosing information. As a result some fear patient care concerns, if not patient satisfaction issues. Following is a road map for creating a framework that provides reasonable assurances to those who must apply professional judgment in making disclosures to personal representatives, those involved in a patient's care, and other covered entities.

What Standards Are Involved?

There are a number of standards relating to "who to tell what." Any one of them alone seems to be reasonable. But when considered together, appropriate action seems less clear.

Minimum Necessary

The minimum necessary standard requires uses, disclosures, and requests to be limited to the amount necessary to accomplish the intended purpose. The minimum necessary standard (§164.502(b)) carries two important exceptions:

- It does not apply to disclosures or requests by a healthcare provider for treatment.

- It does not apply to uses or disclosures made to the individual.

Verification Requirements

HIPAA's section on other requirements relating to uses and disclosures of protected health information (PHI) (§164.514) addresses further details of implementing minimum necessary uses, disclosures, and requests and provides a standard on verification requirements.

Source: Amatayakul, Margret. "Due Diligence in Moderation: Disclosing PHI (HIPAA on the Job series)." *Journal of AHIMA* 74, no. 8 (September 2003): 16A–D.

The minimum necessary requirements standard (§164.514(d)(3)) indicates that providers may rely, if reasonable, on a request for disclosure to be the minimum necessary if the information is requested by another covered entity.

The verification standard (§164.514 (h)(1)) requires oral or written documentation, statement, or representation of the identity and authority of any person to have access to PHI if the identity or authority is not known. However, disclosures can be made under the opportunity to agree/object to the standard (§164.510).

Providers have responded to the above two standards in a variety of ways. The typical scenario is that a provider calls to request PHI (such as diagnostic studies results) for an impending visit by the patient or for a patient physically present. Responses have ranged from:

1. Fulfilling the request because it is orally represented as for treatment by another provider

2. Fulfilling the request only if the provider is affiliated (i.e., member of the medical staff)

3. Fulfilling the request only if the provider is a "provider of record"

4. Fulfilling the request only if a written representation is obtained (such as a request faxed on provider letterhead)

5. Fulfilling the request only with the individual's authorization

Any of these responses may be appropriate, depending on the organization's policy, state law, and professional judgment. However, the first two responses are risky.

First, there is no verifiable evidence of identity or authority. In an electronic environment, the requestor would not have access to the information system. Such a response should be avoided or used only in a call-back mode with documentation of the purpose of the disclosure.

In the second case, there is no verifiable evidence of authority. In an electronic environment, access to the PHI should trigger an emergency mode access response (or "break the glass" auditable action). In the paper world, the equivalent probably should be a call back with documentation of the purpose of the disclosure.

The third response makes the assumption that a provider of record has been identified and has authority. It may be appropriate to describe in the policy the time frame or events that would constitute the definition of "provider of record." This would serve not only in the paper world, but would also establish parameters for access to electronic PHI.

The fourth response could be acceptable if the patient's appointment is for a later date, although it could be spoofed. If the provider making the request is not affiliated or a provider of record, this response may be just as risky as the first response. Remember, relying on a request for disclosure from another covered entity only applies when the request is for the minimum necessary. Identity and authority should also be verified. Such a written request probably should not be fulfilled unless verification of identity and authority is performed by a call back.

The fifth response is always acceptable as a means to verify identity and authority. Because an authorization is not required by HIPAA when there is a treatment relationship, some providers may balk at getting an authorization. Be aware, however, that some state laws require an authorization when health information is released to an unrelated entity. Furthermore, it may be the only means to ensure that there is a treatment relationship.

Personal Representatives

Another due diligence issue that relates to the personal representative standard requires the covered entity, with certain exceptions, to treat a personal representative as the individual for purposes of the privacy rule. This means that because minimum necessary does not apply to the individual, it also does not apply to the individual's personal representative.

There are two key issues to address:

- Who is a personal representative?

- When do exceptions apply?

When identifying a personal representative, first determine who your state law considers a personal representative. Figure 4.4, Legal Definitions of Representation, lists a number of terms that may be used in your state to describe various forms of representation.

Next, you'll need to know who is a legitimate personal representative. If such a person is present, the person should have the formal documentation as indicated in Figure 4.4. If the person is not present or there is an emergency wherein the person cannot produce such documentation, then healthcare providers should apply professional judgment in communicating about an individual's health status with an informally recognized next of kin or significant other. Most healthcare professionals have experience questioning an individual to get a good sense of the nature of the relationship and therefore how much to say.

Opportunity to Agree/Object

An opportunity to agree or object to inclusion in a facility directory must be provided via the notice of privacy practices (NPP). Some providers are being proactive and advising individuals at the time of registration that, unless they object at that time, the provider will disclose to persons who ask for the individual by name his or her location in the facility and condition in general terms that do not communicate specific medical information. In addition, religious affiliation will be provided to the clergy.

An opportunity to agree or object to uses and disclosures for involvement in the individual's care is also a required statement in the NPP. Providers should probably be more proactive. If the individual can respond, providers should ask if:

- The person accompanying them should remain with the individual during care and if that person should be provided information about caring for the individual. If so, the disclosures should be limited to that which is directly relevant to such person's involvement with the individual's care or payment for care.

- The person who is involved in care and calls can be provided more information than that permitted through the facility directory. A means to identify the person should be agreed on and recorded in a readily accessible location. As with a person accompanying an individual, the disclosures should be limited to that which is directly relevant to such person's involvement with the individual's care or payment for care.

If the individual is not present or is incapable of agreeing or objecting, professional judgment should be applied. Such judgment has long been based on:

- Previous knowledge of the individual's relationships, if known

- The individual's best interest

Figure 4.4.   Legal definitions of representation

Type	Definition/Documentation	Access to PHI
Attorney in fact	Person given *durable power of attorney* to make certain decisions for an individual. In most states, this does not authorize a person to make life support decisions.	If power of attorney extends to making healthcare decisions when an attending physician deems the individual unable to make his or her own decisions, then access is same as individual with exceptions as noted.
Conservator of estate	Person *appointed by a probate court* to make financial decisions for an incapable individual	Limited to that relating to financial issues, such as Medicaid application or claim
Conservator of person	Person *appointed by a probate court* to make personal decisions for an incapable individual	Access same as individual with exceptions as noted
Guardian of a mentally retarded patient	Person *appointed by a probate court* to supervise some or all aspects of the care of a mentally retarded adult	Access same as individual with exceptions as noted
Guardians of an unemancipated minor	Father and mother, unless deceased or parental rights terminated, in which case another person *appointed by a probate court*	Access same as individual with exceptions for unemancipated minors as noted
Healthcare agent	Person appointed via a *document signed by the individual* providing authority to communicate (life support and comfort care) decisions in the event the individual becomes incapable of making those decisions	Limited to that relating to making life support and comfort care decisions when such decisions need to be made
Next of kin	Person who provides a *notarized request in writing* stating there is no estate and is next of kin. Generally next of kin are: • Spouse • Adult children • Parents • Adult sibling • Grandparents or adult grandchildren • Adult nephews, nieces, uncles, or aunts	Used in lieu of conservator with exceptions as noted. In an emergency, healthcare providers will apply professional judgment in communicating about an individual's health status with an informally recognized next of kin or significant other. See also "Involved in care."

Exceptions:
- A provider may elect not to treat a person as a personal representative if there is reason to believe the individual has been or may be subjected to domestic violence, abuse, or neglect; it could endanger the individual; or the provider decides that it is not in the best interest of the individual to treat the person as the individual's personal representative.
- In the case of an unemancipated minor, a parent, guardian, or other person acting *in loco parentis* is the personal representative with respect to PHI. However, if the minor has the authority under state law to consent to or obtain healthcare service without consent of the parent, guardian, or other person acting *in loco parentis* (usually for HIV testing and treatment, treatment for alcohol and drug abuse, outpatient mental health treatment, and treatment of sexually transmitted diseases), the provider must refer to state law to disclose PHI to the parent, guardian, or other person acting *in loco parentis*:
  —If permitted or required by state law, disclosure or provision of access to PHI about an unemancipated minor may be made to a parent, guardian, or other person acting *in loco parentis*
  —If prohibited by state law, disclosure or provision of access to PHI about an unemancipated minor may not be made to a parent, guardian, or other person acting *in loco parentis*
  —If state law is silent and the parent, guardian, or other person acting *in loco parentis* is not designated by the unemancipated minor as the personal representative, a licensed healthcare professional should exercise professional judgment in making or not making a disclosure or provision of access to PHI about the unemancipated minor to the parent, guardian, or other person acting *in loco parentis*

Just as if the individual were physically present or capable, the disclosure of PHI should be limited to that which is directly relevant to such a person's involvement with the individual's care or payment for care. For example, if an individual is calling about another individual's bill, it would be appropriate to verify that the person has the bill in front of them, such as by requesting the account number and amount of charges. Typically, medical information should not be discussed, but rather instructions on whom, when, and what to pay can be provided.

Reasonable Due Diligence

Due diligence is important to verify identity and authority, but should not impede patient care. Professional judgment and reasonableness are required by HIPAA—and should be liberally applied.

Part 5

Copying, Printing, and Transmitting Health Information

Transfer of Patient Health Information across the Continuum

Gwen Hughes, RHIA, CHP

Background

In order to assure continuity of patient care, healthcare providers disclose to subsequent health-care providers the health information that is necessary to facilitate a smooth transition and efficient and effective care. Such disclosures occur verbally, when a referring physician telephones a consultant, or through the provision of documentation originated by the first provider and sent to the second.

As advances in technology provide for the automation of these information transfers, it is important that members of the health information management and information services team understand the data that must be transferred as identified in law, accreditation, or professional practice standards.

Legal and Regulatory Requirements

Federal

The *Medicare Conditions of Participation for Hospitals* state, "The hospital must transfer or refer patients, along with necessary medical information, to appropriate facilities, agencies or outpatient services, as needed, for follow-up or ancillary care." (42 CFR 482.43)

The *Requirements for States and Long Term Care Facilities* state:

- "The resident's right to refuse release of personal and clinical records does not apply when the resident is transferred to another health care institution or record release is required by law." (42 CFR 483.10)

- "In cases of transfer of a resident with mental illness or mental retardation from a nursing facility to a hospital or to another nursing facility, the transferring nursing facility is responsible for ensuring that copies of the resident's most recent PASARR and resident assessment reports accompany the transferring resident." (42 CFR 483.106)

Source: Hughes, Gwen. "Transfer of Patient Health Information across the Continuum (AHIMA Practice Brief)" (Updated June 2003).

The *Conditions of Participation for Home Health Agencies* state:

- "All personnel furnishing services maintain liaison to ensure that their efforts are coordinated effectively and support the objectives outlined in the plan of care. The clinical record or minutes of case conferences establish that effective interchange, reporting, and coordination of patient care does occur. A written summary report for each patient is sent to the attending physician at least every 60 days." (42 CFR 484.14)

- "The home health agency must inform the attending physician of the availability of a discharge summary. The discharge summary must be sent to the attending physician upon request and must include the patient's medical and health status at discharge." (42 CFR 484.48)

- "If a patient is transferred to another health facility, a copy of the record or abstract is sent with the patient." (42 CFR 484.48)

The *Conditions of Participation for Comprehensive Outpatient Rehabilitation Facilities* state:

- "All patients must be referred to the facility by a physician who provides the following information to the facility before treatment is initiated:

    —The patient's significant medical history

    —Current medical findings

    —Diagnosis(es) and contraindications to any treatment modality

    —Rehabilitation goals, if determined." (42 CFR 485.58)

- ". . . A physician must establish a plan of treatment before the facility initiates treatment. . . ." (42 CFR 485.58)

The *Conditions of Participation for Clinics, Rehabilitation Agencies, and Public Health Agencies as Providers of Outpatient Physical Therapy and Speech-Language Pathology Services* state:

- "The following are obtained by the organization before or at the time of initiation of treatment:

    —The patient's significant past history

    —Current medical findings, if any

    —Diagnosis(es), if established

    —Physician's orders, if any

    —Rehabilitation goals, if determined

    —Contraindications, if any

    —The extent to which the patient is aware of the diagnosis(es) and prognosis

If appropriate, the summary of treatment furnished and results achieved during previous periods of rehabilitation services or institutionalization." (42 CFR, 485.711)

The federal government permits the disclosure of protected health information to another healthcare provider for treatment, payment, and certain healthcare operations in the privacy rule (*Standards for Privacy of Individually Identifiable Health Information* [45 CFR164.506]).

State

Individual states may also have laws or regulations that require one healthcare provider to provide specific health information to another caring for a patient.

Accreditation Standards

Standard CC.5 in the Joint Commission's automated *Comprehensive Accreditation Manual for Hospitals* states, "Appropriate information related to the care and services provided is exchanged when a patient is accepted, referred, transferred, discontinued service, or discharged to receive further care or services . . ." The corresponding statement of intent says, "Information shared with other providers consists of relevant information, including: the reason for transfer, referral, discontinuation of services, or discharge; the patient's physical and psychosocial status; a summary of care provided and progress toward goals; and community resources or referrals provided to the patient."

The Joint Commission's automated *2002–2003 Comprehensive Accreditation Manual for Ambulatory Care,* standard CC.5, states: "Appropriate information related to the care and services provided is exchanged when a patient is accepted, referred, transferred, discontinued service, or discharged to receive further care or services." The corresponding statement of intent says: "Information shared with other providers consists of relevant information, including: the reason for transfer, referral, discontinuation of services, or discharge; the patient's physical and psychosocial status; a summary of care provided and progress toward goals; and community resources or referrals provided to the patient."

Standard CC.5 in the Joint Commission's *2002–2003 Comprehensive Accreditation Manual for Long Term Care* states, "Appropriate information related to the care and services provided is exchanged when residents are accepted, referred, transferred, discontinued service, or discharged to receive further care or services." Standard IM 7.5 states, "Discharge information is provided to the resident or to the receiving organization." The corresponding intent statement says, "The organization provides relevant information to the resident, family, or another entity accepting the resident when the resident is transferred or discharged. The information includes:

- Medical findings, diagnosis(es), and treatment orders

- A summary of the care and services provided and progress toward achieving goals

- Diet orders and medication orders

- Behavioral status, ambulation status, nutrition status, and rehabilitation potential

- The resident's physical and psychosocial status

- Nursing information useful in resident care

- Advance directives

- Referrals provided to the resident

- The reason for transfer, discharge, or referral

- The physician's orders for the resident's immediate care

- Instructions given to the resident before discharge

- The referring physician's name, and

- The physician who has agreed to be responsible for the resident's medical care and treatment, if other than the referring physician"

In the Joint Commission's *2003 Comprehensive Accreditation Manual for Home Care,* standard CC.4.1 states, "As appropriate to the scope of care or services, the organization provides the responsible physician with information on the patient's condition, the outcome of current treatment, and the patient's response."

In the corresponding intent statement, the manual also states, "There is ongoing communication between organization staff and the patient's physician as appropriate to the scope of care or services. The organization provides information on a timely basis and as required by law and regulation. The information includes the patient's current condition, changes in the patient's condition, the outcome of care and service, the patient's response to current treatment and medication, changes in caregiver support or the environment, or results of relevant laboratory tests when they become available."

In addition, standard CC.5.2 states, "Appropriate patient information is exchanged when the patient is referred, transferred or discharged."

In the corresponding statement of intent, the manual states, "The organization communicates appropriate patient information to any health care organization or provider to which the patient is referred, transferred, or discharged. Relevant information includes (when appropriate):

- The reason for transfer, referral or discharge

- The patient's physical and psychosocial status at the time of transfer

- A summary of the care or services provided and progress toward goals

- Continuing symptom management needs (for example, pain, nausea, dyspnea)

- Instruction and referrals provided to the patient, and

- The existence of any advance directives

The physician(s) who ordered care or service is notified if the patient is referred, transferred, or discharged. When required by law and regulation, written discharge summaries are provided to the patient's physician." The intent statement also says, "When a hospice patient is transferred from home care to inpatient service, or vice versa, the service transferring the patient provides a summary including: the care or services provided; specific medical, psychosocial, or other problems requiring intervention or follow-up; and any follow-up to be provided by an interdisciplinary team member from the service that is transferring the patient."

Standard CC.5 in the Joint Commission's *2003–2004 Comprehensive Accreditation Manual for Health Care Networks* states, "The network facilitates timely communication of information among components and practitioner sites to support continuity of care." The corresponding intent statement says, "Information necessary to provide continuity of care is given to any health care component or practitioner or other clinical care site to which the member is admitted, referred, or discharged." The intent statement also says, "The network provides the receiving component or practitioner site with relevant member information including: care requested; the reason for changing the site of care; a summary of care provided and progress toward achieving goals; and instructions or referrals provided to the member."

The Accreditation Association for Ambulatory Care's *Accreditation Handbook for Ambulatory Health Care 2003* states, "When necessary for ensuring continuity of care, summaries or records of a patient who was treated elsewhere (such as by another physician, hospital, ambulatory surgical service, nursing home, or consultant) are obtained. When necessary for ensuring continuity of care, summaries of the patient's records are transferred to the health care practitioner to whom the patient was transferred and, if appropriate to the organization where future care will be rendered."

Recommendations

In order to ensure continuity of care, healthcare providers should:

- Identify existing federal and state requirements relative to the transfer of information between providers.

- Identify applicable accreditation requirements.

- Establish policies and procedures to facilitate appropriate provision of patient health information when referring, transferring or discharging patients.

- Educate staff as to policies and procedures for transferring information to other health-care providers.

- Audit processes against established policies and procedures and implement corrective action when indicated.

References

Accreditation Association for Ambulatory Health Care, Inc. *Accreditation Handbook for Ambulatory Health Care.* Wilmette, IL, 2003.

Centers for Medicare & Medicaid Services, Department of Health and Human Services. "Conditions of Participation: Specialized Providers." *Code of Federal Regulations,* 2001. 42 CFR, Chapter IV, Part 485.

Centers for Medicare & Medicaid Services, Department of Health and Human Services. *Conditions of Participation for Home Health Agencies.* Code of Federal Regulations, 2001. 42 CFR, Chapter IV, Part 484.

Centers for Medicare & Medicaid Services, Department of Health and Human Services. *Conditions of Participation for Hospitals.* Code of Federal Regulations, 2001. 42 CFR, Chapter IV, Part 482.

Centers for Medicare & Medicaid Services, Department of Health and Human Services. "Requirements for States and Long Term Care Facilities." *Code of Federal Regulations* 2001. 42 CFR, Chapter IV, part 483.

Joint Commission on Accreditation of Healthcare Organizations. *Automated Comprehensive Accreditation Manual for Ambulatory Care.* Oakbrook Terrace, IL: Joint Commission 2002–2003.

Joint Commission on Accreditation of Healthcare Organizations, *Comprehensive Accreditation Manual for Home Care.* Oakbrook Terrace, IL: Joint Commission 2003.

Joint Commission on Accreditation of Healthcare Organizations. *Automated Comprehensive Accreditation Manual for Hospitals.* Oakbrook Terrace, IL: Joint Commission 2003.

Joint Commission on Accreditation of Healthcare Organizations. *Comprehensive Accreditation Manual for Health Care Networks.* Oakbrook Terrace, IL: Joint Commission 2003–2004.

Joint Commission on Accreditation of Healthcare Organizations, *Supplement to the Automated Comprehensive Accreditation Manual for Long Term Care.* Oakbrook Terrace, IL: Joint Commission 2002–2033.

"Standards for Privacy of Individually Identifiable Health Information; Final Rule" 45 CFR, Part 160 and 164. *Federal Register* 67, no. 157 (August 14, 2002).

Provider–Patient E-Mail Security

Jill Burrington-Brown, MS, RHIA
Gwen Hughes, RHIA, CHP

E-mail communication has become "as common as the fax machine in business settings."[1] In fact, the American Medical Association reports that 96 percent of physicians send or receive e-mail, and 25 percent of those physicians use e-mail to communicate with patients.[2] Clearly, e-mail is becoming another communication tool in healthcare.

Advantages

The advantages of e-mail communication between providers and patients are numerous. For example, e-mail:

- Is an efficient way to respond to multiple nonurgent messages
- Is retrievable at any site (for more mobile physicians)
- Eliminates the "telephone tag" problem
- Is communication that may be saved and stored in a way that telephone and face-to-face communications cannot
- Can be used to send test results with interpretations and treatment recommendations
- Can be used to clarify treatment instructions or medication administration
- May be used to direct a patient to a specific Web site for more information

When used in addition to, rather than as a substitute for, face-to-face communication, e-mail may also enhance the patient–provider relationship.

Risks

In addition to the benefits, there are risks associated with the use of e-mail by patients and providers to discuss health-related matters, including privacy breaches, data integrity violations, repudiation, and others. Following is a brief overview of the major issues:

Source: Burrington-Brown, Jill, and Gwen Hughes. "Provider–Patient E-Mail Security (AHIMA Practice Brief)" (Updated June 2003).

Confidentiality Concerns

- Employers and online services retain the right to archive and inspect messages transmitted through their systems.[3] Personal messages between patient and physician would not be considered confidential.

- E-mail, because it is usually unencrypted, can be intercepted.[4] Although the probability of interception is low, the results of such interception can be harmful.

- An individual might accidentally send e-mail to the wrong person because addresses are not always intuitive and frequently change.

- E-mail might be left visible on an unattended terminal.

- E-mail can be printed, circulated, forwarded, and stored in numerous paper and electronic files.

- E-mail may be discoverable for legal purposes.

- A person authorized to access the information might use it for an unauthorized purpose or disclose it to an unauthorized party.

- Confidential health information might be obtained by an unauthorized entity from discarded media.

- E-mail may be vulnerable to computer hackers who could transmit information for illegitimate purposes.

- Phony e-mail could dupe legitimate users into voluntarily giving up sensitive information or receiving incorrect or maliciously generated information.

Data Integrity Violations

- E-mail can be used to introduce malicious software into computer systems.

- An impostor can forge e-mail.

- E-mail can be altered, forwarded, and stored without detection.

Repudiation

- A party to the communication could falsely deny that the exchange of information took place.

Other Risks

- The sender may assume, but doesn't necessarily know, that his or her message was delivered.

- The recipient might not check his or her messages within the time frame the sender expects.

- The attachments embedded in the e-mail might be in a format the recipient's software can't read.

- E-mail can be misinterpreted. Without verbal and nonverbal feedback, the sender can't confirm that his or her messages are understood.

Safeguards can be devised and implemented against most threats. However, these are not without costs.

Legal and Regulatory Requirements

Federal statutes and regulations that address patients' rights to privacy of health information include HIPAA, the Medicare Conditions of Participation, and the Code of Federal Regulations relative to alcohol and drug abuse.

HIPAA contains requirements that health information be protected against threats to security, integrity, and authorized use. The final privacy rule, published August 14, 2002, mandates standards to protect the privacy of individually identifiable health information maintained or transmitted electronically in connection with certain administrative and financial transactions.

The final security rule, published February 20, 2003, also mandates standards to ensure the confidentiality, integrity, and availability of all electronic protected health information the covered entity creates, receives, or transmits.[5] The security rule indicates that covered entities must perform a risk analysis and then determine the level of e-mail security that is needed.

The Conditions of Participation, with which healthcare facilities must comply to be eligible for Medicare funds, vary based on the healthcare entity. The conditions are as follows:

- Hospitals: "The hospital must have a procedure for ensuring the confidentiality of patient records. Information from or copies of records may be released only to authorized individuals, and the hospital must ensure that unauthorized individuals cannot gain access to or alter patient records."[6]

- Home health agencies: "Clinical record information is safeguarded against loss or unauthorized use."[7]

- State and long-term care: "The resident has the right to personal privacy and confidentiality of his or her personal and clinical records."[8]

- Comprehensive outpatient rehabilitation facilities: "The facility must safeguard clinical record information against loss, destruction, or unauthorized use."[9]

- Critical access hospitals (CAHs): "The CAH maintains the confidentiality of record information and provides safeguards against loss, destruction, or unauthorized use."[10]

- Outpatient physical therapy services furnished by physical therapists in independent practice: "Clinical record information is recognized as confidential and is safeguarded against loss, destruction, or unauthorized use."[11]

The Privacy Act of 1974 mandates that federal information systems must protect the confidentiality of individually identifiable data. Section 5 USC 552a (e)(10) of the act is very clear: federal systems must "establish appropriate administrative, technical, and physical safeguards to ensure the security and confidentiality of records and to protect against any anticipated threats or hazards to their security or integrity which could result in substantial harm, embarrassment, inconvenience, or unfairness to any individual on whom information is maintained."[12]

Further, a Department of Health and Human Services (HHS) policy (still referred to as the HCFA Internet Security Policy) issued in November 1998 states that "a complete Internet communications implementation must include adequate encryption, employment of authentication or identification of communications partners, and a management scheme to incorporate effective password/key management systems."[13] The policy is meant to establish the basic security requirements that must be addressed to transmit HIPAA-protected information over the Internet.

Excerpt from HCFA Internet Security Policy

Acceptable Encryption Approaches

Note: As of November 1998, a level of encryption protection equivalent to that provided by an algorithm such as Triple 56 bit DES (defined as 112-bit equivalent for symmetric encryption, 1024-bit algorithms for asymmetric systems, and 160 bits for the emerging Elliptical Curve Systems) is recognized by HCFA as minimally acceptable. HCFA reserves the right to increase these minimum levels when deemed necessary by advances in techniques and capabilities associated with the processes used by attackers to break encryption (for example, a brut-force exhaustive search).

Hardware-based Encryption

1. Hardware encryptors: While likely to be reserved for the largest traffic volumes to a very limited number of Internet sites, such symmetric password "private" key devices (such as link encryptors) are acceptable.

Software-based Encryption

2. Secure Socket Layer (SSL) (sometimes referred to as Transport Layer Security-TLS) implementation: At minimum SSL level of Version 3.0, standard commercial implementations of PKI, or some variation thereof, implemented in the Secure Socket Layer are acceptable.

3. S-MIME: Standard commercial implementations of encryption in the e-mail layer are acceptable.

4. In-stream: Encryption implementations in the transport layer, such as pre-agreed passwords, are acceptable.

5. Offline: Encryption/decryption of files at the user sites before entering the data communication process is acceptable.

These encrypted files would then be attached to or enveloped (tunneled) within an encrypted header and/or transmission.

Acceptable Authentication Approaches

Authentication: This function is accomplished over the Internet and is referred to as an "in-band" process.

1. Formal certificate authority-based use of digital certificates is acceptable.

2. Locally managed digital certificates are acceptable, providing all parties to the communication are covered by the certificates.

3. Self-authentication, as in internal control of symmetric "private" keys, is acceptable.

4. Tokens or "smart cards" are acceptable for authentication. In-band tokens involve overall network control of the token database for all parties.

Acceptable Identification Approaches

Identification: The process of identification takes place outside of the Internet connection and is referred to as an "out-of-band" process.

1. Telephonic identification of users and/or password exchange is acceptable.

2. Exchange of passwords and identities by US Certified Mail is acceptable.

3. Exchange of passwords and identities by bonded messenger is acceptable.

4. Direct person contact exchange of passwords and identities between users is acceptable.

5. Tokens or smart cards are acceptable for identification. Out-of-band tokens involve local control of the token databases with the local authenticated server vouching for specific local users.[14]

While specific medical e-mail legislation, other than previously mentioned in the security rule, has not emerged at the federal level, Congress has included e-mail within the definition of "telemedicine." Thus, any telemedicine interaction between a patient and provider requires informed consent, not only because medical information might be obtained, transmitted, or stored during the telemedicine consultation, but also because patients are engaging in a specific medical procedure.[15]

Because states determine policy on licensure to practice medicine within state boundaries, a practitioner with a license in one state may be at risk of violating another state's licensing laws when engaging in e-mail consultation, diagnosis, or treatment in another state. Prior to engaging in an electronic consultation with or about a patient, physicians should be aware of potential licensing issues, particularly when interacting across state lines.[16]

The HIPAA privacy rule addresses disclosure of information concerning the care and treatment of a patient. Many states have additional protections outlining the disclosure of patient information relative to mental health, substance abuse, and sexually transmitted disease.

Ethical Considerations

The medical profession recognizes the ethical necessity of patient privacy. The Hippocratic Oath declares, "Whatever, in connection with my profession, or not in connection with it, I may see or hear in the lives of men which ought not to be spoken abroad I will not divulge as reckoning that all should be kept." Further, the American Medical Association's Report of the Council on Ethical and Judicial Affairs addresses e-mail as follows: "When using e-mail communication, physicians hold the same ethical responsibilities to their patients as they do during other encounters."[17]

Accreditation Standards

The Joint Commission on Accreditation of Healthcare Organizations' hospital, ambulatory care, behavioral health, home health, networks, critical care hospital, and long-term care standards IM.2 require that "confidentiality, security, and integrity of data and information are maintained."

Recommendations

Prior to establishing e-mail communication with patients, providers should:

1. Conduct a risk assessment that includes consideration of applicable laws and standards.

2. Establish a rigorous information security infrastructure that includes policies and procedures; training and awareness; and appropriate technology and architecture to protect health information against threats to security and integrity, unauthorized access, and repudiation.

3. Explain the inherent risks and benefits to patients, and obtain an informed consent relative to both the use of e-mail and telemedicine consultations.

4. Describe the types of individuals who may see patient e-mail messages, such as office staff, consultants, or those covering during physician absence.

5. Inform the patient that e-mail correspondence will be maintained in the individual health record.

6. Inform the patient about intended response time.

7. Provide patients with e-mail guidelines for communicating with providers.

8. Consider using an automatic reply to acknowledge receipt of the patient's initial message. Modify the auto reply if circumstances are such that no one will be responding to e-mail for an extended period of time.

9. Generate a new reply e-mail message upon completion of the patient's request.

10. Include footers that invite telephone calls or office visits if the patient would like further contact.

11. Maintain all messages, message replies, and confirmation receipts electronically or in hard copy in the patient's healthcare record.

12. Recognize that all e-mail is discoverable in legal proceedings.

13. When sending group e-mail, address the e-mail to the sender in the blind copy section of the e-mail address in order to keep recipients invisible to one another.

14. Do not use patient e-mail addresses in marketing without the patient's consent.

15. Never forward patient-identifiable data to a third party without the patient's express permission.

In communicating with providers, patients should:

1. Understand the risks associated with using electronic mail to discuss private health information with healthcare providers.

2. Understand the risks associated with telemedicine consultations.

3. Include their full name in the first line of the body of their message.

4. Maintain a copy for their personal records.

Both patients and providers should:

1. Double-check the recipient's address.

2. Protect the security of their passwords.

3. Be careful about leaving programs operational and/or documents visible when computer terminals are unattended.

4. Make use of screen savers with private passwords or automatic sign-off.

5. Communicate via e-mail only information they're comfortable having forwarded.

6. Avoid using e-mail for particularly sensitive matters.

7. Avoid using e-mail for time sensitive messages.

8. Take time to make sure the message is clear and concise and cannot be misconstrued.

Notes

1. Sands, Daniel Z. "Guidelines for the Use of Patient-centered E-mail." Massachusetts Health Data Consortium, Inc., 1999. Available at www.mahealthdata.org (accessed March 9, 2004).

2. Mindy Schneiderman, director of market research and analysis, American Medical Association, telephone interview by author, March 2003.

3. Spielberg, Alissa. "Online without a Net: Physician–Patient Communication by Electronic Mail." *American Journal of Law and Medicine* 25, no. 2/3 (1999): 282.

4. Ibid., 270.

5. "Health Insurance Reform: Security Standards Final Rule." 45 CFR, Part 164.306(a)(1). *Federal Register* 68, no. 34 (February 20, 2003).

6. Centers for Medicare & Medicaid Services, Department of Health and Human Services. "Conditions of Participation for Hospitals." *Code of Federal Regulations,* 2002. 42 CFR, Chapter IV, Part 482.24.

7. Centers for Medicare & Medicaid Services, Department of Health and Human Services. "Conditions of Participation for Home Health Agencies." *Code of Federal Regulations,* 2002. 42 CFR, Chapter IV, Part 484.48.

8. Centers for Medicare & Medicaid Services, Department of Health and Human Services. "Conditions of Participation for State and Long Term Care Facilities." *Code of Federal Regulations,* 2002. 42 CFR, Chapter IV, Part 483.10.

9. Centers for Medicare & Medicaid Services, Department of Health and Human Services. "Conditions of Participation for Specialized Providers." *Code of Federal Regulations,* 2002. 42 CFR, Chapter IV, Part 485.60.

10. Centers for Medicare & Medicaid Services, Department of Health and Human Services. "Conditions of Participation for Specialized Providers." *Code of Federal Regulations,* 2002. 42 CFR, Chapter IV, Part 485.638.

11. Centers for Medicare & Medicaid Services, Department of Health and Human Services. "Conditions for Coverage of Specialized Services Furnished by Suppliers." *Code of Federal Regulations,* 2002. 42 CFR, Chapter IV, Part 486.161.

12. The Privacy Act of 1974, Section 5 U.S.C. 552a. Available online at www.usdoj.gov/foia/privstat.htm (accessed March 9, 2004).

13. "HCFA Internet Security Policy." Issued November 24, 1998. Available online at www.cms.hhs.gov/it/security/docs/internet_policy.pdf (accessed March 9, 2004).

14. Ibid.

15. Spielberg, Alissa R. "Online without a Net: Physician–Patient Communication by Electronic Mail." *American Journal of Law and Medicine,* 1999: 25, nos. 2 and 3: 287–289.

16. Ibid. 291.

17. American Medical Association. "Guidelines for Physician–Patient Electronic Communications" (2002). Available online at www.ama-assn.org/ama/pub/category/2386.html (accessed March 9, 2004).

References

Ford, Warwick. *Computer Communications Security: Principles, Standard Protocols and Techniques.* New Jersey: Prentice Hall PTR, 1994.

Health Data Management. *Comprehensive Guide to Electronic Health Records.* New York: Faulkner and Gray, Inc., 1999.

Joint Commission on Accreditation of Healthcare Organizations. *Comprehensive Accreditation Manual for Ambulatory Care:* 2002. Oakbrook Terrace, IL: Joint Commission, 2002.

Joint Commission on Accreditation of Healthcare Organizations. *Comprehensive Accreditation Manual for Hospitals: The Official Handbook.* Refreshed Core January 2002. Oakbrook Terrace, IL: Joint Commission, 2002.

Joint Commission on Accreditation of Healthcare Organizations. *Comprehensive Accreditation Manual for Long Term Care: 2002.* Oakbrook Terrace, IL: Joint Commission, 2002.

Kane, Beverley, and Daniel Z. Sands. "Guidelines for the Clinical Use of Electronic Mail with Patients." *Journal of the American Medical Informatics Association* 5, no. 1 (1998).

Sherman, Lynn, and Mark Adams. "Patients and E-Mail: Technology Means Increased Confidentiality Concerns." *Wisconsin Medical Journal* (May/June 1999).

Facsimile Transmission of Health Information

Gwen Hughes, RHIA, CHP

Background

The quality of healthcare is enhanced when patient clinical information is readily available to healthcare providers. As a result, facsimile (fax) machines and fax software have become commonplace in healthcare organizations. Fax machines work by scanning a document and converting the text to electronic impulses that are then transmitted over telephone lines. The receiving fax then converts the electronic impulses back to text. Physicians who need to share clinical information about a patient use fax machines, for example, when intercampus or regular mail delivery proves too slow. Similarly, hospital transcription departments use facsimile software to deliver a copy of a dictated report to the physician's office as soon as the report is transcribed.

Although fax equipment and software can enhance the quality of healthcare by facilitating rapid transmission of clinical information, this same equipment and software opens up the possibility that information will be misdirected or intercepted by individuals to whom access is not intended or authorized. In recent years, there have been numerous reports describing events wherein patient health records were inadvertently faxed to a newspaper office, for example, rather than the intended recipient.

Legal and Regulatory Requirements

Most federal regulatory requirements such as HIPAA, the Medicare Conditions of Participation, and the Confidentiality of Substance Abuse Patient Records do not specifically address the use of fax equipment or copies.

State laws vary and may address the use of facsimile equipment in licensing or health information laws or regulations, or possibly those related to specific types of diseases, such as sexually transmitted disease or mental health problems.

More than half of the states have adopted rules based on the Federal Rules of Evidence or Rule 803 of the Uniform Rules of Evidence (URE). The URE recognizes that business records created and relied on in the ordinary course of business possess a circumstantial probability of

Source: Hughes, Gwen. "Facsimile Transmission of Health Information (AHIMA Practice Brief)" (Updated). *Journal of AHIMA* 72, no. 6 (2001): 64E–F.

trustworthiness and are admissible as evidence. According to the URE, "a duplicate is admissible to the same extent as an original unless (1) a genuine question is raised as to the authenticity or continuing effectiveness of the original, or (2) in the circumstances it would be unfair to admit the duplicate in lieu of the original."

A number of states have adopted the Uniform Photographic Copies of Business and Public Records Act, which authorizes the admissibility of reproductions made in the regular course of business without need to account for the original. Some states have adopted the Uniform Business Records as Evidence Act, which also addresses the admissibility of record reproductions.

The Bureau of Policy Development of the Health Care Financing Administration (HCFA) addressed the subject of transmitting physicians' orders to healthcare facilities via fax machine. In Letter No. 90-25, dated June 1990, the Bureau states:

> The use of fax to transmit physicians' orders is permissible. When fax is used, it is not necessary for the prescribing practitioner to countersign the order at a later date. Note, however, that fax copies may fade and may need to be photocopied. Healthcare facilities should be advised to take extra precaution when thermal paper is used to ensure that a legible copy of the physician's order is retained as long as the medical record is retained.

Recommendations

1. Establish fax policies and procedures based on federal and state law and regulation and consultation with legal counsel.

2. Include in your organization's Notice of Information Practices uses and disclosures of individually identifiable health information made via facsimile machine or software where appropriate.

3. Obtain a written authorization for any use or disclosure of individually identifiable health information made via facsimile machine or software when not otherwise authorized by the individual's consent to treatment, payment, and healthcare operations, or federal or state law or regulation.

4. Take reasonable steps to ensure the fax transmission is sent to the appropriate destination. Preprogram and test destination numbers whenever possible to eliminate errors in transmission from misdialing. Periodically remind those who are frequent recipients of individually identifiable health information to notify you if their fax number is to change (for example, include a piece in medical staff newsletters where transcriptionists automatically fax reports to physician offices). Train staff to double check the recipient's fax number before pressing the send key.

5. Attach a confidentiality statement on the cover page when transmitting individually identifiable health information. (See Figure 5.1, Sample Confidentiality Notice.)

6. Contact the receiver and ask that the material be returned or destroyed if the sender becomes aware that a fax was misdirected.

7. Place fax machines in secure areas.

8. Unless otherwise prohibited by state law, information transmitted via facsimile is acceptable and may be included in the patient's health record.

Figure 5.1.   **Sample confidentiality notice [for fax cover page]**

The documents accompanying this transmission contain confidential health information that is legally privileged. This information is intended only for the use of the individual or entity named above. The authorized recipient of this information is prohibited from disclosing this information to any other party unless required to do so by law or regulation and is required to destroy the information after its stated need has been fulfilled.

If you are not the intended recipient, you are hereby notified that any disclosure, copying, distribution, or action taken in reliance on the contents of these documents is strictly prohibited. If you have received this information in error, please notify the sender immediately and arrange for the return or destruction of these documents.

References

"Facsimile Transmission of Health Information Position Statement." AHIMA, May 1994.

Letter No. 90-25. Bureau of Policy Development, Health Care Financing Administration, June 1990.

Tomes, Jonathan P. *Healthcare Records Management, Disclosure and Retention: The Complete Legal Guide.* Chicago, IL: Probus Publishing Company, 1993.

Release of Information for Marketing or Fund-Raising Purposes

Harry Rhodes, MBA, RHIA, CHP

Requests for individually identifiable patient health information for use in marketing and fund raising are not uncommon. Within a healthcare organization, patient information might be used to identify potential benefactors or those interested in one of the facility's new services. Externally, medical, surgical, and pharmaceutical companies want information to identify potential customers. Yet, healthcare consumers want protection from unwanted marketing solicitations. Organizations must establish clear policies and procedures that address the use of individually identifiable patient health information for marketing and fund raising.

Standards for Use and Disclosure of Protected Health Information for Marketing

The HIPAA standards for privacy of individually identifiable health information require covered entities (health plans, healthcare clearinghouses, and healthcare providers that transmit certain transactions electronically) to adhere to certain standards relative to the use and disclosure of individually identifiable health information for marketing and fund-raising purposes. Briefly, the standards state that the amended privacy rule under 164.508 requires that an authorization be obtained for activities that meet the definition of marketing.

The amended rule defines marketing as "to make a communication about a product or service that encourages recipients of the communication to purchase or use the product or service." The new definition includes the selling of protected health information by a covered entity to another company or provider for the marketing of that company's products and services.

The amended privacy rule also clarifies that nothing in the marketing provisions of the privacy rule is to be construed as amending, modifying, or changing any other federal or state statutes or regulations, such as antikickback, fraud and abuse, or self-referral statutes or regulations.

Although the amended rule requires an authorization for uses or disclosures of protected health information (PHI) for marketing communications, it exempts two types of marketing activities. They are:

- Face-to-face communication between the individual and the covered entity
- When the marketing communication involves a promotional gift of nominal value

Source: Rhodes, Harry. "Release of Information for Marketing or Fund-Raising Purposes (AHIMA Practice Brief)" (Updated October 2002).

Communications that are specifically excluded in the definition of marketing are:

- Communications that describe the covered entity's health-related products or services (or payment for such products or services) provided by or included in a plan of benefits of the covered entity making the communication (i.e., brochures)

- Communications that describe the health plan or participating providers in a network. Communications that inform health plan enrollees of participating physicians and hospitals are not considered marketing

- For treatment of the individual, such as recommending a medication. In addition, prescription refill or appointment reminders are not considered marketing under the amended privacy rule

- Case management or care coordination for the individual or directions or recommendations for alternative treatments, therapies, healthcare providers, or settings of care to the individual

Marketing activities that do not use PHI to target market a specific group of individuals are not subject to HIPAA. Mass mailings and communications, such as newsletters that do not use PHI to identify the recipients of the mailing, would not fall under the HIPAA regulations.

State Law

Individual states may also have laws or regulations relative to the use of patient health information for marketing or fund raising. As the HIPAA standards for privacy will preempt state law (except where state law is more stringent than HIPAA or provides individuals with greater control over their PHI), health organizations may find it necessary to consult legal counsel when developing their own policies and procedures.

Standards for the Use and Disclosure of Protected Health Information for Fund Raising

Section 164.514(f) of the HIPAA amended final rule does not require an authorization from the individual if the fund-raising activity is for the covered entity and the only PHI used or disclosed is demographic information and dates of service.

Nonprofit organization fund-raising activities that use PHI to target individuals for awareness, research, or other disease-related efforts require an authorization. The final rule allows a covered entity to use or disclose PHI to a business associate without an authorization to identify individuals for fund raising for its own benefit.

The organization's notice of privacy practice must include a description about the use or disclosure of individually identifiable health information for fund raising, including information on how to opt out of future fund-raising mailings.

Recommendations

- Become knowledgeable about the standards and any other federal and state laws and regulations for your facility's population that address the use of individually identifiable patient health information for marketing or fund-raising purposes.

- Draft policies and procedures to address handling requests for individually identifiable patient health information for marketing or fund-raising purposes. One possible approach would be to enlist the expertise of the appropriate oversight committee or to identify a committee responsible for approving or rejecting requests.

- Ask legal counsel to review draft policies and procedures.

- Establish a system wherein patients who sign authorizations to allow for the use and disclosure of their PHI for targeted marketing can be identified and tracked.

- In the organization's notice of privacy practices, include a description about the use or disclosure of individually identifiable health information for marketing or fund raising that requires the patient's specific written authorization. Include definitions of communications that are specifically excluded from the definition of marketing.

- Educate staff about the issues, policies, and procedures related to health information for marketing and fund raising.

- Monitor adherence to policies and procedures and implement corrective action where indicated.

References

"Standards for Privacy of Individually Identifiable Health Information; Final Rule." 45 CFR Parts 160 and 164. *Federal Register* 67, no. 157 (August 14, 2002).

"Standards for Privacy of Individually Identifiable Health Information; Final Rule." 45 CFR Parts 160 and 164. *Federal Register* 65, no. 250 (December 28, 2000).

Part 6

Establishing Health Record Security

Information Security—An Overview

Carol Ann Quinsey, RHIA, CHPS
Mary D. Brandt, MBA, RHIA, CHE, CHP

Background

Maintaining the security of health information used to be a fairly straightforward process. When most clinical information systems were introduced, they were implemented using limited-function workstations physically attached to a designated processor so end users could be limited to specific applications. User access to protected health information generally could be prevented through the security administration available in most health information applications.

Today, powerful workstations are attached to networks on which multiple applications reside, and end users are just a password away from accessing a wide variety of information. Inappropriate access to information could occur if security is not closely monitored.

The increasing use of health information systems in both inpatient and outpatient settings and the linking of systems as the healthcare industry consolidates bring still more challenges. Information systems that once resided in a single facility are being expanded and integrated to simultaneously serve the needs of hospitals, home health agencies, long term care facilities, ambulatory care services, physicians, payers, employers, and others. System boundaries that historically were contained within the walls of an institution may now span multiple states or even nations.

Electronic health records (EHRs) offer the potential for maintaining health information on individuals across all care settings and throughout their lifetimes. With proper design and monitoring, EHRs can offer greater protection for protected information than paper-based patient records afford today.

The Health Insurance Portability and Accountability Act (HIPAA) Final Security Rule approved in February 2003 establishes a baseline for securing health information for covered entities. However, there is flexibility for covered entities to choose security measures in accordance with their risks and operational needs.

Basic Concepts

Information security is undertaken to preserve the confidentiality, integrity, and availability of computer-based information. Security controls reduce the effects of security threats and

Source: Quinsey, Carol Ann, and Mary D. Brandt. "Information Security—an Overview (AHIMA Practice Brief)" (Updated November 2003).

vulnerabilities to a level acceptable to the organization. A major focus of information security is preventing unauthorized individuals from accessing, creating, or modifying information.

Risk assessment is the identification of information resources, the threats to those resources, and the vulnerabilities that may be exploited by those threats, thus exposing the resources to a loss of confidentiality, integrity, or availability.

Risk analysis is the formal process of examining potential threats and identified vulnerabilities discovered during the risk assessment and prioritizing those risks based upon probability and impact. A risk analysis includes a cost and benefit comparison to justify and determine appropriate security controls. Risks may be mitigated, transferred, or accepted, depending upon which option is the most reasonable for the organization.

Risk management is the ongoing process of managing identified risks to an acceptable level by applying security controls and measures to maintain a predetermined level of risk. Security systems cannot withstand every possible threat, and therefore there is no such thing as absolute security. Instead, health information professionals must weigh risks to their systems against the criticality and confidentiality of the information they contain and focus on developing, implementing, and maintaining appropriate security controls.

Cost-effective security controls and safeguards appropriate to the level of risk should be implemented by covered entities. Good security measures do not have to be very expensive, and they should not affect system speed or performance or make legitimate access to systems a hassle. The HIPAA Security Rule clearly indicates that cost alone does not relieve a covered entity of the responsibility of applying appropriate security measures to their systems.

Separation of duties ensures that checks and balances are designed into the system to limit the impact of any given end user. Roles and responsibilities should be divided so that a single end user cannot subvert a critical process. This practice divides the tasks related to maintaining system security among different personnel such that no single individual could compromise system security.

Least privilege means users should be granted access to only the information and functions they need to do their jobs. Functions should be restricted according to the user's job duties. For example, many employees may need "read-only" access. If their jobs do not require them to enter, change, or delete information, copy files, or print reports, they should not be given those capabilities. This supports the 'minimum necessary' requirement of the HIPAA Privacy Rule.

Types of Controls

Broadly speaking, there are three types of controls used in information security: management controls, operational controls, and technical controls.

Management controls are issues that must be addressed by management in the organization's information security program. Generally, these issues focus on management of the information security program and the management of risk within the organization. Management controls include security policies, procedures, and plans that incorporate all applicable laws and regulations and meet the organization's needs.

Operational controls are implemented and executed by staff at all levels of an organization; sometimes consultants and vendors also are asked to do this work. Operational controls include contingency planning, user awareness and training, physical and environmental protections, computer support and operations, and management of security breaches.

Technical controls focus on controls that are executed by information systems. These controls include user identification and authentication, access control, audit trails, and cryptography.

Roles and Responsibilities

Ultimately, everyone who interacts with a computer system is responsible for its security, but several groups have specific responsibilities.

Executives and senior managers have the overall responsibility for the security of information. They also must provide the necessary resources and support for the program.

Information systems security professionals have the technical expertise and knowledge of options available to ensure security. They are responsible for implementing and maintaining information security.

Data owners must assist in determining the data's sensitivity and classification levels and should have an active role in designing access controls for their systems. They should be accountable for the accuracy of the information. Data owners should also assist in designing audit systems for their systems, and they accept the risk for their systems in the organization's current configuration.

HIM professionals should be an integral part of their organization's information security program because of their expertise in confidentiality and legal and regulatory compliance. They must be knowledgeable about the management, operational, and technical controls required to appropriately secure systems and networks and should help determine access control privileges. HIM professionals may design or assist in designing access control and other security policies, standards, guidelines, and procedures. They may serve as privacy or security officers for the organization.

Security officers should provide regular reports to senior management on the effectiveness of the security controls based on periodic audits. Security officers should also ensure that the security policies and procedures comply with industry standards. The information security program may have designated staff, or it may be handled through a committee or department. An officer's duties include design, implementation, management, and review of security policies, standards, guidelines, and procedures.

System managers and administrators program, operate, and fix computer systems. They are responsible for implementing technical security measures.

Users include individuals who are authorized to access a system for their own use as well as those who use information from reports and those who input data into the system. Users are responsible for following established policies and procedures and for alerting managers, data owners, or security officers of security breaches.

Threats and Vulnerabilities

Threats are events that may cause significant damage to information systems and the sensitive information they contain. Threats may be malicious or accidental, but they can damage a system or cause loss of confidentiality, integrity, or availability.

Vulnerabilities are system weaknesses that can be exploited by a threat. Reducing system vulnerabilities can significantly reduce the risk and impact of threats to the system.

Threats to information security include but are not limited to:

- **Physical problems:** Losses may result from power failure (including outages, spikes, and brownouts), utility loss (such as power, air conditioning, or heating), water outages and leaks, sewer problems, fire, flood, earthquakes, storms, civil unrest, or strikes.

- **Disgruntled employees:** The greatest risk of sabotage to computer systems comes from an organization's own employees and former employees. Sabotage may include destroying hardware or facilities, planting "logic bombs" that destroy programs or data, entering data incorrectly, crashing systems, deleting data, and changing data. Because of this threat, it is critical that system access and passwords be deleted immediately when an employee resigns or is discharged.

- **Malicious code:** Malicious code can attack both personal computers and more sophisticated systems. It includes viruses, worms, Trojan horses, logic bombs, and other software. Malicious code programs may play harmless pranks, such as displaying unwanted phrases or graphics, or create serious problems by destroying or altering data or crashing systems. The increasing use of corporate networks, electronic mail, and the Internet provides fertile ground for the development of new strains of viruses and other malicious code. It is critical that antiviral software be kept up to date.

- **Hackers:** Hackers are individuals who gain illegal entry into a computer system, often without malicious intent but simply to see if they can do it. While insiders constitute the greatest threat to information security, the hacker problem is serious. Other terms sometimes used in this context are "crackers" and "attackers." Actions taken by hackers, crackers, and attackers may be limited to simply browsing through information in a system or may extend to stealing, altering, or destroying information. Systems accessible via modem are particularly vulnerable to hacker activity.

- **Theft:** Desktop and laptop computers and the data they contain are vulnerable to theft from inside or outside the organization. The increasing use of personal digital assistants and other handheld devices makes potential inappropriate access to protected health information a greater threat. Measures must be implemented to ensure that patient and corporate data are protected if devices are stolen or misplaced by users.

- **Errors and omissions:** End users, data entry clerks, system operators, and programmers may make unintentional errors that contribute to security problems by creating vulnerabilities, crashing systems, or compromising data integrity.

- **Browsing:** Legitimate users may sometimes attempt to access information they do not need to do their jobs simply to satisfy their curiosity. Extremely sensitive information such as human immunodeficiency virus test results may be vulnerable to this threat if not adequately protected in system or security design.

Establishing Security Policies

Information security policies are required for every organization and form the basis for an information security program. To be effective, policies must be issued at the highest level of the organization and apply to all units of the organization. Security policies should apply to all members of the workforce, including medical staff, volunteers, students, independent contractors, and vendors. Organizations must issue security policies to:

- Create its information security program and assign responsibility for it

- Outline its approach to information security

- Address specific issues of concern to the organization

- Outline decisions for managing a particular system

Figure 6.1, Security Issues, presents a list of the kinds of specific issues that should be addressed when developing organizational and departmental policies and procedures. Multiple issues may be included in a single policy or procedure if appropriate.

Conclusion

Organizational policies and procedures regarding security must be reasonable, cost effective, and appropriate to the risks identified through the risk assessment and analysis process. Keep in mind that good security does not have to be very expensive, nor should it hinder business operations. In fact, security practices may be implemented in a way that enhances business operations. The references included below are a valuable source of additional information on this subject.

Figure 6.1.   Security issues

Access controls	Malicious code
Acquisition of software	Media reuse
Acquisition of hardware	Passwords and other access authentication measures
Antiviral software use	Personal digital assistants
Audit controls, trails, and system logs	Privacy rights (including patients, families,
Audit procedures to avoid discrimination	caregivers, employees, and research)
Audit trail retention	Protection of confidential and proprietary
Back-up, archive, and restore procedures	information
Bringing in software, diskettes, or other media	Remote access to information systems
from outside the organization	Retention, archiving, and destruction of electronic
Business associates	and paper-based information
Change management	Risk analysis
Configuration management	Sanctions and penalties for violations of privacy
Contingency plan	and confidentiality
Dictation and transcription systems	Security incident reporting and response
Disaster recovery	Staff responsibility for data accuracy and integrity
Disposal of media (including disks, hard drives,	Termination procedures
computers, and printed reports)	Training and awareness
Electronic data interchange	Use and monitoring of security alarms
Encryption of files and electronic mail	Use of electronic mail (including the level
Facility security plans	of privacy users may expect)
Firewalls	Unauthorized software
Home use of organization hardware or software	Vendor access to information systems
(such as telecommuting)	Workforce security
Internet access	Workstation use and security

References

An Introduction to Computer Security: The NIST Handbook. Washington, DC: National Institute of Standards and Technology, 1994.

"Guidelines for Establishing Information Security Policies at Organizations Using Computer-based Patient Record Systems." Schaumburg, IL: Computer-based Patient Record Institute, 1995.

"Guidelines for Managing Information Security Programs at Organizations Using Computer-based Patient Record Systems." Schaumburg, IL: Computer-based Patient Record Institute, 1995.

"Health Insurance Reform: Security Standards." Final Rule. 45 CFR Parts 160, 162, 164. *Federal Register* 68, no. 34 (February 20, 2003).

Krutz, Ronald L., and Russell Dean Vines. *The CISSP Prep Guide: Gold Edition.* Wiley Publishing, 2003.

Margret\A Consulting, LLC. "Maps of Final Security Rule to Proposed Rule: Final Security Rule to NPRM and NPRM to Final Security Rule." Copyright 2003. Unpublished.

Rada, Roy. *HIPAA@ IT Reference, 2003: Health Information Transactions, Privacy, and Security.* Hypermedia Solutions Limited, 2003.

"Standards for Privacy of Individually Identifiable Health Information." Final Rule. 45 CFR Parts 160 and 164. *Federal Register* 65, no. 250 (December 28, 2000).

"Take Four Steps to Address 'Addressable' Implementation Specifications." *HIPAA Security Compliance Insider,* April 2003. Brownstone Publishers.

A HIPAA Security Overview

Carol Ann Quinsey, RHIA, CHPS

A great deal has been published about the HIPAA security rule in the past year. This practice brief will provide a succinct overview of the security rule, along with some of the background and basic concepts needed to understand it. In addition, the article will outline some of the skills HIM professionals have that may aid in implementing the security rule in their organizations. Also included is a list of resources that may be useful in furthering your knowledge of this subject.

Background

The final HIPAA security regulations were published on February 20, 2003, by the Department of Health and Human Services. As with the HIPAA privacy rule, its roots are found in the Health Insurance Portability and Accountability Act of 1996. As with the privacy rule, covered entities have two years to comply with the security rule. Most covered entities must comply no later than April 21, 2005. (Small health plans have until April 21, 2006, to comply.)

While the privacy rule covers all protected health information (PHI) in an organization, the security rule is narrower in scope, with the focus solely on *electronic* PHI. Section 164.530 of the privacy rule requires "appropriate administrative, technical, and physical safeguards to protect the privacy of protected health information." The final security rule approved in February 2003 complements the privacy rule by establishing the baseline for securing electronic health information for covered entities.

The security rule is based on three principles: comprehensiveness, scalability, and technology neutrality. The rule addresses all aspects of security, ensures that the rule can be implemented effectively by organizations of any type and size, and does not require specific technology to achieve effective implementation.[1]

Basic Concepts

Covered entities include healthcare plans, healthcare clearinghouses, and healthcare providers who electronically maintain or transmit PHI.

Source: Quinsey, Carol Ann. "A HIPAA Security Overview (AHIMA Practice Brief)." *Journal of AHIMA* 75, no. 4 (2004): 56A–56C.

Electronic protected health information (EPHI) is PHI maintained or transmitted in electronic form. The security rule does not distinguish between electronic forms of information. Some examples of EPHI are patient information stored on magnetic tapes or disks, optical disks, hard drives, and servers. Examples of transmission media include Internet and extranet technology, leased lines, private networks, and removable media such as disks.

Some examples of information that would not be covered by the security rule include information not in electronic form before the transmission, messages left on voice mail, or paper-to-paper faxes that were not in electronic form prior to the transmission. For purposes of the security rule, copy machines are not considered electronic.

Implementation specifications provide direction as to how the standards should be executed. All standards must be implemented. However, implementation specifications may be "required" or "addressable." Required implementation specifications must be implemented. Addressable implementation specifications must be implemented as stated in the rule or in an alternate manner that better meets the organization's needs. This offers some flexibility to organizations in implementing the standard. Organizations must document why the implementation specification in the security rule was implemented in an alternate manner.

Information security is the preservation of confidentiality, integrity, and availability of electronic patient information used for clinical decision making or healthcare operations.

Safeguards are described in the final rule to include administrative, physical, and technical issues an organization must consider in its plans to implement the standards and implementation specifications included in the security rule. Safeguards are not limited to technology; they also require policies and procedures for the work force to follow and sanctions for noncompliance.

Scalability allows an organization to decide on security measures appropriate to its operational risks. Such things as the organization's size and complexity, hardware and software, costs of implementing additional security, and the threats and vulnerabilities identified in a risk analysis guide an organization in implementing appropriate measures.

The Security Rule at a Glance

Security rule standards are grouped into five categories: administrative safeguards, physical safeguards, technical safeguards, organizational standards, and policies, procedures, and documentation requirements. One of the most important steps you will take in preparing to implement the security rule is to read and study the rule. The most important elements are summarized below:

Administrative safeguards (164.308) include nine standards:

- **Security management functions** (four implementation specifications) require organizations to analyze their risks to security and implement policies and procedures that prevent, detect, and correct security violations and to define appropriate sanctions for security violations.

- **Assigned security responsibility** (no implementation specifications) requires that organizations identify the individual responsible for overseeing development of the organization's security policies and procedures.

- **Work force security** (three implementation specifications) requires organizations to have policies and procedures to ensure that members of the work force have access to information appropriate for their jobs and clear termination procedures.

- **Information access management** (three implementation specifications) requires organizations to implement procedures authorizing access to EPHI.

- **Security awareness and training** (four implementation specifications) requires a security awareness and training program for all members of the work force, including management.

- **Security incident procedures** (one implementation specification) requires that there be policies and procedures for reporting and responding to security incidents.

- **Contingency plan** (five implementation specifications) requires an organization to have policies and procedures for responding to an emergency or occurrence (such as fire, vandalism, or natural disaster) that damages equipment or systems containing EPHI such that information is not available to caregivers when and where it is needed.

- **Evaluation** (no implementation specifications) requires that organizations periodically monitor adherence to security policies and procedures, document the results of monitoring activities, and make appropriate improvements in policies and procedures.

- **Business associate contracts and other arrangements** (one implementation specification) require that contracts between a covered entity and business associates provide satisfactory assurance that appropriate safeguards will be applied to protect the APHI created, received, maintained, or transmitted on behalf of the covered entity.

Physical safeguards (164.310) include four standards:

- **Facility access controls** (four implementation specifications) require limitations on physical access to equipment and locations that contain or use EPHI.

- **Workstation use** (no implementation specifications) requires descriptions of what tasks can be performed at each workstation, the manner in which tasks can be performed, and the physical attributes of areas where workstations with access to EPHI are located.

- **Workstation security** (no implementation specifications) requires a description of how workstations permitting access to EPHI are protected from unauthorized use, including portable workstations such as laptops and PDAs.

- **Device and media controls** (four implementation specifications) require organizations to address the receipt and removal of hardware and electronic media that contain EPHI. This includes the use, reuse, and disposal of electronic media containing EPHI both within and outside the organization (for example, a third-party vendor's potential reuse of back-up tapes).

Technical safeguards (164.312) include five standards:

- **Access control** (four implementation specifications) requires policies and procedures limiting access to EPHI to persons or software programs requiring the EPHI to do their jobs.

- **Audit controls** (no implementation specifications) require installation of hardware, software, or manual mechanisms to examine activity in systems containing EPHI.

- **Integrity** (one implementation specification) requires policies and procedures that protect EPHI from being altered or destroyed in any way.

- **Person or entity authentication** (no implementation specifications) requires implementation of measures to prevent unauthorized users from accessing EPHI.

- **Transmission security** (two implementation specifications) requires mechanisms to protect EPHI that is being transmitted electronically from one organization to another.

Organizational requirements (164.314) include two standards:

- **Business associate contracts or other arrangements** (two implementation specifications) require organizations to document that their business associate contracts or other arrangements comply with the security measures when handling EPHI.

- **Requirements for group health plans** (one implementation specification) require each organization to ensure that its plan documents that appropriate safeguards will be implemented for EPHI.

Policies, procedures, and documentation requirements (164.316) include two standards:

- **Policies and procedures** (no implementation specifications) state that organizations must implement reasonable and appropriate policies and procedures to comply with the standards, implementation specifications, and other requirements of the security rule.

- **Documentation** (one implementation specification) requires that written or electronic records of policies and procedures implemented to comply with the security rule be maintained for a period of six years from the date of creation or the date when last in effect.

HIM Professional's Skills and Responsibilities

HIM professionals have knowledge and skills that can add value to the planning and implementation of security measures to comply with the HIPAA security rule. These include:

- Understanding of federal and state law and accreditation standards as they relate to confidentiality and privacy of PHI in all formats

- Expertise about electronic disclosures that can and should be made versus those that should not

- Experience defining appropriate access to PHI based on the needs of the patient, work force, and federal and state laws and regulations

- Knowledge of the organization's compliance efforts with the privacy rule

- Development of policies, procedures, standards, and guidelines

- Educating the work force relative to privacy- and security-related policies and procedures

- Experience measuring effectiveness and compliance with requirements for licensure and accreditation

- Design of audit processes and programs

- Strong organizational and collaborative skills

- Service as privacy or security officers for the organization

HIM professionals are often in a position to foresee the effect of security systems on work flow throughout the organization and can assist in achieving compliance with such systems. Typically, they have strong communication links with members of the executive, nursing, ancillary, and medical staffs, so they can be of great assistance in implementing required work flow changes.

HIM professionals can also make great trainers for privacy and security because of their ability to tie the theory behind the rules to actual practice for those being affected by changes. Their knowledge of various departments' roles in delivering healthcare can help them create realistic examples for staff in multiple departments and can make an enormous contribution to effective training and successful implementation.

Conclusion

The first step in the journey toward implementing security is to read the security rule. The rule is organized in a way that flows logically from conducting a risk analysis through implementing systems, policies, and procedures that allow you to comply with the rule. Many organizations already have excellent information security provisions in place. Nothing in the rule requires costly system changes unless they are deemed appropriate to an organization, nor does the rule require implementing systems that will impair your ability to do business in an efficient and cost-effective way. It seems imminently reasonable to think that the implementation of good security practices could enhance the business of delivering healthcare. The next step is to get involved in your organization's efforts to comply with implementation of the HIPAA security rule.

Note

1. Amatayakul, Margret et al. *Handbook for HIPAA Security Implementation.* Chicago: AMA Press, 2004, p. 8.

References

Amatayakul, Margret. "Finding Quality HIPAA Security Resources." *Journal of AHIMA* 75, no. 1 (2004): 58–59.

Amatayakul, Margret. "Security Risk Analysis and Management: An Overview." *Journal of AHIMA* 74, no. 0 (2003): 72A–72G.

Cooper, Ted, et al. "CPRI Toolkit: Managing Information Security in Healthcare, Version 4." Available online at www.himss.org/asp/cpritoolkit_toolkit.asp.

CPRI Workgroup on Confidentiality, Privacy, and Security. *Guidelines for Establishing Information Security Policies at Organizations Using Computer-Based Patient Record Systems.* Schaumburg, IL: Computer-Based Patient Record Institute, 1995.

CPRI Workgroup on Confidentiality, Privacy, and Security. *Guidelines for Managing Information Security Programs at Organizations Using Computer-Based Patient Record Systems.* Schaumburg, IL: Computer-Based Patient Record Institute, 1995.

"Eight Key HIPAA Security Terms and What They Mean." *HIPAA Security Compliance Insider* (September 2003).

"Eight Security Compliance Tasks You Can Start Now." *Health Information Compliance Insider* (April 2003).

"Get Set to Comply with Final HIPAA Security Regs." *Health Information Compliance Insider* (April 2003).

Hjort, Beth. "Practice Brief: Security Audits (Updated)." 2003.

Krutz, Ronald L., and Russell Dean Vines. *The CISSP Prep Guide: Gold Edition.* New York: John Wiley & Sons, 2003.

National Institute of Standards and Technology. "An Introduction to Computer Security: The NIST Handbook." Available online at http://csrc.nist.gov/publications/nistpubs/800-12/handbook.pdf.

Quinsey, Carol Ann. "Practice Brief: Information Security—An Overview (Updated)." 2003.

"Security Standards Final Rule." 45 CFR Parts 160, 162, and 164. *Federal Register* 68, no. 34 (February 20, 2003).

"Standards for Privacy of Individually Identifiable Health Information; Final Rule." 45 CFR Parts 160 and 164. *Federal Register* 65, no. 250 (August 14, 2003).

"Take Four Steps to Address 'Addressable' Implementation Specifications." *HIPAA Security Compliance Insider* (April 2003).

A Primer on Network Security

Margret Amatayakul, MBA, RHIA, CHPS, FHIMSS

The lack of specificity in HIPAA's transmission security standard for "guarding against unauthorized access to electronic protected health information (EPHI) that is being transmitted over an electronic communications network" may leave you a bit cold, especially the portion of the preamble that states, "Features . . . associated with a proposed requirement for 'Communications/network controls' . . . have been deleted since they are normally incorporated by telecommunications providers as part of network management and control functions that are included with the provision of network services."

While telecommunications providers and vendors of network devices do supply a lot of security features, how you construct your internal network has a lot to do with your ability to prevent external attacks from doing harm to EPHI that resides in your systems and to reduce internal threats to EPHI. Security depends on the type of systems deployed and the scope of connectivity required.

Know Your Environment: Network Security Scenarios

Mainframe Environment

Some providers may still have some legacy systems that deploy a mainframe computer and "dumb" terminals. These systems do not connect to the Internet and do not afford remote access as we know it today. In a mainframe environment, remote access essentially was how far you could string cable to connect your terminals. As such, little additional technical security was needed beyond access, authentication, audit, and integrity controls for data at rest.

Client–Server Environment

Most providers have adopted a client–server computing environment. Local area networks (LANs) manage access by client computers to data and applications held within server computers. A network operating system (NOS) runs the networked computers. The most common NOS platforms are Windows 2000, Windows NT, Novell, and UNIX.

Source: Amatayakul, Margret. "A Primer on Network Security (HIPAA on the Job)." *Journal of AHIMA* 75, no. 3 (March 2004): 56–57.

Each computer or other peripheral device (for example, a printer) must have a network interface card (a NIC), or LAN adapter, to enhance the digital signals of data for transmission through the network cabling. Various types of cabling are used, including hardwire (copper cable that transmits electrical pulses or fiber-optic cable that transmits light pulses) or wireless (using radio or light waves). One or more wiring hubs, depending on the type and configuration of the network cabling (for example, Ethernet, token-ring), may be used to manage the cabling.

LANs can be self-contained within a facility, or they can connect to the Internet. Modems may be used to dial up to the Internet through the plain old telephone system (aka POTS), or a terminal adapter may be used to attach phones to an integrated services digital network (ISDN) line.

There are various ways to configure a LAN to reduce cost and heighten security. For example, some providers use "thin" clients with minimal or no processing and storage capability. As a LAN grows, a network management system may be necessary to monitor network activity, and network partitioning may be used to create discrete security zones. Still, if the LAN has no connection to the external world (either directly to the Internet or to other LANs that have such a connection), it is less vulnerable to external security threats.

Integrated healthcare delivery systems need to connect one LAN to another. A variety of communication links may be used, with distance, speed, volume, connection time (permanent or temporary), and cost contributing to the choice.

Until recently, most conservative providers preferred to use private frame relay, ISDN, or digital T1 lines leased from telephone companies. Bridges, routers, and switches are used to connect and disconnect remote users. Asynchronous transfer mode (or ATM) services permit transmission of video and digitized sound data. For greater distances (in wide area networks, or WANs), microwave or satellite services may be used. Digital subscriber line (DSL) and cable services may also be used, although these tend to be used by small offices or for connectivity from home. Again, your security threats are lower if you can be certain that there is no external connectivity within any of the components of your LAN or WAN—although today this is virtually impossible to ensure.

Browser-based Computing Environment

The Internet has brought not only convenient messaging and access to an amazing web of information, but it has also brought new technologies to information management. Many of these new technologies are finding their way into healthcare computing.

An intranet is essentially a LAN (or WAN) that provides Internet-like services for authorized members of the work force and others. These services include access to internal e-mail and the means to provide secure e-mail with patients and business associates. The Internet's Standard Generalized Markup Language (SGML) and derivatives provide the ability to search for and share documents across any computing platform.

An intranet adopts this browser-based technology to help authorized users gain access quickly and easily to policies and procedures, training materials, and other resources that the organization may provide through its intranet. An extranet may extend such access to affiliates, business associates, and patients.

Finally, some providers are beginning to use a virtual private network (VPN) to transmit data through the Internet using a special protocol to create a proprietary tunnel.

From the Top Down: Network Security Layers

As greater connectivity occurs, even with trusted partners and most certainly via the Internet, providing transmission security is no longer just about having antivirus software and a firewall.

Many security experts believe a layered approach is necessary to thwart unauthorized access, alteration of data, and denial-of-service attacks.

In a layered approach, your risk analysis determines exactly what controls are needed at each level:

- **Perimeter** is the outermost layer (the next layer out being the Internet or any other network with a different level of trust associated with it). Within the perimeter, the most common security controls include one or more firewalls and a set of strictly controlled servers managing other security functions located in a portion of the perimeter often referred to as the "demilitarized zone" (DMZ). Servers in the DMZ, such as e-mail servers, may contain software to protect against malicious code. An intrusion detection system can be added to detect intrusions that have circumvented or passed through the firewall or are occurring within the LAN behind the firewall. VPNs typically terminate within the perimeter layer.

- The **network** layer of security should have access controls and authentication services for both users and devices connected to the network. Other protections may include intrusion detection systems (IDSs), if they are not located within the perimeter layer, and network vulnerability assessment services that scan devices within the network for flaws and vulnerabilities that could be exploited by harmful traffic.

- The **host** layer of security focuses on individual devices such as workstations and network devices. Access controls, authentication measures, and IDSs can be applied here, although managing them at this level can be extremely time consuming, especially in a heterogeneous environment. Most providers reserve such controls for special-function servers. Modems are another source of vulnerability, permitting dial-up access from a workstation, even in some cases where there is hardwire connectivity. Downloads, instant messaging, and other unprotected connectivity are huge threats. A large organization may want a "war dialer" to identify open modem lines that normally should be off or are unauthorized. A similar tool should be used to detect rogue wireless access points in a wireless LAN. Another host-level security function is "platform hardening" to ensure that unnecessary services, software, and users are removed from all platforms on which Web pages, databases, and other types of applications, data, or software reside.

- The **application** layer of security is where controls for data at rest are generally applied. Application-layer firewalls may also be installed on Web servers, e-mail servers, and other special devices to thwart internal attacks. Integrity controls in the form of data edits are not strictly security controls, but they could prevent keying errors from causing alteration or destruction of data.

- **Data**-layer security controls are the last line of defense. An important control here is contingency planning, including data redundancy and backup. Integrity controls ensure that data are not altered when stored or transmitted. Encryption is the strongest form of data security. Encryption for data at rest is an addressable implementation specification within HIPAA. Most providers will use encryption primarily when data are transmitted outside of a proprietary communication link.

Arranged like the layers of an onion, security layers protect against single points of failure in your network.

Security Risk Analysis and Management: An Overview

Margret Amatayakul, MBA, RHIA, CHPS, FHIMSS

The HIPAA security rule requires every covered entity (CE) to conduct a risk analysis to determine security risks and implement measures "to sufficiently reduce those risks and vulnerabilities to a reasonable and appropriate level."[1] The concept of risk management is not new to healthcare. But making decisions about how to comply with a regulation using a risk-based approach is new.

In addition, deciding and documenting the appropriate level of controls based on potential threats that might exploit vulnerabilities is not a customary practice. But the preamble to the security rule makes it clear that regulators recognize that "use of electronic technology . . . results in many new and potentially large risks. These risks represent expected costs, both monetary and social. Leaving risk assessment up to individual entities will minimize the impact and ensure that security effort is proportional to security risk."[2]

This practice brief reviews the regulatory requirements for security risk analysis and management, provides an overview of the types of risk analysis that can be performed, and offers a practical approach on how to comply with these requirements.

Regulatory Requirement

The security rule requires a CE, in accordance with the security standards general rules (§164.306), to have a security management process in place "to implement policies and procedures to prevent, detect, contain, and correct security violations."[3]

The security standards general rules include general requirements to:

- Ensure the confidentiality, integrity, and availability of all electronic protected health information the CE creates, receives, maintains, or transmits.

- Protect against any reasonably anticipated threats or hazards to the security or integrity of such information.

- Protect against any reasonably anticipated uses or disclosures of such information that are not permitted or required under the privacy rule.

- Ensure compliance with this subpart by its work force.

Source: Amatayakul, Margret. "Security Risk Analysis and Management: An Overview (AHIMA Practice Brief)." *Journal of AHIMA* 74, no. 9 (October 2003): 72A–G.

The standards are flexible in regards to approach:

- CEs may use any security measures that allow the CE to reasonably and appropriately implement the standards and implementation specifications as specified in this subpart.

- In deciding which security measures to use, a CE must take into account the following factors:

    —The size, complexity, and capabilities of the CE

    —The CE's technical infrastructure, hardware, and software security capabilities

    —The costs of security measures

    —The probability and criticality of potential risks to electronic protected health information

In applying flexibility, however, the preamble to the security rule states, "Cost is not meant to free covered entities from this [adequate security measures] responsibility."[4]

Risk Analysis Approaches

Risk analysis and risk management are two of the required implementation specifications within the security management process standard. The security rule does not specify exactly how a risk analysis should be conducted, but it does reference the National Institute of Standards and Technology (NIST) Special Publication 800-30, "Risk Management Guide for Information Technology Systems."[5]

The NIST publication offers a comprehensive approach to incorporating risk management into the system development life cycle. Threats in the environment are identified, then vulnerabilities in information systems are assessed. Threats are then matched to vulnerabilities to describe risk.

The NIST document includes a description of the roles of various persons in risk analysis and management. It emphasizes the key role senior management plays in understanding security risk, establishing direction, and supplying resources.

HIPAA requires assigning responsibility to the security official for the development and implementation of security policies and procedures. This individual may lead the team that actually performs the risk analysis, do much of the policy and procedure writing, and recommend or even select many of the controls.

The fact that NIST identifies the chief information officer, system and information owners, business and functional managers, information technology (IT) security analysts, and trainers recognizes the importance of a team that extends beyond IT and encompasses users.[6] In a clinical setting, users not only can assist in providing application and data criticality information, but must also be involved in determining which mitigation strategies will work.

Because healthcare has so many regulations to comply with, it is also helpful to "piggyback" security onto other functions where possible. For example, a safety officer may make rounds that could include the review of workstation locations. Physical plant security personnel (also known as protective services personnel) may already be monitoring that members of the work force are wearing badges and checking that doors are locked. Communicating these issues with the information security official is critical to compliance.

Qualitative Approach

The NIST approach is generally considered qualitative, because it relies heavily on narrative descriptions of risk. The NIST approach addresses cost/benefit analysis, but not as an integral determinant of risk. Other security experts offer methodologies that rank risks or are highly quantitative.

Ranking Approach

Because the security rule's flexible approach calls for the identification of probability and criticality of potential risks as well as cost considerations, a ranking approach may provide compliance justification and be more conducive to budgeting than a qualitative approach alone.

In a ranking approach, each vulnerability/threat pair can be rated as high-medium-low on a probability scale and a criticality scale. Together the ratings combine scores that can be used to prioritize the risks and therefore identify where the CE needs to put its attention. (The "Practical Methodology" section, below, is an example of this approach.)

Quantitative Approach

A quantitative risk analysis attempts to assign monetary values to the potential losses that might occur as a result of a threat exploiting a vulnerability.

A quantitative risk analysis requires that information assets be valued by some sort of common standard. (See Figure 6.2, Sample Quantitative Risk Analysis Calculation.) There are typically three elements that determine the value of an information asset:

1. Initial and ongoing cost of purchasing, licensing, developing, and supporting the information asset

2. Value of the information asset to the organization's operations, research, and business model viability

3. Value of the information asset established in the external marketplace and the estimated value of the intellectual property such as trade secrets, patents, or copyrights

For healthcare, such an evaluation process may be very difficult and not fully applicable. The first value should be something that can be identified but is not commonly available. While the second value is applicable, it is very difficult to determine, and can probably only be estimated.

For example, one would have to conduct an exercise to determine if certain patient information is not available in an information system, would it be available elsewhere and, if so, in a timely manner? Is it likely that the absence of the information will result in harm? Can the value of the harm be measured?

Finally, value in the marketplace generally does not apply to healthcare, though if the first two values could be determined, this value being zero would not be a problem.

After information assets are valued, the rate of occurrence of threats exploiting vulnerabilities must be quantified. For example, a vulnerability may be a port left open for the information systems vendor to provide patches and troubleshoot system problems. How frequently, then, does this open port get exploited by others who do not have legitimate access? This would need to be quantified, such as once a year or once a week.

From the value of the loss and the rate of occurrence of threats exploiting vulnerabilities, annualized loss expectancy can be determined. This would be the monetary value of the risk. The result of this analysis can then be compared to what it would cost to institute security controls that would reduce the risk.

Figure 6.2.   Sample quantitative risk analysis calculation

Information Asset: Lab results from remote access reference lab

Vulnerability: Open port

Threat: Exploitation of open port by disgruntled former employees of the hospital or lab to gain unauthorized access to lab results

Calculation: Value of asset: (1) Amortized initial cost plus annual costs + (2) Cost to process an OCR complaint, fine for one violation, and risk manager's estimate of likelihood and cost of a lawsuit = $500,000

Rate of Occurrence: Since the system was installed two years ago, there has been one successful hacker who obtained test results that resulted in a breach of confidentiality, a privacy complaint to the Office for Civil Rights, and an out-of-court settlement. Rate of occurrence is one every two years, or 0.5.

Annualized Loss Expectancy: $500,000 × .5 = $250,000

Analysis: It has been determined that the only viable risk reduction strategy would be to keep the port closed at all times and have the reference lab call to request a staff member open it when the lab is ready to send information. This has been determined to cost $50,000 per year in staff time. Because the cost of risk reduction is less than the annualized loss expectancy, security experts would recommend adopting the security control.

Note: If there had been no exploitation of the vulnerability, the annualized loss expectancy would have been 0, in which case, a cost of $50,000 to introduce a control could be considered an unnecessary expense. Some security experts suggest that the potential for exploitation of a threat be estimated and used instead of actual occurrences. The potential for threat could be estimated from other healthcare providers' experiences, if known, or an estimate based on senior management's risk profile (how risk tolerant or risk averse they are). For example, senior management may indicate that in all cases, a factor of .2 should be used to estimate annualized loss expectancy, in which case the result in this example would be $100,000, still within the range where the control should be implemented.

Reprinted with permission from Margret\A Consulting, LLC.

Practical Methodology to Risk Analysis, Management

While the quantitative approach may produce a seemingly straightforward answer as to when risk mitigation strategies should be employed, it is time-consuming to use and highly dependent on estimation. The principles behind the process, however, are sound and can be used as part of one's thinking process while conducting a more qualitative or ranking-oriented risk analysis.

Practical approaches to conducting and documenting a risk analysis for the HIPAA security rule may be to:

- Inventory information systems, their present security controls, and criticality of the applications and their data. Understand senior management's risk profile.

- Identify threats in the environment.

- Identify vulnerabilities that threats could attack.

- Determine the probability that a threat could attack a vulnerability, analyze the criticality of the impact, and summarize the risk.

- Determine risk mitigation strategies, implement applicable controls, and report residual risk to senior management.

- Document the process.

- Using information from an information system activity review, track results of controls; monitor changes in the environment, information systems, and security technology; update the risk analysis; and implement any other controls.

Inventory Information Systems

A Y2K inventory or information systems review for the privacy rule may already be available. It is a good idea to track date acquired, license, location, vendor, maintenance agreements, current version, functions, and data owners or system administrators for all major hardware, operating systems, and application software. Such an inventory should encompass all information systems, whether they are located in the data center or not.

For each application, identify and describe the security features. These would include the ability to support unique user identification, access controls, emergency mode access, automatic logoff, audit controls, authentication, data integrity, encryption, and backup. Reference the policy and procedure in which each control is documented. For example, under authentication, you may describe that the application supports only up to a six alphanumeric character password (no special characters).

Part of contingency planning is assessing the relative criticality of specific applications and data in support of other contingency plan components. Criticality can be rated on a high-medium-low scale. For example, the criticality of an intensive care information system is probably high, where the criticality of an order communication system is medium (for example, orders are recorded on paper and it is feasible to call or send copies to ancillary departments).

A good way to assess criticality is to determine the amount of time the system could be down before patient care would be affected (high criticality), before operations would be significantly impacted (medium criticality), or if paper/independent computer systems could be used to load batches at a later time (low criticality).

Identify Threats

A threat is an indication or warning of trouble. In security, a threat is anything that could harm information. Most security experts consider that there are three components to a threat:

- Target: The object of a threat. HIPAA identifies confidentiality, integrity, and availability as potential targets of a threat. Many add "accountability" to the list.

- Agent: The motivation or resources for carrying out the threat. Motivation is a human characteristic and could include accidental threats such as input errors, inappropriate activities such as wasting corporate resources, and intentional and illegal acts such as theft and sabotage. These may be internal or external. There are also natural acts and environmental threats that are the source of power outages, building explosions, etc.

- Event: The result of a threat. In general, there are four types of events: unauthorized access (breaching confidentiality), modification (causing a data integrity problem), denial of service (rendering data unavailable), and repudiation (the inability to identify the source and hold someone accountable for an action).

The healthcare delivery system has typically taken the approach that "this won't happen here." Unfortunately, there have been many security-related incidents that have reached newsworthy proportion, many more that have been handled without media attention, and some that may even have gone unnoticed. As part of HIPAA's risk analysis, your organization should make an honest appraisal of what might realistically happen.

Consider the location of the facility. Is the data center located over a flood plain? Are utility cables above ground where damage is more likely to occur? Some threats may be temporary. For example, is there new construction nearby? Understand the community and population that serve as a source of work force members and patients.

Some threats result from information system configuration. It may be that a best of breed environment is more prone to threats than a best of fit simply because there are fewer different people to deal with and things to learn about and remember to do.

Identify Vulnerabilities

A vulnerability is a flaw or weakness in information system security policies and procedures, design, implementation, or controls that could be accidentally triggered or intentionally exploited by one or more threats previously identified. Many healthcare organizations performed a "gap analysis" or "privacy and security assessment" as part of their privacy rule preparedness. This is a good place to start to identify security vulnerabilities in information systems. Other internal sources may be auditors' reports and risk management reports.

As privacy complaints begin to occur, review them to determine if there is a security component. Privacy and security may have a cause and effect relationship. Another approach is to simply conduct a walk-through, both literally in the physical environment and figuratively in terms of information systems. Vulnerability scanning tools can be used and penetration tests performed to identify vulnerabilities in information systems.

External sources of information about vulnerabilities include hardware and software vendor Web sites that might describe incidents others have had and provide patches or service packs to mitigate some of these. Many security associations produce online and print newsletters. Even local business groups, colleges or universities, and the police department may be good sources of information.

Summarize Risk

Typically, threats are paired with vulnerabilities, although it is not necessarily a one-to-one relationship. Many threats may exploit a single vulnerability. One threat may exploit many vulnerabilities.

One way to ensure your organization is both complete in your assessment and comprehensive in your compliance with the security rule is to document vulnerabilities and threats as they relate to each security standard. Once you have the threats and vulnerabilities documented, assign a high-medium-low rating to each threat/vulnerability pair with respect to probability and criticality. (See Figure 6.3, Rating Risk.)

The ratings may be combined to create a numeric ranking as shown in Figure 6.4, Risk Ranking Scale. This type of chart can be used to summarize the risk and prioritize remediation. Bear in mind, however, that every security rule standard must have a compliance plan. Implementation specifications may be required or addressable. The risk analysis is critical in determining how you will treat the addressable implementation specifications. Based on the risk analysis, it may be necessary to address the implementation specification as described in the rule. Alternatively, a medium to low ranking may suggest that an alternative is satisfactory.

It is possible that an implementation specification does not apply. For most hospitals and large physician offices, however, most implementation specifications will probably apply. Remember also that even though an implementation specification may not apply, the standard itself must be complied with.

Figure 6.3.   Rating risk

Rating	Probability	Criticality
High	• You have experienced an incident • Controls are not very effective	• Results include human death or serious injury • Inability to recover critical data or high cost of recovery • Major lawsuit • Loss of licensure or accreditation
Medium	• You have been alerted to threat • Controls may impede threat	• Results include human injury/harm • Complaint to federal government • Significant cost of recovery • Minor lawsuit • Public relations issue
Low	• No one in community has experienced threat • Controls will greatly deter or prevent success of a threat	• Complaint • Loss of productivity • Nuisance • Embarrassment

Reprinted with permission from Margret\A Consulting, LLC.

Figure 6.4.   Risk ranking scale

Rating	Criticality		
High	3	6	9
Medium	2	4	6
Low	1	2	3
	Low	Medium	High

Risk Mitigation

Once risk is understood, risk mitigation strategies can be developed and controls implemented. The NIST "Risk Management Guide for Information Technology Systems" lists six options for risk mitigation[7]:

- Risk assumption: The acceptance of the potential for risk. Controls may be used to lower risk, but not to the extent they could be if more resources are applied. This may be an acceptable strategy if risk is determined to be low and the cost of mitigation is high.

- Risk avoidance: The act of eliminating the risk cause. Generally this means foregoing certain functions in the system or shutting the system down. This strategy is not often used, but may be necessary on a temporary basis.

- Risk limitation: The implementation of controls that minimize the adverse impact of a threat exploiting a vulnerability. These controls would help deter, detect, and react to a potential threat.

- Risk planning: The management of risk by prioritizing, implementing, and maintaining controls. This is essentially the process of conducting risk analysis as outlined here.

- Research and acknowledgment: The acknowledgment that a vulnerability exists and the process to research appropriate controls. This should be considered a temporary strategy reserved for use during the implementation phase of the security rule, the implementation of a new information system, or when a completely new threat becomes known.

- Risk transference: The selection of other options to compensate for loss, such as purchasing insurance. This generally will be used in combination with other strategies.

These options recognize that controls cannot totally eliminate risk. In general, controls may be categorized as:

- Preventive: Inhibiting a threat, such as by access controls, encryption, and authentication requirements.

- Deterrent: Keeping the casual threat away, such as strong passwords, two-tiered authentication, and Internet use policies.

- Detective: Identifying and proving when a threat has occurred or is about to occur, such as audit trails, intrusion detection, and checksums.

- Reactive: Providing a means to respond to a threat that has occurred, such as an alarm or penetration test.

- Recovery: Control that helps retrieve or recreate data or application, such as backup systems, contingency plans.

In addition to what the security controls address, control strategies should include administrative, physical, and technical components. The HIPAA security rule standards themselves offer guidance on what general types of controls are required.

The security rule also references two other NIST Special Publications, "Generally Accepted Principles and Practices for Securing Information Technology Systems" (800-14) and "Underlying Technical Models for Information Technology Security" (800-33). The NIST Web site features many other helpful special publications. Many information system vendors have also posted information about what plans they have for enhancing security features.

Policy provides the overall direction for the controls. If senior management directs that controls should be preventive to the extent possible, then controls must necessarily be stronger than those where management indicates deterrent or detective controls are adequate.

Procedures will spell out the details of how specific controls will be implemented. While security policies should be known by all members of the work force, some security procedures may need to be considered sensitive information.

In this case, only a limited number of persons with a need to know should have access to procedures such as how to set passwords or the encryption methodology employed. While procedures may be sensitive and the number of persons with a need to know limited, there should always be more than one person who knows each procedure (backup) and no one person should know all procedures for all controls (separation of duties).

A final step in risk mitigation is to determine and report residual risk to senior management. Because no system can be made risk free, residual risk is that risk remaining after the implementation of new or enhanced controls. In an age of due care and ultimate responsibility for mission accomplishment, an estimate of residual risk should be made and presented to senior management. If the residual risk has not been reduced to an acceptable level, the risk analysis cycle must be repeated to identify a way of lowering the residual risk to an acceptable level.

Just as with the risk analysis itself, residual risk can be qualitatively or quantitatively described. For example, a security expert may indicate that the probability of a threat exploiting a given vulnerability is less than 10 percent. Residual risk may be described in monetary terms if a quantitative risk analysis was performed.

In the example used in Figure 6.2, Sample Quantitative Risk Analysis Calculation, the estimate of asset value was based on a breach of confidentiality, a privacy complaint to the Office for Civil Rights, and a settlement, which cost the organization $500,000. The control recommended would prevent most hackers. Additionally, a security expert could offer a judgment on the likelihood that a social engineer could spoof members of the work force and get them to open the port to an unauthorized hacker.

It is conceivable, however, that the cost of the remediation could be even higher if a major lawsuit was involved. A risk manager might provide an estimate of $2 million. The likelihood of a threat still occurring with the control and the higher cost estimate would be residual risk information that senior management should understand.

Document

HIPAA requires documentation of the risk analysis and that it be retained for six years. Documentation is critical in proving that the analysis was performed. Even if you are in the "research and acknowledgment" phase, it is good practice to document exposures.

Once again, HIPAA does not specify the form of documentation a risk analysis should take. Many organizations will use some type of spreadsheet, especially if they have ranked risks or use any quantitative approach. The format in Figure 6.5, Risk Analysis and Management Documentation, may be used to create a spreadsheet to document the risk analysis and conduct ongoing risk management.

Risk Management

Risk management is the act of implementing the security measures. It also entails monitoring for changes and responding with enhanced strategies. The security standards general rules also address maintenance (§164.306(e): "Security measures implemented to comply with standards and implementation specifications adopted . . . must be reviewed and modified as needed to continue provision of reasonable and appropriate protection of electronic protected health information."

The Information System Activity Review implementation specification under the security management process standard requires records of audit logs, access reports, and incident tracking reports. These and other internal and external documents should be periodically reviewed to determine if risk has increased. In addition, technology itself changes. Where it may have

Figure 6.5.   Risk analysis and management documentation

Standard	Vulnerability	Threat	Probability	Criticality	Risk Score	Control	Residual Risk	Review Date
§ 164.308 (a)(1)(ii) (A) Risk analysis	Only gap analysis performed to date	Existence of threats not documented	M	H	6	Risk analysis	Not all threats may be identified	April 20, 2004

been difficult and costly in the past to institute single sign-on, new standards may make it easier to implement this measure that helps users manage their authentication process.

If specific reports do not trigger a review of risk, it may be suitable to institute specific indicators or future review dates. Federal government agencies are required by law to reassess risk to information systems every three years. This is a good benchmark from which to determine an appropriate time frame.

One measure that the final security rule does not explicitly address is configuration management. The rule's preamble explains this was eliminated as a separate standard (previously included in the proposed security rule) because it was believed to be incorporated in other standards. Configuration management is essentially change control. Many organizations apply configuration management to information technology to manage versions of software and prioritize requests for changes to systems. A formal change control procedure should also address security. Any time a change in a system takes place, two key elements should be reviewed:

1. Are security controls in place? Were any security controls temporarily shut off to install an upgrade? Have they been reinstated? Are there default controls in the new system that should be customized to your environment?

2. Should new controls be adopted? Are changes to the system or new systems such that old controls don't work or newer controls will apply? Are there additional controls that are needed for the upgrade or new system?

Keys for Success

The NIST "Risk Management Guide for Information Technology Systems" concludes with some suggested "keys for success." In summarizing these and offering practical guidance to HIM professionals, a successful risk analysis and management program depends on people—people given the authority and assuming responsibility for complying with policy and following procedure, for awareness and reporting incidents, and for offering suggestions for mitigating risk.

The security rule contains many more administrative and physical safeguard standards than technical standards. Even as it only addresses protected health information in electronic form, it is people that make security happen.

Notes

1. "Health Insurance Reform: Security Standards; Final Rule." 45 CFR parts 160, 162, and 164. *Federal Register* 68, no. 34, page 8377 (February 20, 2003).

2. Ibid., page 8364.

3. Ibid., page 8377.

4. Ibid., page 8343.

5. NIST. Special Publication 800-30, "Risk Management Guide for Information Technology Systems." Chapters 2 and 3.

6. Ibid., page 6.

7. Ibid., page 27.

Security Audits

Beth Hjort, RHIA, CHP

Access controls are critical tools for ensuring privacy and security of electronic protected health information (PHI). They serve as gatekeepers for front-end compliance with the privacy standard of "minimum necessary" and the security principle of "need-to-know." But even with an ideal access-control plan, the complexities of the healthcare environment are unavoidable. Security audits must be performed to hold the users of information systems accountable for their actions.

Protection of individually identifiable health information is a patient right. Besides being mandated by the Health Insurance Portability and Accountability Act of 1996 (HIPAA), security audits offer a back-end look at system and policy effectiveness for ensuring that patient right. Audit information may also be useful as forensic data during investigations of security incidents and breaches to patient privacy.

Job positions with broad, random functions may require electronic access to at least select portions of all patients' medical files. Without such access, employee and provider effectiveness could be significantly inhibited. For paper records, a locked file room and record-request system provide control over the physical record, but these measures offer no control over what is viewed when a complete record is accessed. For electronic records, access may be controlled down to the data-item level, but it is much more difficult to control and defend when random access is required. Decisions to grant broad access should be carefully evaluated and justified.

Unlike paper records, where evidence of inappropriate viewing can be nonexistent, computerized audit logs of electronic file access make tracking possible. IT systems have the capability of logging key activities. Audit trails—computer reports showing threads of activity occurring within the electronic system—can be used to investigate individual access patterns, either by user or for a particular file.

Audit logs are records of system activity. Reports of this activity can be produced according to predetermined report parameters. Security audits use audit trails and audit logs to compare actual system activity to expected activity. It's helpful to distinguish the difference in these terms: Audit logs are records of activity maintained by the system. An audit trail consists of the log records identifying a particular transaction or event. An audit is the process of reviewing those records. An audit can be a periodic event or it can be done as a result of a patient complaint or suspicion of employee wrongdoing.

Source: Hjort, Beth. "Security Audits (AHIMA Practice Brief)" (Updated November 2003).

Legal and Regulatory Requirements

HIPAA security regulations directly and indirectly relating to audits include:

- Information system activity review (required): "Implement procedures to regularly review records of information system activity, such as audit logs, access reports, and security incident tracking reports." (164.308(a)(1)(ii)(c))

- Evaluation (required): "Perform a periodic technical and nontechnical evaluation, based initially upon the standards implemented under this rule and subsequently, in response to environmental or operational changes affecting the security of ePHI, that establishes the extent to which an entity's security policies and procedures meet the requirements [of the Security Rule]." (164.308(a)(2)(8))

- Audit controls (required): "Implement hardware, software, and procedural mechanisms that record and examine activity in information systems that contain or use electronic protected health information." (164.312(1)(b))

The basic tenets of the Privacy Act of 1974 apply to any organization. The act directs that data may be used only for the purpose for which it was collected.

Accreditation Requirements

The 2004 Joint Commission on Accreditation of Healthcare Organizations hospital standards have been modified to be consistent with HIPAA. Standards IM.2.10 and IM.2.20 respectively address a healthcare organization's responsibility to maintain privacy and security.

IM.2.10 states, "Information privacy and confidentiality are maintained."

IM.2.20 states, "Information security including data integrity is maintained."

Elements of performance for both of these standards require written policies, an effective process for enforcing policies, monitoring policy compliance, and the use of monitoring of information to improve privacy, confidentiality, and security.

Recommendations

Security audits, besides being a mechanism to address regulatory and accreditation responsibilities, are an investment in risk reduction. A confidentiality task force can be an excellent opportunity for key individuals to explore and determine a security audit procedure that protects the entire organization. Such a task force would typically include the privacy officer, security officer, the CIO, representation from HIM, risk management, legal affairs, human resources, quality management, the medical staff, IS, and compliance officer and internal audit and data analysis experts as appropriate.

Approach

When setting up a security audit process, consider:

- Your system(s) capabilities; disparate systems may require modified audit plans

- Creating screen warning banners to notify computer users that activities are being monitored and audited

- Involving data owners when appropriate (often the same as department or unit leadership) to determine what activities should trigger an entry into audit trails

- Having audit trails reviewed by department or unit leadership to determine appropriateness of PHI access based on workforce roles and tasks

- Directly involving department or unit leadership most familiar with job responsibilities in interpreting findings and identifying questionable circumstances needing further investigation

- Determining how random audits will be conducted

- Obtaining human resource department involvement when a manager suspects employee wrong-doing and requests review of employee activities via an audit trail (for protection of employee rights)

- Adding a provision to contractual agreements requiring adherence to privacy and security policies, cooperation in security audits, and investigation and follow-through when breaches occur

- The impact of running audit reports on system performance

- Conducting occasional "check the checker" audits, whereby an individual is assigned to assess viewing access of those who are conducting the department, unit, or entity audits

- Ensuring top-level administrative support for consistent application of disciplinary and plenary actions

- Enhancing the quality management process to enfold security audit responsibility into each department's, unit's, or entity's performance improvement monitors

Security Audit Process

It would be prohibitive to perform security audits on every data field. Good-faith efforts to investigate the compliance level of individuals educated on privacy issues can be achieved through a well-thought-out approach.

Identify "trigger events"—criteria that raise awareness of questionable conditions of viewing of confidential information. Some will be appropriately applied to the whole organization, some will be department- and unit-specific.

Examples include:

- Users that have the same last name, address, or street name as in the patient file being viewed

- VIPs (board members, celebrities, governmental or community figures, authority figures, physician providers, management staff, or other highly publicized individuals)

- Patient files with isolated activity after no activity for 120 days

- Employees viewing other employee files; this should be cross-departmental as well as interdepartmental (set parameters to omit legitimate caregiver access)

- Diagnosis related (set parameters to omit caregivers)

- Sensitive diagnoses such as psychiatric disorders, drug and alcohol problems, AIDS

- Files of minors who are being treated for pregnancy or sexually transmitted diseases

- Department- or unit-specific circumstances (brainstorm a customized approach according to function and job responsibilities):

  —Nurses viewing files of patients on other units (e.g., medical and surgical nurses viewing files of patients treated only in emergency services or psychiatric services)

  —Transcriptionists viewing files of services or patients for whom they did not transcribe reports

  —Emergency department nurses viewing files of emergency patients from shifts and days when they were not working

  —Medicare billers viewing insurance categories they do not process

- Terminated employees (checks that access has been rescinded)

- Employees with home access

- Physicians viewing records of patients they did not treat as attending physician, consultant, or surgeon

- Nonclinical staff audit (nonclinical staff viewing clinical information inappropriately)

- All-hits audit (a random review that checks who users are, where they work, and if they should be accessing the file)

- Focused audit (use to investigate periodic patient or staff complaints of suspected breaches)

Sample size: When possible, use a 100-percent capture in an ongoing manner for trigger events that identify only inappropriate access. Some triggers will be unwieldy at 100 percent, so consider performing a 100-percent audit for a shorter time period. Some trigger factors will lend themselves to application within certain departments, units, or services. For triggers with expectations of large-volume logs, consider drilling down on a select number (e.g., every third file until a sample of 30 is accrued).

Frequency: Security audits can encourage the swift detection of security breaches. To encourage immediate review and investigation, examine your organization's ability to generate ongoing reports for trigger factors that are expected to be infrequent. Define sporadic and random monitoring periods for triggers that are not ongoing and are more effectively reviewed for patterns one day of the week (rotate the day), one week out of the quarter, one entire month, et cetera. Not every trigger event needs to be audited every period. Consider rotating trigger events so that different audits are conducted each period. Include follow-up audits for those triggers previously uncovering problem areas.

Scope: The extent of the audit can likewise be varied according to department, unit, or corporate entity. A department may choose to monitor all employees viewing other employee files during one monitoring period and elect to review only third shift for another. The following elements can help to focus the scope and make it more meaningful:

- Day of the week or time of day the access occurred

- Where the access occurred

- Number of accesses

The number of trigger factors and the breadth of the coverage chosen should be paced for reasonableness by the individuals reviewing the audit logs.

Educate, Educate, Educate

Make certain that patient rights and policies and procedures related to privacy and security are understood by all involved employees, providers, associates, and contractual partners. Inform them of the security audit practice and management support to enforce it, but do not reveal the details of the audits themselves (e.g., trigger points, timing, scope, and frequency). Include this focused training in orientation for all new employees.

Signed confidentiality statements are a mechanism of documentation showing completion of training and employee commitment to comply with expectations. Consider initiating these with completion of the initial privacy and security training and renewing the signature commitment each year. Some organizations find annual appraisal intervals to be the most consistent. Warning statements placed on network and application sign-on screens help ensure top-of-mind awareness of monitoring and audit practices for the workforce and physicians.

Evaluating Findings

It is recommended that organizations work through management staff for deciphering pertinent report results. As department and unit leaders, they know the job functions of their staff and, in some cases, can quickly discern need for further investigation. Formation of a computer incident response team can be very beneficial in the investigation of abnormal audit findings. This team may be the same as the confidentiality team mentioned earlier. Significant involvement of the security officer is recommended for focused and consistent handling of all aberrant activity.

Be thorough in your investigation. As appropriate, get human resources, risk management, and legal counsel involved before confronting an individual. Even after all likely factors are exhausted, an individual may have good reason for out-of-the-ordinary access; treat the questioning as an inquiry, rather than interrogation. Consistency in application of policy is critical. Making exceptions can be dangerous, both for maintaining workforce trust and in legal defense. Provide for a graduated penalty process so that the punishment fits the crime. Policy should not be so rigid that it does not allow flexibility in taking action against breach activity.

The idea that individual behavior may be altered when individuals know they are being monitored, known in research circles as the Hawthorne effect, can be valuable. For example, if an employee becomes a patient of the hospital in which he or she works, hospital policy may allow the employee to request an audit trail of access to his or her PHI. If this is feasible within the system, existence of the policy may discourage employees from looking at the medical information of their coworkers.

Reporting Findings

Security audits constitute a monitoring practice that lends itself to performance improvement for responsibilities with high-risk potential. Security audit activities can be appropriately tied to quality-improvement reporting for executive-level involvement all the way to the board of directors.

Protecting and Retaining Audit Logs

To demonstrate compliance with HIPAA regulations, it is important to institute an audit protection and retention policy. These reports detail any findings and demonstrate regulatory compliance.

Consider these important elements in creating your plan:

- Storing audit logs and records on a server separate from the system that generated the audit trail

- Restricting access to audit logs to prevent tampering or altering of audit data

- Retaining audit trails for network activity and application activity based on a schedule determined jointly by IS and department or unit leadership

Know your state's statute of limitations relative to discoverability. Should you need to take disciplinary action against an employee or contracted agent, these records will also allow the facility to demonstrate consistent disciplinary action and policy enforcement.

Audit information may also be useful as forensic data during investigations of security incidents and breaches to patient privacy. A structured audit process—with strong controls, oversight, document protections, and appropriate record retention policies and procedures—will ensure that audit findings stand up to challenges of accuracy and validity.

References

Borten, Kate. "Using an Audit Facility to Protect Patient Data at the Massachusetts General Hospital." Presented at *Toward an Electronic Patient Record,* 1995.

Derhak, Mike. "Uncovering the Enemy Within: Utilizing Incident Response, Forensics." *In Confidence* 11, no. 9 (2003).

Henenberg, Joel. "Developing a Computer Incident Response Team." *In Confidence* 7, no. 5 (1999).

Joint Commission on Accreditation of Healthcare Organizations. *2004 Accreditation Standards for Hospitals.* Oakbrook Terrace, IL.

Jones, Russell L. "The Internet and Healthcare Information Systems: How Safe Will Patient Data Be?" *Information Systems Control Journal* 1 (1998).

Mead, Kevin. "An Internal Audit Model for Information Security." *In Confidence* 8, no. 4 (2000).

O'Donnell, Charles P. "Constructing Effective Audit Trails." *In Confidence* 7, no. 4 (1999).

Rhodes, Harry. "Physician Peer Review: A Response to Confidentiality Breaches." *In Confidence* 7, no. 4 (1999).

Security Standards Final Rule. 45 CFR Parts 160, 162, 164. *Federal Register* 68, no. 34 (February 20, 2003).

HIPAA and the EHR: Making Technical Safeguard Changes

Joseph Fodor

As electronic health records (EHRs) become more commonplace in healthcare, changes, adjustments, and improvements will be inevitable. When designing, implementing, upgrading, or remediating an EHR system, your organization's implementation team should consider the impact of complying with the HIPAA security rule by April 2005.

The HIPAA security standards apply to electronic protected health information (PHI) as it relates to health plans, healthcare clearinghouses, and healthcare providers that transmit any health information in electronic form in connection with a HIPAA-covered transaction. This article will explore what your organization should consider when making system changes to be in compliance with HIPAA security technical safeguards.

Understanding Standards and Safeguards

HIPAA security standards address the confidentiality, integrity, and availability of electronic PHI in three main categories—administrative, physical, and technical. This discussion is limited to the technical safeguards as they relate to the EHR. Defined in the technical safeguards are standards that in most cases have associated implementation specifications, some of which are required and others that are addressable. Addressable implementation specifications are to be implemented if they are deemed reasonable and appropriate. Those standards that do not have an associated implementation specification are by default required.

Technical safeguards include:

- Access to electronic PHI (accessing information through unique user identifications and controlling system access)

- Monitoring or auditing access

- Helping to ensure data integrity and detecting any alteration or destruction of electronic PHI

- Authentication (identity confirmation for individuals and entities)

- Monitoring the transmission of electronic PHI over an open network

Source: Fodor, Joseph. "HIPAA and the EHR: Making Technical Safeguard Changes." *Journal of AHIMA* 75, no. 1 (January 2004): 54–55.

Of the technical safeguards, audit controls and authentication are two standards that do not have associated implementation specifications, but they must be implemented.

Determining Policies and Procedures

Access control policies and procedures must exist over the EHR. There must be a policy that addresses the minimum amount of information necessary for an individual to perform his or her job, and a procedure must be in place to grant that access. For instance, a manager should authorize and approve role-based access to the EHR according to appropriately approved and documented policies.

A provision needs to be made for identifying and tracking activity by user via a unique user name or number. This is addressed by login name into the EHR, which is generally six to ten alphanumeric characters, a combination of the user's first and last name, or a less meaningful combination of characters and numbers. The benefit of using the user's name when performing a review of the audit logs is that it makes it easier to quickly identify which user accessed which data. The risk to using a name is that it may be easier to guess that user's password and thereby circumvent security.

Procedures must exist to verify that a person or entity seeking access to electronic PHI is who he or she claims to be. This verification typically takes the form of a unique user ID and password. EHR systems must provide for audit logging controls that record and examine activity of the use of electronic PHI. Additionally, there must be procedures for obtaining necessary electronic PHI during an emergency. With regard to EHR systems the significance is clear. If the system is not available, patient care could suffer. In light of events like power outages or terrorist attacks, it is imperative that contingencies exist for these types of events as well as hard drive and network failures.

Several addressable implementation specifications such as automatic logoff, encryption, and decryption are highly dependent on the EHR systems that have been deployed and the location of the workstations that access the EHR. For instance, a security executive may determine that a terminal located in an emergency room may be set to automatically log off after a greater period of time or not at all, as opposed to a workstation in a less critical patient care area that is set to lock out a user after a shorter period of inactivity.

Evaluating Specifications

There are two encryption and decryption specifications. One is relevant for electronic PHI at rest or data stored on a device. Examples may include workstations, tablet PCs, personal PCs, personal digital assistants (PDAs), or other enablers of EHR technologies.

The other encryption specification addresses data as it is being transmitted. Encryption methods are usually deployed for data that is transmitted wirelessly or remotely, but encryption is not likely if the data is transmitted across a local area network (LAN) or stored on a device. Management must evaluate whether LAN traffic should be encrypted, whether policies should exist restricting the storage of electronic PHI on various devices, and whether encryption technologies should be implemented for portable terminals, laptops, or PDAs.

Another set of addressable implementation specifications includes integrity controls over stored and transmitted electronic PHI. With respect to stored data, mechanisms should be in place to corroborate that electronic PHI has not been altered or destroyed in an unauthorized manner. For transmitted data, measures should ensure that this data is not improperly modified without detection. The EHR system may be capable of tracking all changes made to the electronic PHI. Addressing the transmission encryption specification will go a long way toward mitigating the risk that electronically transmitted PHI is improperly modified.

Technical safeguards defined within the final HIPAA security rule must be addressed as they relate to EHR systems. The covered entity must ensure the confidentiality, integrity, and availability of the EHR. In addition, covered entities should protect this information against any reasonably anticipated threats or hazards to the security or integrity of the data, protect it against any reasonably anticipated uses or disclosures that are not permitted, and ensure that its work force is in compliance with the regulations. With appropriate planning and execution an entity can comply with the HIPAA security regulations and help contribute to effective patient care.

Finding Quality HIPAA Security Resources

Margret Amatayakul, MBA, RHIA, CHPS, FHIM

Many of us struggled to understand the HIPAA privacy rule and initially had few resources to turn to for help. As your organization begins planning for security rule compliance, however, many of you may be finding that you're overwhelmed with the volume of potential resources available.

Virtually every vendor that sells anything related to information security is attempting to sell products or provide giveaways that can help your organization comply with HIPAA security requirements. While many vendors offer valuable information and certainly many good products, it may be helpful to cast your net a bit wider when looking for security resources. This article offers suggestions on how to find quality resources to help your organization prepare for security rule compliance.

Sorting through Freebies

There are many free resources available on the Web, at trade shows, in trade journals, or presented as advertisements in the mail. Do not discard these resources, as many of them can be valuable. You just need to know how they can be of value to you.

Web Resources

If you want to understand a security concept, the Internet can be an excellent source of information. But be careful—you will need to filter your surfing. Look for "white papers," "models," or actual documents in the descriptions of resources. Also look at the source—generally if a resource is from a university, professional or trade association, or from a covered entity directly, it can be reliable. However, be sure to review the document's date—you'll be surprised how many documents are several years old.

You will want to review several documents on the same topic, as you will also be surprised at the variability of interpretations, even from reputable sources. Vendors will also offer white papers, and many can be enlightening, but you may have to register with the site to view the document (which means you may get a marketing e-mail or call from the vendor). When you review white papers you will also need to mentally filter out what is related to the vendor's

Source: Amatayakul, Margret. "Finding Quality HIPAA Security Resources." *Journal of AHIMA* 75, no. 1 (January 2004): 58–59.

product versus what is just generic information. You may be tempted by various freeware or shareware, but you should never download anything that is executable without checking with your organization's IT department first.

Professional and Trade Association Offerings

Though you may obtain free material from professional and trade associations on the Web, these resources are somewhat different than those obtained through idle Internet surfing. Typically, these sponsors can provide best practices by benchmarking their members or subscribers, offering product comparisons, and providing an interpretation of security concepts applicable to their target audience.

To find associations and publications applicable to security, search the Web using the HIPAA security standards as key words. For example, if you look for "disaster recovery" you will find *Disaster Recovery Journal,* a quarterly publication for contingency planners. Several association Web sites include excellent glossaries and references to textbooks.

To Spend or Not to Spend

Not surprisingly, there are plenty of sources that come at a cost. Some of the Web sites you visit sell policy and procedure templates, document generators, and other products. Unless you have exhausted all other resources, however, you may want to hold off on spending.

Some security resources are standards or guidelines from standards development organizations for which a small fee is charged. As long as the organization is reputable, preferably accredited by the American National Standards Institute (ANSI), you may want to consider paying for these resources, as they typically go to support the work of the organization.

Help from the Government

NIST Resources

The National Institute of Standards and Technology (NIST) is part of the US Department of Commerce. It is responsible for developing standards and guidelines in support of government computing systems. Its security documents are many, varied, and generally easy to read. In addition to their narrative content, these documents include illustrations, glossaries of terms, references to additional resources, and model documents.

Three NIST documents are specifically referenced in the preamble to the HIPAA security rule, so you should feel comfortable using NIST's documents as resources. However, you should also be aware that the documents are written for government agencies, not HIPAA covered entities. You will need to adapt them to the healthcare environment in which you work.

Most of the NIST documents applicable to HIPAA security come from its Computer Security Resource Center Special Publications 800 series. To view a full list, visit http://csrc.nist.gov/publications/nistpubs. The following are some resources that may be especially helpful for your HIPAA compliance activities:

SP 800-64   "Security Considerations in the Information System Development Life Cycle" (October 2003) describes how to incorporate security into all phases of systems acquisition, through use to disposal.

SP 800-50 "Building an Information Technology Security Awareness and Training Program" (October 2003) is an excellent resource to help you comply with section 164.308(a)(5). Note that the earlier SP 800-16, "Information Technology Security Training Requirements" (April 1998), is referenced in the HIPAA security rule preamble. SP 800-50 complements and expands on the earlier work.

SP 800-34 "Contingency Planning Guide for Information Technology Systems" (June 2002) will help you understand disaster recovery and emergency mode operations plans for compliance with section 164.308(a)(7).

SP 800-33 "Underlying Technical Models for Information Technology Security" (December 2001) was referenced in the HIPAA security rule and is useful for understanding various technical controls, especially audit controls.

SP 800-30 "Risk Management Guide for Information Technology Systems" (January 2002) will help you conduct your risk analysis in compliance with section 164.308(a)(1).

SP 800-26 "Security Self-Assessment Guide for Information Technology" (November 2001) provides a tool to use in identifying vulnerabilities as part of your risk analysis.

SP 800-14 "Generally Accepted Principles and Practices for Securing Information Technology Systems" (September 1996) is a fairly old reference, but it is also referenced in the HIPAA security rule preamble and is considered a classic for understanding an overall framework for information security.

In addition to these references, the SP 800 series also provides standards and guidelines on specific technical topics such as wireless networks, telecommuting, e-mail, network security testing, firewalls, handling security patches, PKI, intrusion detection systems, and more.

CMS Resources

Although they are not referenced in HIPAA, the Centers for Medicare and Medicaid Services (CMS) provides a number of very useful documents on its IT Web page at http://cms.hhs.gov/it/security/References/ps.asp. These documents are primarily policies for CMS's Automated Information Systems Security Program or for its business partners and contractors, but, with some adaptation, they are very relevant to HIPAA security. Because CMS is responsible for security rule enforcement, its interpretation of the security rule may be influenced by its own documents. Of particular interest are the following:

- "CMS Internet Security Policy"
- "CMS Threat Identification Resource"
- "CMS Information Security Risk Assessment Methodology"
- "CMS System Security Plans Methodology"

International Standards and Open-Source Materials

Another resource that might be helpful for benchmarking specific controls is the International Standard ISO/IEC 17799, "Information Technology—Code of Practice for Information Security

Management" 2000. The International Organization for Standardization and the International Electrotechnical Commission develop international standards, and the ISO/IEC 17799 provides recommendations for controls associated with most of the HIPAA security rule standards. In the US, the document is available from ANSI (www.ansi.org) for a processing fee.

While you are looking for security resources, you may also find what are called "open-source" software or methodologies. An example is the "Open-Source Security Testing Methodology Manual," copyrighted by Peter Vincent Herzog and available for free dissemination under the GNU General Public License (visit www.isecom.org/projects/osstmm.htm for more information).

While open source may be most closely associated with the Linux operating system, it has come to mean any software or methodology that is licensed for free distribution. The purpose of the license is to protect the integrity of the original work. Open-source material may be developed through a group consensus, individual, or other process.

If you find a resource you like online, bookmark the URL and consider saving the document (and catalog it). Many of the materials available on the Web disappear or are updated rapidly—make sure you're not missing any valuable information.

Moving toward a Unified Information Security Program

Michael Ruano, CHS

Is your organization up to the challenge of creating a unified information security program?

A unified information security program has been all but mandated for healthcare organizations by the federal government. HIPAA requires that electronic, paper, and oral patient identifiable information be protected to a prescribed minimum level. This regulation also calls for the creation of formal responsibility for these protections.

Prior to this legislation, healthcare organizations protected information through various mechanisms and many separate departments. These departments commonly created and policed their own security standards in relative autonomy. Now, HIPAA provides the challenge of gathering up these parts into a single system for the management of information security. This article presents guidance to help your organization navigate this challenge.

Up to the Challenge

Each department (such as HIM, information management services, human resources, compliance, and others) has already created a section of what must be coordinated. One critical success factor is effective communication among different departments. By now, you should have already started the process of pulling together all critical departments and processes into one newly coordinated information security management process. This is no simple task, especially within a defined time frame.

There will be issues to resolve concerning guidelines, incident response, and sanctions. Much discussion is needed to create workable new processes, as departments will have already developed their own processes concerning these issues. All departments must participate in discussions to reach a consensus on these issues.

Necessary Guidelines

Guidelines will be required to set an organization's internal standards for incident response, sanctions, and many other day-to-day operations affected by the HIPAA regulations. To provide

Source: Ruano, Michael. "Moving toward a Unified Information Security Program." *Journal of AHIMA* 74, no. 1 (2003): 66, 68.

direction and define intent, high-level guidelines should be developed before detailed procedures are developed. This will allow the creation of focused and consistent policies and procedures for both incident response and sanctions.

Examples of the types of guidelines that will be required are defining what information is within the organization and developing a categorization scheme of its criticality to the organization. A definition of information security incidents and the response to these incidents according to information criticality levels is also needed. Based on high-level statements for these issues, the creation of appropriate and consistent policies and procedures becomes much easier to accomplish.

Preparing an Incident Response System

Information security incidents that involve computers, networks, and other technical aspects of the organization may already be reported through the information management services department and might be the easiest to discover and document. Incidents that involve employees and medical staff will usually be reported to the human resources department or medical staff office. In these situations, notification of other departments and managers outside of human resources or the medical staff office may be minimal.

Current communications mechanisms were most likely developed from existing need-to-know standards. The list of those with a need to know must now include those individuals named responsible for privacy and security as required by HIPAA. They may be reluctant at first to share information concerning personnel with other departments or areas, including the new information security function.

HIPAA requires a formally documented process for incident response and damage mitigation. This must include the notification of the privacy and security officers when an information security incident occurs. HIPAA requires the officers to be responsible for the management of personnel in relation to privacy and security mandates. At a minimum, this will mean the input from the security officer on the new incident process as well as routine reporting of incidents to them for auditing and process improvement. At the maximum, the security officer will be involved actively in the incident response process and may in fact act independently of other areas in these situations.

Sorting Out Sanctions

Sanction policies and processes related to information security incidents will need to be reviewed and made cross relational, meaning they need to be consistent with HIPAA regulations, with existing and newly HIPAA-required organizational policy, and with each other. These new sanction policies and processes will need to be formally documented and applied consistently.

They will apply to all personnel as well as to external organizations that may have access to the covered entity's facilities, information processes and systems, and information. In certain instances, coordination with other departments may become necessary, as is the case with incident response processes. These instances will include the participation of the security officer in the guideline and process redesigns required to comply with the regulations. There will also be additional issues to resolve with the legal department and other areas that are responsible for contracts with business associates, as sanctions are also necessary in some of these situations.

The sanctions put in place may vary from what each organization has in place today. It will be imperative to make every effort to educate all staff, business associates, and others regarding expectations of the organization regarding sanctions. If successful, this education will probably be the best and most cost-effective method of reducing the likelihood of personnel-related information security incidents.

Communication Is Key

In response to HIPAA regulations, healthcare organizations are challenged to create a single view for the management of information security. The HIM department and others will have to resolve issues concerning guidelines, incident response, and sanctions. Only through effective communications can these issues be resolved within these short time frames.

Final Security Regulations Present Challenges, Opportunities for HIM

Dan Rode, MBA, FHFMA

With the release of the final HIPAA security regulations in February, HIM has taken yet another step toward the transition from paper to the electronic health record (EHR). This article discusses key areas of security compliance and how your organization can be prepared.

When PHI Goes Electronic

Electronic protected health information (PHI), essentially defined as PHI in an electronic medium or transaction, becomes the key focus under the security rule. An organization's efforts to meet the requirements for PHI are the basis for the protection of electronic versions of PHI.

The rule underscores the HIM professional's role in moving the industry to the EHR by establishing standards by which organizations must address administrative, technical, and physical aspects of electronic PHI. It reinforces the idea that electronic PHI security is an administrative activity, not an information technology activity. It recognizes, however, that information technology will be part of the resources used to meet the obligations HIPAA creates for the organization.

The rule also requires that an organization not only address the confidentiality of electronic PHI but also take steps to assess risks and protect the availability and integrity of health records through the implementation of risk assessment, policies, procedures, and training. The industry's concurrent moves toward the EHR and a national health information infrastructure will make these activities even more critical.

Taking the Lead

HIM professionals have the challenge and the opportunity to take the lead not only in implementing the EHR, but also in ensuring ongoing confidentiality and security of the EHR and electronic PHI. The rule also gives guidance in the latter process that is useful today, even though the deadline for compliance is 2005.

Source: Rode, Dan. "Final Security Regulations Present Challenges, Opportunities for HIM." *Journal of AHIMA* 74, no. 5 (May 2003): 14ff.

For example, the rule says an organization must:

- Ensure the confidentiality, integrity, and availability of all electronic PHI it creates, receives, maintains, or transmits

- Protect against any reasonably anticipated threats or hazards to the security or integrity of such information

- Protect against any reasonably anticipated uses or disclosures of such information that are not permitted under the privacy rule

- Ensure compliance by the organization's work force

There are 18 standards, and each has implementation specifications that are required or could be addressed. Like the privacy rule, the security rule provides for a flexible approach. The standards take into account that no two covered entities are alike, nor are they on the same timetable for EHR implementation. But all entities must understand, address, and respond to the issues appropriately based on their environment, situation, and resources.

Dealing with Designated Record Sets

As the profession addressed the privacy rule and PHI, we had to take into account an organization's "designated record sets" that contain PHI. One of the challenges of privacy rule implementation is that paper and electronic records are often used all over an organization. For example, there may be electronic PHI in diagnostic areas, electronic claims in patient accounting or billing, and paper records as well. Conversion to the EHR will be paralleled by conversions in other systems within an organization. Organizations will need to address not only what goes out of the EHR but where incoming information comes from and where it is going.

The security rule calls for "administrative safeguards," and the Department of Health and Human Services (HHS) indicates that covered entities must implement policies and procedures to prevent, detect, contain, and correct security violations. This involves an organization's risk analysis, risk management, sanctions, and information system review activities. HHS not only suggests that these should be among the first steps of the organization's security rule implementation, but also suggests that this be an ongoing process, especially as the industry becomes more electronically based.

The rule also calls for a security official who is responsible for development and implementation of the policies and procedures required by the security rule. This individual ideally should be the organization's privacy officer—a perfect role for an HIM professional.

Training: A Familiar Refrain

The rule's call for work force security training also resembles the requirements established for privacy. It includes initial and ongoing training of the entire work force, including senior management, as well as sanctions for those who do not abide by policies and procedures related to the rule. Covered entities are to include security reminders as part of their compliance processes.

Like the privacy rule's concept of "minimum necessary," the security rule addresses information access as a standard. While the implementation specifications are addressable, meaning the covered entity must assess whether the standard is reasonable and appropriate for the entity and would contribute to the protection of electronic PHI, this section directly affects anyone with access to electronic PHI. In addition to the limitations surrounding access, the security rule also requires the monitoring of log-ins and password management, along with some response to security incidents.

The security rule also addresses the security of data from the perspective of having it available when it is needed and ensuring data integrity—clear requirements of any record system. The rule provides a contingency plan requirement and calls for three plans:

- A data back-up plan

- A disaster recovery plan

- An emergency mode operation plan

These requirements should be part of every organization's disaster plan, whether records are paper or electronic.

Technical Expertise Is Key

In the electronic environment, many of these activities will call for technical options. Organizations will need to have the technical knowledge internally, use the technical knowledge available within the organization (usually a function of the information technology department), or purchase the knowledge elsewhere. At a minimum, HIM professionals must have basic information system knowledge in order to request support or determine options for resource consulting or purchase. This same knowledge is also needed for EHR implementation.

The security rule also calls for a number of "technical safeguards." The extent to which an organization will have to address these requirements is directly proportional to the degree of electronic systems and data it possesses. User IDs, emergency access procedures, automatic log-off, encryption and decryption, audit controls, integrity, electronic authentication, and transmission security should be addressed. The more "electronic" an organization is, the better the chance that technology expertise and resources are already available to the implementation team.

Physical Security in a PDA World

There are also requirements covering physical security and organizational items such as adding language to business associate agreements to cover security. Physical security covers looking at contingency operations, security plans for physical access, tampering, and theft, access controls, including "visitors" (including the potential for patient access to EHR), and maintenance of records. Workstation security is key—not only for desktop computers and central systems but laptops and PDAs as well.

The surge in the use of laptops and PDAs containing electronic PHI will be a challenge for a variety of healthcare entities, especially those that provide care in patients' homes or outside the organization. This will call for technical security to prevent inappropriate access and medical record policies regarding information outside the traditional system or record.

What Comes First?

First, it is important to thoroughly read the security rule. AHIMA has also provided an analysis on the rule available online at www.ahima.org/dc. More materials will be forthcoming.

Next, any purchase of information systems or technology now needs to be considered with the final security rule in mind. Organizations should not make or plan for a purchase without including pertinent information that covers the rule in a request for proposal. Any purchase should be made with compliant security components or with an agreement that the purchase will be upgraded to include all components needed to meet the security rule's provisions. Because most organizations take some time to make these purchases, it is not too early to begin your security process. This would be especially important for organizations in the process of purchasing EHR systems.

Remember, the April 21, 2005, implementation date is an "implementation by" date; there is no penalty for implementing early. (The compliance date does not apply to small health plans as defined in the HIPAA regulations.) Given that the security rule is also a good business rule, implementing early will be to the advantage of your organization.

Like any challenge, meeting the rule's requirements will take time and effort. But HIM professionals, many already on the road to the EHR, have the experience and education to promptly get on the path to compliance.

Five Principles for Protecting Information

In March, AHIMA presented an audio seminar on the security rule's impact on privacy and HIM. Speaker Bill Braithwaite, MD, PhD, a principal author of the HIPAA regulations, mentioned five "principles of fair information practices" that the HIPAA privacy and security rules follow—principles very close to tenets followed by AHIMA. These include:

- Notice: Existence and purpose of a record-keeping system must be known to the individual whose information is the subject of the record, thus the notice of privacy practices required under the HIPAA privacy regulation.

- Choice: Information is collected only with knowledge and permission of the subject and used only in ways relevant to the purpose for which the data was collected and disclosed only with permission or overriding legal authority.

- Access: The individual, the subject of the record, has the right to see the record and ensure quality of information, meaning also the requirement that the record holder maintains accurate, complete, and timely information.

- Security: Reasonable safeguards for confidentiality, integrity, and availability of information are in place.

- Enforcement: Violations of an organization's privacy and security standards or policies result in reasonable mitigation and penalties.

Translating the Language of Security

Margret Amatayakul, MBA, RHIA, CHPS, FHIMSS

There were no big surprises in the final security rule. As promised, it has been reconciled with the privacy rule and most redundancies were removed. The security rule addresses only electronic protected health information (ePHI), though we must not forget the privacy rule's "minisecurity rule" (the requirement for administrative, physical, and technical safeguards to protect the privacy of protected health information) (Sec. 164.530[c][1]).

The final security rule emphasizes risk analysis to determine how to address the requirements. Possibly the only surprise is the "required" and "addressable" designations for implementation specifications. This treatment of how to implement the standards provides even more scalability, flexibility, and technical neutrality than the proposed rule. Coupled with the fact that the term "reasonable" appears 57 times throughout the 49 pages of preamble and standard, the final rule is even less black and white than the proposed rule, something IT professionals will find even more troubling.

To develop security regulations applicable to every form of covered entity—from a small dentist office to a huge, multistate health plan—the government had to modify its primary source of information security principles (the Department of Defense) for a vastly different industry. Then it attempted to use a regulation predicated on mainframe technology, update it, and make it last for many years.

This article aims to translate parts of the final security standards into principles that may afford more definitive best practices for healthcare today.

What Does "Best" Really Mean?

The term "best practice" is a good place to start. It should be understood that "best" does not mean "most," as in most expensive or most organizations practice this way. A best practice is a way to do something that is most efficient and effective.

For example, if a hospital is having difficulty getting users to save documents to a network rather than the hard drive on their workstations, a best practice may be to name the network drive "C," which is typically the hard drive, and rename the hard drive something else.

Source: Amatayakul, Margret. "Translating the Language of Security (HIPAA on the Job series)." *Journal of AHIMA* 74, no. 6 (June 2003): 16A–D.

Get the Terms Straight

Required and Addressable

The terms *required* and *addressable* are also critical to understand. Just because they are a pair of terms does not mean that the opposite of *required* is *not required.* Addressable means that the proposed way to implement a standard needs to be evaluated for the environment. If the proposed implementation specification makes sense, it should be adopted. If there is a better alternative, the alternative should be justified and adopted. If the implementation is not applicable, this should be described.

Addressable only applies to implementation specifications. All standards are required. For example, the standard on transmission security has two implementation specifications: integrity controls and encryption, both of which are addressable. This does not mean that a covered entity does not need to secure its transmission of PHI; it just means that it needs to describe how it will implement integrity controls and encryption when transmitting PHI.

Risk Analysis and Gap Analysis

Another pair of terms to distinguish is *risk analysis* and *gap analysis.* The final rule does not use the term *gap analysis,* but many organizations conducted a gap analysis for privacy, security, and transactions when the privacy rule was published. The gap analysis identified the elements that may have been missing in the organization, such as the notice of privacy practices, audit trails for security, or a translator to create X12N transactions.

Very few organizations conducted an actual risk analysis in which each gap in security (known as a vulnerability) is evaluated in light of potential threats to determine level of risk. For example, not having an audit trail is a vulnerability. The threat is inappropriate access that is difficult to prove.

Risk is described in the final rule as a combination of the probability the threat will occur and the criticality the threat poses to the organization. (See Figure 6.6, Assessing Probability, Criticality of Potential Risks to ePHI.) Thus, the risk of not having audit trails is a violation of the regulation and the potential inability to impose sanctions for breach of confidentiality or prove that access occurred or was a violation.

A qualitative risk analysis describes probability and criticality by ratings such as high, medium, and low. This is a good way to start the process, but obviously does not provide any measure of return on investment in security controls. In an environment where budgets are tight and the rule is gray, it may be worth the effort to be more quantitative.

There are several degrees of quantification. A simple quantification might assign a numeric value to the combination of probability and criticality. This helps to prioritize remediation of risks.

A cost-based risk analysis may be calculated by estimating loss (for example, the cost of fines, a lawsuit, or public relations effort to regain consumer confidence) and comparing it to the cost of remediation (for example, purchasing a new system, recovering data, or ongoing maintenance). Such an estimate, however, does not consider the probability that the threat would occur. For example, a lawsuit may cost $1 million and remediation costs $100,000. But if the CEO believes the likelihood of a lawsuit is one in a million, then he or she could argue that any cost to remediate more than $1 is too much.

Security experts use an annualized loss expectancy calculation that factors in the probability of the threat and its criticality. This calculation must be performed with relatively accurate information for it to be worth the effort, but it provides a much more realistic picture and justification for security controls.

Figure 6.6.   Assessing probability, criticality of potential risks to ePHI

Use this matrix to determine the probability and criticality each threat imposes on a vulnerability. Multiply the probability level by the criticality level to determine your level of risk. (Example: A medium (2) probability and a medium (2) criticality would result in a 4 level of risk.) Use the level of risk to prioritize activities to mitigate the risk.

Vulnerability: _____

		Risk Level		
Probability of threat occurring at this vulnerability	**High (3):** Threat has occurred here, and/or controls are only reactive/recovery	3	6	9
	Medium (2): Threat has not occurred here, but in other similar organizations, and/or controls are deterrents	2	4	6
	Low (1): Threat has not occurred here, and rarely in other similar organizations, and/or controls are preventative	1	2	3
		Low (1): Impact is an internal annoyance, potential risk to licensure and/or compliance fines, and/or requires considerable recovery effort	**Medium (2):** Impact on consumer confidence of data could cause patient care issue or breach of confidentiality harms patient (resulting in lawsuit or civil/criminal penalties)	**High (3):** Impact on availabilty or integrity

Criticality of threat to this vulnerability

Information Access Management, Work Force Security as Complements

The information access management and work force security standards in the final rule may appear to include some redundancy and may suggest some missing elements or relaxed requirements. The standards are complementary and each has an important, unique function. Best practice suggests strengthening controls, potentially through use of a centralized suite of controls.

Information access management includes implementation specifications on authorization, establishment, and modification of access privileges. Establishing access for a new or transferred member of the work force is often less than timely and sometimes results in decentralizing the function at the department level.

Note that the duties of access authorization and establishment should be separated and taken very seriously. In fact, the issue of access may be the largest area of potential risk that the healthcare industry has not acknowledged because in the past, many information systems were not mission-critical and access controls were generally weak.

For example, a manager who authorizes Mary's access "just like" Sharon's is not taking care to ensure that Mary really needs the same access. A harried employee in IT who takes John's word for the fact that he needs his old access reinstated is succumbing to social engineering—an increasingly common technique to gain inappropriate access. Administration that does not support tighter controls is operating under the mistaken impression that security breaches won't happen at their facility.

Complementary to access authorization and establishment are work force security standards. These include authorization/supervision (a holdover from mainframe days), clearance checks (which should be done before access authorization), and termination procedures (for which managers should be held at least equally if not more accountable than for access authorization).

A Closer Look at Access Controls, Authentication

The final security rule provides an additional challenge in the removal of implementation specifications relating to types of access controls. No longer are user-based, role-based, or context-based access controls identified. Some infer, therefore, that these are not necessary. However, in keeping with the intent to make the rule timeless, these options were simply not enumerated because there are currently other forms of access controls and new forms may yet be invented. The minimum necessary use requirement in the privacy rule, however, makes it very clear that classes of workers needing access, categories of PHI to which access is needed, and conditions appropriate to such access need to be defined. Such access classes, categories, and conditions require, at a minimum, what is typically called role-based access controls, if not context-based controls.

While access controls establish the means to achieve minimum necessary use, emergency access procedures, automatic logoff, and encryption/decryption are included in this standard as well.

The rule defines emergency access procedures as "procedures for obtaining necessary ePHI during an emergency." Considering that there are emergency mode procedures under contingency planning, this definition seems either redundant or inconsistent with the commonly considered meaning of emergency access procedures as "break-the-glass" functionality. Break-the-glass (which draws its name from breaking the glass to pull a fire alarm) refers to a quick means for a person who does not have access privileges to certain information to gain access when necessary. Typically, a special audit trail is created to monitor such access.

Access controls should be established with sufficient rules to minimize the number of times break-the-glass needs to occur. That emergency mode procedures are a required implementation specification suggests that strong access controls are expected.

Automatic logoff is designated as an addressable implementation specification of access controls—so that the environment can help determine whether this is needed and the timing for which the logoff should be set. For example, automatic logoff could be set for a full day in the office of a small physician's practice that is inaccessible by the public, in comparison to a few minutes for a hospital's registration area.

Encryption/decryption is also addressable in the access control standard. The final rule supposedly does not distinguish controls for data at rest (that is, within an information system) from data en route (that is, transmitted through a network). However, there is a separate standard for transmission security with its own addressable implementation specification for encryption. This suggests that the intent is for encryption to be employed in both cases as appropriate. It is certainly greater protection than typically afforded data at rest. But perhaps this is a case of the government anticipating the future, where data in mobile computing devices should be encrypted because the device itself moves and is prone to loss.

Finally, authentication refers to the mechanism to prove the person seeking access is the one claimed. Obviously, it relates very closely to access. The healthcare industry has usually managed the various components of access separately. Best practice, however, would suggest stronger overall management and centralization. A single suite of products may be able to manage authorization, establishment, termination, and adherence to password policy. Single login, with or without biometrics, may be another suite of products to manage this process.

HIPAA Lessons Learned

This article addresses only a portion of the security controls required in the final rule. Healthcare organizations, however, should consider lessons learned from the privacy rule. Security controls are generally costlier to purchase, implement, and manage on an ongoing basis than privacy controls. The requirement for security risk analysis was placed first in the rule to emphasize its importance and prioritization. It is the key to budgeting for the rest of security and should be done well in advance of when the controls need to be implemented, tested, trained on, and revised as necessary prior to the compliance date of April 20, 2005.

Securing Executive Support for Security

Margret Amatayakul, MBA, RHIA, CHPS, FHIMSS

Many information privacy officials (IPOs) and information security officials (ISOs) may be facing what seems like an uphill battle to gain support for security measures believed to be necessary to comply with the HIPAA security rule. There are a number of converging factors that can influence executive management and a number of steps IPOs and ISOs can take to help their cause.

Executive Support

Executive support is obviously needed for the assignment of resources for a security official and budget for security controls. Some executives may think compliance with the "minisecurity rule" in the privacy rule is sufficient. They may also decide that with little evidence of privacy rule enforcement and without the occurrence of an adverse security incident that current security measures are sufficient. The key, however, is that without a risk analysis that matches threats and vulnerabilities in your environment to the actual risk executive management is willing to assume, it is impossible to determine whether current security measures are sufficient.

Executive management support is needed not only to assign the appropriate individual to the function of information security, but to:

- Define their risk position and establish a risk mitigation strategy.

- Approve security controls and understand their residual risk.

- Support ongoing security monitoring.

- Create an environment of security awareness.

External Influencers

An important business case can be made to support security by referencing the Sarbanes-Oxley Act (Public Law 107.204), but a connection may need to be made between securing electronic

Source: Amatayakul, Margret. "Securing Executive Support for Security (HIPAA on the Job Series)." *Journal of AHIMA* 75, no. 2 (February 2004): 54–155.

protected health information (EPHI) and what may be perceived as solely an accounting issue. Signed into law after the Enron and other public company accounting practice scandals, the act is controversial, only applies to publicly traded companies, and therefore directly affects only a certain segment of the healthcare industry. It requires an adequate internal control structure and procedures for financial accounting and reporting. Many industry observers, however, note that a secure information infrastructure is central to internal controls and that the act's principles will transfer to nonprofits as a standard of practice.

Another important factor for executive managers to consider is increasing risk of identity theft and other cyber crimes. These criminal acts frequently are not targeted at EPHI, but at the identity of patients, and possibly even the provider's own identity, for perpetrating other types of crimes such as writing illegal prescriptions. Many of the techniques used to carry out such crimes involve no technology or low technology and must be thwarted by continual awareness. With increasing issues surrounding health insurance and costs of drugs, heightened interest in electronic health records, and the finalization of the HIPAA National Provider Identifier expected this winter, healthcare may become an even easier target for cyber crimes in the future.

Internal Considerations

Having built a case for support, IPOs and ISOs also need to do their part. The best IPOs and ISOs will be passionate about privacy and security, but must be equally capable of using a strategic approach that is:

- Reasonable. Especially for general security professionals, it must be recognized that the traditional approach drawn from the US Department of Defense (DOD) does not work in healthcare. Some risk is unavoidable in order to provide proper healthcare to patients. In fact, recognizing that EPHI would be classified as "confidential" in the range of "top secret" to unclassified, and that systems would be rated C2 by DOD standards, may help put HIPAA security into perspective.[1] HIPAA supports a reasonable approach through its risk analysis requirement and addressable implementation specifications.

- Synergistic. There are many competing demands for executive attention and support. Coupling discussion of HIPAA security with other strategic initiatives will build awareness with executives and support integration of security. This should not diminish the importance of security, but rather it will make it an integral part of all internal control requirements. IPOs and ISOs should cultivate relationships with those responsible for other internal controls, such as in patient financial services, pharmacy, and HIM, and gather momentum for security through a well-planned and coordinated approach.

- Channeled. As much as IPOs and ISOs may want the HIPAA security rule to be on every executive's agenda, it may be necessary to work through channels within the organization. It can help to identify who or what has the most attention currently and channel security through them or their initiatives. Using corporate compliance, risk management, and an executive sponsor are also built-in channels to deploy for success.

- Documented. HIPAA requires documentation, so IPOs and ISOs should use this to their advantage. But rather than just applying documentation from the perspective of documentary evidence, documentation of threats and vulnerabilities, costs and benefits, and alternative control mechanisms may point to more cost-effective and efficient means of accomplishing the desired security. For example, if an intrusion detection system is on your "must-have" list, do the math and you may find that a more layered firewall configuration may be just as effective, with lower capital outlay and much less labor.

Pick Your Battles

There are many clichés that could apply to the position IPOs and ISOs find themselves in with respect to getting executive attention for HIPAA security rule compliance. "Pick your battles" may be apropos. Executives deal with strategy, which was originally a military term that meant the art of planning and directing large-scale military movements (e.g., a war). IPOs and ISOs deal with tactics, which, in the military sense, means the art of deploying forces and maneuvering them in battles.

In addition to providing perspective, these definitions recognize that both planning and maneuvering are art forms. IPOs and ISOs should cultivate the art of recognizing where they must be reasonable. Remember, just as the commander in chief plans the war, executives determine their risk position. While that in itself is not an easy task for healthcare executives, once defined, the IPO and ISO should rely on that as their benchmark for recommending controls—so long as the residual risk in those controls is clear.

Note

1. US Department of Defense. "Trusted Computer System Evaluation Criteria." DoD 5200.28-STD. 1985.

A Reasonable Approach to Physical Security

Margret Amatayakul, MBA, RHIA, CHPS, FHIMSS

Of all the components of HIPAA, physical security may be the most challenging and costly to address. After all, how do you move walls or create doors in open space? This article will show how physical security can be flexible, scalable, and reasonable for healthcare facilities.

What Is Physical Security?

HIPAA's proposed security rule defines physical safeguards as including assigned security responsibility, media controls, physical access controls, workstation location and use, and security awareness training. Although this may seem to be an eclectic mix of requirements, the best practice ideas and cautionary tales below will demonstrate how these items relate.

Who Will Be Responsible?

Many organizations have not yet designated an information security official, partly because the rule has not been finalized, but also because many are trying to decide to whom that responsibility should be assigned. Candidates include the physical plant's security officer, safety officer, information systems analyst, HIM professional, chief information officer, and many others. In short, there is no one "right" person, and in fact, the right person is likely to vary from organization to organization and even over time within an organization.

As you consider candidates, ask who most people turn to when concerned about security. The answer is probably the facility's current security officer. Security officers are highly trained in security awareness and gathering evidence, which makes them excellent in identifying potential incidents and their causes and avoiding future incidents. Security personnel are also upgrading their training in electronic security systems, including thwarting computer hackers and managing physical barriers to wireless data transmission.

Regardless of the choice for information security official, he or she should not work in a vacuum. A team of individuals with a variety of knowledge and skills should work together with the information security official as point person.

Source: Amatayakul, Margret. "A Reasonable Approach to Physical Security (HIPAA on the Job series)." *Journal of AHIMA* 73, no. 4 (2002): 16A–C.

A Closer Look at Media Controls

The HIPAA requirements for managing media controls include access controls, accountability, back-up, storage, and disposal.

Access controls on media can refer to many things. The proposed security rule does not provide much detail, but many have interpreted this to include protecting fax transmissions, verifying who has print and local save capability on computers, and determining who has access to file rooms, data centers, back-up tape vaults, and even portable devices (such as personal computers and personal digital assistants).[1] Many facilities are removing floppy, CD, and even hard drives from workstations. When acquiring new workstations, facilities are buying "thin clients" for most users, which are essentially stripped-down workstations that serve as "dumb terminals."

Accountability is defined by HIPAA as the "property that ensures that the actions of an entity can be traced uniquely to that entity." In its purest form, accountability would require biometric identification for physical access. Today, however, entities can improve signage to provide greater awareness of confidentiality needs, adopt sign-in sheets for visitors to non-public areas, escort visitors, supervise maintenance personnel, keep logs of when locks are changed, and use swipe cards to track personnel entrance and exit.

The physical security section also highlights the need for safeguarding back-ups. The healthcare industry has never considered backing up its paper-based medical records, although some portions are stored in electronic form and copies of some documents that are routinely distributed to physician offices may not be accessible in the event of a disaster. Extra environmental precautions are required by the Joint Commission on Accreditation of Healthcare Organizations and other licensing and accrediting agencies, although satellite file areas and warehouses for older records do not always get the same attention. It is not uncommon for these file areas to be used for numerous other storage and functional needs, including housing utility meters accessible directly by workers and storage for everything from old beds to food.

Back-up details for electronic information should be spelled out in a back-up plan (referenced in the administrative section of the security rule). These plans should identify what is backed up (i.e., protected health information [PHI], the application software, other information), the frequency of the back-up process, on what media the back-ups are stored, how they are tested, and where they are stored.

PHI, obviously, should be backed up. In small offices or for departmental systems, however, it is important to ensure that any components of the operating system that change as data are processed are also backed up. A copy of the application software may be available through the vendor, but not if the software has been customized by the provider.

It is prudent to back up PHI at least daily and essential applications should have redundant or mirrored systems that perform continuous back-up. A frequent error is the lack of routine back-up system testing. Error-check programs can ensure the integrity of the back-up, but full restoration testing should also be performed. Finally, it is not uncommon to find that back-ups for stand-alone systems are often stored right beside the system itself. While this is adequate when the goal is only to protect against system failure, the systems can be easily lost or stolen and do not, therefore, safeguard confidentiality.

In addition to storing back-ups, all PHI storage is included in the physical security requirement. Healthcare facilities are cautioned that the weakest link in securing health information is often not in the file area, data center, or even warehouse, but in storage of shadow records, stand-alone servers, individual databases, copies, preliminary reports, drafts, worksheets, and other documents that are not a part of the official medical record but still contain health information.

Safe disposal is also a critical step in the physical security process. Many organizations have begun using a shredder service. This is a good practice, but only if everyone follows the shredding program faithfully. There may be confusion about the containers for PHI and for recycling.

Because most paper discarded in a healthcare facility contains individually identifiable health information, it may be easier to simply focus on shredding everything but Styrofoam, cans, and bottles. Check with the shredding service vendor to determine what other materials can be shredded, such as labels, IV bags, and plastic medicine vials. (Incineration, in which steam from the process is recycled, is an alternative to shredding.)

Finally, all steps in the shredding process need to be protected. Overflowing shred boxes, unsecured shred bins, and bags of material waiting to be shredded need as much security as the shredding itself.

How to Control Physical Access

Physical access controls refer to having appropriate safeguards wherever PHI may be used or stored. Locked doors are an obvious solution. Most healthcare facilities have very open campuses in which multiple external doors are locked only at night. Some facilities are looking to the hotel industry or other more security-conscious businesses as models for maintaining employee entrances, guard services, camera monitoring of entrances, and more.

Internal doors also require scrutiny. Evaluate the HIM department's proximity to a photocopier, fax, public areas, or even other departments. Security can be compromised by a back door to a file room or space shared with another department.

In one facility, the HIM department shared space with a social services department that reported to a different executive and had very different policies for allowing visitors. Such visitors included family members and friends of staff and posed a vulnerability for the HIM department.

Or, recall the case in a Florida hospital in which an HIM staff member's child changed HIV test results that were mailed to patients and one patient who received an altered result attempted suicide.

Other areas to watch are entrances with the physicians' dictation area, unlocked file cabinets of old explanation of benefits forms in the reception area of the billing office, shadow records stored near an elevator and out of a staff member's line of sight, or any other potential physical access vulnerabilities.

Sometimes we may be so familiar with the current physical plan that it is difficult to recognize that greater physical access controls are needed. One way to see the forest for the trees is to tour the facility while checking each door for public access, standard lock, and secure lock requirements.

Although termination procedures are included in the security rule's administrative requirements, facilities should keep in mind that voluntary terminations are not always "friendly," and that such employees who know about lax security practices pose a threat. Conduct a physical inventory of doors to determine how frequently locks are changed and confirm that they are always changed whenever an employee leaves.

HIPAA's View of Workstation Use and Location

Workstations should be positioned away from public view or screened so that casual observers cannot view the contents displayed on a monitor. Workstation location could also be interpreted in light of the privacy rule's requirements for confidential communications and include any location where "work" takes place and working papers are in public view, such as sign-in sheets, schedules, white boards, chart racks and chart boxes, and even locations where shift reports or rounds are conducted. Reexamining workstation location may lead to installing staff elevators where patients can be transported away from visitors and protection such as walls or partitions between examining rooms or bed rooms.

The privacy rule's guidelines have provided information that recognizes that reasonable approaches to such work location issues need to be taken. A hospital cannot be expected to convert to all private rooms. Communications should not be impeded by requiring rounds to be held in a conference room away from access by nursing personnel. But awareness of one's surroundings should be considered when PHI is used or disclosed in the course of treatment, payment, and operations.

Some good sources to consider as models for all areas of the healthcare facility include the added protections afforded psychiatric services, and more recently, obstetric and newborn areas. Attention to safeguarding information affects not only the confidentiality of health information but patient care as well. For example, a pediatrician conducting rounds stopped in front of a pre-teen patient's room. The pediatrician had not finished discussing the previous patient's case and proceeded to describe the gravity of the illness and some alternative surgical approaches. Because the door to the preteen patient's room was ajar, the entire conversation was overheard, personalized, and caused the young patient to become very distraught. The situation could have been avoided first by completing the discussion away from the different patient and, second, by simply closing the door.

Workstation use refers to procedures for functions associated with one's workstation. The proposed security rule uses the example of instructing users to always log off a workstation when leaving it unattended. While this is important and should be done any time the user will be away for an extended period of time or a different user will be using the workstation, the busy environment of most healthcare facilities may make this difficult to achieve. Instead, it may be appropriate to implement automatic log off (also required under HIPAA) set to a relatively short period of time.

Some other functions to consider include the access workstations afford to the network, back office applications, and the Internet. If employees have Internet access, proper use of the Internet should be included in the instructions for proper workstation use. Create a policy on introducing foreign software on a workstation, downloading executable files, uploading documents/creating attachments, and which Internet sites may be banned if there are no site or keyword filters at the firewall. One of the purposes of awareness training and a role for the information security official may be to randomly check computers for downloaded screensavers as a clue that employees may be using the Internet improperly.

Training: Make It Creative

Finally, physical security is very much about being aware of one's surroundings. Who can overhear conversations about PHI? Who can see identifying data? What information is accessible to those without clearance?

Security awareness training needs to be simple, random, targeted, and varied. It should fit the culture of the organization and the needs of current security issues. Signage reminding employees that "the walls have ears" may be ineffective if not varied over time. In fact, most organizations find such signs unsightly and prohibit them. More subtle, but equally powerful, opportunities exist. Creativity is required in building a security campaign that is effective and efficient.

Note

1. AHIMA's practice brief, "Facsimile Transmission of Health Information (Updated)" is an excellent resource for creating a fax protection policy. It can be found in the June 2001 *Journal of AHIMA* (vol. 72, no. 6) or online in the FORE Library: HIM Body of Knowledge.

Part 7

Securing the Superhighway

An IT Contingency Plan to Meet HIPAA Security Standards

Sandra Nutten
Chris Mansueti

HIPAA security standards require your organization to have a contingency plan. Here's the how-to for a plan that measures up.

The final rule for HIPAA security standards, published in the *Federal Register* on February 20, 2003, clearly states that a covered entity must protect the integrity, confidentiality, and availability of electronic protected health information (PHI). With the compliance dates on the horizon, this article explains how HIM staff can develop, maintain, and test a contingency plan to meet the security standards.

The One-minute HIPAA Security Pretest

1. What is your deadline for complying with HIPAA's security standards?

2. Why do you need a contingency plan for HIPAA security?

3. Who is responsible for making sure that your entity is in compliance with the security standards?

4. Where is your contingency plan—physically, where is it?

5. When do you invoke the contingency plan?

6. How do you prove that your contingency plan will work?

Kudos to anyone who can answer all six questions right now in 10 seconds or less. Most of us, however, are in the planning stage of HIPAA security compliance and may only have the answers to the first three questions.

By April 21, 2006, if you are a small health plan (under HIPAA, a plan with annual receipts of $5 million or less), or by April 21, 2005, for all other covered entities, you should know the answers to all six questions.

Source: Nutten, Sandra, and Chris Mansueti. "An IT Contingency Plan to Meet HIPAA Security Standards." *Journal of AHIMA* 75, no. 2 (February 2004): 30–37.

The Contingency Planning Process

The Centers for Medicare and Medicaid Services (CMS) define a contingency plan as "an alternate way of doing business when established routines are disrupted." CMS offers the following seven steps as general guidelines for creating that plan: (1) assess your situation, (2) identify risks, (3) formulate an action plan, (4) decide if and when to activate your plan, (5) communicate the plan, (6) test your plan, and (7) treat your contingency plan as an evolving process.[1]

In addition to planning against disruptions in routines, healthcare entities are required to develop a HIPAA security contingency plan in the event of a security breach that jeopardizes PHI. HIPAA security standards require covered entities to "ensure the confidentiality, integrity, and availability of all electronic protected health information the covered entity creates, receives, maintains, or transmits" (§164.306(a)) and to "protect against any reasonably anticipated threats or hazards to the security or integrity of such information" (§164.306(a)).

But HIPAA regulations specifically direct healthcare entities to develop and implement a number of safeguards that are categorized according to operational focus areas. References to contingency planning and contingency operations can be found in the sections on administrative safeguards (§164.308) and physical safeguards (§164.310). While there is no mention of contingency planning in the section covering technical safeguards (§164.312), it is this section that provides the standards that actually provide the secure environment.

Prior to HIPAA, there was no universal means with which to identify whether a healthcare business was securing information to the best of its ability. That is the crux of what HIPAA asks of healthcare providers now: secure electronic PHI to the best of their ability, within reason and without bias. Defining, documenting, and demonstrating ability, reason, and nonbiased approach to electronic health information security is the cornerstone of HIPAA compliance.

The following HIPAA security contingency planning process has six fundamental components, usually taken in the following sequence:

1. Appoint members to the HIPAA security task force.

2. Name a project manager from the task force membership.

3. Establish task force protocols.

4. Identify milestone dates, working backward from your internal compliance date.

5. Define your method of analyzing risk for your entity.

6. Develop, test, and maintain the contingency plan.

Applying the principles of "define, document, and demonstrate," let's lay out the framework for the plan. Project plans can be created in very sophisticated and user-friendly software, but unless every member of the task force has mastered the application, you will find yourself wasting precious meeting time navigating the tool instead of navigating the content. A simple table or spreadsheet will suffice for initial contingency plan development. An example using the first five components of the planning process is shown in Figure 7.1, The Contingency Planning Process, Parts 1–5.

Contingency Plan Standards

As noted above, the HIPAA security standard states that a covered entity must ensure the confidentiality, integrity, and availability of electronic PHI. The standard also states that a contingency plan must be put in place and the implementation specifications of the contingency plan support one or more of the confidentiality, integrity, or availability requirements.

Figure 7.1.   The contingency planning process, parts 1–5

	Action Item	Definition	Documentation	Demonstration of Compliance
1.	Appoint task force	a. Appointments to task force by the security officer (named by the CEO and endorsed by the board) b. Appointment shall be for a duration of at least 15 months c. Appointee shall be a full-time work force member or business associate	i. E-mail request with task force member's response confirmed ii. Appointee will acknowledge time commitment in acceptance response iii. Task force appointment shall be included in job performance evaluation or business associate agreement (BAA)	Correspondence from work force participants and BAAs on file. Due Date: March 1, 2004
2.	Name project manager	a. Appointment by executive leadership or task force election	i. Project manager for HIPAA security contingency plan job description	Duties of project manager listed in job description, evaluated by executive leadership Due Date: March 15, 2004
3.	Establish task force protocols	a. Empower task force to develop HIPAA security contingency plan b. Task force may be identified as permanent or project-specific body c. Recurring, mandatory meeting dates and times to be established d. Authority to create, edit or amend policies and procedures specific to HIPAA security e. Define limits of authority: monetary or scope of change f. Define project documentation requirements and format— create status report template	i. Written task force charter, endorsed by executive leadership and/or board ii. Charter to include scope and limits of task force iii. Meeting dates and times agreed upon during initial session published (15 months minimum) iv. Task force charter validates approving body for HIPAA security contingency plan policies and procedures v. Limits of task force to be declared in charter—scope of task force identified vi. Written status reports will be submitted for each project deliverable	Task force charter published and kept with HIPAA security contingency plan documents Due Date: March 15, 2004
4.	Identify project milestones	a. Select end date for HIPAA security contingency plan compliance, preferably 30 to 60 days prior to the mandatory date b. Build project due dates to correspond to the internal compliance due date	i. Project plan documentation will be date specific	Project plan deliverables and variances will be documented in status reports
5.	Define risk analysis method	a. Task force will identify method to assign a risk value to each HIPAA security standard (both required and addressable)	i. Method will be published in task force meeting minutes and incorporated into a policy; associated procedures will be declared prior to security standard review	Each security standard will be analyzed for its risk value to the entity. Assignment of risk will be matched to each standard

Figure 7.2, The Contingency Planning Process, Part 6, presents a continuation of the preceding plan, mapping out the process to completion using both required and addressable standards. Underneath each required action item is a section specifically illustrating how an HIM department can apply the law to its work.

A Practical Approach to Contingency Planning

In addition to complying with the contingency planning standard within HIPAA security, healthcare organizations must also approach contingency planning with an eye on sound business practices. Organizations should implement a business continuity plan that fits their business operations, allowing them to continue to deliver care in case of disaster or system outage. Within an overall business continuity plan, a technology contingency plan must be implemented and tested to ensure that mission-critical systems, networks, applications, and data are available to support the business operations.

Complementary to the technology contingency plan, organizations must also develop contingency plans related to nontechnical aspects of their operations (e.g., work flow, staffing, physical facilities) as part of their overall business continuity plan. These aspects must be addressed to ensure they can continue to deliver quality patient care during a disaster or system outage. The following discussion focuses on the technology contingency plan related to systems, networks, applications, and data.

Business Impact Analysis and Risk Assessment

Most organizations do not have unlimited funds to invest in technical contingency plans. Limited funds must be spent wisely to ensure that organizational risk is minimized and that mission-critical applications and data are available in the case of an emergency.

To determine the best investment in a contingency plan, organizations should first conduct a business impact analysis (BIA) and risk assessment. This process also supports compliance with the HIPAA application and data criticality analysis (§164.308 (a)(7)(ii)(E)). During the BIA, each mission-critical application, system, and business process is inventoried and prioritized. This step, in turn, assists in determining the sequence of their recovery. The cost of downtime is calculated for each entry on the list.

A risk assessment should be conducted to determine the business risk associated with the inoperability of each of these systems. Once organizations understand the risks and costs associated with downtime, they can determine where to spend limited funds to ensure that the availability of the most critical applications is maximized and the business risk is minimized.

Disaster Recovery Planning

Upon completion of the BIA and the risk assessment, organizations are then in a position to develop a cost-effective disaster recovery plan (DRP). This plan supports compliance with the HIPAA requirement in §164.308 (a)(7)(ii)(B). At a base level, the proper policies, processes, and technologies must be put in place to ensure that electronic PHI is backed up regularly and can be restored (this supports compliance with the HIPAA requirement for a data backup plan in §164.308 (a)(7)(ii)(A)). Processes and solutions for good backup and recovery are well documented and should be standard procedure within IT departments.

Figure 7.2.   The contingency planning process, part 6

	Action Item	Definition	Documentation	Demonstration of Compliance
6.	Contingency planning			
§164.308 (a)(2)	Assigned security responsi-bility	Identify the security official who is responsible for the development and implemen-tation of the policies and procedures required by this subpart for the entity	Task force charter will require members of the task force to acknowledge and support the security official with a public endorsement	Security official assignment
	HIM department	Name the person within your department that will be called by your entity's security official when a threat to your department occurs and estab-lish a call-out roster to be used if more personnel are required to handle the emergency. Include volunteers in this list, if they already work in your department	Address the emergency call-out list in your monthly department meetings. Keep the list posted in the department, in the security official's office, and in an off-site location accessible to an HIM department staff member	Meeting minutes
§164.308 (a)(7)(i)	Administra-tive safe-guards: Contingency plan	Establish (and implement as needed) policies and proce-dures for responding to an emergency or other occurrence (e.g., fire, vandalism, system failure, or natural disaster) that damages systems containing electronic PHI	HIPAA security policy, *Emergency Response to Disasters Impacting Electronic PHI*	Policies and procedures written and approved by task force. Training of work force on policies and procedures to this policy completed. Procedures of the contingency plan tested on a regular basis, no less than annually
	HIM department	Identify what, if anything, is evacuated with personnel if a direct threat occurs in the department	Add HIM-specification items to entity contingency plan. Discuss all procedures in department meetings	
§164.308 (a)(7)(ii) (A)	Administra-tive safe-guards: Contingency plan: Imple-mentation specification: Data backup plan (required)	Establish and implement procedures to create and maintain retrievable exact copies of electronic PHI	Backup and recovery procedures	Implement backup and recovery procedures Test backup and recovery procedures on a regular basis

(Continued on next page)

Figure 7.2. **(Continued)**

	Action Item	Definition	Documentation	Demonstration of Compliance
	HIM department	Identify where backup systems are located. Name the personnel who will be held accountable for assisting with the capture of redundant information back to operations	Add HIM specific action items to entity contingency plan. Discuss all procedures in department meetings.	Consider adding line items into HIM position descriptions that identify what the individual's duty will be in disaster recovery mode, including working at other entity locations until normal business functions are restored
§164.308 (a)(7)(ii) (B)	Administrative safeguards: Contingency plan: Implementation specification: Disaster recovery plan (required)	Establish (and implement as needed) procedures to restore any loss of data	Disaster recovery plan	Implement a disaster recovery plan Test the disaster recovery plan
	HIM department	Identify if any HIM staff will actually be required in the restoration process	Name personnel by position, name, and contact information. The duties of these personnel will be reassigned to other HIM staff until restoration process is complete	List of personnel who will be dedicated to the actual recovery actions to be given to security official
§164.308 (a)(7)(ii) (C)	Administrative safeguards: Contingency plan: Implementation specification: Emergency mode operations plan (required)	Establish (and implement as needed) procedures to enable continuation of critical business processes for protection of the security of electronic PHI while operating in emergency mode	Emergency mode operations plan	Implement an emergency mode operations plan. Test the emergency mode operations plan
	HIM department	Inventory all HIM applications Rank each application as mission critical or mission noncritical	Mission-critical applications will be reviewed for HIPAA protections as they come back online by IT department, validated by HIM personnel Mission-noncritical applications in HIM will not be addressed	During a threat to PHI, all HIM staff will double check validity of data requests that are not via mission-critical applications Maintain a log of PHI requests, disclosures, and refusals during the emergency operations mode

Figure 7.2. (Continued)

	Action Item	Definition	Documentation	Demonstration of Compliance
§164.308 (a)(7)(ii) (D)	Administrative safeguards: Contingency plan: Implementation specification: Testing and revision procedures (addressable)	Implement procedures for periodic testing and revision of contingency plans	Contingency plan ongoing test plan Contingency plan ongoing maintenance plan	Test the contingency plan on a regular basis and document the results Execute the ongoing maintenance plan with input from the ongoing test plan
§164.308 (a)(7)(ii) (E)	Administrative safeguards: Contingency plan: Implementation specification: Application and data criticality analysis (addressable)	Assess the relative criticality of specific applications and data in support of other contingency plan components	Business impact analysis and risk assessment	Complete and document the business impact analysis and risk assessment
§164.310 (a)(2)(i)	Physical safeguards: Facilities access control: Implementation specification: Contingency operations (addressable)	Establish (and implement as needed) procedures that allow facility access in support of restoration of lost data under the disaster recovery plan and emergency mode operations plan in the event of an emergency	Emergency facility access control plan	Test and document results of the emergency facility access control plan on a periodic basis
§164.312 (a)(2)(ii)	Technical safeguards: Access control: emergency access procedures (required)	Establish (and implement as needed) procedures for obtaining necessary electronic PHI during an emergency	Emergency access control procedures	
	HIM department	Inventory all HIM applications Establish role-based access procedure for emergency operations	Publish list of the HIM personnel by position and name, with contact information, who are permitted to access electronic PHI during an emergency operation mode	Role-based access during emergency operations will be defined as those HIM personnel who are permitted to function as gatekeepers of PHI—maintaining a disclosure log and tracking activity

The approaches and options for developing a DRP are much more diverse than those for backup and recovery. Consequently, it is a valuable exercise to assess the various disaster recovery options applicable to an organization's environment. Based on the BIA and the risk assessment, the most appropriate disaster recovery approach can be selected to ensure that critical applications are recoverable at acceptable levels of risk. This approach must cover emergency procedures, business and technical processes, organizational and staffing requirements, duplication and continued access to required physical assets. It must also address technical solutions that include duplicated systems, applications, networks, and data and the ability to switch processing from a failed system to the duplicate system.

Disaster Recovery Plan Implementation

After development, review, and approval of the DRP, the plan is ready for implementation. This stage verifies that all features are in place, preparing the organization against disasters.
Implementation includes the following components:

- Technical implementation, including backup and recovery systems, high-availability systems, duplicate networks, business partner and technology service provider availability (e.g., telecommunications providers), and sites to which processing for systems and staffing can be switched in the case of a failure

- Procedural implementation, including off-site storage of the DRP, backup and recovery procedures, off-site backup facilities, escalation procedures, recovery and fail-over procedures, and technical and nontechnical manual processes required when systems are unavailable (in compliance with the HIPAA requirement for an emergency mode operations plan, §164.308 (a)(7)(ii)(C))

- Organizational implementation that addresses organizational issues to ensure adequate response to a disaster, such as:

  —Assignment of specific roles and responsibilities in the case of an emergency

  —Proper training of all staff members on their roles in case of disaster or outage— both staff directly involved in the recovery process and those delivering healthcare services

Disaster Recovery Plan Testing

Testing the DRP is a crucial step, and further, it complies with the HIPAA requirement for testing and revision procedures (§164.308 (a)(7)(ii)(D)). On a basic level, testing backup and recovery of data must occur periodically and when new systems and applications come online.
Organizations must take a very structured approach to testing their plans. Testing must occur on a scale much larger than simply recovering information from a failed disk drive. Appropriate testing includes simulation of a disaster or major system outage. By nature, such tests may be disruptive to the healthcare delivery process, but there is no substitute to testing the DRP in order to uncover issues and problems that could occur in a real emergency. It is far less costly in time, money, and human capital to discover these issues during a simulated test than during a real disaster.

After issues and problems are identified and assessed, the DRP can be adjusted to correct the issues or minimize their impact. The DRP related to systems, applications, and networks should be tested on a periodic basis, with a portion tested every year. For example, an organization may test their entire DRP every three years and one-third of the systems, applications, and network annually.

In addition to periodic testing, the DRP must be maintained and updated as organizational environments change. Facilities may be changed or added, new applications may be implemented, service providers may change, or the technical infrastructure may be upgraded. When these events occur, the DRP must be updated to reflect these changes. It may mean revisiting the BIA, or it may be as simple as retesting the DRP to ensure that the change has not altered recovery capabilities. Changes must be addressed in the context of the DRP, verifying that the DRP can accommodate the additions and changes in the case of a disaster or system outage.

Disaster Recovery Plan Executions

Once the DRP has been implemented, the organization is in a position to execute the plan in case of a disaster or system outage. Backup and recovery of data should occur on a regular basis as part of normal IT operations. Hardware failures are a regular occurrence, and recovery of data from these situations will occur. These are relatively normal, ongoing activities.

Executing a DRP in an emergency situation is an activity that most organizations would prefer to avoid. A sound DRP addresses "disasters" in all shapes and sizes—a system going down, telecommunication lines being severed by construction crews, a fire in the data center, a hurricane or earthquake, or an act of terrorism. Each of these events will trigger the DRP, and the organization will respond as the plan dictates.

The depth of planning and testing that went into the DRP will quickly become apparent during the emergency. After recovery is complete, organizations should assess their performance and identify areas for improvement. Incorporating improvements into the DRP is essential to ensuring improved performance in the case of another disaster or system outage.

Take the pretest again with your HIM work force. As you carry out your compliance and contingency planning, document each action in your process. Your efforts will be rewarded if your organization ever finds itself enacting a contingency plan.

Note

1. The CMS steps, which specifically targeted the October 16, 2003, deadline for transactions and code set compliance, may be found on the CMS Web site at www.cms.hhs.gov/hipaa/hipaa2/general/default.asp#contingency_ guide. See "Steps for Contingency Planning."

Portable Computer Security

Carol Ann Quinsey, RHIA, CHPS

Background

Portable computers can be efficient and effective in documenting patient care and treatment, particularly when healthcare professionals move between nursing units, healthcare facilities, or patient homes. Not only can they save users time, portable computers can facilitate the collection of more complete and accurate information. Unlike networked desktop computers, however, portable computers are easily stolen and thus pose increased risks to the security of patient health information.

Legal and Regulatory Requirements

The Health Insurance Portability and Accountability Act of 1996 (HIPAA) requires that health information be protected against threats to security, integrity, and unauthorized use.

The final privacy standards (45 CFR, Parts 160 and 164) were set forth to protect the privacy of individually identifiable health information maintained or transmitted electronically in connection with certain administrative and financial transactions.

The final security rule (45 CFR Parts 160, 162, and 164) covers electronic protected health information (ePHI), which is the electronic subset of protected health information (PHI) addressed in the privacy rule.

Section 164.306 of the security rule covers some general rules for all covered entities, including general requirements and crossover requirements with the privacy standards. Specifically, this section covers four things that must be done under the security rule:

- Ensure the confidentiality, integrity, and availability of all ePHI the covered entity creates, receives, maintains, or transmits.

- Protect against any reasonably anticipated threats or hazards to the security or integrity of such information.

Source: Quinsey, Carol Ann. "Portable Computer Security (AHIMA Practice Brief)" (Updated June 2003).

- Protect against any reasonably anticipated uses or disclosures of such information that are not permitted under the privacy subpart.

- Ensure compliance with the security subpart by the entity's work force.

This section describes implementation specifications for each of the security standards as either "required" or "addressable." If a standard is required, covered entities must implement the implementation specification. If a standard is addressable, the covered entity must assess whether the implementation specification is reasonable in their environment and document the results of their assessment. If it is found to be reasonable and appropriate, the covered entity must implement. (It is permissible to implement an alternative measure that is determined to be more reasonable and appropriate.) If the assessment does not conclude the implementation specification to be reasonable or appropriate, then the covered entity is not required to implement.

Several references in 164.310 are made specifically to workstations. This section requires a covered entity to "implement policies and procedures that specify the proper functions to be performed, the manner in which those functions are to be performed, and the physical attributes of the surroundings of a specific workstation or class of workstation that can access ePHI." It further requires that the entity "implement physical safeguard for all workstations that access ePHI to restrict access to authorized users" and requires the implementation of "policies and procedures that govern the receipt and removal of hardware and electronic media that contain ePHI into and out of a facility and the movement of these items within the facility."

- Disposal (required): The entity must "implement policies and procedures to address the final disposition of ePHI and/or the hardware or electronic media on which it is stored."

- Media reuse (required): Likewise, the entity must "implement procedures for removal of ePHI from electronic media before the media are made available for reuse."

- Accountability (addressable): The entity must "maintain a record of the movements of hardware and electronic media and any person responsible therefore."

- Data backup and storage (addressable): The entity must "create a retrievable, exact copy of ePHI, when needed, before movement of equipment."

Covered entities must account for the fact that many workstations are small and easy to move. As a result, they may be used almost anywhere; for instance, many employees work from home. As with the privacy rule, an entity will have to consider the security questions surrounding such practices.[1]

Section 164.312 says that a covered entity must "implement technical policies and procedures for electronic information systems that maintain ePHI to allow access only to those persons or software programs that have been granted access rights as specified in the "administrative safeguards" section (164.308). To do this, a covered entity must initiate four implementation specifications:

- Unique user identification (required): The entity must "assign a unique name and/or number for identifying and tracking user identity."

- Emergency access procedure (required): An entity must "establish (and implement as needed) procedures for obtaining necessary ePHI during an emergency."

- Automatic logoff (addressable): The entity must "implement electronic procedures that terminate an electronic session after a predetermined time of inactivity."

- Encryption and decryption (addressable): The entity must "implement a mechanism to encrypt and decrypt ePHI" as needed.

While the requirements that mention encryption in this section and elsewhere are short, a longer discussion in the preamble also contains important information. HHS is not suggesting encryption always must be done, but each aspect of ePHI should be reviewed to determine if encryption makes sense. Decision makers should take into account that encryption is rapidly changing.[2]

The Medicare Conditions of Participation for healthcare facilities also address information security with the following requirements:

- Hospitals: "The hospital must have a procedure for ensuring the confidentiality of patient records. Information from or copies of records may be released only to authorized individuals, and the hospital must ensure that unauthorized individuals cannot gain access to or alter patient records."[3]

- Home health agencies: "Clinical record information is safeguarded against loss or unauthorized use."[4]

- State and long-term care: "The resident has the right to personal privacy and confidentiality of his or her personal and clinical records."[5]

- Comprehensive outpatient rehabilitation facilities: "The facility must safeguard clinical record information against loss, destruction, or unauthorized use."[6]

- Critical access hospitals: "The facility maintains the confidentiality of record information against loss, destruction, or unauthorized use."[7]

- Outpatient physical therapy services furnished by physical therapists in independent practice: "Clinical record information is recognized as confidential and is safeguarded against loss, destruction, or unauthorized use."[8]

The Privacy Act of 1974 mandates that federal information systems must protect the confidentiality of individually identifiable data. Section 5 U.S.C. 552a (e) (10) of the act is very clear: federal systems must "establish appropriate administrative, technical, and physical safeguards to ensure the security and confidentiality of records and to protect against any anticipated threats or hazards to their security or integrity which could result in substantial harm, embarrassment, inconvenience, or unfairness to any individual on whom information is maintained."[9]

The *Code of Federal Regulations* relative to Alcohol and Drug Abuse, 42 CFR, Chapter I, Part 2, Section 2.1, states that records of the identity, diagnosis, prognosis, or treatment of any patient that are maintained in connection with the performance of any drug abuse prevention function conducted, regulated, or directly or indirectly assisted by any department or agency of the United States shall be confidential and disclosed only for the purposes and under the circumstances expressly authorized.

In addition, individual states may have laws or regulations that require health information to be protected against threats to security, integrity, and unauthorized use.

Accreditation Standards

The Joint Commission on Accreditation of Healthcare Organizations' hospital, ambulatory care, and long-term care standard IM.2 reads "Confidentiality, security, and integrity of data and information are maintained."

Recommendations

The risks of portable computer and associated information theft can be minimized when healthcare facilities:

- Improve access and physical controls.
- Provide employees with theft awareness instruction.
- Make small investments in computer accessories.

In terms of establishing appropriate controls, healthcare facilities should:

- Establish written policies and procedures covering the loan and use of portable computers.
- Purge user data from returned portable computers prior to assigning the same portable computer to the next user.
- Require all borrowers to sign a copy of the policy statement or guidelines for portable computers.
- Avoid maintaining patient health information on portable computers. Instead, store the information on the healthcare facility's network so the information can be backed up and maintained more securely. When network storage is not possible, maintain the patient information on disk(s), storing and transporting the disks separately from the computer carrying case, or encrypt the information to protect it from unauthorized access should the computer be stolen.
- Require written authorization by the HIM director when portable computers are to be used to collect and/or maintain patient health information.
- Limit use of the assigned portable computer to the employee.
- Hold the computer borrower responsible and accountable for the safety and security of the assigned equipment and information.
- Maintain a current list of portable computer users and borrowers, assigned equipment serial numbers, and software.
- Audit policies, procedures, and assigned equipment and software lists regularly
- Perform loss investigations on all stolen equipment.
- Secure portable computers, offices, and meeting rooms when equipment is left unattended.
- When purchasing portable computers, consider those with local repair facilities to avoid potential theft during shipment to or from the factory when computers are sent for repair.
- Require the use of strong passwords of at least seven to eight characters, including alphanumeric and special characters.

In terms of theft awareness and instruction, healthcare facilities should:

- Require that employees be familiar with the facility's policies and procedures relative to portable computer use prior to being assigned such equipment.

- Require that employees be familiar with the facility's policies and procedures relative to confidentiality of patient health information.

- Educate employees about the potential risks caused by computer or information theft or loss.

- Provide employees with computer and data theft precaution and deterrent information. Examples might include instructions to:

  —Avoid using portable computers where they can be easily stolen.

  —Transport a portable computer in a car's trunk rather than on a seat, thereby keeping it hidden.

  —Carry the computer in something other than a readily identifiable computer carrying case.

  —Carry disks separately from the case containing the portable computer.

  —When possible, place a portable computer on an airport conveyor after the preceding individual has cleared the metal detector.

  —Place unattended portable computers in room safes when leaving a hotel room. (Some hotel room safes include an AC adapter so that the computer can be recharged while locked away.)

  —Lock the room or place the computer in a laptop depository when leaving a portable computer in an unattended meeting room. (A laptop depository is a portable safe in which computers can be placed. An alarm will sound if the depository is moved after it is closed.)

  —Avoid setting a portable computer down in a public place.

  —Avoid accessing patient identifiable health information where it might be seen by individuals without a legitimate need to know.

In terms of making investments in computer accessories that will minimize the risk of theft, facilities should:

- Provide employees with the best accessories available to protect their portable computers and require use of these devices. Examples include:

  —Carrying cases that do not appear to contain computers

  —Cables with locks that hook to desks or tables and that once removed do not allow a thief to turn the computer on

  —Lock down enclosures, proximity alarms, and software programs that instruct computers to "phone home" to report their location

- Install and use appropriate password, security, and encryption programs.

- Use an antitheft plaque or etching tool to engrave the company name/ID on all portable computers. (Some antitheft plaques contain a metallic bar code and registration number. If a thief tries to pry off the plaque, the computer casing will be damaged, decreasing the resale value. If the thief succeeds in removing the plaque, the computer will still bear the imprint of the words "stolen property" on its shell.)

Notes

1. AHIMA's Policy and Government Relations Team. "Final Rule for HIPAA Security Standards," February 2003. Available in the FORE Library: HIM Body of Knowledge at www.ahima.org.

2. Ibid.

3. Health Care Financing Administration, Department of Health and Human Services. "Medicare Conditions of Participation for Hospitals." *Code of Federal Regulations,* 1999. 42 CFR Ch. IV, Part 482.24.

4. Health Care Financing Administration, Department of Health and Human Services. "Medicare Conditions of Participation for Home Health Agencies." *Code of Federal Regulations,* 42 CFR Ch. IV, Part 484.48.

5. Health Care Financing Administration, Department of Health and Human Services. "Medicare Conditions of Participation for States and Long-Term Care Facilities." *Code of Federal Regulations,* 42 CFR, Ch. IV, Part 483.10.

6. Health Care Financing Administration, Department of Health and Human Services. "Medicare Conditions of Participation for Specialized Providers." *Code of Federal Regulations,* 1998. 42 CFR Ch. IV, Part 485.60.

7. Health Care Financing Administration, Department of Health and Human Services. "Medicare Conditions of Participation for Specialized Providers." *Code of Federal Regulations,* 1998. 42 CFR Ch. IV, Part 485.638.

8. Health Care Financing Administration, Department of Health and Human Services. "Medicare Conditions of Participation for Specialized Services Furnished by Suppliers." *Code of Federal Regulations,* 1998. 42 CFR, Ch. IV, Part 486.161.

9. Health Care Financing Administration. "HCFA Internet Security Policy." November 24, 1998. (www.cms.hhs.gov/it/security/docs/internet_policy.pdf).

References

Briggs, Bill, ed. *Comprehensive Guide to Electronic Health Records.* New York, NY: Faulker and Gray, Inc., 2000.

Joint Commission on Accreditation of Healthcare Organizations. *2002–2003 Comprehensive Accreditation Manual for Ambulatory Care.* Oakbrook Terrace, IL: Joint Commission on Accreditation of Healthcare Organizations, 2003.

Joint Commission on Accreditation of Healthcare Organizations. *2003 Comprehensive Accreditation Manual for Hospitals: The Official Handbook.* Oakbrook Terrace, IL: Joint Commission on Accreditation of Healthcare Organizations, 2003.

Joint Commission on Accreditation of Healthcare Organizations. *2002–2003 Comprehensive Accreditation Manual for Long Term Care.* Oakbrook Terrace, IL: Joint Commission on Accreditation of Healthcare Organizations, 2003.

"Standards for Privacy of Individually Identifiable Health Information; Final Rule." (45 CFR, Parts 160 and 164) (August 14, 2002).

"Health Insurance Reform: Security Standards; Final Rule (45 CFR Parts 160, 162, and 164). (February 20, 2003).

Safe at Home: Remote Coding Meets HIPAA

Tim Keough, MPA, RHIA

Remote coding offers big benefits and unique security challenges. Here's how one organization moves patient data securely across the Internet.

"Whatever, in connection with my professional practice, or not in connection with it, I see or hear, in the life of men, which ought not to be spoken of abroad, I will not divulge, as reckoning that all such should be kept secret." These words, written by Hippocrates, the father of medicine, demonstrate that preserving patient health information in a confidential and secure manner was as of extreme importance in the fifth century B.C. as it is today.

Tremendous modern advances in information technology add an entirely new level of complexity to keeping secret that "which ought not be spoken of abroad." Health information management professionals face the challenge of leveraging the power of information technology while simultaneously preserving patients' rights to confidentiality and security. Perhaps nowhere is this challenge more acute than in organizations employing the benefits of remote coding technology under HIPAA privacy and forthcoming security rules.

Finding a Remote Coding Solution

In 2001 Community Medical Center's HIM department faced the common issues that confront most acute care facilities at some time or another: lack of space, an abundance of paper-based patient medical records, need for simultaneous access to patient records, a desire to improve employee satisfaction, and of course, a need to reduce the revenue cycle by attracting and retaining the best and the brightest coders to the facility.

For Community—a 596-bed, acute care facility with a volume of more than 225,000 visits per year, part of the Saint Barnabas Healthcare System in Toms River, NJ—home-based coding was the answer. Allowing coding to be performed off site would give Community the ability to accommodate improved coding processes, provide authorized clinicians with simultaneous access to patient information, and allow coders to work out of their homes.

Community's HIM department, in conjunction with the center's information technology and services department, reviewed many vendor product offerings, seeking a cost-effective and operationally efficient document imaging system. Of equal importance was the need for the

Source: Keough, Tim. "Safe at Home: Remote Coding Meets HIPAA." *Journal of AHIMA* 75, no. 2 (February 2004): 42–46.

chosen system to meet confidentiality and security requirements for protected health information (PHI), both as they exist today and as they will evolve with the implementation of HIPAA's security and electronic signatures standards in April 2005.

Community chose a feature-rich and secure system that captures scanned images and transmits them to authorized users. The process is administered through a third-party vendor, the application service provider (ASP) who developed the software. The system offers high-speed scanning, essential and intuitive coding work flow tools, and advanced supervisory controls. In addition, the system could be implemented without great expense for hardware, since the hospital already had the network infrastructure and sufficient bandwidth to accommodate the transfer of image information.

Prior to making the final purchase decision, a project management team reviewed the goals of the project and identified the operational, confidentiality, and security risks and challenges that such a system would present. To accomplish this review, expertise was sought from representatives of the HIM department, the chief privacy officer, the information technology and services department, physician leadership, and representatives from clinical departments including the emergency department, cardiology, and nursing.

The project management team reviewed the risks and potential weaknesses of an electronic record system and began to design work flows and network topologies to establish a secure approach to remote coding. Figure 7.3 illustrates the final work flow of Community's home-based coding system.

Multiple Locations, One Set of Security Regulations

The proposed HIPAA security regulations provided the project management team with the security goals for the new coding system. The tenets of the security rule indicated that there was no recognized single standard but that any standard chosen would be technology neutral. The rule also noted that technical solutions should be flexible and scalable for providers, clearinghouses, and plans. The general approach within the rule states that covered entities must ensure that electronic information pertaining to individuals remains secure.

The security rule delineates recommendations in three distinct categories: (1) administrative procedures; (2) physical safeguards; and (3) technical security services and mechanisms. Given Community's remote coding work flow, the center had to address the recommendations for three types of workers in three types of facilities. Here's how the center approached these requirements.

Administrative Procedures

Generally, the security rule requires that covered entities establish administrative procedures and measures to protect data and regulate the conduct of employees in the use of PHI. Complying with this requirement was fairly straightforward, since Community already had established policies and procedures for information management that addressed data validity and integrity, security and control, and confidentiality. In addition, the center also had a clearly defined sanction policy for confirmed breaches of confidentiality.

In addition to policies governing use of information, employee training related to the HIPAA rules and confidentiality and security in general were very important. These issues are addressed upon hire during employee orientation and are reinforced throughout the year in mandatory code of conduct classes, departmental meetings, and a biweekly employee newsletter.

Figure 7.3.   Home-based coding work flow

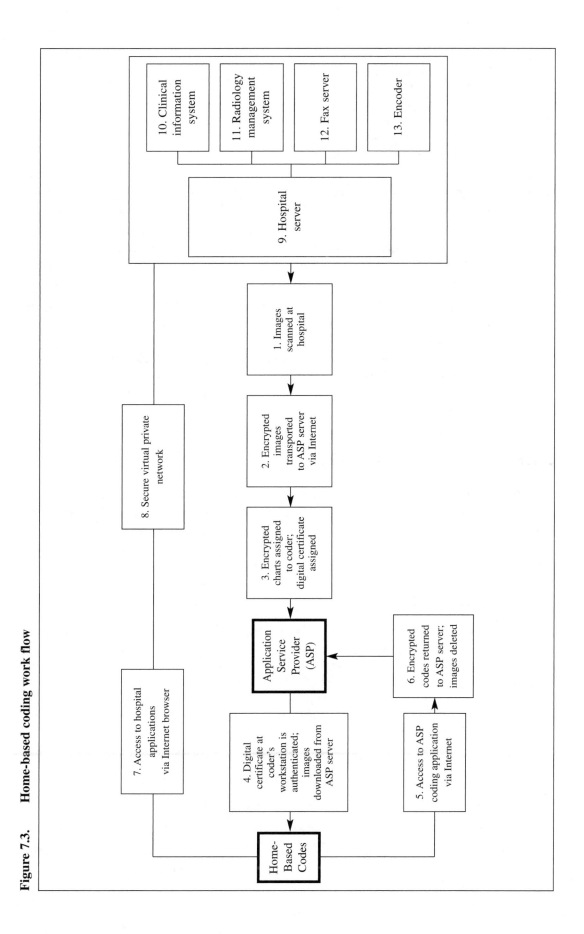

309

However, to drive the point home for users of the home-based coding system, additional administrative measures were taken to ensure data integrity, confidentiality, and privacy. These include:

- Home-based coding telecommuting policy and agreement. A new policy was developed for eligible employees requiring them to maintain confidentiality and security of information in their home by providing a private and secure workplace. The policy also requires that use of computer equipment is for coding purposes only. The agreement must be signed by all employees after it is reviewed with them by their supervisor.

- Electronic record policy and procedure. This new policy and procedure was developed to enhance the existing information management policy and to address new processes of accounting for records in an electronic format, scanning and indexing charts, and home-based coding and online viewing of records by authorized clinicians and HIM staff members.

- Down-time procedure. If for any reason coders are not able to perform their work due to Internet connectivity issues or other technical problems, the supervisor has the ability to recall the employee to work from the hospital until the problem is resolved. Currently Community has this ability because all employees live within commuting distance of the hospital. For clinical staff needing access to records during down time, the HIM department will retrieve the paper-based chart and bring it to the requesting department.

Physical Safeguards

The HIPAA rule addresses the physical protection of computer systems from events such as fire or environmental hazards and the use of locks or other security features to control access to systems and facilities. Since Community was implementing a remote coding program managed by a third party, the center had to address three areas for physical safeguard compliance: the vendor facility, the hospital, and the employee's home.

The Vendor

Since Community's new system involved sending scanned medical records via the Internet to be stored at the vendor's location, much attention had to be given to the physical safeguards of the vendor's facility. During the request for proposal process, the safeguards listed below were identified and verified:

- All servers located at a secure location monitored 24/7 by security personnel and closed-circuit television.

- Access to locked server location only through badge-card scan and palm scan.

- Access to server location limited to authorized technical staff only.

- Servers backed up on digital tape drives on a nightly basis.

- Servers have short-term battery back-up power and long-term diesel back-up power.

- Data stored as mirror image on two computer drives; in the event that one drive fails, data may be removed from the failed drive on the fly. Secondary cooling fans available to keep equipment at safe operating temperatures.

The Hospital

To effectively code from home, employees needed access to all the tools and systems available at the hospital. Just as radiology reports, lab findings, or other clinical findings may be missing from a paper chart at the time of coding, they may also be missing from the scanned electronic chart. While working within the hospital, coders had access to laboratory, radiology, and clinical information systems in addition to encoder and fax servers.

To replicate access to these systems and to provide for an additional layer of security, Community installed a secured socket layer (SSL) virtual private network (VPN). This system enables coders to connect to all necessary hospital systems through their home-based computer and a Web browser. Data and information flowing from hospital-based systems are protected behind a firewall, and information is encrypted between the SSL VPN site and the home-based coder.

Other physical safeguards used by the hospital include storage of computer equipment in locked, climate-controlled computer rooms where access is controlled through identification cards.

The Coders

To enhance physical computer safeguards for the employee working from home, Community had to take a realistic approach. Naturally, it was not cost effective or practical for the center to install dry fire-extinguishing systems or elaborate computer rooms in each coder's home or for the center to provide back-up systems. However, there were reasonable and practical things that Community could do to improve safeguards, keeping in mind that safeguards must be scaled to what was reasonable for an employee's home.

The first safeguard was the requirement that computers placed in the employees' homes are used exclusively for home-based coding. Employees sign a user's agreement and receive training so that they understand they may not alter or circumvent Web browser restrictions, which could open the computer to unsecured Web sites and increase the risk of exposure to viruses or hacking attempts. Further, all connections to the Internet are regulated through routers that include built-in firewall protection. Employees working from home also acknowledge in the user's agreement that they should not install any other personal software on their home-based coding computer.

The service provider's software does not allow the employees to print, screen capture, or transmit an electronic record from their computers to any other users. Further, following completion of coding, the program does not store copies of patient records on the home-based computer's hard drive, either as files or as cookies. Programming in the software negates this possibility. PHI is not stored on the computers.

Technical Services and Mechanisms

HIPAA requires that technical security services and mechanisms be in place to prevent unauthorized access to data transmitted over a communications network. Community's home-based coding program met these recommendations through a number of measures. The center employs digital certificates and data encryption, and all systems run updated virus protection software and are protected behind a firewall.

Access to the system is restricted by password, which employees choose themselves. The system gives the facility the option of requiring users to change their passwords according to a fixed schedule. Community requires employees to change their passwords every six months.

Access to electronic records is restricted according to predefined rules based on employee role. Community's established roles and privileges are as follows:

- Administrators can change system settings, create new users, and delete former users. They also have the ability to delete records or correct record indexing problems.

- Coders can only access and view charts assigned to them by their supervisors. This ensures that they only access records on a "need to know" basis.

- Online viewer status is granted to clerical employees within the HIM department and authorized clinical staff. Online viewers can be restricted to only viewing records onscreen, or they can be designated to print material.

- Scan technicians have the ability to scan, index, and upload images to the vendor's server.

- Supervisors have access to scanned records and can assign records to individual coders. They may also set additional rules to select a sample of records to be reviewed for coding accuracy.

In a paper-based world, it is very difficult, if not impossible, to know who has looked at a record, when they looked at it, and what they may have copied from the chart. Community experienced a significant auditing benefit by migrating to the new electronic system, because each employee accessing a record now leaves behind an electronic fingerprint. The audit trail allows the center to enhance its ability to verify that records are only accessed on a need-to-know basis.

Audit trails can be run either by patient name—listing all employees having looked at the electronic chart—or by employee, listing all patient records that an individual has accessed. Reports can be defined by time period, as well. Information captured in the audit trail includes employee name, patient name, date accessed, the function performed, the pages accessed, and the pages printed.

From the onset of scanning paper charts to electronic files at Community, technological security measures are in place, all of which are documented in policies and procedures. Paper-based records are scanned by a designated scan technician within 24 hours of discharge. The images are encrypted and transmitted via the Internet to the vendor's facility. As noted, the vendor protects data in their custody by securing their equipment, limiting access, and providing necessary back-ups and system redundancy.

Access to an electronic record can only occur after an authorized coder logs into the system with their user name and password and only after the coder's computer digital certificate is authenticated by the vendor site. For users designated as online viewers, an administrator can restrict viewing capabilities to a specific computer if desired.

A Program Worth the Effort

As with most things that are worth accomplishing, Community found that establishing a home-based coding program was not easy to achieve but certainly was worth the time and effort. To date, the center employs eight coders working from home, processing all emergency department and outpatient records. In the final phase of the program, inpatient medical records also will be coded from home.

Home-based coding allowed Community to accomplish its established goals and to do so without any compromise to the confidentiality or security of patient records. In fact, the features and safeguards of the new system provide better control over records than the center could have ever achieved in a paper-based environment.

Make Your Telecommuting Program HIPAA Compliant

Margret Amatayakul, MBA, RHIA, CHPS, FHIMSS

An increasing number of healthcare workforce members are telecommuting. As transcriptionists, coders, customer service representatives, and others are working from home, many providers are weighing the benefits against potential privacy and security risks.

Who Is Working from Home?

There are two general types of home-based workers: those contracted by a provider and those employed by a provider. Although the organizational relationship may make no difference in terms of what the risk is and how it should be mitigated, the relationship does determine how a provider controls the risk.

For the contractor, the provider must have a business associate agreement to establish a contractual arrangement for safeguarding protected health information. The provider generally does not directly evaluate the home-based worker of the contractor. However, the guidelines offered here could be used by the contractor to establish safeguards and for the provider to establish contractual obligations.

Specific types of workers who may work from home may be considered narrowly or broadly from a HIPAA perspective. Transcriptionists are perhaps the most common home-based workers. Increasingly, coders are looking to work from home as well. Other groups of home-based workers are business office customer service representatives and staff who perform preregistration, eligibility verification, and precertification.

In interpreting the home-based worker role more broadly, however, one could include virtually anyone who has remote access to protected health information, brings work home on floppy disks or laptops containing protected health information—even only occasionally—or uses personal e-mail to communicate with patients.

What Protected Health Information Do Telecommuters Need?

Each type of home-based worker has different needs for protected health information. These needs already determine the feasibility of performing the task at home and should be carefully evaluated against minimum necessary criteria and potential for deidentification.

Source: Amatayakul, Margret. "Make Your Telecommuting Program HIPAA Compliant." *Journal of AHIMA* 73, no. 2 (2002): 16A–C.

HIPAA should help us challenge current thinking about what and how all protected health information is used and disclosed. For example, home-based or not, transcriptionists and coders may actually not need patient identity to transcribe or code records. From a practical perspective, however, it may be difficult to deidentify the dictation or the record content, but this is becoming easier with new technology. Some systems today are capable of randomly assigning a document number to dictation that can be converted back to the medical record number when the transcription is transmitted back for filing.

Document scanning systems can be programmed to replace a patient identification bar code with a randomly assigned number. Not only would this remove patient identity from the documents used by the coder, but it would serve as a check on the contents of the paper chart to ensure that all relate to the same patient.

Employees who occasionally take work home on floppy disks would rarely, if ever, need protected health information. However, if there is identifying information in spreadsheets or databases that are used for processing at home, take steps to separate the identifying information from the information to be processed where possible.

Measures such as assigning a code to replace the patient name and medical record number or deleting an identifying column on a spreadsheet do not fully deidentify the patient, according to the 19 data elements required by HIPAA for deidentification. These measures, however, go a long way toward addressing minimum necessary use requirements and protecting transmission of data to remote locations when the worker would ordinarily have access to patient identity.

Such deidentification, however, does not apply to all who may work remotely. For example, physicians who may access the hospital system or their office system would need the identity of the patient. Visiting nurses could also be considered home based even though the patients' homes they visit are not their own. Other workers, such as customer service representatives, may also need patient identity—both to gain access to information to respond to requests as well as to validate with whom they are speaking. While deidentifying information used in these circumstances is not possible, steps recommended for all telecommuters can be used to better protect individually identifiable health information in these circumstances.

What Are the Risks at Home?

Many risks in the home environment are the same as in the provider setting, but the risks tend to be intensified. While most HIM departments, business offices, and other such operational areas generally are not open to the public, there is a small risk of coworkers who do not have a need to know having access to protected health information. This risk is further minimized on site by the fact that these persons are members of the work force, have received privacy and security training, and have agreed to abide by the policies of the organization under penalty of sanctions up to and including termination. Homes are not areas where members of the "public" have great access, but persons who may visit the home are not under the same obligations as coworkers on site. In the home, there is significantly greater risk of casual observation or overhearing of protected health information by persons not in the employer's work force.

Unscrupulous workers can exist both on site and at home. When on site, however, there are usually fewer opportunities to divert, alter, or destroy information than in a home, where there is no other person to oversee what is being done to the information. In the home environment, transcribed documents, coded encounter forms, and other forms of protected health information can be saved to floppy disks, printed and retained in hard copy, or saved to alternative hard drives or servers. There are also greater risks of errors occurring at home, where there is not direct access to technical support. These problems can result in loss of data, misrouting of information, or accidental access by a person who is not a member of the provider's work force.

Finally, connectivity is an issue for telecommuters. Most security experts believe that the greatest threat to protected health information is still internal—that is, accidental or intentional misuse or disclosure by a member of the work force (whether on site or at home). There is, however, greater possibility of wire tapping, service disruption, or mail interception when connecting from the single point of a home. The courier who routinely transports documents from the home to the provider could be secretly copying contents or gaining unlawful access to the information contained in the documents being transported.

How Can I Achieve Security and Privacy Compliance in the Home?

There are three key steps to providing security and privacy protections for telecommuters. The first is to hire employees or engage contractors who have been adequately screened and with whom there is regular privacy and security communication. Out of sight should not be out of mind. Know who is performing the work and how the work is being performed. Every telecommuter should receive privacy and security training, regular updates, and the same (or greater) level of awareness building as those on site. For regular telecommuters, this may include random site visits, e-mail, telephone calls, or other means to provide communications. This not only directs communications to the telecommuter, but also permits them to communicate any concerns they may have.

A second key step is to ensure that the environment is suitable to afford protections. For members of the work force who take work home only occasionally or connect remotely for only part of their time, ensure that they too have been appropriately trained and agree to follow appropriate safeguards. The picture of the physician accessing patient information while eating breakfast with the family may be endearing, but it is not necessarily the ideal image of privacy. Not only should the telecommuting environment be ergonomically appropriate and conducive to productivity, but physical and technical safeguards should be provided. Each telecommuting function will have its own set of technical features that must be considered. In addition to these, however, the Sample Telecommuter Safeguards Checklist in Figure 7.4 is a good place to start for any form of telecommuting.

Figure 7.4.   Sample telecommuter safeguards checklist

This list represents only a sample of approaches to structuring a telecommuting security policy. For a complete list, see the AHIMA Practice Brief "Telecommuting" published in February 1999 and available online at www.ahima.org.

____ Work location in separate room or room unused by others during work time

____ Private area for connectivity/remote access and/or telephone conversations

____ Separate phone line if remote connection to provider or contractor

____ Smoke detector/alarm present and functional in area of workstation

Date last checked:_____

____ Fire extinguisher near work area and accessible

____ Power surge protector available for workstation

____ Equipment out of direct sunlight and away from heaters

____ Lock on work area door/workstation

____ Workstation password protected

The third factor is contractual. Even if the telecommuter is an employee, it is advisable to have an agreement with the facility concerning ownership and use of equipment and rights to information. When contracting with a service, the provider may want to include in the business associate contract how the contractor ensures that its work force is trained, information is protected, and the legal obligation to conform to requirements. Figure 7.5, Sample Telecommuter Obligations, identifies elements that should be included in a telecommuter's agreement or contract. These would be in addition to the elements required by HIPAA for the business associate contract.

Figure 7.5.   Sample telecommuter obligations

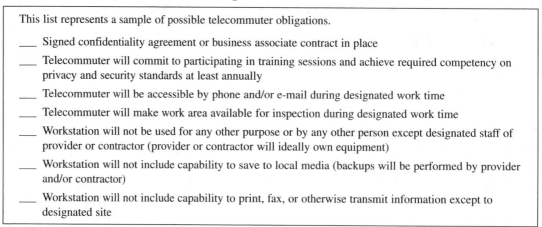

This list represents a sample of possible telecommuter obligations.

___ Signed confidentiality agreement or business associate contract in place

___ Telecommuter will commit to participating in training sessions and achieve required competency on privacy and security standards at least annually

___ Telecommuter will be accessible by phone and/or e-mail during designated work time

___ Telecommuter will make work area available for inspection during designated work time

___ Workstation will not be used for any other purpose or by any other person except designated staff of provider or contractor (provider or contractor will ideally own equipment)

___ Workstation will not include capability to save to local media (backups will be performed by provider and/or contractor)

___ Workstation will not include capability to print, fax, or otherwise transmit information except to designated site

Selecting Strong Passwords

**Margret Amatayakul, MBA, RHIA, CHPS, FHIMSS
Tom Walsh, CISSP**

Are the majority of passwords in your organization something like "Spot1," "Spot2," "Spot3" (for Joe, whose password expires every 90 days and whose dog's name is Spot)? If so, your organization could be at risk. Here's what you need to know about HIPAA requirements for establishing and managing passwords.

What Does HIPAA Require?

HIPAA requires a two-tier form of entity authentication. Entity authentication is defined as "the corroboration that an entity [person or system] is the one claimed." A unique user identifier and one of the following are required: biometric identification (such as fingerprint or retinal scan), password, personal identification number (PIN), telephone call-back procedure, or token. Most healthcare vendors provide a unique user identifier and a password. However, the system with which passwords are administered and passwords themselves are not as strong as they could be. A strong password is easy for the user to remember and difficult for anyone else to guess.

What Is Entity Authentication?

The whole process of entity authentication includes definition of access privileges, access authorization, access establishment (including verification, training, and assignment of authentication), password management, and audit controls. Access control should also include modification of access when a user changes jobs within the organization, emergency-mode access, automatic log-off, and termination procedures to ensure access is removed when a user terminates association with the organization.

What Are Access Privileges?

Access privileges should be defined at the time a system is installed. HIPAA permits one of the following:

- User-based access control identifies the user to the system, and the user has access to all information. Many hospitals grant physicians user-based access controls on the

Source: Amatayakul, Margret, and Tom Walsh. "Selecting Strong Passwords (HIPAA On the Job series)." *Journal of AHIMA* 72, no. 9 (2001): 16A–D.

premise that, in an emergency, a physician should not be restricted from accessing any information. Such access privileges, however, can be improved through the use of emergency-mode access controls, also required by HIPAA. These controls limit access only to information in which the user is a user of record but permit access to other information when there is a demonstrable need for access.

- Role-based access control assigns privileges based on the role of the user. A nurse on one unit may be able to access records of only the patients on that nursing unit. A laboratory technician may be able to view all patients in-house but may not write to any record except in the laboratory information system. Most vendors supply some form of role-based access control today and are looking to enhance this for HIPAA.

- Context-based access control assigns privileges based on a much more detailed level. It controls access to given data elements and will change the level of access based on the role being assumed at a given time. For example, a nurse in the emergency department may have access to all patients' medication histories but not to detailed reports of histories and physical exams.

The American Society for Testing and Materials' (ASTM) E1986 Standard Guide for Information Access Privileges to Health Information further clarifies these access levels and recommends that both data elements and healthcare personnel warrant differing levels of access control.

How Is Access to Information Controlled?

Once access privileges are defined, HIPAA's information access control requirements describe how access is authorized, established, and modified. Access authorization policies and procedures should require manager approval for assignment of a specific access privilege. Access establishment policies and procedures commonly require a controlled number of individuals who may receive the access authorization and assign access rights. The process should entail:

- Verification of the individual to whom the access is granted. There should always be a positive form of identification made before assigning a password. If a password is not assigned in person with a photo ID, then some other system, such as a secret question and response, should be used to verify identity.

- Training in selection of passwords and other aspects of workstation use. This should be performed at the time access is established. In addition to selecting a strong password, users should be trained in virus protection, to monitor for unsuccessful log-ins, and how to report security incidents.

- Assignment of a one-time password that permits access to the system and creation of the user's own password. Today, many systems assign a default password that allows users to use the password several times, if not indefinitely. Time is critical in a healthcare environment, so it may be appropriate to set the initial password to a two-time use, but retaining this password beyond that is extremely risky.

Access modification policies and procedures apply when a user changes jobs or believes a password has been compromised. Access modification requires coordination between transferring managers.

What's the Best Way to Choose a Password?

In evaluating the options permitted for the second tier of entity authentication (in addition to the unique user identifier), the password is the most common. A PIN is typically considered the weakest. Biometrics and tokens are considered the strongest, but they are also the most expensive. Telephone callback is generally inconvenient and not totally reliable. Good business practice suggests that a password would be adequate authentication as long as there is strong password management (as described above) and:

- Self-selection of a strong password

- Controlled frequency of change of password

- Passwords should not be reused

- Same password for multiple applications/systems per user

Selecting a strong password is something users should be taught to how to do. The password characteristics should match the operating system requirements. For example, under Windows 95, 98, and NT, passwords of seven characters are best because of the way Microsoft stores the password. UNIX passwords are best at eight characters; in fact, additional characters in the UNIX password are ignored.

Passwords made up of alphabetic, numeric, and special (if possible) characters in upper and lower case (if possible) are best. These passwords should be easy to remember and difficult for others to guess. Some suggestions include:

- Two short, disassociated words combined with or containing special characters and upper- and lower-case characters (for example, k!s$rugS [kiss rugs])

- A short phrase spelled in a unique way (for example, buy3w@y [by the way])

- A mnemonic, also including numbers and special characters (for example, Owt$gm1 [Oh When The Saints Go Marching I(1)n])

Avoid using:

- Words that are easy to guess (for example, "Cubbies," for a baseball fan who lives in Chicago)

- Words that convey personal information (for example, license plate, spouse name, or other identifier typically associated with an individual, such as a unique physician identification number or an employee's badge number)

- Single words found in a dictionary of any language

- Repeat characters (for example, AAA222)

Information security professionals disagree on the exact frequency with which passwords should be changed, but they do agree that the stronger the password, the less frequently it needs to be changed. The environment may dictate frequency, but six months to one year can be appropriate for many organizations, as long as the password is strong.

Ideally, a "single sign-on" system would authenticate users to all applications to which they have access privileges, making it necessary for users to have only one password. Because of the potpourri of systems in hospitals today, a single sign-on is not totally feasible. There-fore, users should be encouraged to use the same password for every application/system to which they have access.

While there is a risk that one compromised password would compromise all systems, it is more likely that one remembered password would be less frequently compromised than many passwords that cannot be remembered and have to be recorded somewhere. To the extent possible, users should not be able to reuse passwords once they have changed the password.

Some schools of thought encourage the subsequent password to be a spin-off of the first, such as changing one number in sequence, again to promote memorization. Others consider this to be too close to not changing the password at all and encourage an entirely different password. The likelihood of password compromise should dictate recommendations concerning password construction.

Automatic log-off of systems after a set period is also associated with password management. HIPAA requires automatic log-off but does not specify the time. Each organization should evaluate the location of the workstations and set times that reflect the risk of inappropriate access.

What Are Audit Controls?

Some information systems specialists suggest that strong access controls negate the need for audit controls. While the prevention afforded by access control is better than the remediation provided by audit controls, audit controls are a requirement under HIPAA and a key element in supporting access controls. Audit controls, including audit trails, ensure that access controls work. They provide proof of access that may be allowed based on the access privileges, but is inappropriate.

How Should I Handle Sanction Policy and Termination?

The proposed security rule defines sanction policy as "such policy regarding disciplinary actions which are communicated to all employees, agents, and contractors, for example, verbal warning, notice of disciplinary action placed in personnel files, removal of system privileges, termination of employment and contract penalties."

The rule references ASTM standard E1869 (Confidentiality, Privacy, Access, and Data Security Principles for Health Information Including Computer-based Patient Records). E1869 states that "All organizations and individuals shall adopt and use sanctions to deter inappropriate access, misuse of data, unauthorized release of data and sharing of access mechanisms." It further indicates that "Intentional violations should be penalized more severely. Response to negligent, inadvertent, or accidental violations should include the reeducation of the individual as well as a review of related policies and procedures. Penalties should be adjusted to fit the situation ranging from dismissal from the job or loss of contract to lesser sanctions."

HIPAA also requires formal, documented instructions, including appropriate security measures, for the termination of a user's access. Whether friendly/voluntary or unfriendly/involuntary, all terminations should be treated equally.

Because a number of parties (including management, human resources, payroll, and information systems) are often involved in a termination, a system of checks and balances is needed to ensure that all parties have performed their tasks on time. The manager should be responsible for the initial notification and verifying removal of access. For employees, an automatic link between processing the last paycheck and access removal would be desirable. If this is not possible or not reliable, it is advisable to purge accounts after a defined period of inactivity.

Managing termination of access for agents and contractors is always more difficult, but it can be the weakest link. Agent or contractor access can be controlled by setting up their access accounts to automatically suspend on the date their contract ends and by assigning them unique user identifications that can be easily tracked for activity (for example, all temporary unique user identifications begin with the letter T). A list of unique user identifiers with active accounts should be generated regularly and used by applicable parties to validate continued requirements for the account. Any changes or terminations that have not been removed will appear on the list.

Computer Recycling: Are You Legally Prepared?

Joseph P. Harford, MS

As the healthcare industry continues to prepare for HIPAA compliance, two obstacles are emerging—the safe and legal disposal of outdated computer equipment and the digital or physical data destruction of patient information contained on them. This equipment comes in the form of computer monitors, hard drives, printers, copiers, and more. In the past, this equipment may have been placed into storage, donated to a school, or sent to the dumpster.

None of these methods of disposal address healthcare organizations' environmental or legal responsibilities. But how do you know if your organization is legally positioned to handle disposal of computer equipment? This article will address these concerns.

What Is Legal?

To determine if your organization is legally prepared in terms of computer equipment, three questions should be addressed:

- Does your organization have a plan in place for the removal and disposal of outdated computer equipment?

- Does your plan adhere to appropriate local, state, and federal environmental laws for equipment removal or recycling?

- Does your plan follow the appropriate local, state, and federal laws regarding the privacy of patient data that may still reside on the equipment in question?

The 1976 Resource Conservation and Recovery Act addresses the proper disposal of hazardous materials. Computer monitors contain an average of five to eight pounds of lead in the glass. Computer equipment also contains materials categorized as hazardous such as mercury, cadmium, and arsenic. Dumping large amounts of this equipment into a landfill is against the law.

In summer 2002, the Environmental Protection Agency filed fines for the improper disposal of hazardous waste that included computer monitors. For more information on such fines, go to www.epa.gov.

Source: Harford, Joseph P. "Computer Recycling: Are You Legally Prepared?." *Journal of AHIMA* 74, no. 3 (2003): 54.

It is estimated that by 2004 there will be 350 million obsolete computers in the US with no clear channel for removal, recycling, or disposal. This volume of equipment not only poses an environmental nightmare but also a challenge regarding the protection of privacy. Many states are attempting to enact legislation that will control the disposal of this equipment. Massachusetts and New Jersey have created a ban on dumping it into landfills. Pennsylvania will soon require a permit for companies that want to be involved with electronic recycling.

Protecting PHI

Although it is not directly addressed by HIPAA, it is obvious that proper recycling of computer equipment that contains protected health information (PHI) is just as important as following the guidelines for secure document storage and document destruction. The removal and recycling of computer equipment should be partnered with the need to properly and securely destroy PHI.

Healthcare organizations are aware of the need to work with a trustworthy document storage and destruction company. However, in many cases, the electronic source of all of these paper documents is forgotten. There have been numerous cases in which drives have not been properly "cleansed" and information has been inadvertently given away.

Destroying Data

Data destruction is not as simple and straightforward as "formatting" the hard drive of a computer. In fact, simply formatting the hard drive is in no way secure, comprehensive, or reliable. It is critical to implement responsible practices that consider the fiduciary responsibility of a healthcare provider to its patients.

The US Department of Defense has set forth standards for the reliable and secure destruction of both electronic and physical data that resides on a computer hard drive. In the absence of standards of this type, healthcare organizations may want to consider adopting these standards when completing the task of secure data destruction. It may be helpful to refer to the standards listed in the National Industrial Security Program Operating Manual at www.dss.mil/isec/nispom.htm.

Healthcare organizations may find the internal task of electronics recycling to be a daunting one and may decide that the identification, inventory management, destruction, and certification of private data should be left in the hands of reputable recyclers.

While it is always necessary to perform due diligence on a vendor, it is critical in this case in light of the potential environmental and confidentiality liabilities that organizations face. Ideally, an electronics recycler would perform both certified digital and physical data destruction services. Simply purchasing software or removing and destroying the hard drive is not adequate to protect an organization from an information breach.

The information that is solicited from a potential recycler or destruction vendor should be similar to that collected about the document storage or destruction vendor that may already be working for the organization. When choosing a recycling/destruction vendor, consider the following issues:

- Landfill policy
- Employee training
- Background review and bonding
- Data destruction practices and insurance coverage

Even with a vendor in hand, the liability associated with improper computer disposal or data loss ultimately remains with the accused institution. Make sure your organization is prepared.

Part 8

Roles and Training
for HIPAA Compliance

Privacy Official: Position Statement

The American Health Information Management Association (AHIMA) recognizes the increased complexity of protecting patients' privacy while managing access to, and release of, information about patients and other healthcare consumers.

Credentialed health information management (HIM) professionals—because of their academic preparation, work experience, commitment to patient advocacy, and professional code of ethics—are uniquely qualified to assume positions as designated privacy officials as required by the Health Insurance Portability and Accountability Act (HIPAA).

Background

Healthcare is a service industry that relies on information for every facet of its delivery. Health information has value to the patient it describes, the provider it serves, and the organization it supports, in addition to society as it directs the health of the population. It must be protected as a valuable asset, and in its primary form as the medical record of a unique individual, it must be safeguarded.

Privacy concerns grow as technology increases access to health information. Mental health, substance abuse, sexually transmitted disease, and now genetic information create a heightened awareness of the need for privacy. Documented cases of the use of health information to make decisions about hiring, firing, loan approval, and to develop consumer marketing have sensitized the public to the risks of sharing information with their healthcare provider.

For years, states have written laws and regulations to protect their citizens' privacy by limiting release of information based on the requester, the type of information, and the use of that information. Due to the complexity of the issue, the number of concerned parties, and the variety of health information, no two states have the same laws.

Over the last 10 years, the federal government has tried to address the patchwork nature of state laws by developing comprehensive federal legislation, but has failed to complete that task. In an effort to ensure all citizens have a standard minimum protection, the Department of Health and Human Services has promulgated regulation under the authority of HIPAA to provide a universal floor of protection. However, the industry is already concerned with meeting this new minimal level.

Source: AHIMA Position Statement (February 2001).

To ensure the necessary leadership for compliance, the Standards for Privacy of Individually Identifiable Health Information released in December 2000 require that each health plan, healthcare clearinghouse, and certain healthcare providers must designate a privacy official who is responsible for the development and implementation of their policies and procedures relative to privacy.

HIM professionals have effectively managed the release of information in healthcare organizations for decades. Establishing policy, training staff, developing consents, releasing information, and documenting information use are key elements of the HIM role. Coursework that prepares HIM professionals to fulfill this role has long been included in the curriculum of all accredited HIM academic programs, and is included in the certification examination for both registered health information administrators and technicians. Since its formation in 1928, AHIMA has supported its members in their efforts to protect patient privacy.

Support for the Position

To maintain the privacy, confidentiality, and security of health information, AHIMA members assume a leadership role in compliance with state and federal laws, develop appropriate organizational initiatives, and exercise ethical decision making. HIM professionals are uniquely qualified to assume the role of privacy officials, because we:

- Interpret state and federal laws that apply to the use of health information, into policy

- Understand the decision-making processes throughout healthcare that rely on information

- Direct the flow of information within healthcare organizations and throughout healthcare

- Apply HIM principles to information in all its forms

- Understand the content of health information in its clinical, research, and business contexts

- Apply the technologies used to collect, access, store, and transmit information in all its forms

- Establish and recognize best practices in the management of privacy of health information

- Collaborate with other healthcare professionals to ensure appropriate security measures are in place

- Historically managed the release of information function

- Advocate for the patient, relative to health information confidentiality

- Live by a Professional Code of Ethics specific to maintenance of patient privacy

Are You Ready to Be a Privacy Officer?

David A. Sobel, PhD, CHP

As an HIM professional, you may be asked to serve as your organization's first privacy officer. While serving as privacy officer will give you the opportunity to play a new and more profound role in safeguarding patients' privacy rights, it will also provide you with new challenges.

Are you ready to take on this role? This article will explore some of the issues you should consider before accepting the position of privacy officer.

Know Your Position Description

Your new responsibilities will include developing and administering a privacy program and ensuring that all staff, including physicians, are educated in safeguarding protected health information (PHI). Successful privacy officers have a formal position description that contains clearly defined responsibilities.

When looking at a position description for a privacy officer, you should ask yourself the following:

- Has executive leadership developed formal position responsibilities for the privacy officer?

- Is this a full-time or part-time position?

- Would this be an addition to your current HIM director responsibilities and, if so, is it possible to do both jobs?

- It is also important to consider whether information security responsibilities are assigned to another person. If not, will you be required to serve as both the privacy and security officer?

New Reporting Relationships

To ensure that authority matches the level of job responsibility, privacy officers should report to the highest levels of management such as a chief financial officer, chief operating officer, or

Source: Sobel, David. "Are You Ready to Be a Privacy Officer?" *Journal of AHIMA* 74, no. 4 (April 2003): 60, 62.

chief information officer. Before accepting the privacy officer position, it is imperative that you know what management expects of you and your new reporting relationship. This is a challenging position that will be significantly more difficult without a formal position description and the outright support of executive leadership.

Successful privacy officers enjoy a degree of independence similar to that of an internal auditor. In addition to reporting to a member of senior management, it is recommended that you have a secondary reporting relationship to an appropriate committee of the organization's governing board such as the quality assurance or audit committee. Providing the governing board with quality progress reports is one of the responsibilities of the privacy officer.

Consider the situation of a privacy officer at a teaching hospital who recently reported a breach of confidentiality to the appropriate department director for further investigation and disposition. As the investigation unfolded, it became clear that the person responsible for the breach was related by marriage to the department director, the individual in charge of investigating the incident. Despite convincing evidence, no formal action was taken against this employee by the department director.

By reporting to the chief financial officer, with a secondary relationship to the audit committee of the board of governors, the privacy officer was able to present this case to committee members. The end result was that an additional investigation was conducted and both the director and employee received disciplinary action consistent with human resource policies.

Privacy Oversight Committee: A Must

All privacy officers quickly learn that to be successful, it is necessary to work with a strong and representative oversight committee such as an information security and privacy committee. Some questions to consider are:

- Does your organization have an oversight committee, or is one being established?

- Who chairs this committee?

- Is the committee made up of key members who have responsibilities for maintaining the confidentiality, security, and integrity of all information, but particularly PHI?

- What is the role of the privacy officer as a member of this committee?

Everybody Needs Back-up

Every privacy officer needs a back-up person. Healthcare information privacy is a very time-consuming obligation. If you accept the position of privacy officer, you will need a back-up to assume your responsibilities when you are away.

Your back-up should be familiar with your responsibilities and be able to step in at a moment's notice. He or she should be competent to deal with policy matters, answer employee and patient questions, and manage serious incidents.

A Balanced Budget?

Successful privacy officers have a budget. Does a budget exist within your organization or will you have a role in developing the budget? Will you be responsible for developing the budget in subsequent years?

Like all programs, there are costs associated with managing a privacy program. You may need to purchase resource materials, order subscriptions to industry publications, and perform research. You may want to attend a state or national conference. And you will certainly need to devote financial resources to educating employees, physicians, and volunteers.

Rewards with Responsibility

Finally, consider the position's salary. Will your salary be adjusted to reflect your new responsibilities?

You may be asked to develop and administer policies, ensure compliance with state and federal regulations, work with all levels of management, manage privacy and security incidents, and serve as the in-house consultant to executive leadership for all matters pertaining to protection of health information. It is reasonable to assume that privacy officers should be properly compensated with respect to their position's responsibilities.

Serving as a privacy officer is both an exciting and daunting role. With the outright support of the governing board and executive leadership, a solid position description, a good reporting relationship, a necessary degree of independence, a strong oversight committee, a reliable back-up, and a realistic budget, you should be well on your way to experiencing success in this new position.

Success at Every Level: A Career Ladder for Privacy Officers

Gwen Hughes, RHIA, CHP

Considering a career in privacy? AHIMA's Career Progression Ladder for Privacy Officers reveals the education, skills, and support you need to succeed.

The HIPAA privacy rule requires that covered entities designate a privacy official responsible for the development and implementation of privacy-related policies and procedures. HIM professionals are in a unique position to assume the privacy officer role because of their comprehensive understanding of how patient health information is requested, used, and disclosed. Additionally, HIM professionals are committed to protecting patient health information while ensuring that information is readily available to legitimate requesters.

With this in mind, AHIMA developed the Career Progression Ladder for Privacy Officers. This ladder provides information about privacy officer career options and the professional development steps required to reach each level. As you examine this career ladder, it is important to note that AHIMA strongly encourages hiring RHITs and RHIAs for privacy officer roles.

Keep in mind that there are many ways to climb the privacy officer career ladder. While some people may prepare for a privacy officer role through the traditional HIM or patient accounts roles illustrated on this ladder, others may obtain the necessary knowledge, skills, and experience through roles in education, research, or information systems. Finally, your place on the career ladder is determined by what you want to accomplish—there is no one "right" rung. Reaching the next rung is up to you.

Career Progression Ladder for Privacy Officers

Level One: Clerk

Educational preparation: High school diploma or equivalent; successful completion of a health record clerk program or equivalent education or on-the-job training program

Privacy-related knowledge needed:

- Medical terminology

- Health record content

Source: Hughes, Gwen. "Success at Every Level: A Career Ladder for Privacy Officers." *Journal of AHIMA* 74 no. 2 (February 2003): 52–56.

- Basic understanding of patients' rights to privacy and facility's responsibilities for ensuring privacy

Skills needed:

- Ability to apply privacy concepts, policies, and procedures to requests for protected health information
- Ability to recognize potential risks and situations in which supervisor should be consulted

Duties:

- Evaluates authorizations, court orders, and subpoenas for validity
- Applies minimum necessary standard or criteria to requests
- Evaluates requested content to determine if any of the information should be withheld from the requester
- Discloses information according to federal and state law and facility policy
- Submits certifications and disclosures made in response to a court order or subpoena to supervisor for approval
- Denies access or disclosure in accordance with policies and procedures
- Consults supervisor with questions or areas of concern

Salary data: None available

Job titles: Health information disclosure coordinator, health information disclosure clerk, release of information clerk, release of information coordinator

Where to look for jobs: Positions most common in large physician practices and hospitals; can be found in either patient account or health information management departments; can also be found in any healthcare provider or third-party payer setting

Level Two: Supervisor

Educational preparation: Successful completion of vocational program in HIM or a closely related field with courses that address medical terminology, health record content, and legal aspects of health records; RHIT certification preferred

Privacy-related knowledge needed:

- Medical terminology
- Health record content
- Federal and state laws relative to requesting, using, and disclosing health information

Skills needed:

- Ability to explain privacy policies and procedures to staff and requesters of information
- Ability to lead staff effectively
- Ability to monitor privacy-related compliance with federal and state law and facility policy
- Ability to deny access to individuals, law enforcement, attorneys, members of the work force, physicians, and business associates in a constructive manner

Duties:

- Trains clerks to disclose health information in accordance with federal and state law and facility policy

- Trains clerks to differentiate between valid and invalid authorizations, court orders, and subpoenas

- Trains clerks to apply minimum necessary standards or criteria

- Trains staff to identify information that should be withheld from access or disclosures

- Monitors disclosures for compliance with federal and state laws and facility policies

- Checks and approves certifications and disclosures made in response to subpoenas and court orders

- Documents and reports to privacy officers any incidents wherein disclosures did not comply with laws, regulations, policies, and procedures

- Serves as a resource to clerks who have questions about applying laws, regulations, policies, and procedures

Salary data: None available

Job titles: Supervisor, HIM; supervisor, medical records; supervisor, patient accounts; supervisor, copy service; supervisor of compliance and regulatory management

Where to look for jobs: Positions most common in large provider settings, such as physician practices and hospitals; can be found in either patient account or HIM departments; can also be found in any third-party payer setting

Level Three: Manager or Assistant Director

Educational preparation: RHIT certification or an associate's degree in accounting (or related field) with courses that address medical terminology, health record content, and legal aspects of health records

Privacy-related knowledge needed:

- Medical terminology

- Health record content in both paper-based and computer-based systems

- Information privacy laws

- Ethical privacy standards

- Access, use, and disclosure of health information

- Access control technologies

- Presentation techniques

Skills needed:

- Ability to simplify and teach others privacy-related concepts, federal and state law, and facility policy related to privacy

- Ability to lead staff effectively

- Ability to write policies and procedures that are accurate and understandable

- Ability to work with others to ensure compliance

- Ability to establish and implement logical systems that meet federal, state, or facility privacy standards

- Ability to deny access to any requester in a constructive manner

Duties:

- Manages day-to-day operations in HIM, patient accounts, or equivalent department in a health plan

- Authors department-level or organization-wide policies and procedures

- Educates and trains members of the organization's work force

- Establishes systems as needed to implement compliance with federal and state laws and regulations, standards of practice, organizational policy, and departmental goals and objectives

- Works with other departments to monitor compliance with laws, regulations, standards, policies, and procedures

- Designs and takes corrective action when indicated by monitoring

- Reports the results of performance monitoring activities to appropriate organizational authority

Salary data: $30,000–$75,000

Job titles: Health information manager; assistant director, HIM; patient accounts manager; assistant director, patient accounts; compliance manager

Where to look for jobs: Provider organizations including hospitals, nursing homes, physician practices, and home health organizations; health plans; organizations that contract with providers to provide release of information or other patient information-related services

Level Four: Director

Educational preparation: RHIA certification or a bachelor's degree and RHIT certification
Privacy-related knowledge needed: Same as above
Skills needed: Same as above
Duties:

- Directs HIM, patient accounts, business office, or equivalent function in a health plan

- Authors organizational and department policies and procedures

- Educates administration, members of the work force, the medical staff, and others as to laws, regulations, standards, policies, and procedures

- Works with administration to acquire the resources needed to implement organizational initiatives

- Works with others to ensure organizational and departmental compliance with laws, regulations, standards, policies, and procedures

Salary data: $35,000–$80,000

Job titles: Director, HIM; director, patient accounts; director of corporate compliance

Where to look for jobs: Provider organizations, health plans, and organizations that contract with those organizations to provide health information-related services

Level Five: Manager or Director of One or More Departments with the Responsibilities of a Privacy Officer

Educational preparation: RHIA certification or a bachelor's degree and RHIT certification; AHIMA certification as a privacy officer

Privacy-related knowledge needed: Same as above, plus:

- Ethical and accreditation standards
- Adult learning
- Gap analysis
- Risk management analysis
- Compliance
- Accepted physical and security systems
- Auditing systems
- Storage, retention, and destruction of health information

Skills needed: Same as above, plus:

- Ability to write and speak persuasively
- Ability to administer an appropriate organizational infrastructure for privacy
- Ability to coordinate facility-wide projects
- Ability to update, coordinate, and implement privacy-related policies and procedures facility wide

Duties:

- Directs the HIM, patient accounts, or other departments or services
- Works with other departments to develop and implement privacy-related policies and procedures that adhere to federal and state laws and regulations
- Fosters privacy awareness
- Serves on or as a liaison to the organization's institutional review board or privacy committee
- Works with the security officer to ensure alignment between privacy and security practices
- Represents the organization's information privacy interests to internal and external groups

Salary data: $50,000–$100,000

Job titles: Director, HIM; director, patient accounts; director, information services; director, corporate compliance; chief information officer; privacy officer

Where to look for jobs: Provider organizations, health plans, and organizations that contract with those organizations to provide health information services

Level Six: Facility Privacy Officer (Single Facility)

Educational preparation: AHIMA certification as a privacy officer
  Privacy-related knowledge needed: Same as above
  Skills needed: Same as above, plus:

- Ability to simplify and teach others privacy-related concepts, federal and state law, ethical standards of practice, and facility policy related to privacy

- Ability to establish and administer an appropriate organizational infrastructure for privacy

Duties: Same as above, plus:

- Manages the development and implementation of privacy-related policies and procedures that adhere to federal and state laws and regulations

- Fosters privacy awareness

- Serves on or as a liaison to the organization's institutional review board or privacy committee

- Works with the security officer to ensure alignment between privacy and security practices

- Represents the organization's information privacy interests to internal and external groups

Salary data: $50,000–$100,000
Job title: Privacy officer
Where to look for jobs: Provider, health plan, and business associate enterprises

Level Seven: Enterprise Privacy Officer (Privacy Officer for More Than One Facility)

Educational preparation: AHIMA certification as privacy officer
  Privacy-related knowledge needed: Same as above
  Skills needed: Same as above, plus:

- Ability to lead effectively; skills must be particularly strong due to breadth of position and absence of direct-line authority in most cases

- Ability to understand the unique operational aspects of each facility within the enterprise

- Ability to coordinate enterprise-wide projects

Duties: Same as above, plus:

- Develops and implements privacy-related policies and procedures that adhere to federal and state laws and regulations among numerous organizations in an enterprise

- Fosters privacy awareness

- Serves on or as a liaison to the organization's institutional review board or privacy committee

- Works with the security officer to ensure alignment between privacy and security practices

- Represents the organization's information privacy interests to internal and external groups

Salary data: $70,000–$125,000
Job title: Privacy officer
Where to look for jobs: Large provider, health plan, and business associate enterprises

Level Eight: Chief Privacy Officer (Enterprise Privacy Officer to Whom Other Privacy Officials Report)

Educational preparation: AHIMA certification as a privacy and security officer; master's or doctorate degree in HIM, information systems, law, or a related field
Privacy-related knowledge needed: Same as above, plus:

- Strategic planning

- Enterprise information systems

- Knowledge management

Skills needed: Same as above, plus:

- Ability to manage enterprise-wide projects

Duties:

- Develops and implements privacy-related policies and procedures that adhere to federal and state laws and regulations among numerous organizations in an enterprise through other privacy officers

- Fosters privacy awareness

- Serves on or as a liaison to the enterprise's institutional review board

- Ensures alignment between enterprise privacy and security practices

- Represents the organization's information privacy interests to internal and external groups

Salary data: $125,000 or more
Job titles: Chief privacy officer; vice president, privacy; vice president, privacy and security; vice president, information services
Where to look for jobs: The largest provider, health plan, and business associate enterprises

References

Scichilone, Rita. "Climbing the Coding Career Progression Ladder." *Journal of AHIMA* 73, no. 4 (2002): 32–36. Available online in the FORE Library: HIM Body of Knowledge at www.ahima.org.

2002 Salary Survey. Rockville, MD: HIPAA Compliance Alert, 2002.

"New Survey Shows Privacy Officers Take Hold in Key Consumer Industries and Report to Top Management." *Privacy & American Business* (December 6, 2001). Press Release.

Privacy and Security: Are Two Hats Better Than One?

William Woloszyn, RHIA

Who, me? Work as both a privacy officer and a security officer? It may seem impossible, but it can be done. While the roles of privacy officer and security officer are often presented as two distinct jobs in relation to HIPAA, if a lack of resources or personnel demand it, a daring HIM professional can take on both at the same time.

Don't assume, however, that combining the functions of these two roles will be an easy solution. Disagreements and conflicts often arise. Each individual's role should be well defined in order to prevent conflicts.

Drawing the Line

There seems to be a distinct overlap in terms of the definition of both the security and privacy officer jobs. According to AHIMA's privacy officer job description, the privacy officer "oversees all ongoing activities related to the development, implementation, maintenance of, and adherence to the organization's policies and procedures covering the privacy of, and access to, patient health information in compliance with federal and state laws and the healthcare organization's information privacy practices."[1]

The proposed HIPAA security rule defines the security officer's duties as "the management and supervision of (1) the use of security measures to protect data, and (2) the conduct of personnel in relation to the protection of data." This assignment is critical to provide an organizational focus and importance to security and to pinpoint responsibility.

HIPAA includes administrative procedures as a component of the security measures, arguably a function of both privacy and security officers. This provokes a conflict and raises the question: where do you draw the line between security and privacy policy and procedures? This question will need to be addressed as organizations develop policies and procedures.

A Basis for Comparison

The skills required for a privacy officer and security officer are similar. This person must be decisive, firm, and a clear communicator. Both the privacy and the security officer must have

---

Source: Woloszyn, William. "Privacy and Security: Are Two Hats Better Than One?" *Journal of AHIMA* 73, no. 6 (2002): 59.

an eye for detail and clear ideas of right and wrong. Privacy (protection from wrongful disclosure) and security (protection from destruction, tampering, and unavailable access) are unique and yet unavoidably connected. Both positions share similar skills and responsibilities, but they may vary in regard to the interpretation of risk and agreement of solutions to apply.

A Matter of Opinion

The two roles may differ in other ways as well. One example is the way they view solutions to different problems. A technical solution may be ironclad and "secure" but in all practical ways useless because it has unacceptable "response time." A practical solution may be found in policy to "log all disclosures," but the question arises: technically, how will this happen? Will it happen by having centralized control of all disclosures? Are the two positions' understanding of operations broad enough to ensure consideration of the impact to clinical care or patient satisfaction when making decisions? Another challenge will be applying sanctions equally—from the CEO to the file clerk. Both are liable under HIPAA if they violate a rule. When one person fills both roles, using both perspectives may be a challenge.

Privacy and security officers both need to be able to consider technical solution limitations in practical versus theoretical terms. How can you really have a grasp on what needs to happen if you don't understand the options for getting there?

The Best of Both Worlds

There are advantages to having two people fill the privacy and security roles. Potentially, they can produce more work together than individually. If they work as a team, they can act as checks and balances in tough decisions and directing initiatives. And, ultimately, they can provide backup for each other.

It is clear that HIPAA makes both privacy and security roles important, but it does not mandate separation of the two roles. However, if resources or organizational limits require, the functional overlap permits one person to hold both roles. Wearing two hats may not be for everyone, but an awareness of the challenges can help navigate around the pitfalls.

Note

1. AHIMA. Position Statement: Privacy Official. February 2001. Available at www.ahima.org/infocenter/index.html.

HIPAA Privacy and Security Training

Beth Hjort, RHIA, CHP

HIM professionals have long known and upheld the legal and ethical obligations of consumer privacy protection of health information. Advocacy of these principles within healthcare organizations has been based on professional accountability and external directives. However, depending on an organization's state of residence (state laws), program participation (such as Medicare, alcohol and drug abuse programs, and accreditation programs), and applicable federal laws, this protection may be fragmented at best.

The extent of work force awareness and degree of privacy and security restrictions for patient health information have varied due to the delicate balance of privacy with the benefits of sharing and using information, job position influence or parameters, leadership interpretation of existing directives, and implementation cost. Though implicit, these requirements for upholding privacy and security of health information have seldom required work force training.

HIPAA requires formal education and training of the work force to ensure ongoing accountability for privacy and security of protected health information (PHI). HIPAA's privacy rule and security rule independently address training requirements. Like the majority of the standards, the training requirements are nonprescriptive, giving organizations flexibility in implementation. This practice brief offers guidelines to covered entities to aid in implementation of the training standards and suggests the efficacy of combining efforts.

Federal Requirements

HIPAA Privacy Rule

Section 164.530 of the HIPAA privacy rule states:

> (b) 1. Standard: training. A covered entity must train all members of its work force on the policies and procedures with respect to PHI required by this subpart, as necessary and appropriate for the members of the work force to carry out their function within the covered entity.

Source: Hjort, Beth. "AHIMA Practice Brief: HIPAA Privacy and Security Training" (Updated November 2003).

(b) 2. Implementation specifications: training.

    i. A covered entity must provide training that meets the requirements of paragraph (b)(1) of this section, as follows:

- To each member of the covered entity's work force by no later than the compliance date for the covered entity

- Thereafter, to each new member of the work force within a reasonable period of time after the person joins the covered entity's work force

- To each member of the covered entity's work force whose functions are affected by a material change in the policies or procedures required by this subpart, within a reasonable period of time after the material change becomes effective in accordance with paragraph (i) of this section

    ii. A covered entity must document that the training as described in paragraph (b)(2)(i) of this section has been provided, as required by paragraph (j) of this section

(j) 1. Standard: documentation. A covered entity must:

    i. Maintain the policies and procedures provided for in paragraph (i) of this section in written or electronic form

    ii. If a communication is required by this subpart to be in writing, maintain such writing, or an electronic copy, as documentation

    iii. If an action, activity, or designation is required by this subpart to be documented, maintain a written or electronic record of such action, activity, or designation

(j) 2. Implementation specification: retention period. A covered entity must retain the documentation required by paragraph (j)(1) of this section for six years from the date of its creation or the date when it last was in effect, whichever is later.

Summary: A covered entity must train the entire work force on HIPAA-directed privacy policies and procedures necessary to comply with the rule through execution of organizational operations. Small health plans have an extension to April 14, 2004, one year beyond the implementation date for most covered entities. All must provide for ongoing updates and evidence of compliance must be documented in either written or electronic form and be retained for a minimum of six years from the implementation date.

HIPAA Security Rule

HIPAA's security standard 164.308(a)(5)(i) states:

" . . . Implement a security awareness and training program for all members of its work force (including management)."

(ii) Implementation specifications. Implement:

- Security reminders (addressable)

- Protection from malicious software (addressable)

- Log in monitoring (addressable)

- Password management (addressable)

Section III, analysis of and responses to public comments on the proposed rule, clarifies that "the amount and type of training needed will be dependent upon an entity's configuration and security risks." It further states, "Business associates must be made aware of security policies and procedures, whether through contract language or other means. Covered entities are not required to provide training to business associates or anyone else that is not a member of their work force." Further, it states, "Training can be tailored to job need if the covered entity so desires."

Summary: The entire work force, including management, must be trained on security issues respective of organizational uniqueness. The requirement for periodic security updates ensures the ongoing nature of the effort.

State Laws and Regulations

Though few states have had regulations specifically requiring training for privacy and security, any existing regulations are preempted by HIPAA except in cases of a more stringent status designation. Organizations should be aware of state circumstances.

Accreditation

Joint Commission Standards

The 2004 hospital standards were modified to be consistent with HIPAA. The prepublication Web edition addresses privacy and security:

IM.2.10 states, "Information privacy and confidentiality are maintained." The second element of performance addresses privacy training and updates: "The organization's policy, including significant changes to the policy, has been effectively communicated to applicable staff."

IM.2.20 states, "Information security including data integrity is maintained." The same element of performance applies for security as for privacy noted in IM.2.10 above.

The Accreditation Association for Ambulatory Health Care and the American Osteopathic Association standards do not explicitly cover privacy and security training.

Recommendations

If you have HIPAA privacy and security training responsibilities in your organization, following are considerations for program development.

General

Determining the best training approach for your organization is a significant task. Healthcare organizations may be able to reduce the administrative burden and cost of privacy and security training by making it part of a comprehensive HIPAA educational program or part of an even broader educational program. While the training standards apply to a universal audience when other portions of the administrative simplification act may not, organized planning can address audience overlap and reduce redundancies in reaching large groups with varying messages.

Obtaining support and conducting high-level training for administration and senior management is critical due to the magnitude, cost, and ongoing nature of the requirements.

Similarities in the privacy and security requirements invite combined training efforts. Both rules include training of all personnel, ongoing training, and documentation. Below are points to consider when implementing a successful training process:

- Make training your mantra—it may be your best privacy asset.

- Develop an enduring program that perpetuates itself and becomes part of the culture of your organization.

- Document your organizational privacy and security training program. It should cover education (knowledge and understanding), training (how-to), and ongoing awareness. The compliant approach includes PHI in all forms including verbal, written, and electronic. Timelines for initial efforts and subsequent new employee orientation according to date of hire should also be included.

- Use effective training structures and methods already in place when possible.

- Present an understanding of the spirit of HIPAA as it applies to the individual consumer to personalize it. Make each employee your deputy in compliance. Emphasize the need for cultural change and the need to resist the natural tendency toward curiosity.

- Develop a responsive communication process to address questions that arise after training and in an ongoing manner. Implementation questions may point out holes in the program that need to be addressed.

- A reference repository of up-to-date policies and procedures is critical. A centralized composite on the intranet can be a dependable and easily updated resource. Employer-endorsed Web sites can provide a mechanism for individuals to stay current on privacy issues and legislation.

- Develop a process for evaluating training program effectiveness, reliability, and validity. This should include a provision for updating the trainers on any changes or enhancements.

- Make a commitment to follow industry best practices, benchmarks, and standards regarding training as healthcare settles into this new way of life. No two programs will be identical, yet much can be gained from networking.

Who Is Trained

HIPAA's privacy rule defines work force as "employees, volunteers, trainees, and other persons whose conduct, in the performance of work for a covered entity, is under the direct control of such entity, whether or not they are paid by the covered entity." It further directs that training include "all members of its work force," "each new member of the work force," and "each member of the covered entity's work force whose functions are affected by a material change in the policies or procedures."

The security rule states, "all members of its work force (including management")." Understanding the breadth of the training audience is critical for both initial and ongoing training. An organization should define its audience according to structure and operations with particular respect for access to PHI, responsibilities presenting compliance risk, and the ripple nature of PHI access through contractual relationships. Careful evaluation may introduce the importance of including individuals outside of the rule definitions. Individuals to be considered include part-time, contractual, temporary, home-based, and remote employees, management, board of directors, physicians (on site, in offices, and remote), educators, students, researchers, and maintenance personnel.

Who Trains

Existing organizational structure will help to direct a logical, workable approach for identifying trainers and accommodating HIPAA requirements. The need to establish clear accountability, appoint knowledgeable, qualified trainers, and clarify timelines and ongoing roles is critical in every setting. Questions to consider include:

- Who are the effective trainers in your organization now?

- Has a HIPAA oversight team been appointed?

- Do your privacy officer and security officer positions or functions work together to encourage a unified, coordinated approach?

- What role is appropriate for the human resources department, especially for reaching new hires with general training?

- If a train-the-trainer method is chosen, what key individuals are competent and are they appropriate for ongoing, instructor-led training?

- Does management have a role? Would management conduct general training or role- or job-specific training?

- Should you use point persons for department, section, or unit training?

- Will your organization retain consultant services for training? What will be covered?

What to Cover

The privacy rule states that the following should be covered in an organization's privacy program: "Policies and procedures with respect to protected health information . . . as necessary and appropriate for the members of the work force to carry out their function within the covered entity."

The security rule includes four "addressable" topics:

- Periodic security updates

- Procedures for guarding against, detecting, and reporting malicious software

- Procedures for monitoring log-in attempts and reporting discrepancies

- Procedures for creating, changing, and safeguarding passwords

Customizing Training

The rules address minimum training requiring scalability to be applied. Programs can and should be customized to your organization, operational nuances, and job position uniqueness. HIPAA-related gap and risk analyses are valuable references to fortify training outline. As you compile policies and procedures for training purposes, it will be evident that some are universal in application while others are unique to roles and select positions. Consider creating levels of training. Level I, for example, would entail the universally important education and training topics. Level II would include those particular to a role or job position and would be closely aligned with the need-to-know parameters identified for varying positions.

Additional training levels may be needed when increased knowledge and skills are necessary to carry out operations in a compliant manner. For example, management/supervisory staff may need specific training due to their involvement in compliance functions. High-level training may be developed for the information systems staff who must apply privacy policies in administering technological responsibilities. Be flexible by applying as many varied levels as needed to accomplish your goals. (See Figure 8.1, Sample HIM Department Privacy and Security Training Plan.)

It could be helpful to prioritize the training protocol by weighing issues and group impact. For example, greatest volume, information sensitivity levels, and areas of heightened risk concern would be addressed more urgently than groups needing only periodic access.

Figure 8.1.   Sample HIM department privacy and security training plan

Training Level	Target Audience	Privacy Topics	Security Topics
1	All employees Contractual coders Volunteers Students New employees	• General confidentiality • Training requirements • Patient rights (general) • Reporting known or suspected breaches • Sanctions • E-mail • Faxing • Complaints	• General security policies • Physical and workstation security • Periodic security reminders • Virus protection • Importance of monitoring log-ins • Password management • Audits
2	All employees Volunteers Students	• Special record handling	• Department security procedures • Software discipline
2	ROI staff management staff	• Federal and state laws • Consents and exclusions • Psychotherapy notes • Uses and disclosures/ authorizations • Patient rights • Subpoenas, court orders • Copy charges	• Audit trails
3	Management staff	• Department privacy and security training • Role and position assessments • Training program evaluations • Remediation procedures • Sanctions	

Level I/General Training Examples

- General confidentiality: governing laws and regulations and organizational policies

- Training requirements

- General patient rights

- General security policies: consider including a security primer to increase understanding of information security and technology

- Physical/workstation security

- Periodic security reminders: why they are important, how they will be accomplished

- Virus protection: potential harm, how to prevent it and how to report it

- Importance of monitoring log-in success/failure and how to report discrepancies

- Password management: keeping private, procedures for creating or changing, and other access management

- Ramifications of breaches to the organization and the individual

- Monitoring procedures

- Reporting known or suspected breaches

- Sanctions (organizational and individual)

- Role of the Office for Civil Rights, the agency charged with enforcing the privacy regulations

- E-mail

- Faxing

- Complaints

- Verbal confidentiality

Consider adopting Level I training content into new employee orientation, taking over when the first wave of training is complete. Be clear in communicating to new employees plans for department or unit customized training to supplement general training.

For Level II or job-specific training, drill down to necessary detail to evaluate positions effectively. Determine how a position uses health information, then fashion training accordingly. Assessment tools can be useful in determining appropriate inclusions for specific positions. Such tools provide a list of privacy and security topics. Using available information sources, determine applicable topics, including use and sensitivity levels when appropriate. Information sources could include job descriptions, observation, and discussion. (See Figure 8.2, Sample Privacy and Security Position Assessment.)

Figure 8.2. Sample privacy and security position assessment

Role/Position Assessment For:

Role/Job Title: _____

Behavioral Health Unit _____

Date: _____

Training Topic			
Sensitivity Level (high, medium, low)	**Use Level (0–5)**	**Include in Training? (Yes/No)**	
Treatment/Payment/Operations	high	5	yes
Notice of privacy practices	medium	3	yes
Marketing	low	0	no
Psychotherapy notes	high	5	yes
Business associate agreements	low	0	no
Disclosures: routine	medium	5	yes
Patient rights: access	medium	3	yes
Patient rights: amend	medium	2	yes
Photographs	low	1	yes

Level II Training Topic Examples

- Federal laws, state laws, regulations
- Treatment/payment/operations
- Notice of privacy practices
- Facility directories
- Access
- Business associate agreements
- Marketing
- Fund raising
- Psychotherapy notes
- Photography
- Disclosure, authorizations, routine, restrictions
- Redisclosure
- Patient rights: access, amend, accounting of disclosures, confidential communication
- Research
- Destruction of sensitive information
- Copy charges
- Deidentification
- Retention
- Minimum necessary
- Aggregate data
- Mitigation

For appropriate groups, cover:

- Policies for geographical considerations: on site, remote, at home, physician offices
- Equipment nuances: laptops, personal digital assistants, cell phones, pagers

Level III Training Example

Management-specific training might include:

- Review of policies or specific roles in department or section training
- Role and position assessments and training
- Audits
- Training program evaluations and modifications
- Ongoing awareness training or change updates
- Remediation procedures
- Sanctions

Training Delivery

Delivery method is important to the understandability of the information. Make an effort to use a variety of learning techniques and considerations as they relate to targeted groups or individuals and that optimally present the material to be covered. Below are important points to consider:

- When planning audience participation, consider different knowledge levels.

- Consider how you can reach the most influential people in your organization.

- Recognize the potential for information overload during training.

- Varying learning techniques can help address different learning styles in group presentations.

- Instructor-led classrooms may work best for in-depth training and when interaction or Q&A sessions are desired.

- Rotate presenters in instructor-led sessions.

- Computer-based training (PC, Intranet, and Internet) can be effective for reaching large groups (this can include online assessments/quizzes for immediate feedback).

- Training labs provide hands-on opportunity.

- Videotapes can be used for varying audiences.

- Videoconferencing.

- Distance training takes advantage of teaching tools developed by others such as Web casts, informational Web sites, and online classes.

- Frequently asked questions and discussion threads can be valuable when they are easily accessible.

- If using handouts, display the information differently from your slides and choose the best time to distribute them according to your approach.

- Consider developing training manuals to ensure consistency of coverage among trainers (these should be easily updated).

Ongoing Training

According to the privacy rule, "a covered entity must provide training . . . to each member of the covered entity's work force whose functions are affected by a material change in the policies or procedures required . . . within a reasonable period of time after the material change becomes effective." The security rule requires "security reminders."

Ongoing training is the process of keeping the issues in front of the work force. It is important to determine how often reminders will be circulated in addition to those triggered by change or new information. It is also important to identify which part of the work force needs which communications.

Optional methods of periodic reminders include sign-on security reminders, company newsletters, meetings, training programs, lunchtime sessions, promotional products, e-mail messages, banners and screen savers, fliers or handouts, posters, cafeteria tent cards, Web pages, teachable moments, grapevine, and literature and case law circulation, if only to select groups. Ensure a mechanism for updating the content of various training levels to reflect policy and procedure changes for affected individuals.

Documentation

The privacy rule requires that "a covered entity must document that the training . . . has been provided." The security rule addresses documentation in a general manner for all appropriate security standards in 164.316, requiring the maintenance of policies and procedures as necessary to comply with the requirements. It further states "if an action, activity, or assessment is required by this subpart to be documented, maintain a written (which may be electronic) record of the action, activity, or assessment."

Documentation bearing evidence that training has been completed is likely to be combined for privacy and security. It is recommended that the documentation include content, training dates, and attendee names. Methods of documenting training efforts could include the following:

- Training program sign-in sheets, retention of training aids, and handouts
- Signed confidentiality statements acknowledging receipt and understanding of any training level attended
- Electronic access trails to record computer-based training completion or quiz results
- Meeting handouts and minutes
- Retention of e-mail messages
- A compliance training database recording details such as broadcast e-mails, flier distribution, screen saver or banner launching, or cafeteria tent displays

Ensure a documentation provision for recording training program assessments and updates, and apply HIPAA's retention requirement of six years.

References

Amatayakul, Margret, Joe Gillespie, and Tom Walsh. "What's Your HIPAA ETA?" *Journal of AHIMA* 73, no. 1 (2002): 16A–16D.

"Five Topics to Include in Initial HIPAA Security Awareness Training Session." *Health Information Compliance Insider,* August 2001.

"Gap and Risk Analysis: Get Started Now—and Not Just for HIPAA's Sake." *HIPAA note 1,* no. 55 (December 5, 2001).

"Guidelines for Academic Medical Centers on Security and Privacy." *Association of American Medical Colleges* (2001).

Joint Commission on Accreditation of Healthcare Organizations. 2004 Pre-publication Web edition *Accreditation Standards for Hospitals.* Oakbrook Terrace, IL: Joint Commission, 2003.

"Policy for Education, Training, and Awareness of the Health Insurance Portability and Accountability Act (HIPAA)." State of Maryland Department of Health & Mental Hygiene. September 28, 2001.

"Question of the Week." *hcPro's HIPAA Weekly Advisor,* December 31, 2001. Available online at www.himinfo.com/hipaa_ezine/hipaa_arc.cfm?&content_id=19650.

Security Standards Final Rule. 45 CFR Parts 160, 162, and 164. *Federal Register* 68, no. 34 (February 20, 2003).

"Standards for Privacy of Individually Identifiable Health Information; Final Rule." 45 CFR Parts 160 and 164. *Federal Register* 67, no. 157 (August 14, 2002).

Upham, Randa. "Educating the Organization." *HIPAA Watch* (December 2001).

Walsh, Tom. "Building Effective Training Programs to Make Cultural and Behavioral Changes." Presented at the Joint Healthcare Information Technology Alliance Conference in La Jolla, CA, May 23, 2001.

Compliance in the Crosshairs: Targeting Your Training

Margret Amatayakul, MBA, RHIA, CHPS, FHIMSS
Merida L. Johns, PhD, RHIA

Depending on how you count them, there are anywhere from 20 to 60 new policies, procedures, forms, and other related documents required by HIPAA. Its training requirements specify that all members of the work force must be trained on policies and procedures with respect to protected health information.

The training component of HIPAA may be one of the largest tasks and certainly the most important in achieving compliance. It could also be the most expensive and least effective if not performed properly. This article provides some suggestions on targeting training to meet specific work force needs.

Policies and Procedures Lay the Groundwork

The groundwork for HIPAA training is policies and procedures. Because HIPAA requires training specific to the policies and procedures, it is important to begin planning for training while writing policies and procedures.

Healthcare organizations are taking a variety of approaches to policy and procedure development. Some already have policies and procedures that address many of the topics covered by HIPAA while others have very few. Organizations with many existing policies and procedures may plan to revise or modify existing policies and procedures to include HIPAA directives, hoping that it will be a more efficient or less expensive approach. Or they may argue that members of their work force are already familiar with these policies and procedures and they can achieve better compliance without new ones.

Other organizations are approaching HIPAA with a clean slate by developing all new policies and procedures, assuming that the cost of developing them is the same whether the research and development is directed at modifying existing policies or creating new ones. Or they may believe that tracking down all the policies to be revised may be an additional burden.

The approach an organization takes will depend on its size, how centralized the policy and procedure development currently is, and whether well-documented policies and procedures on HIPAA topics already exist. Most organizations will likely approach policy and procedure development from a combination of these two approaches by capitalizing on what they can,

Source: Amatayakul, Margret, and Merida L. Johns. "Compliance in the Crosshairs: Targeting Your Training (HIPAA on the Job series)." *Journal of AHIMA* 73, no. 10 (2002): 16A–F.

adding new policies and procedures to address topics not otherwise covered, ensuring that conflicting documents are retired, and then training on all new and revised policies and procedures.

Cross-References Ensure Complete Coverage

Whether revising existing policies or creating new ones, organizations will need to determine whether to address each of the HIPAA standards as individual topics or to combine or group standards where they may be logically related. Once a thorough study of HIPAA's requirements is conducted, it is obvious that there are many relationships among the standards.

To a certain extent, the granularity of the policies and procedures depends on whether the organization has the ability to cross-reference documents in an automated environment, such as on an intranet. Addressing only one topic per policy and procedure may result in many policies and procedures but may reduce confusion because each topic is discrete. This may also make the training easier to manage because there is a one-to-one relationship between a document and required training. Alternatively, combining related topics results in fewer documents and demonstrates relationships but may make targeting training more of a challenge.

Again, organizational philosophy and culture will drive how the policies and procedures are ultimately constructed. It is a good practice, however, to ensure that related policies and procedures are identified. This can be achieved by putting cross-references in the documents. It is ideal if these cross-references can be created as links to the other policies and procedures on an intranet.

Consider identifying key words in the policies and procedures. Again, if they are online, these key words should be searchable and, ideally, linked to a glossary of terms that provides their definition. This also helps to keep them shorter and more consistent because terms do not have to be redefined in each document. (Key definitions of terms should be able to be printed with the policy and procedure when a paper copy is requested.)

Figure 8.3, Sample Policy and Procedure Development Reference Tool, illustrates how an organization may ensure that all HIPAA standards are addressed. Related standards are identified from references in the regulation, as well as other references the organization believes apply.

In the sample tool, the first privacy rule standard references nine different standards directly. The second privacy rule standard references four standards and one other subpart. It does not directly reference the standard relating to minimum necessary requirements, but the organization considers it an important cross-reference.

Next, the organization identifies the specific policy and procedure that addresses the standard itself. In this case, the organization has modified its corporate code of conduct to reflect that it will only use or disclose protected health information as permitted or required by the privacy rule for the first standard. It has created a new policy and procedure on minimum necessary use, disclosure, and request that will encompass both when minimum necessary applies and does not apply (for the second listed standard), as well as the specific requirements. The organization has created or modified several other policies that are cross-referenced with each of these standards.

Customize Training by Audience

This preparatory work will assist in identifying members of the work force who need to be trained on specific policies and procedures. There are a variety of approaches. Some organizations have identified people who will be affected by certain policies and procedures. In addition, there will be some policies and procedures for which the need for training will be incremental.

Figure 8.3.   Sample policy and procedure development reference tool

Standard	Related Standards	Policy and Procedure	Cross-references
§164.502(a) Permitted and required uses and disclosures	§164.506 Uses and disclosures to carry out treatment, payment, and operations §164.502(b) Minimum necessary application §164.530(c) Safeguards to limit incidental uses and disclosures §164.508 Authorization required §164.510 Opportunity to agree or object to a use or disclosure for facility directory and involvement in care §164.512 Authorization not required §164.514(e)(f) Limited data set, fund raising §164.524 Access §164.528 Accounting for disclosures	Corporate code of conduct as modified April 14, 2003	Policy and procedure on uses and disclosures requiring and not requiring authorization Policy and procedure on minimum necessary use, disclosure, and request Security policy Policy and procedure on admission under an alias Policy and procedure on providing patients opportunity to agree or object to uses and disclosures for involvement in care Policy and procedure on creating a limited data set and obtaining a data use agreement Policy and procedure on fund raising Policy and procedure on accounting for disclosures
§164.502(b) Minimum necessary application	§164.502(a) Does not apply to disclosures to provider for treatment or to individual §164.508 Does not apply pursuant to authorization Subpart C of Part 160 Compliance reporting to Secretary of HHS §164.512(a) Does not apply to uses and disclosures required by law §164.514(d) Minimum necessary requirements	Policy and procedure on minimum necessary use, disclosure, and request	Corporate code of conduct Policy and procedure on uses and disclosures requiring and not requiring authorization Policy and procedure on corporate compliance reporting

AHIMA's practice brief, "HIPAA Privacy and Security Training," *Journal of AHIMA* 73, no. 4 (April 2002), describes three levels of training and offers topics for each level within HIM. The three levels are:

- Level I: general training

- Level II: job-specific training

- Level III: management-specific training

This is a good place to start in addressing the level of specificity for training on each policy and procedure throughout the organization.

For example, while a housekeeper does not need any training on a policy and procedure on fund raising and many other HIPAA standards, he or she will need general training on confidentiality, ramifications of breaches of confidentiality including sanctions for workers and penalties to the organization, and reporting known or suspected breaches. The housekeeper may need more job-specific information on workstation location, media disposal, and physical access controls for specified areas. Alternatively, the office dealing with fund raising would need in-depth training on giving patients an opportunity to opt out of fund raising, general information on patients' rights, and some of the same information on confidentiality, ramifications of breaches of confidentiality including sanctions for workers and penalties to the organization, and reporting known or suspected breaches. They may not need, however, the same examples used to train the housekeeper.

Because the training must reflect the policies and procedures, it may be helpful to list the policies and procedures in a matrix and identify:

- Which groups of workers represent synergistic training opportunities
- The degree to which groups of workers need to be trained on each of the policies and procedures

Develop Training Targets

Every provider organization will want to develop its own training target list. This target list may or may not be similar to those used for providing other types of training. HIPAA defines work force as all "employees, volunteers, trainees, and other persons whose conduct, in the performance of work for a covered entity, is under the direct control of such entity, whether or not they are paid by the covered entity. "Most provider organizations are including physicians in training program planning because they must adhere to the organization's policies and procedures by virtue of their medical staff membership. Considerations in developing the target list should include:

- Degree of direct patient contact and the setting in which such contact occurs, which will influence the amount of information needed on patients' rights
- Custodial responsibilities for components of the designated record set, which would require significant information on uses and disclosures
- Access to the organization's information systems, either as a user or for technical support, which affects the extent of security-related information required
- Administrative responsibility for organizational relationships and compliance, which focuses on administrative issues, as well as a broader view of all aspects of HIPAA
- Typical learning styles and preferences, which focus less on content and more on delivery. Consider which groups may have numerous questions, which groups will listen and accept, and which groups may need shorter training sessions.

Given these various considerations and the three general levels of training, the training matrix in Figure 8.4 may be helpful. Several work force categories are identified here. The work force members included in each general category would be defined by the organization.

Core Training

Before other specific training is provided, every target group will need a core set of content as a baseline. This training would briefly cover:

- That there is a federal law that pertains to permitted and required uses and disclosures of protected health information; what protected health information is

Figure 8.4.   Sample targeted training matrix

In the matrix below, the level of training needed for each work force category is noted for each policy and procedure.

Policy and procedure	Nursing personnel	Other clinicians	Nonclinical administrative personnel	Nonclinical support personnel	Physicians	Board and senior managers	Volunteers	Researchers
Corporate code of conduct	I	I	I	I	I	I	I	I
Policy and procedure on uses and disclosures requiring and not requiring authorization	I	I	I II: HIM	I	I		I	
Policy and procedure on minimum necessary use, disclosure, and request	II	I	I II: HIM, patient financial services		II			
Security policy	I	I	II: IT	I		I		
Policy and procedure on alias	I	I	II: Patient access, HIM, patient financial services		I		I	
Policy and procedure on providing patients opportunity to agree or object to uses and disclosures for involvement in care	II	II	I		II		I	
Policy and procedure on creating a limited data set and obtaining a data use agreement			I: HIM, quality assurance		I			II
Policy and procedure on compliance reporting			III: Corporate compliance			III		

- What confidentiality means

- What rights patients have to their information

- What the ramifications of violations are to each member of the work force and the organization

- Where to obtain policies and procedures on privacy and security

- The importance of reporting—without fear of retaliation—any suspected breaches of confidentiality

Even this information might have to be delivered in a variety of ways. Departmental meetings with nonclinical support staff may be used to convey information about HIPAA and additional training planned.

Consider developing brochures to supply to all physicians, board members, and senior management, again with some targeted training opportunities provided at meetings or via a CD with additional information.

Consider delivering core content via computer-based training for all nurses, other clinicians, and nonclinical administrative staff, with follow-up on job-specific functions through computer-based or classroom training.

Job-specific Training

The practice brief on privacy and security training provides sound advice on training delivery, including varying learning techniques to address different learning styles and the issue of information overload.

Too much or too detailed information can be easily forgotten. Covering every single privacy standard and the numerous related policies and procedures in one long training session is too much for most members of the work force. Short sessions will work far better.

The training matrix provides some suggestions on job-specific training requirements. It may be appropriate to add an initial training timeline and delivery method to the matrix.

Further, while HIPAA requires training on the privacy policies and procedures before April 14, 2003, it does not specify the manner in which the training must be given. Also, while it requires documentation that training occurred, it does not require certification (i.e., administration of a test or other form of competency determination) of the training. Organizations can decide for themselves which groups might benefit from certification.

Training Delivery Options

There are a variety of options for delivering HIPAA training including classroom delivery, use of print materials or video, and computer-based training. The delivery method should be shaped by the training objectives and the target audience.

HIPAA training should not be a one-shot inoculation. The goal of the training is for the work force members to internalize proper behaviors and be able to apply these behaviors in specific situations. To help ensure that work force members can remember the rules and apply them, it is critical that the training program be built on sound training principles.

Research has shown that learners have a limited ability to retain information and that information delivery must be presented in manageable pieces. HIPAA rules and their exceptions contain complex information, and policies and procedures reflecting implementation of the rules are likely to be complex as well. Therefore, it is important to present privacy and security rules in logical sequence and in small sections.

Adults also learn best when training is limited to what they need to know. In the job situation, work force members don't want to learn everything—rather, just what they need to know to perform their jobs. Therefore, HIPAA training needs to focus on specific policies required for specific job functions. Additionally, an important part of adult training is feedback. Adult training is more successful when a mechanism exists for learners to provide feedback about the training.

Sometimes entertainment is misconstrued as training. Training that primarily seeks to entertain reduces the actual learning that occurs. The use of irrelevant stories and extraneous words, pictures, and graphics can interfere with the learning process.[1] Therefore, in whatever delivery strategy used, it is critical that training materials be developed by using sound instructional design and adult learning principles.

The Next Step Is Maintenance

HIPAA requires training of all new members of the work force and whenever there are changes to policies and procedures. Training is the key to compliance. Most organizations will find they need some ongoing method of education, training, and awareness to routinely help members of the work force understand the nuances of HIPAA requirements and to remind them of their obligations. In fact, a comprehensive training matrix could include a component that identifies when retraining on each policy and procedure may be appropriate.

Note

1. Mayer, Richard E. *Multi-Media Learning*. Cambridge: Cambridge University Press, 2001.

Tough Questions? Scripts Provide Easy Answers

Margret Amatayakul, MBA, RHIA, FHIMSS, CHPS

What do members of your work force say when:

- A patient asks what the notice of privacy practices is.

- An individual states that her mother already signed the notice of privacy practices.

- A physician office claims that authorization from the patient isn't needed for your hospital to send a copy of the discharge summary to the office.

- An individual asks for access to lab results that have just become available.

These and many other questions may surprise members of your work force even if they have received training on HIPAA policies and procedures. To best prepare those staff members with direct patient contact, it is a good idea to anticipate the types of questions that will be asked and write a brief script that can be used in response.

What Is Scripting?

Scripting is anticipating patient questions and writing short responses, providing workers with key words to use or not use, and giving directions for when to refer questions to others. It's common for public relations departments to use prewritten scripts to help them respond appropriately to questions from the press. In a healthcare organization, scripting responses for patient questions is an excellent way to prepare members of the work force.

When Are Scripts Needed?

Every member of the work force who has direct contact with patients may be in the position of responding to HIPAA questions, although those in patient access, HIM, patient financial services, and patient relations are likely to be asked the most questions. See Figure 8.5, Who Needs Scripts?, for categories of workers and common questions.

Consistency and accuracy are the primary reasons for scripting. The questions at the beginning of this article are examples of the types of questions for which answers can be scripted.

Source: Amatayakul, Margret. "Tough Questions? Scripts Provide Easy Answers (HIPAA on the Job series)." *Journal of AHIMA* 74, no. 5 (May 2003): 16A–D.

Figure 8.5.   Who needs scripts?

Worker Categories	Potential Questions
Patient access: Including admission, registration, schedulers, call centers, and other staff members where patient access may occur without a registrar (for example, emergency department charge nurse, retail pharmacy)	• Why do I have to sign the notice? I already signed the notice. I don't want to sign the notice. • What does this notice mean? • I don't want anyone to know I'm here. How do I keep [a person or class of persons] outside of the organization from knowing I'm here? I don't want [a person] inside the organization knowing I'm here.
Switchboard operators	• I'd like to speak to [patient name]. (Patient is on the do not publish list.) • Is [patient name] in the hospital? • Is [patient name] ready to go home from clinic?
Unit coordinators	• How do I keep [a person or class of people] outside of the organization from knowing I'm here? I don't want [a person] inside the organization knowing I'm here. • How do I get a copy of my records? • I want to know who has seen my record. • We [another provider] need information about [patient name].
HIM and patient financial services	• I want to correct my record. I want my record changed. • I want to know who has seen my record. • I don't want my records sent to my [provider or facility name].
Healthcare professionals	• I don't want anyone/[name] to know I am here. • Did you tell [person or class of persons] I was here/what was wrong with me? • That information is wrong. • I want to see everything written in my record.
Patient relations/information privacy officer	• What does this [statement or phrase] mean in the notice of privacy practices? • Why was I sent [marketing material] when I had requested information be sent only to [alternative address for confidential communication]?

While scripting can be extremely effective, be cautious about overscripting responses or using scripts when professional judgment should be applied. Further, staff members who must memorize or make reference to a scripting resource will only be able to effectively handle a relatively small number of scripts, with a minimum of verbiage. They may also spend too much time searching the script to find the question and deliver the answer. Remember that scripts are aids. They should instill confidence that the response is correct and complete—not give the impression that the staff member does not know the answer.

The number of scripted questions and answers for each type of staff member should be limited to three to six, with guidance that refers the individual asking the question to a limited number of resources. For example, complaints or detailed questions about the notice should be directed to the information privacy officer or patient relations while questions about the designated record set should go to HIM or patient financial services. All other questions should be referred to a thoroughly knowledgeable person, such as the information privacy officer.

Beyond staff members committing the responses to memory, scripting resources may include a quick reference guide that includes a set of questions and check boxes on the computer or a flip chart device placed on an easel or attached to the computer monitor. The resource should be easily accessible. (See Figure 8.6, Sample Quick Reference Guide.)

Generally, scripts are not appropriate for situations requiring professional judgment. HIPAA includes a number of references to the fact that a licensed healthcare professional should use judgment in making certain decisions. For example, HIPAA permits a covered entity to "reasonably infer from the circumstances, based on the exercise of professional judgment, that the individual does not object to a disclosure" relative to a person's involvement in care. In these cases, the professional should be sufficiently knowledgeable about HIPAA requirements as well as professional protocols to make a case-by-case decision.

How Should Scripts Be Written?

Write scripts in a style that will most closely reflect the nature of the question and the manner in which the response should be given. HIPAA requires the notice of privacy practices to be written in plain language. Despite this, some of the required content results in use of phrases and terms that may not be commonly understood words. For example, many questions about the notice of privacy practices may simply be related to the meaning of words like disclosure, amendment, accounting, and restriction.

Figure 8.6.   Sample quick reference guide

HIPAA Privacy Standard	Related Questions	See Our Policy and Procedure on
Safeguard against incidental disclosures of protected health information (PHI) because disclosures can be perceived as lax privacy protection.	• How do I discard labels? • Should I report a misdirected fax? • The patient sent me PHI via e-mail. How should I respond?	• Confidentiality/security of PHI • Transmission via fax or e-mail
Give patients an opportunity to accept or reject disclosure of limited information to a family member or friend for their involvement in the patient's care.	• How do I know if I can disclose information to a person accompanying a patient? • Can I disclose information to the parent?	• Opportunity to accept/reject uses and disclosures of PHI • Personal representatives
Other than for use in treatment, use or disclose only the minimum necessary information needed to perform the task.	• What is a minimum necessary use? • How much is minimum necessary for a specific disclosure?	• Minimum necessary uses, disclosures, and requests
Get an authorization from the patient or an institutional review board waiver for use of PHI in all research on human subjects. To use PHI preparatory to research, you must present a representation that you will not remove any PHI.	N/A	• Uses and disclosures of PHI for research
Patients have new or enhanced rights in their information.	• What restrictions requested by patients can we accept? • Where do we record a patient's request for confidential communications to be sent to an alternative address?	• Handling patient requests for restrictions/confidential communications

Scripts are often useful when there is a choice of actions. For example, if the patient refuses to sign the acknowledgment of receipt of the notice of privacy practices, there may be different ways to proceed based on date of service, or reason given by patient. See Figure 8.7, Sample Scripts, for some choices. You will need to customize the script for your facility to reflect its procedures.

Will Scripts Work?

While writing the script, be sure to request input from those who will be required to use it. While those writing the policies and procedures will know what message needs to be conveyed, the staff members delivering the message must feel comfortable with it. The same staff members often can anticipate questions because they may have the same questions as they are being trained. It may also be useful to test the scripts using volunteers from other departments.

As staff members become more familiar with the questions and learn which responses work best, the scripts may not be needed. However, the questions and answers should still be monitored. With repeated use, the responses may be altered slightly for convenience, but result in a different message than intended. Furthermore, questions may change over time, especially as more patients will have read privacy notices.

Finally, workers need to have confidence that the message in the script is, in fact, the message the organization wants to convey and will stand behind. Some messages may relate to denial of patient rights, or directions to other providers that may not seem convenient. Well-written scripts are intended to minimize negative effects of potentially negative messages or messages where the organization must stand firm to afford proper privacy protection. Staff members who find that patients or others respond negatively should immediately report the issue to their supervisors. Then, the supervisors can review procedures and consider rewriting scripts. Like other HIPAA preparations, scripting may be an evolving process.

Figure 8.7.   Sample scripts

Notice of Privacy Practices
Check YES on registration screen for "Acknowledgment Signed." If NO:
This is our notice of privacy practices. It tells you about how we may use your information in caring for you, getting your bill paid, and ensuring quality services. It also describes your privacy rights for your information. Please sign this page so we know you have received this notice.

Patient Question	Action/Script
Why do I need to sign this?	*It helps us keep track that we gave you the notice.*
Does this mean you can give out my information?	*The notice describes when we may release your information and when we need to get your permission.*
I already signed this.	*Thank you for letting us know. Do you recall when you got it and who may have given it to you?* If within our organized healthcare arrangement (OHCA): *Thanks. You may keep that as an extra copy.* Record that patient claimed that notice was signed [approximate date/location in facility] and extra copy provided. If not within our OHCA: *I do not seem to have a record that you signed it. If you wouldn't mind signing it again I'd appreciate it.* If patient objects: *All right, please keep that copy anyway.* Record: • Patient claimed that notice was signed [approximate date/location in facility] and extra copy provided • Patient refused to sign and copy provided • Patient refused to sign and copy rejected

Protecting Confidentiality in Healthcare Education Programs

Beth Hjort, RHIA, CHP

For decades, medical education programs and student affiliations have served as an important means of preparing students to move into professional roles contributing to our nation's healthcare services. The value of real world experience is evident, as individuals are guided and mentored to deal with human lives directly and indirectly after graduation. Didactic and hands-on education approaches are an immeasurably valuable combination for learning. Multiple types of academic healthcare programs are structured to include both methods of instruction, among them programs in HIM, nursing, medical doctor programs, osteopathic doctor programs, physical therapy, occupational therapy, and laboratory technology.

The high national incidence of hospital medical errors enumerated by the Institute of Medicine's November 1999 report "To Err Is Human" encourages serious reflection on the importance of high-quality educational programs. Healthcare employers commonly seek recruits with demonstrated experience, but seasoned individuals are not always available due to healthcare worker shortages. Educational programs include practical experience sought by employers. The need for high-quality, meaningful educational programs cannot be overstated.

An important element of educational programs is the expectation for protection of trainee-acquired confidential information. Federal privacy regulations implemented through HIPAA in April 2003 have prompted covered entities (CEs) to reevaluate affiliation practices and raise new concerns about organizational risk from exposing the trainee population to protected health information (PHI).

Traditionally, patient privacy rights have been protected through affiliation agreements between university or college medical education programs and healthcare practice sites. Commonly, a confidentiality statement has broadly addressed the trainee obligation in a secondary manner, placing it in the shadow of the more focused concern—physical liability protection. This brief will address HIPAA privacy and security rule interpretations related to educational program affiliations where students/trainees are exposed to PHI.

Legal and Regulatory

State and Federal

Prior to HIPAA, healthcare organizations/education affiliation sites have been governed by privacy guidance within state laws, healthcare licensing acts, and applicable federal regulations.

Source: Hjort, Beth. "Protecting Confidentiality in Healthcare Education Programs (AHIMA Practice Brief)." *Journal of AHIMA* 74, no. 8 (September 2003): 64A–D.

Like all healthcare workers, students have been required to adhere to these laws through compliance with organizational policies, procedures, and practices on which they were based. Because many state privacy laws are more stringent than HIPAA privacy regulations, state laws preempt the privacy rule and must continue to be upheld via an organization's administrative directives, even as HIPAA requirements are added.

HIPAA Privacy Regulations

The privacy rule reminds us approximately 180 times of the intention that CEs implement "reasonable" privacy procedures and practices. The overarching spirit of the rule is to protect privacy rights at the same time appropriate healthcare activities continue uninterrupted.

The topic of education programs is not conveniently located within the privacy and security standards. However, considered collectively, several definitions and references create comfortable and safe conditions for addressing confidentiality concerns within educational program affiliations. These HIPAA considerations work in tandem with state and federal privacy obligations previously in place for healthcare organizations:

1. Trainees are part of the healthcare work force.

Privacy rule definitions describe "work force" as "employees, volunteers, trainees, and other persons whose conduct, in the performance of work for a covered entity, is under the direct control of such entity, whether or not they are paid by the covered entity."

2. Education programs are part of healthcare operations.

In Section 164.501, Definitions, the privacy rule addresses training programs in the definition of "healthcare operations": "Healthcare operations means any of the following activities of the covered entity to the extent that the activities are related to covered functions . . . conducting training programs in which students, trainees, or practitioners in areas of healthcare learn under supervision to practice or improve their skills as healthcare providers."

Standard 164.508, "uses and disclosures for which an authorization is required," further clarifies the acceptability of the use of psychotherapy notes in training programs without authorization: "Authorization required: psychotherapy notes . . . except: (B) Use or disclosure by the covered entity for its own training programs in which students, trainees, or practitioners in mental health learn under supervision to practice or improve their skills in group, joint, family, or individual counseling."

The December 3, 2002, Privacy Guidance similarly reiterates the expectation of PHI-sharing with students and trainees when addressing minimum necessary applicability to training programs. It states that "Covered entities can shape their policies and procedures for minimum necessary uses and disclosure to permit medical trainees' access to patients' medical information, including entire medical records."

3. Most training program relationships do not require business associate agreements.

From stated provisions, it can also be concluded that when students are considered part of the work force, compliance with the business associate standards is not required. The privacy rule defines a business associate as "with respect to a covered entity, a person who, on behalf of such covered entity or of an organized healthcare arrangement . . . but other than in the capacity of a member of the work force . . . performs or assists in the performance of a function or activity involving the use or disclosure of individually identifiable health information . . . " The absence of a business associate agreement indicates the work force definition applies.

When students are directly supervised by college or university instructors rather than staff, and the work force definition of "under the direct control of such entity" is not met, affiliate organizations should evaluate the appropriateness of a business associate agreement. When direct training responsibility is shared by academic instructors and affiliate staff, the affiliate may choose the approach best suited to the circumstances, a business associate agreement or a work force/operations approach with use of an affiliation agreement.

When students are instructed exclusively by university staff within a university teaching hospital setting, a business associate agreement may not be necessary if the hospital and university are considered components of the same organization.

4. Students must be trained in privacy and security relative to the policies, procedures, and practices of the affiliation site and specific trainee position.

Training programs are defined in the privacy rule as part of healthcare operations. CEs are required to ensure privacy training for "each new member of the work force within a reasonable period of time after the person joins the covered entity's work force" and for "each member of the covered entity's work force whose functions are affected by a material change in the policies or procedures . . ."

In addition to recognizing security requirements nestled within the privacy rule, the security rule separately provides for "security training for all staff regarding the vulnerabilities of the health information in an entity's possession and procedures which must be followed to ensure the protection of that information."

As such, CEs must include all trainees in privacy and security training, including initial, broad awareness training and customized training relative to particular areas of affiliation. If signed confidentiality statements are the practice, trainees should likewise be asked to sign. (See Figure 8.8, Employee/Student/Volunteer Nondisclosure Agreement.) For the duration of the affiliation relationship, students should be included in periodic and update training relative to paper-based, hybrid, and electronic environments. Documentation of student training should be retained for the required six-year period, as for all training records.

Recommendations

General

Unique User Identifiers

Security rule section 164.312(a)(1) requires the use of unique user identifiers, an important factor within educational programs. Group passwords and employee-shared access are not supportive of a HIPAA-compliant environment where specific accesses must be individually assigned and trackable.

Termination Procedures

The student segment of the work force must not be overlooked at time of termination. Similar to out-processing steps completed for employees, severance of access to all PHI should be completed immediately at the time of student separation. In addition to discontinuing electronic and physical access, it is recommended that the student be requested to sign a termination confidentiality agreement as a reminder of the ongoing privacy expectation of position-acquired PHI. (See Figure 8.9, Termination Nondisclosure Agreement for Employees/Students/ Volunteers.)

Figure 8.8.   Employee/student/volunteer nondisclosure agreement

[*Name of healthcare provider*] has a legal and ethical responsibility to safeguard the privacy of all patients and protect the confidentiality of their health information. In the course of my employment/assignment at [name of healthcare provider], I may come into possession of confidential patient information, even though I may not be directly involved in providing patient services.

I understand that such information must be maintained in the strictest confidence. As a condition of my employment/assignment, I hereby agree that, unless directed by my supervisor, I will not at any time during or after my employment/assignment with [name of healthcare provider] disclose any patient information to any person whatsoever or permit any person whatsoever to examine or make copies of any patient reports or other documents prepared by me, coming into my possession, or under my control, or use patient information, other than as necessary in the course of my employment/assignment. When patient information must be discussed with other healthcare practitioners in the course of my work/assignment, I will use discretion to ensure that such conversations cannot be overheard by others who are not involved in the patient's care.

I understand that violation of this agreement may result in corrective action, up to and including discharge.

_____

Signature of Employee/Student/Volunteer

_____

Date

Note: This sample form was developed by AHIMA for discussion purposes. It should not be used without review by your organization's legal counsel to ensure compliance with local and state laws.

Photography

Use of individually identifiable photographs for teaching purposes requires inclusion of policies in a CE's notice of privacy practices and patient authorizations. These policies must be carefully developed and administered within educational programs.

Deidentification

Distinction should be made in the approaches taken for exposing students to PHI at affiliation sites versus within the academic setting. Appropriate methods of deidentification for hard copy records and data scrubbing for electronic data must be applied to PHI adapted for use in classroom instruction. Some academic settings reinforce deidentification efforts by having students sign a confidentiality pledge in the event identifying information is missed in the deidentification process. Likewise, student assignments requiring transport of medical information from the affiliation site to the academic setting should involve only unidentifiable PHI.

Students as Volunteers

Students who volunteer their time in healthcare organizations would be appropriately guided by the CE, as with any volunteer assignment. As members of the work force, volunteers and students require general and customized privacy and security training for adherence to all related policies, procedures, and practices.

Class Tours

Often, educators arrange for student tours within healthcare organizations as part of the educational experience. While students are on site, incidental exposure of PHI may occur. Academic programs and affiliate organizations may mutually wish to address confidentiality expectations of students within affiliation agreements to cover these occasions.

Figure 8.9.   Termination nondisclosure agreement for employees/students/volunteers

[*Name of healthcare provider*] has a legal and ethical responsibility to safeguard the privacy of all patients and protect the confidentiality of their health information. In the course of my employment/assignment at [name of healthcare provider], I may have come into possession of or overheard confidential patient information, even though I may not have been directly involved in providing patient services.

I understand that such information must be maintained in the strictest confidence. I hereby agree that I will not at any time after my employment/assignment with [name of healthcare provider] disclose any patient information, in any form, to any person whatsoever.

I understand that violation of this agreement may result in civil action.

_____   _____
Signature of Employee/Student/Volunteer   Witness

_____
Date

Note: This sample form was developed for AHIMA for discussion purposes. It should not be used without review by your organization's legal counsel to ensure compliance with local and state laws.

Academic Settings

- Create or update affiliation agreements with liability insurers and legal counsel to address intent of student compliance with all affiliate privacy and security policies and procedures, including HIPAA.

- Consider addressing confidentiality expectations for student tours within affiliation agreements if appropriate.

- Integrate general, preaffiliation privacy and security training into course syllabi to precondition trainees to the importance of this aspect of the affiliation experience.

- Encourage students to be vigilant in applying HIPAA knowledge, including accepting only unidentifiable copies of medical information for projects or samples for use in academic settings.

- Anticipate an approach for use in affiliation site recruitment. Be prepared to address hesitation due to HIPAA interpretation concerns. Consider the following sample language: "We have investigated HIPAA issues. HIPAA considers training programs to be part of healthcare operations and defines 'trainees' as part of a covered entity's work force. No business associate agreement is required. Our affiliation agreement continues to require student compliance and has been expanded in the area of confidentiality to encompass the new federal law. Likewise, our program preconditions students to the importance of confidentiality by conducting preaffiliation general training, and we expect student involvement in all privacy and security training and operations directives throughout the affiliation."

Affiliation Sites

- Review current and newly offered student affiliation agreements with liability insurers and legal counsel to ensure adequate coverage of student adherence to all organizational privacy and security policies, procedures, and practices.

- Consider addressing confidentiality expectations for student tours within affiliation agreements if appropriate.

- Ensure that privacy and security policies and procedures are applied for students as for other members of the work force:

    —Train students on privacy and security, customizing the training to reflect the affiliation position

    —Stress the importance of the ongoing nature of confidentiality, extending throughout the affiliation and after separation

    —Obtain signed confidentiality statements from students during orientation and training and at time of termination if this practice applies to the entire work force (see Figure 8.8, Employee/Student/Volunteer Nondisclosure Agreement, and Figure 8.9, Termination Nondisclosure Agreement for Employees/Students/Volunteers)

    —Orient students to the organization's legal obligation to carry out enforcement policies

    —Maintain documented student training records for six years

- Ensure consistent, unique user identification assignment and monitoring practices for students with electronic access.

- Complete termination or out-processing steps at time of student completion of site affiliation.

- Recognize special case conditions for use of identifiable photographs in teaching programs. (For more information, refer to AHIMA's Practice Brief "Patient Photography, Videotaping, and Other Imaging (Updated)" available in the FORE Library: HIM Body of Knowledge.)

Affiliation Sites: Business Associate Approach

- Ensure the agreement covers all HIPAA-required elements. (Refer to AHIMA's Practice Brief "Letters of Agreement/ Contracts (Updated)" available in the FORE Library: HIM Body of Knowledge for more information.)

- Require student/trainee participation in all work force privacy and security training as a condition of the business associate agreement. Ensure customized training as appropriate.

Training Benefits All

For most CEs, becoming HIPAA compliant has required creation or enhancement of policies, procedures, and training practices to ensure operational implementation by the entire work force. By ensuring that these efforts are extended to the student population, those CEs choosing to be affiliation sites establish an equally appropriate environment for protection of PHI in educational activities. Enhancement of affiliation agreements to encompass HIPAA-related expectations enables comfortable arrangements on the part of both academic programs and affiliation sites. Review of agreement content by professional liability insurers and legal counsel of both parties should ensure bilateral concurrence.

Through participation in educational programs, healthcare organizations are contributing to the industry's need for well-trained graduates and to the perpetuation of healthcare privacy. As members of the work force or as business associates, students experience the applied law firsthand and live in the HIPAA environment, preparing them to serve as privacy advocates within the healthcare industry as employees and practitioners.

References

"Health Insurance Reform: Security Standards." 45 CFR Part 164.312(a)(1). *Federal Register* 68, no. 34 (February 20, 2003).

Hjort, Beth. "Practice Brief: Patient Photography, Videotaping, and Other Imaging (Updated)." *Journal of AHIMA* 72, no. 6 (2001): 64M–Q.

Kohn, L., J. Corrigan, and M. Donaldson, eds. Committee on Quality of Health Care in America, Institute of Medicine. *To Err Is Human: Building a Safer Health System.* Washington, DC: National Academies Press, 2000.

Leape, Lucian L. "Institute of Medicine Medical Error Figures Are Not Exaggerated." *JAMA* 284, no. 1 (2000): 95–97.

Office for Civil Rights. "Guidance Explaining Significant Aspects of the Privacy Rule." December 3, 2002. Available at www.hhs.gov/ocr/hipaa/privacy.html.

Parker, Susan. "Mining Diamonds in the Rough: How to Hire New Graduates." *Journal of AHIMA* 74, no. 6 (2003): 58–59.

Rhodes, Harry. "Practice Brief: Letters of Agreement/Contracts (Updated)." April 2003. Available in the FORE Library: HIM Body of Knowledge at www.ahima.org.

"Standards for Privacy of Individually Identifiable Health Information; Final Rule." 45 CFR Parts 160 and 164. *Federal Register* 67, no. 157 (August 14, 2002). Available at http://aspe.hhs.gov/admnsimp.

Part 9
Appendices and Index

Appendix A

HIPAA Questions and Answers

Q: What is a "shadow record?"

A: A shadow record is a duplicate record kept for the convenience of a department or health-care provider. For instance, many emergency departments keep copies of an ER record for a few days or weeks in case of a readmission of a patient.

While shadow records have been around a long time, they are in the spotlight now because covered entities must determine what records are included in their designated record set, which must be available for patient review. If a shadow record is used to make determinations about a patient's care, then it may be necessary to identify it as part of the designated record set.

A key element is whether or not the shadow record has any other information not recorded in the original record. If information such as phone calls to check on the patient or notes by the clinician is not transferred to the original record, the shadow record should be included in the designated record set. Organizations should identify where shadow records are kept and the reasons for their use and then develop policies and procedures that explain their exclusion or inclusion in the designated record set.

Source: *Journal of AHIMA* 74, no. 1 (2003).

Q: Is it legal for our facility to provide an individual with an abbreviated version of the notice of privacy practices with the full version available only upon request?

A: If an abbreviated version of the notice is given to an individual, it must contain all the required elements from the privacy rule.[1] Rather than an abbreviated version, the Office for Civil Rights suggested a layered notice in which a brief cover sheet (or short notice) is provided that is easier to read and understand. The more detailed, full notice would be layered beneath the short notice. Technically, you could provide an abbreviated notice as long as the version provided to the individual met all the requirements of the privacy rule.

Note

1. Office for Civil Rights. "OCR Guidance Explaining Significant Aspects of the Privacy Rule." December 4, 2002.

Reference

"Standards for Privacy of Individually Identifiable Health Information; Final Rule." 45 CFR Parts 160 and 164. *Federal Register* 67, no. 157 (August 14, 2002).

Source: *Journal of AHIMA* 74, no. 4 (2003).

Q: An attorney recently told our facility that we need to retain records for at least 10 years to comply with the False Claims Act (FCA). Our state law only requires seven years. Which takes precedence?

A: The FCA (31 USC§3729-3733) applies to actions, jurisdiction, and procedures related to submitting a fraudulent or false claim for payment by the US government. It is the backbone for fraud and abuse investigations and penalties.

Section 3731 of this law addresses the statute of limitations. A claim of fraud can be made up to 10 years from the date a violation was committed. The law further states that materials must be available for inspection and copying by the false claims investigator.

For facilities retaining records longer than 10 years, this record retention guideline will not change their practice. Facilities regularly destroying billing and clinical records in less than 10 years should change their retention schedule because the risk of a fraud investigation is always present for all healthcare organizations. If you do not believe your facility has a compliance problem, consult legal counsel on the legal risks of destroying billing and clinical records before the statute of limitations expires.

Source: *Journal of AHIMA* 74, no. 4 (2003).

Q: What are a covered entity's legal responsibilities when a former employee breaches confidentiality of information gained during his or her employment period?

A: Individual state laws would affect the outcome of litigation if charges were pressed through civil action. If the organization is a covered entity, HIPAA sanctions could apply if the breach involves noncompliance with the law. It would be in a covered entity's best interest to anticipate this scenario and seek legal advice when reviewing and enhancing employee termination procedures related to privacy and security.

Generally, a covered entity can fortify its defense position by ensuring and retaining clear evidence that a former employee was trained and expressed understanding of privacy and security polices and procedures. Thorough documentation of ongoing HIPAA training will demonstrate a covered entity's efforts during the employment period. Addressing postemployment responsibilities in initial training is advised. Ability to iterate periodic reminders and retraining is important as well as evidence of initial orientation. In addition to attendance or completion logs, many organizations are requiring the work force to sign a confidentiality statement demonstrating understanding of critical elements of privacy practices.

Extending confidentiality awareness beyond termination is an important consideration. Organizations can reinforce the living nature of privacy expectations by asking staff to sign an additional confidentiality statement at the time of termination. This form should be designed especially for termination circumstances and should serve as a final warning regarding privacy of information gained during the employee's time as a staff member.

For involuntary terminations, obtaining a signed statement may be more difficult. An organization can verbally explain the expectations to an individual and document refusal to sign or send a letter after separation, taking precautions to demonstrate receipt, such as a certified or registered letter.

Some organizations use out-processing checklists to help ensure that important steps like this one and immediate cancellation of system access are not missed during the termination process.

Source: *Journal of AHIMA* 74, no. 6 (2003).

Q: When is it legal to disclose protected health information to clergy?

A: If the individual is informed in advance of the possible disclosure and has the opportunity to object, the HIPAA privacy rule allows a covered entity to disclose directory information to clergy. Directory information includes the individual's name, location in the facility, general condition, and religious affiliation.

The directory information may be disclosed to anyone who asks for the individual by name. However, only clergy have access to religious affiliation. For example, a Catholic priest may obtain the names of all the Catholic patients in a facility, except those patients who have stated an objection to having that information disclosed. The covered entity should not disclose religious affiliations to different clergy, such as disclosing the names of Protestant patients to a rabbi.

Source: Journal of AHIMA 74, no.1 (2003).

Q: Does reporting cancer surveillance to the state have to be tracked under the accounting of disclosure requirement in the HIPAA privacy rule?

A: Reporting cancer surveillance to a state agency does require tracking under HIPAA. State laws should be checked to determine if the other types of disclosures—to an accrediting body and between covered entities for maintenance of the cancer registry—would require tracking too.

When your organization is required by law to report information to a public health authority or state agency, the disclosure falls outside of treatment, payment, and operations (TPO) and must be part of an individual's accounting of disclosure.

Some accreditation organizations require maintenance of a cancer registry. Reporting information for accreditation purposes falls under healthcare operations and is excluded from an accounting of disclosure. Disclosures made for TPO purposes are excluded from an accounting of disclosure.

There are also disclosures made between covered entities for surveillance and maintenance of the registry. Covered entities may disclose information with another covered entity for treatment, payment, and healthcare operations purposes. Disclosures made for maintaining a registry often fall under the treatment or operations exclusion and would not need to be tracked.

Reference

"Standards for Privacy of Individually Identifiable Health Information; Final Rule." 45 CFR Parts 160 and 164. *Federal Register* 67, no. 157 (August 14, 2002).

Source: *Journal of AHIMA* 74, no. 4 (2003).

Q: Under the privacy rule, how should a physician's office handle a request from parents for a written statement recommending limitation of their child's activities at school?

A: Most covered entities have policies requiring written requests or authorizations for disclosure of protected health information (PHI) as a control feature and to aid in documentation practices.

While the privacy rule doesn't specifically address this scenario, it does call for "reasonable" implementation as many as 180 times. Covered entities have latitude for customization within stated mandates. In this case, requiring a written request or authorization from the personal representative of the one who owns the PHI may seem unreasonable. Busy parents could be significantly inconvenienced if policies delay processing by requiring them to write a letter, stop in the physician's office to sign an authorization, or interact via fax or mail to complete an authorization.

A physician's office may consider waiving the normal written requirement in favor of documenting a note in the medical record recording the verbal request if existing state regulations don't mandate a written request.

The request could be met through a letter to the parents, rather than to the school. By addressing and disclosing the letter to the parents, it becomes their decision whether to verbally explain the physician's recommendation to school officials or to provide the school a copy of the letter. The privacy rule does not govern redisclosure by an individual or personal representative. The rule specifically states that releases to the individual are an exception to the accounting of disclosures standard. Keeping a copy of the letter, however, is advised.

If a covered entity chooses to exercise policy flexibility via acceptance and documentation of verbal requests for disclosure, policies and procedures should reflect that. A statement such as "[Physician office name] retains the prerogative to accept a verbal request for disclosure in lieu of a written request by documenting the request in the medical record" is adequate. General verbiage leaves a policy open to interpretation based on individual circumstances. When considering special policy approaches, a covered entity should also evaluate whether the allowed reasonable charges will be applied or similarly waived.

Source: *Journal of AHIMA* 74, no. 6 (2003).

Q: Under HIPAA, how should covered entities respond to requests from public health officials who state that they need protected health information (PHI) to carry out their duties?

A: The privacy rule recognizes that PHI may be needed to respond to threats to public health, including the need to investigate alleged or suspected bioterrorism. Covered entities may disclose PHI without the patient's authorization to public health authorities acting in response to an emergency or threat of bioterrorism (see 45 CFR 164.512 (b)).

The rule states that PHI may be disclosed to "a public health authority that is authorized by law to collect or receive such information for the purpose of . . . public health investigations and public health interventions."

The rule also supports release of PHI if the covered entity in good faith believes the use or disclosure is necessary to prevent or lessen a serious or imminent threat to the health or safety of a person or the public (45 CFR 164.512 (j)). Disclosure of PHI without an individual's permission may also be made by a covered entity if circumstances implicate law enforcement activities (45 CFR 164.512(f)), national security and intelligence activities (45 CFR 164.512 (k)(2)), or judicial and administrative proceedings (45 CFR 164.512 (e)).

Some agencies and states have proposed or enacted rules that provide for routine review of emergency department logs with health department staff to determine if threats to public health are emerging. Criteria are usually developed to screen for illnesses such as respiratory infections with fever, botulism-like syndromes, or febrile illnesses with rash. These symptoms could indicate disease outbreaks. If the screening criteria are met, medical records may be reviewed to determine if there is a need for further investigation or action.

Staff should verify the identity of persons requesting PHI under these sections of the rule and determine their authority to obtain such information. Public health disclosures of PHI must be included in disclosure accountings provided to patients.

References

Department of Health and Human Services. "Questions & Answers." Updated March 11, 2003. Available at http://answers.hhs.gov.

"Standards for Privacy of Individually Identifiable Health Information; Final Rule." 45 CFR Part 164.512. *Federal Register* 67, no. 157 (August 14, 2002). Available at http://aspe.hhs.gov/admnsimp.

Source: *Journal of AHIMA* 74, no. 8 (2003).

Q: Does the privacy rule allow us to release patient information over the telephone without authorization? How do I decide when I should ask for verification of a treatment relationship with the patient?

A: In the past, HIM professionals have carefully guarded the releasing of patient information. It seems contrary to usual standards of HIM practice, therefore, to release health information without authorization. However, the privacy rule now allows the release of health information without an authorization from the patient in certain situations:

- For treatment (by the patient's or another covered entity)

- For payment

- For healthcare operations

The biggest challenge for most HIM departments is determining if there is a treatment relationship between the patient and the requesting provider. While the privacy rule allows the release of health information without authorization for specific purposes, it also requires verification of the identity of the person requesting health information. In Section 164.514(h), the rule requires the covered entity to "verify the identity of a person requesting protected health information and the authority of any such person to have access to protected health information under this subpart, if the identity or any such authority of such person is not known to the covered entity." Within this challenge is the knowledge that urgent requests for patient information and unauthorized requests for information come to an HIM department via telephone. It is the HIM department's responsibility to be as careful as possible when verifying identity and to treat the request as urgently as is necessary to assist in patient care delivery.

What steps should a covered entity take to be in compliance with the privacy rule? When written requests are received from other covered entities, the HIM department's policy should be to:

- Determine if the covered entity is known to your facility. If the requester is a current medical staff member, a former medical staff member, or a local covered entity, then you have verified the covered entity's identity and have met the intent of the rule.

- If the requester is unknown to you, you can verify that he or she has authority to request the information by:

—Checking the local telephone book or Internet business pages for a business address.

—Calling the switchboard of the requesting facility and verifying identity of the practitioner making the request.

—Verifying whether the clinician is an MD by visiting the American Medical Association's (AMA) Web site at www.ama-assn.org (the site lists all MDs, not just AMA members). Doctors of Osteopathy (DOs) who are members of the American Osteopathic Association can be located at www.aoa-net.org.

- If the identity of the clinician cannot be verified, contact the patient or individual who is the subject of the request to notify him or her of such request and to obtain authorization to release the information. Your organization may decide that getting an oral authorization is sufficient for this purpose.

- Send the information when the identity is verified or when the patient has authorized the release of information.

When your HIM department receives a telephone request, policy should require staff to:

- Verify the identity and business address of the covered entity.

- If the covered entity is unknown to you, but verifiable, ask for a (faxed) written request for PHI in order to have a record of the request.

- If you cannot verify the identity of the covered entity, obtain the authorization from the patient or individual who is the subject of the request. Again, your organization may choose to consider verbal verification and authorization as meeting your procedural guidelines

While the privacy rule has changed some of the ways we do business, HIM professionals still must protect the individual's health information while making sure it is available for treatment. Following the above guidelines will allow compliance with the rule as well as a moderate level of caution.

Reference

"Standards for Privacy of Individually Identifiable Health Information; Final Rule." 45 CFR Part 164.530. *Federal Register* 65, no. 250 (December 28, 2000).

Source: Burrington-Brown, Jill. "On the Line: Professional Practice Solutions." *Journal of AHIMA* 74, no. 9 (October 2003): 62.

Q: Is faxing patient information legal under HIPAA?

A: If the covered entity is permitted to release the information (for treatment purposes or by authorization, for example), then using a fax machine is allowed. The privacy rule requires the entity to provide appropriate administrative, technical, and physical safeguards to protect the privacy of PHI from use or disclosure in violation of the standard. An entity should establish facsimile policies to provide this protection. Such policies might include verifying the fax number of the recipient, requesting a call back when the fax is received, and placing the fax machine in a secure location.

The rule also requires that covered entities employ reasonable procedures. The Bureau of Policy Development of the Health Care Financing Administration (now Centers for Medicare

& Medicaid Services) addressed the subject of transmitting physicians' orders to healthcare facilities via fax machine in letter no. 90-25, dated June 1990:

> The use of fax to transmit physicians' orders is permissible. When fax is used, it is not necessary for the prescribing practitioner to countersign the order at a later date. Note, however, that fax copies may fade and may need to be photocopied. Healthcare facilities should be advised to take extra precaution when thermal paper is used to ensure that a legible copy of the physician's order is retained as long as the medical record is retained.[1]

Note

1. Hughes, Gwen. "Practice Brief: Facsimile Transmission of Health Information (Updated)." *Journal of AHIMA* 72, no. 6 (2001): 64E–64F.

Source: *Journal of AHIMA* 74, no. 1 (2003).

Q: Does HIPAA prohibit physicians from using cell phones to dictate reports?

A: The privacy rule does not address the use of cell phones. Generally, cell phones transmit unencrypted information over insecure lines. These factors alone could be the basis for a policy prohibiting dictation of PHI using cell phones, but there are additional issues that should also be considered when addressing the use of cell phones for dictation.

Transcriptionists have long complained about inconsistent quality of transmission when cell phones are used for dictation. Problems include road and airport noise obscuring words, transmission cutting in and out, and fluctuation in volume. This can be an especially thorny issue when incentive pay models are used to compensate transcriptionists for their work.

Further, consider the locations where cell phones might be used to dictate. In public places, the dictation may be overheard, leaving both the dictator and hospital or clinic vulnerable to a privacy complaint. If the dictator tries to quiet his or her voice, transcriptionists may not be able to accurately decipher what was said.

Perhaps the most difficult issue to consider before policies are developed prohibiting cell phone use for dictation is that of enforcement. If a policy states that cell phones may not be used for dictation of PHI, then covered entities must consistently take corrective action when they are used. Inconsistent enforcement could render a policy void if a cell phone dictator is cited when others have not been sanctioned.

Should you decide to enact such a policy, clear communication of the policy to HIM, transcription, and medical staff is imperative. It must be documented that each dictator was informed about the policy for any subsequent enforcement actions to be upheld.

Acknowledgment: HIPAA Community of Practice Discussion Threads

Source: *Journal of AHIMA* 74, no. 8 (2003).

Q: Because HIPAA gives patients the right to copy their medical records, does my facility have to supply a copy machine for this purpose or allow patients to take their records to a copy center?

A: According to section 164.520 of the HIPAA final privacy rule, an individual has "the right to inspect and copy protected health information as provided by 164.524." Some interpret this phrase to mean that covered entities must hand the health record to the individual and allow them to make their own copies.

However, section 164.530(c)(1) states that covered entities "must have in place appropriate administrative, technical and physical safeguards to protect the privacy of protected health information." In addition, section 164.524 says that except as otherwise provided in the section, individuals have a right of access to inspect or obtain a copy of protected information.

With this in mind, AHIMA encourages HIM professionals to:

1. Evaluate an individual's request to inspect and copy the record and allow the individual access to the entire record or parts thereof in accordance with applicable federal and state laws and regulations, and accepted standards of practice.

2. Provide the individual with assistance as they inspect the record to help locate desired information and safeguard the record.

3. Assist an individual in interpreting records, including abbreviations or medical terminology. Further, as nonclinicians, HIM professionals can assist the individual by putting them in touch with someone better suited to interpret diseases or clinical processes.

4. Provide the individual with copies of materials to which they have a right under applicable federal and state laws and regulations.

References

AHIMA Policy and Government Relations Team's analysis of the final rule for standards for privacy of individually identifiable health information.

"HIPAA Glossary." Workgroup for Electronic Data Interchange.

"Standards for Privacy of Individually Identifiable Health Information; Final Rule." 45 CFR Parts 160 and 164. *Federal Register* 65, no. 250 (December 28, 2000), p. 82462–82829.

Source: *Journal of AHIMA* 72, no. 8 (2001).

Q: What is multi-factor authentication?

A: Multi-factor authentication uses two or all three of the following methods of authentication:

1. Something you know, such as your password, PIN, computer ID

2. Something you have, such as your ATM card, a token, a key, or a swipe-card badge

3. Something you are, such as your fingerprint, voice scan, retina scan, or DNA

Two-factor authentication uses two of the three authentication methods above. Examples include your use of an ATM machine using your ATM card and your PIN (something you have and know); using your credit card and signature (something you have and are); and a PIN and fingerprint to access a secure area (something you know and are).

Using more than one factor of authentication increases the level of security of a system. Your organization will need to go beyond the use of user name and password for authentication. User name and password is only one-factor authentication, because both are what you know.

Reference

Walsh, Tom. "Selecting and Implementing Security Controls." Presented at Getting Practical with Privacy and Security, Denver, CO, 2003.

Source: *Journal of AHIMA* 74, no. 5 (2003).

Q: What is an organized health care arrangement (OHCA) and what are its advantages?

A: The privacy rule defines an OHCA as:

- A clinically integrated care setting in which individuals typically receive healthcare from more than one healthcare provider

- An organized system of healthcare in which more than one covered entity participates and in which the participating entities:

  —Hold themselves out to the public as participating in a joint arrangement

  —Participate in joint activities that include at least one of the following: utilization review, quality assessment and improvement activities, or payment activities

The OHCA agreement only joins the two or more entities for the purposes of HIPAA. This means that the entities are still legally separate entities, both owned and controlled separately. When the entities treat patients in common, or jointly, then the advantages of having an OHCA are evident.

Covered entities participating in an OHCA may jointly provide a notice of privacy practices if:

- The covered entities agree to abide by the terms of the notice.

- The covered entities (or class of covered entities) involved in the OHCA are identified.

- The notice states that the covered entities, if applicable, will share protected health information with each other as necessary to carry out treatment, payment, or healthcare operations relating to the OHCA.

A benefit of participating in an OHCA is that physicians do not have to carry around copies of their notice whenever meeting a new patient outside the office. Physicians, however, might perceive the following as disadvantages of an OHCA:

- They have to agree on the practices outlined in the joint notice.

- If they have multiple OHCAs with various facilities, it might make keeping track of OHCAs difficult for the physician.

- Physicians still have to develop a notice for the patients seen within their practice.

When establishing the OHCA, it is key to reassure the physicians of its purpose, which is solely for HIPAA compliance. Covered entities are still separate entities and responsible for their own business and activities.

References

Amatayakul, Margret. "United under HIPAA: A Comparison of Arrangements and Agreements." *Journal of AHIMA* 73, no. 8 (2002): 24a–24d.

"Standards for Privacy of Individually Identifiable Health Information; Final Rule." 45 CFR Parts 160 and 164. *Federal Register* 67, no. 157 (August 14, 2002).

Source: *Journal of AHIMA* 74, no. 5 (2003).

Appendix B

A HIPAA Glossary

A HIPAA Glossary is reprinted courtesy of the Workgroup for Electronic Data Interchange (WEDI) and Richard Zon Owen. (Copyright © 2001 by WEDI.) The document can be accessed at http://www.wedi.org/public/articles/HIPAA_GLOSSARY.pdf.

Contents

Part I (A HIPAA Glossary & Acronymary) gives general definitions and explanations of HIPAA-related terms and acronyms.

Part II (Consolidated HIPAA Administrative Simplification Final Rule Definitions) shows all definitions included in the final HIPAA A/S rules as of 01/20/2001.

Part III (Purpose & Maintenance) is self-explanatory.

Part I: A HIPAA Glossary & Acronymary

Please note that whenever a definition occurs in both Part I and Part II, the Part II entry will be the more legally compelling one.

AAHomecare: See the *American Association for Homecare*.

Accredited Standards Committee (ASC): An organization that has been accredited by *ANSI* for the development of *American National Standards*.

ACG: Ambulatory Care Group.

ACH: See *Automated Clearinghouse*.

ADA: See the *American Dental Association*.

ADG: Ambulatory Diagnostic Group.

Administrative Code Sets: *Code sets* that characterize a general business situation, rather than a medical condition or service. Under HIPAA, these are sometimes referred to as *non-clinical* or *non-medical code sets*. Compare to *medical code sets*.

Administrative Services Only (ASO): An arrangement whereby a self-insured entity contracts with a *Third Party Administrator (TPA)* to administer a *health plan*.

Administrative Simplification (A/S): Title II, Subtitle F, of HIPAA, which gives HHS the authority to mandate the use of *standards* for the electronic exchange of health care data; to specify what *medical* and *administrative code sets* should be used within those *standards*; to require the use of national identification systems for health care patients, providers, payers (or plans), and employers (or sponsors); and to specify the types of measures required to protect the security and privacy of personally identifiable health care information. This is also the name of Title II, Subtitle F, Part C of HIPAA.

AFEHCT: See the *Association for Electronic Health Care Transactions*.

AHA: See the *American Hospital Association*.

AHIMA: See the *American Health Information Management Association*.

AMA: See the *American Medical Association*.

Ambulatory Payment Class (APC): A payment type for outpatient PPS claims.

Amendment: See *Amendments and Corrections*.

Amendments and Corrections: In the final privacy rule, an amendment to a record would indicate that the data is in dispute while retaining the original information, while a correction to a record would alter or replace the original record.

American Association for Homecare (AAHomecare): An industry association for the home care industry, including home IV therapy, home medical services and manufacturers, and home health providers. *AAHomecare* was created through the merger of the Health Industry Distributors Association's Home Care Division (HIDA Home Care), the Home Health Services and Staffing Association (HHSSA), and the National Association for Medical Equipment Services (NAMES).

American Dental Association (ADA): A professional organization for dentists. The *ADA* maintains a hardcopy dental claim form and the associated claim submission specifications, and also maintains the *Current Dental Terminology (CDT™) medical code set*. The *ADA* and the *Dental Content Committee (DeCC)*, which it hosts, have formal consultative roles under HIPAA.

American Health Information Management Association (AHIMA): An association of health information management professionals. *AHIMA* sponsors some HIPAA educational seminars.

American Hospital Association (AHA): A health care industry association that represents the concerns of institutional providers. The *AHA* hosts the *NUBC*, which has a formal consultative role under HIPAA.

American Medical Association (AMA): A professional organization for physicians. The *AMA* is the secretariat of the *NUCC*, which has a formal consultative role under HIPAA. The *AMA* also maintains the *Current Procedural Terminology (CPT™) medical code set*.

American Medical Informatics Association (AMIA): A professional organization that promotes the development and use of medical informatics for patient care, teaching, research, and health care administration.

American National Standards (ANS): Standards developed and approved by organizations accredited by *ANSI*.

American National Standards Institute (ANSI): An organization that accredits various standards-setting committees, and monitors their compliance with the open rule-making process that they must follow to qualify for ANSI accreditation. HIPAA prescribes that the *standards* mandated under it be developed by ANSI-accredited bodies whenever practical.

American Society for Testing and Materials (ASTM): A standards group that has published general guidelines for the development of standards, including those for health care identifiers. ASTM Committee E31 on Healthcare Informatics develops standards on information used within healthcare.

AMIA: See the *American Medical Informatics Association*.

ANS: See *American National Standards*.

ANSI: See the *American National Standards Institute*. Also see Part II, 45 CFR 160.103.

APC: See *Ambulatory Payment Class*.

A/S, A.S., or AS: See *Administrative Simplification*.

ASC: See *Accredited Standards Committee*.

ASO: See *Administrative Services Only*.

ASPIRE: *AFEHCT's* Administrative Simplification Print Image Research Effort work group.

Association for Electronic Health Care Transactions (AFEHCT): An organization that promotes the use of *EDI* in the health care industry.

ASTM: See the *American Society for Testing and Materials*.

Automated Clearinghouse (ACH): See *Health Care Clearinghouse*.

BA: See *Business Associate*.

BBA: The Balanced Budget Act of 1997.

BBRA: The Balanced Budget Refinement Act of 1999.

BCBSA: See the *Blue Cross and Blue Shield Association*.

Biometric Identifier: An identifier based on some physical characteristic, such as a fingerprint.

Blue Cross and Blue Shield Association (BCBSA): An association that represents the common interests of Blue Cross and Blue Shield *health plans*. The *BCBSA* serves as the administrator for the *Health Care Code Maintenance Committee* and also helps maintain the HCPCS Level II codes.

BP: See *Business Partner*.

Business Associate (BA): A person or organization that performs a function or activity on behalf of a *covered entity*, but is not part of the *covered entity's workforce*. A *business associate* can also be a *covered entity* in its own right. Also see Part II, 45 CFR 160.103.

Business Model: A model of a business organization or process.

Business Partner (BP): See *Business Associate*.

Business Relationships:
- The term *agent* is often used to describe a person or organization that assumes some of the responsibilities of another one. This term has been avoided in the final rules so that a more HIPAA-specific meaning could be used for *business associate*. The term *business partner (BP)* was originally used for *business associate*.
- A *Third Party Administrator (TPA)* is a *business associate* that performs claims administration and related business functions for a self-insured entity.
- Under HIPAA, a *health care clearinghouse* is a *business associate* that translates data to or from a standard format in behalf of a *covered entity*.
- The HIPAA Security NPRM used the term *Chain of Trust Agreement* to describe the type of contract that would be needed to extend the responsibility to protect health care data across a series of subcontractual relationships.
- While a *business associate* is an entity that performs certain business functions for you, a *trading partner* is an external entity, such as a customer, that you do business with. This relationship can be formalized via a *trading partner agreement*. It is quite possible to be a *trading partner* of an entity for some purposes, and a *business associate* of that entity for other purposes.

Cabulance: A taxi cab that also functions as an ambulance.

CBO: Congressional Budget Office or Cost Budget Office.

CDC: See the *Centers for Disease Control and Prevention*.

CDT™: See *Current Dental Terminology*.

CE: See *Covered Entity*.

CEFACT: See *United Nations Centre for Facilitation of Procedures and Practices for Administration, Commerce, and Transport (UN/CEFACT)*.

CEN: European Center for Standardization, or Comite Europeen de Normalisation.

Centers for Disease Control and Prevention (CDC): An organization that maintains several *code sets* included in the HIPAA *standards*, including the *ICD-9-CM* codes.

Center for Healthcare Information Management (CHIM): A health information technology industry association.

CFR or C.F.R.: Code of Federal Regulations.

Chain of Trust (COT): A term used in the HIPAA Security NPRM for a pattern of agreements that extend protection of health care data by requiring that each *covered entity* that shares health care data with another entity require that that entity provide protections comparable to those provided by the *covered entity*, and that that entity, in turn, require that any other entities with which it shares the data satisfy the same requirements.

CHAMPUS: Civilian Health and Medical Program of the Uniformed Services.

CHIM: See the *Center for Healthcare Information Management*.

CHIME: See the *College of Healthcare Information Management Executives*.

CHIP: Child Health Insurance Program.

Claim Adjustment Reason Codes: A national *administrative code set* that identifies the reasons for any differences, or adjustments, between the original provider charge for a claim or service and the payer's payment for it. This *code set* is used in the *X12 835* Claim Payment & Remittance Advice and the *X12 837* Claim transactions, and is maintained by the *Health Care Code Maintenance Committee*.

Claim Attachment: Any of a variety of hardcopy forms or electronic records needed to process a claim in addition to the claim itself.

Claim Medicare Remark Codes: See *Medicare Remittance Advice Remark Codes*.

Claim Status Codes: A national *administrative code set* that identifies the status of health care claims. This *code set* is used in the *X12 277* Claim Status Notification transaction, and is maintained by the *Health Care Code Maintenance Committee*.

Claim Status Category Codes: A national *administrative code set* that indicates the general category of the status of health care claims. This *code set* is used in the *X12 277* Claim Status Notification transaction, and is maintained by the *Health Care Code Maintenance Committee*.

Clearinghouse: See *Health Care Clearinghouse*.

CLIA: Clinical Laboratory Improvement Amendments.

Clinical Code Sets: See *Medical Code Sets*.

CM: See *ICD*.

COB: See *Coordination of Benefits*.

Code Set: Under HIPAA, this is any set of codes used to encode *data elements*, such as tables of terms, medical concepts, medical diagnostic codes, or medical procedure codes. This includes both the codes and their descriptions. Also see Part II, 45 CFR 162.103.

Code Set Maintaining Organization: Under HIPAA, this is an organization that creates and maintains the *code sets* adopted by the *Secretary* for use in the transactions for which *standards* are adopted. Also see Part II, 45 CFR 162.103.

College of Healthcare Information Management Executives (CHIME): A professional organization for health care Chief Information Officers (CIOs).

Comment: Public commentary on the merits or appropriateness of proposed or potential regulations provided in response to an *NPRM*, an *NOI*, or other federal regulatory notice.

Common Control: See Part II, 45 CFR 164.504.

Common Ownership: See Part II, 45 CFR 164.504.

Compliance Date: Under HIPAA, this is the date by which a *covered entity* must comply with a *standard*, an *implementation specification*, or a *modification*. This is usually 24 months after the *effective data* of the associated final rule for most entities, but 36 months after the *effective data* for *small health plans*. For future changes in the *standards*, the *compliance date* would be at least 180 days after the *effective data*, but can be longer for *small health plans* and for complex changes. Also see Part II, 45 CFR 160.103.

Computer-based Patient Record Institute (CPRI) - Healthcare Open Systems and Trials (HOST): An industry organization that promotes the use of healthcare information systems, including electronic healthcare records.

Contrary: See Part II, 45 CFR 160.202.

Coordination of Benefits (COB): A process for determining the respective responsibilities of two or more *health plans* that have some financial responsibility for a medical claim. Also called *cross-over*.

CORF: Comprehensive Outpatient Rehabilitation Facility.

Correction: See *Amendments and Corrections*.

Correctional Institution: See Part II, 45 CFR 162.103.

COT: See *Chain of Trust*.

Covered Entity (CE): Under HIPAA, this is a *health plan*, a *health care clearinghouse*, or a *health care provider* who transmits any health information in electronic form in connection with a HIPAA transaction. Also see Part II, 45 CFR 160.103.

Covered Function: Functions that make an entity a *health plan*, a *health care provider*, or a *health care clearinghouse*. Also see Part II, 45 CFR 164.501.

CPRI-HOST: See the *Computer-based Patient Record Institute - Healthcare Open Systems and Trials*.

CPT™: *See Current Procedural Terminology*.

Cross-over: See *Coordination of Benefits*.

Cross-walk: See *Data Mapping*.

Current Dental Terminology (CDT™): A *medical code set,* maintained and copyrighted by the *ADA*, that has been selected for use in the HIPAA transactions.

Current Procedural Terminology (CPT™): A *medical code set,* maintained and copyrighted by the *AMA*, that has been selected for use under HIPAA for non-institutional and non-dental professional transactions.

Data Aggregation: See Part II, 45 CFR 164.501.

Data Condition: A description of the circumstances in which certain data is required. Also see Part II, 45 CFR 162.103.

Data Content Under HIPAA, this is all the *data elements* and *code sets* inherent to a transaction, and not related to the format of the transaction. Also see Part II, 45 CFR 162.103.

Data Content Committee (DCC): See *Designated Data Content Committee*.

Data Council: A coordinating body within *HHS* that has high-level responsibility for overseeing the implementation of the *A/S* provisions of HIPAA.

Data Dictionary (DD): A document or system that characterizes the *data content* of a system.

Data Element: Under HIPAA, this is the smallest named unit of information in a transaction. Also see Part II, 45 CFR 162.103.

Data Interchange Standards Association (DISA): A body that provides administrative services to *X12* and several other standards-related groups.

Data Mapping: The process of matching one set of *data elements* or individual code values to their closest equivalents in another set of them. This is sometimes called a *cross-walk*.

Data Model: A conceptual model of the information needed to support a business function or process.

Data-Related Concepts:
- *Clinical* or *Medical Code Sets* identify medical conditions and the procedures, services, equipment, and supplies used to deal with them. *Non-clinical* or *non-medical* or *administrative code sets* identify or characterize entities and events in a manner that facilitates an administrative process.
- HIPAA defines a *data element* as the smallest unit of named information. In X12 language, that would be a *simple data element*. But X12 also has *composite data elements*, which aren't really *data elements*, but are groups of closely related *data elements* that can repeat as a group. X12 also has *segments*, which are also groups of related *data elements* that tend to occur together, such as street address, city, and state. These *segments* can sometimes repeat, or one or more segments may be part of a *loop* that can repeat. For example, you might have a claim loop that occurs once for each claim, and a claim service loop that occurs once for each service included in a claim. An X12 *transaction* is a collection of such loops, segments, etc. that supports a specific business process, while an X12 *transmission* is a communication session during which one or more X12 transactions is transmitted. *Data elements* and groups may also be combined into records that make up conventional files, or into the tables or segments used by database management systems, or DBMSs.
- A *designated code set* is a *code set* that has been specified within the body of a rule. These are usually *medical code sets*. Many other *code sets* are incorporated into the rules by reference to a separate document, such as an *implementation guide*, that identifies one or more such *code sets*. These are usually *administrative code sets*.

- *Electronic data* is data that is recorded or transmitted electronically, while *non-electronic data* would be everything else. Special cases would be data transmitted by fax and audio systems, which is, in principle, transmitted electronically, but which lacks the underlying structure usually needed to support automated interpretation of its contents.
- *Encoded data* is data represented by some identification or classification scheme, such as a provider identifier or a procedure code. *Non-encoded data* would be more nearly free-form, such as a name, a street address, or a description. Theoretically, of course, all data, including grunts and smiles, is encoded.
- For HIPAA purposes, *internal* data, or *internal code sets*, are *data elements* that are fully specified within the HIPAA *implementation guides*. For X12 transactions, changes to the associated code values and descriptions must be approved via the normal standards development process, and can only be used in the revised version of the standards affected. X12 transactions also use many coding and identification schemes that are maintained by *external* organizations. For these *external code sets*, the associated values and descriptions can change at any time and still be usable in any version of the X12 transactions that uses the associated *code set*.
- *Individually identifiable data* is data that can be readily associated with a specific individual. Examples would be a name, a personal identifier, or a full street address. If life was simple, everything else would be *non-identifiable* data. But even if you remove the obviously identifiable data from a record, other *data elements* present can also be used to *re-identify* it. For example, a birth date and a zip code might be sufficient to re-identify half the records in a file. The re-identifiability of data can be limited by omitting, aggregating, or altering such data to the extent that the risk of it being *re-identified* is acceptable.
- A specific form of data representation, such as an X12 transaction, will generally include some *structural data* that is needed to identify and interpret the transaction itself, as well as the *business data content* that the transaction is designed to transmit. Under HIPAA, when an alternate form of data collection such as a browser is used, such *structural* or *format-related data elements* can be ignored as long as the appropriate *business data content* is used.
- *Structured data* is data the meaning of which can be inferred to at least some extent based on its absolute or relative location in a separately defined data structure. This structure could be the blocks on a form, the fields in a record, the relative positions of *data elements* in an X12 segment, etc. *Unstructured data*, such as a memo or an image, would lack such clues.

Data Set: See Part II, 45 CFR 162.103.

DCC: See *Data Content Committee.*

D-Codes: A subset of the HCPCS Level II *medical code set* with a high-order value of "D" that has been used to identify certain dental procedures. The final HIPAA transactions and code sets rule states that these *D-codes* will be dropped from the *HCPCS*, and that *CDT codes* will be used to identify all dental procedures.

DD: See *Data Dictionary.*

DDE: See *Direct Data Entry.*

DeCC: See *Dental Content Committee.*

Dental Content Committee (DeCC): An organization, hosted by the *American Dental Association*, that maintains the data content specifications for dental billing. The *Dental Content Committee* has a formal consultative role under HIPAA for all transactions affecting dental health care services.

Descriptor: The text defining a code in a *code set*. Also see Part II, 45 CFR 162.103.

Designated Code Set: A *medical code set* or an *administrative code set* that *HHS* has designated for use in one or more of the HIPAA *standards*.

Designated Data Content Committee or Designated DCC: An organization which *HHS* has designated for oversight of the business data content of one or more of the HIPAA-mandated transaction *standards*.

Designated Record Set: See Part II, 45 CFR 164.501.

Designated Standard: A *standard* which *HHS* has designated for use under the authority provided by HIPAA.

Designated Standard Maintenance Organization (DSMO): See Part II, 45 CFR 162.103.

DHHS: See *HHS.*

DICOM: See *Digital Imaging and Communications in Medicine.*

Digital Imaging and Communications in Medicine (DICOM): A *standard* for communicating images, such as x-rays, in a digitized form. This *standard* could become part of the HIPAA claim attachments *standards*.

Direct Data Entry (DDE): Under HIPAA, this is the direct entry of data that is immediately transmitted into a health plan's computer. Also see Part II, 45 CFR 162.103.

Direct Treatment Relationship: See Part II, 45 CFR 164.501.

DISA: See the *Data Interchange Standards Association*.

Disclosure: Release or divulgence of information by an entity to persons or organizations outside of that entity. Also see Part II, 45 CFR 164.501.

Disclosure History: Under HIPAA this is a list of any entities that have received personally identifiable health care information for uses unrelated to treatment and payment.

DME: Durable Medical Equipment.

DMEPOS: Durable Medical Equipment, Prosthetics, Orthotics, and Supplies.

DMERC: See *Medicare Durable Medical Equipment Regional Carrier*.

Draft Standard for Trial Use (DSTU): An archaic term for any *X12 standard* that has been approved since the most recent release of X12 *American National Standards*. The current equivalent term is "*X12 standard*".

DRG: Diagnosis Related Group.

DSMO: See *Designated Standard Maintenance Organization*.

DSTU: See *Draft Standard for Trial Use*.

EC: See *Electronic Commerce*.

EDI: See *Electronic Data Interchange*.

EDIFACT: See *United Nations Rules for Electronic Data Interchange for Administration, Commerce, and Transport (UN/EDIFACT)*.

EDI Translator: A software tool for accepting an EDI transmission and converting the data into another format, or for converting a non-EDI data file into an EDI format for transmission.

Effective Date: Under HIPAA, this is the date that a final rule is effective, which is usually 60 days after it is published in the Federal Register.

EFT: See *Electronic Funds Transfer*.

EHNAC: See the *Electronic Healthcare Network Accreditation Commission*.

EIN: Employer Identification Number.

Electronic Commerce (EC): The exchange of business information by electronic means.

Electronic Data Interchange (EDI): This usually means X12 and similar variable-length formats for the electronic exchange of structured data. It is sometimes used more broadly to mean any electronic exchange of formatted data.

Electronic Healthcare Network Accreditation Commission (EHNAC): An organization that tests transactions for consistency with the HIPAA requirements, and that accredits *health care clearinghouses*.

Electronic Media: See Part II, 45 CFR 162.103.

Electronic Media Claims (EMC): This term usually refers to a flat file format used to transmit or transport claims, such as the 192-byte UB-92 Institutional EMC format and the 320-byte Professional EMC NSF.

Electronic Remittance Advice (ERA): Any of several electronic formats for explaining the payments of health care claims.

EMC: See *Electronic Media Claims*.

EMR: Electronic Medical Record.

EOB: Explanation of Benefits.

EOMB: Explanation of Medicare Benefits, Explanation of Medicaid Benefits, or Explanation of Member Benefits.

EPSDT: Early & Periodic Screening, Diagnosis, and Treatment.

ERA: See *Electronic Remittance Advice*.

ERISA: The Employee Retirement Income Security Act of 1974.

ESRD: End-Stage Renal Disease.

FAQ(s): Frequently Asked Question(s).

FDA: Food and Drug Administration.

FERPA: Family Educational Rights and Privacy Act.

FFS: Fee-for-Service.

FI: See *Medicare Part A Fiscal Intermediary*.

Flat File: This term usually refers to a file that consists of a series of fixed-length records that include some sort of record type code.

Format: Under HIPAA, this is those *data elements* that provide or control the enveloping or hierarchical structure, or assist in identifying data content of, a transaction. Also see Part II, 45 CFR 162.103. Also see *Data-Related Concepts*.

FR or F.R.: Federal Register.

GAO: General Accounting Office.

GLBA: The Gramm-Leach-Bliley Act.

Group Health Plan: Under HIPAA this is an employee welfare benefit plan that provides for medical care and that either has 50 or more participants or is administered by another business entity. Also see Part II, 45 CFR 160.103.

HCFA: See the *Health Care Financing Administration*. Also see Part II, 45 CFR 160.103.

HCFA-1450: *HCFA*'s name for the institutional uniform claim form, or UB-92.

HCFA-1500: *HCFA*'s name for the professional uniform claim form. Also known as the UCF-1500.

HCFA Common Procedural Coding System (HCPCS): A *medical code set* that identifies health care procedures, equipment, and supplies for claim submission purposes. It has been selected for use in the HIPAA transactions. *HCPCS* Level I contains numeric *CPT* codes which are maintained by the *AMA*. *HCPCS* Level II contains alphanumeric codes used to identify various items and services that are not included in the *CPT medical code set*. These are maintained by *HCFA*, the *BCBSA*, and the *HIAA*. *HCPCS* Level III contains alphanumeric codes that are assigned by Medicaid state agencies to identify additional items and services not included in levels I or II. These are usually called "local codes, and must have "W", "X", "Y", or "Z" in the first position. *HCPCS* Procedure Modifier Codes can be used with all three levels, with the WA - ZY range used for locally assigned procedure modifiers.

HCPCS: See *HCFA Common Procedural Coding System*. Also see Part II, 45 CFR 162.103.

Health and Human Services (HHS): The federal government department that has overall responsibility for implementing HIPAA.

Health Care: See Part II, 45 CFR 160.103.

Health Care Clearinghouse: Under HIPAA, this is an entity that processes or facilitates the processing of information received from another entity in a nonstandard format or containing nonstandard *data content* into standard *data elements* or a standard transaction, or that receives a standard transaction from another entity and processes or facilitates the processing of that information into nonstandard format or nonstandard *data content* for a receiving entity. Also see Part II, 45 CFR 160.103.

Health Care Code Maintenance Committee: An organization administered by the *BCBSA* that is responsible for maintaining certain coding schemes used in the X12 transactions and elsewhere. These include the *Claim Adjustment Reason Codes*, the *Claim Status Category Codes*, and the *Claim Status Codes*.

Health Care Component: See Part II, 45 CFR 164.504.

Healthcare Financial Management Association (HFMA): An organization for the improvement of the financial management of healthcare-related organizations. The *HFMA* sponsors some HIPAA educational seminars.

Health Care Financing Administration (HCFA): The *HHS* agency responsible for Medicare and parts of Medicaid. *HCFA* has historically maintained the UB-92 institutional EMC format specifications, the professional EMC *NSF* specifications, and specifications for various certifications and authorizations used by the Medicare and Medicaid programs. *HCFA* also maintains the *HCPCS medical code set* and the *Medicare Remittance Advice Remark Codes administrative code set*.

Healthcare Information Management Systems Society (HIMSS): A professional organization for healthcare information and management systems professionals.

Health Care Operations: See Part II, 45 CFR 164.501.

Health Care Provider: See Part II, 45 CFR 160.103.

Health Care Provider Taxonomy Committee: An organization administered by the *NUCC* that is responsible for maintaining the Provider Taxonomy coding scheme used in the X12 transactions. The detailed code maintenance is done in coordination with *X12N/TG2/WG15*.

Health Industry Business Communications Council (HIBCC): A council of health care industry associations which has developed a number of technical standards used within the health care industry.

Health Informatics Standards Board (HISB): An ANSI-accredited standards group that has developed an inventory of candidate standards for consideration as possible HIPAA standards.

Health Information: See Part II, 45 CFR 160.103.

Health Insurance Association of America (HIAA): An industry association that represents the interests of commercial health care insurers. The *HIAA* participates in the maintenance of some *code sets*, including the *HCPCS* Level II codes.

Health Insurance Issuer: See Part II, 45 CFR 160.103.

Health Insurance Portability and Accountability Act of 1996 (HIPAA): A Federal law that allows persons to qualify immediately for comparable health insurance coverage when they change their employment relationships. Title II, Subtitle F, of HIPAA gives *HHS* the authority to mandate the use of standards for the electronic exchange of health care data; to specify what *medical* and *administrative code sets* should be used within those standards; to require the use of national identification systems for health care patients, providers, payers (or plans), and employers (or sponsors); and to specify the types of measures required to protect the security and privacy of personally identifiable health care information. Also known as the Kennedy-Kassebaum Bill, the Kassebaum-Kennedy Bill, K2, or Public Law 104-191.

Health Level Seven (HL7): An ANSI-accredited group that defines standards for the cross-platform exchange of information within a health care organization. *HL7* is responsible for specifying the Level Seven OSI standards for the health industry. The *X12 275* transaction will probably incorporate the HL7 CRU message to transmit claim attachments as part of a future HIPAA claim attachments standard. The HL7 Attachment SIG is responsible for the HL7 portion of this *standard*.

Health Maintenance Organization (HMO): See Part II, 45 CFR 160.103.

Health Oversight Agency: See Part II, 45 CFR 164.501.

Health Plan: See Part II, 45 CFR 160.103.

Health Plan ID: See *National Payer ID*.

HEDIC: The Healthcare EDI Coalition.

HEDIS: Health Employer Data and Information Set.

HFMA: See the *Healthcare Financial Management Association*.

HHA: Home Health Agency.

HHIC: The Hawaii Health Information Corporation.

HHS: See *Health and Human Services*. Also see Part II, 45 CFR 160.103.

HIAA: See the *Health Insurance Association of America*.

HIBCC: See the *Health Industry Business Communications Council*.

HIMSS: See the *Healthcare Information Management Systems Society*.

HIPAA: See the *Health Insurance Portability and Accountability Act of 1996*.

HIPAA Data Dictionary or HIPAA DD: A *data dictionary* that defines and cross-references the contents of all X12 transactions included in the HIPAA mandate. It is maintained by *X12N/TG3*.

HISB: See the *Health Informatics Standards Board*.

HL7: See *Health Level Seven*.

HMO: See *Health Maintenance Organization*.

HPAG: The HIPAA Policy Advisory Group, a BCBSA subgroup.

HPSA: Health Professional Shortage Area.

Hybrid Entity: A *covered entity* whose covered functions are not its primary functions. Also see Part II, 45 CFR 164.504.

IAIABC: See the *International Association of Industrial Accident Boards and Commissions*.

ICD & ICD-n-CM & ICD-n-PCS: International Classification of Diseases, with "n" = "9" for Revision 9 or "10" for Revision 10, with "CM" = "Clinical Modification", and with "PCS" = "Procedure Coding System".

ICF: Intermediate Care Facility.

IDN: Integrated Delivery Network.

IIHI: See *Individually Identifiable Health Information*.

IG: See *Implementation Guide*.

IHC: Internet Healthcare Coalition.

Implementation Guide (IG): A document explaining the proper use of a *standard* for a specific business purpose. The X12N HIPAA IGs are the primary reference documents used by those implementing the associated transactions, and are incorporated into the HIPAA regulations by reference.

Implementation Specification: Under HIPAA, this is the specific instructions for implementing a *standard*. Also see Part II, 45 CFR 160.103. See also *Implementation Guide*.

Indirect Treatment Relationship: See Part II, 45 CFR 164.501.

Individual: See Part II, 45 CFR 164.501.

Individually Identifiable Health Information (IIHI): See Part II, 45 CFR 164.501.

Information Model: A conceptual model of the information needed to support a business function or process.

Inmate: See Part II, 45 CFR 164.501.

International Association of Industrial Accident Boards and Commissions (IAIABC): One of their standards is under consideration for use for the First Report of Injury *standard* under HIPAA.

International Classification of Diseases (ICD): A *medical code set* maintained by the *World Health Organization (WHO)*. The primary purpose of this *code set* was to classify causes of death. A US extension, maintained by the *NCHS* within the *CDC*, identifies morbidity factors, or diagnoses. The *ICD-9-CM* codes have been selected for use in the HIPAA transactions.

International Organization for Standardization (ISO): An organization that coordinates the development and adoption of numerous international standards. "ISO" is not an acronym, but the Greek word for "equal".

International Standards Organization: See *International Organization for Standardization (ISO)*.

IOM: The Institute of Medicine.

IPA: Independent Providers Association.

IRB: Institutional Review Board.

ISO: See the *International Organization for Standardization*.

JCAHO: See the *Joint Commission on Accreditation of Healthcare Organizations*.

J-Codes: A subset of the HCPCS Level II *code set* with a high-order value of "J" that has been used to identify certain drugs and other items. The final HIPAA transactions and code sets rule states that these *J-codes* will be dropped from the *HCPCS*, and that *NDC codes* will be used to identify the associated pharmaceuticals and supplies.

JHITA: See the *Joint Healthcare Information Technology Alliance*.

Joint Commission on Accreditation of Healthcare Organizations (JCAHO): An organization that accredits healthcare organizations. In the future, the *JCAHO* may play a role in certifying these organizations' compliance with the HIPAA A/S requirements.

Joint Healthcare Information Technology Alliance (JHITA): A healthcare industry association that represents *AHIMA, AMIA, CHIM, CHIME,* and *HIMSS* on legislative and regulatory issues affecting the use of health information technology.

Law Enforcement Official: See Part II, 45 CFR 164.501.

Local Code(s): A generic term for code values that are defined for a state or other political subdivision, or for a specific payer. This term is most commonly used to describe HCPCS Level III Codes, but also applies to state-assigned Institutional Revenue Codes, Condition Codes, Occurrence Codes, Value Codes, etc.

Logical Observation Identifiers, Names and Codes (LOINC™): A set of universal names and ID codes that identify laboratory and clinical observations. These codes, which are maintained by the *Regenstrief Institute*, are expected to be used in the HIPAA claim attachments *standard*.

LOINC™: See *Logical Observation Identifiers, Names and Codes*.

Loop: A repeating structure or process.

LTC: Long-Term Care.

Maintain or Maintenance: See Part II, 45 CFR 162.103.

Marketing: See Part II, 45 CFR 164.501.

Massachusetts Health Data Consortium (MHDC): An organization that seeks to improve healthcare in New England through improved policy development, better technology planning and implementation, and more informed financial decision making.

Maximum Defined Data Set: Under HIPAA, this is all of the required *data elements* for a particular *standard* based on a specific *implementation specification*. An entity creating a transaction is free to include whatever data any receiver might want or need. The recipient is free to ignore any portion of the data that is not needed to conduct their part of the associated business transaction, unless the inessential data is needed for coordination of benefits. Also see Part II, 45 CFR 162.103.

MCO: Managed Care Organization.

M+CO: Medicare Plus Choice Organization.

Medicaid Fiscal Agent (FA): The organization responsible for administering claims for a state Medicaid program.

Medicaid State Agency: The state agency responsible for overseeing the state's Medicaid program.

Medical Code Sets: Codes that characterize a medical condition or treatment. These *code sets* are usually maintained by professional societies and public health organizations. Compare to *administrative code sets*.

Medical Records Institute (MRI): An organization that promotes the development and acceptance of electronic health care record systems.

Medicare Contractor: A Medicare Part A Fiscal Intermediary, a Medicare Part B Carrier, or a Medicare Durable Medical Equipment Regional Carrier (DMERC).

Medicare Durable Medical Equipment Regional Carrier (DMERC): A Medicare contractor responsible for administering Durable Medical Equipment (DME) benefits for a region.

Medicare Part A Fiscal Intermediary (FI): A Medicare contractor that administers the Medicare Part A (institutional) benefits for a given region.

Medicare Part B Carrier: A Medicare contractor that administers the Medicare Part B (Professional) benefits for a given region.

Medicare Remittance Advice Remark Codes: A national *administrative code set* for providing either claim-level or service-level Medicare-related messages that cannot be expressed with a *Claim Adjustment Reason Code*. This *code set* is used in the *X12 835* Claim Payment & Remittance Advice transaction, and is maintained by the *HCFA*.

Memorandum of Understanding (MOU): A document providing a general description of the responsibilities that are to be assumed by two or more parties in their pursuit of some goal(s). More specific information may be provided in an associated *SOW*.

MGMA: Medical Group Management Association.

MHDC: See the *Massachusetts Health Data Consortium*.

MHDI: See the *Minnesota Health Data Institute*.

Minimum Scope of Disclosure: The principle that, to the extent practical, individually identifiable health information should only be disclosed to the extent needed to support the purpose of the disclosure.

Minnesota Health Data Institute (MHDI): A public-private partnership for improving the quality and efficiency of heath care in Minnesota. *MHDI* includes the Minnesota Center for Healthcare Electronic Commerce (MCHEC), which supports the adoption of standards for electronic commerce and also supports the Minnesota EDI Healthcare Users Group (MEHUG).

Modify or Modification: Under HIPAA, this is a change adopted by the *Secretary*, through regulation, to a *standard* or an *implementation specification*. Also see Part II, 45 CFR 160.103.

More Stringent: See Part II, 45 CFR 160.202.

MOU: See *Memorandum of Understanding*.

MR: Medical Review.

MRI: See the *Medical Records Institute*.

MSP: Medicare Secondary Payer.

NAHDO: See the *National Association of Health Data Organizations*.

NAIC: See the *National Association of Insurance Commissioners*.

NANDA: North American Nursing Diagnoses Association.

NASMD: See the *National Association of State Medicaid Directors*.

National Association of Health Data Organizations (NAHDO): A group that promotes the development and improvement of state and national health information systems.

National Association of Insurance Commissioners (NAIC): An association of the insurance commissioners of the states and territories.

National Association of State Medicaid Directors (NASMD): An association of state Medicaid directors. *NASMD* is affiliated with the American Public Health Human Services Association (APHSA).

National Center for Health Statistics (NCHS): A federal organization within the *CDC* that collects, analyzes, and distributes health care statistics. The *NCHS* maintains the *ICD-n-CM* codes.

National Committee for Quality Assurance (NCQA): An organization that accredits managed care plans, or *Health Maintenance Organizations* (HMOs). In the future, the *NCQA* may play a role in certifying these organizations' compliance with the HIPAA A/S requirements. The *NCQA* also maintains the Health Employer Data and Information Set (*HEDIS*).

National Committee on Vital and Health Statistics (NCVHS): A Federal advisory body within *HHS* that advises the *Secretary* regarding potential changes to the HIPAA standards.

National Council for Prescription Drug Programs (NCPDP): An ANSI-accredited group that maintains a number of standard formats for use by the retail pharmacy industry, some of which are included in the HIPAA mandates. Also see *NCPDP ... Standard*.

National Drug Code (NDC): A *medical code set* that identifies prescription drugs and some over the counter products, and that has been selected for use in the HIPAA transactions.

National Employer ID: A system for uniquely identifying all sponsors of health care benefits.

National Health Information Infrastructure (NHII): This is a healthcare-specific lane on the Information Superhighway, as described in the National Information Infrastructure (NII) initiative. Conceptually, this includes the HIPAA A/S initiatives.

National Patient ID: A system for uniquely identifying all recipients of health care services. This is sometimes referred to as the National Individual Identifier (NII), or as the Healthcare ID.

National Payer ID: A system for uniquely identifying all organizations that pay for health care services. Also known as Health Plan ID, or Plan ID.

National Provider ID (NPI): A system for uniquely identifying all providers of health care services, supplies, and equipment.

National Provider File (NPF): The database envisioned for use in maintaining a national provider registry.

National Provider Registry: The organization envisioned for assigning National Provider IDs.

National Provider System (NPS): The administrative system envisioned for supporting a national provider registry.

National Standard Format (NSF): Generically, this applies to any nationally standardized data format, but it is often used in a more limited way to designate the Professional EMC *NSF*, a 320-byte flat file record format used to submit professional claims.

National Uniform Billing Committee (NUBC): An organization, chaired and hosted by the *American Hospital Association*, that maintains the UB-92 hardcopy institutional billing form and the *data element* specifications for both the hardcopy form and the 192-byte UB-92 flat file EMC format. The *NUBC* has a formal consultative role under HIPAA for all transactions affecting institutional health care services.

National Uniform Claim Committee (NUCC): An organization, chaired and hosted by the *American Medical Association*, that maintains the *HCFA-1500* claim form and a set of *data element* specifications for professional claims submission via the *HCFA-1500* claim form, the Professional EMC *NSF*, and the *X12 837*. The *NUCC* also maintains the *Provider Taxonomy Codes* and has a formal consultative role under HIPAA for all transactions affecting non-dental non-institutional professional health care services.

NCHICA: See the *North Carolina Healthcare Information and Communications Alliance*.

NCHS: See the *National Center for Health Statistics*.

NCPDP: See the *National Council for Prescription Drug Programs*.

NCPDP Batch Standard: An *NCPDP standard* designed for use by low-volume dispensers of pharmaceuticals, such as nursing homes. Use of Version 1.0 of this *standard* has been mandated under HIPAA.

NCPDP Telecommunication Standard: An *NCPDP standard* designed for use by high-volume dispensers of pharmaceuticals, such as retail pharmacies. Use of Version 5.1 of this *standard* has been mandated under HIPAA.

NCQA: See the *National Committee for Quality Assurance*.

NCVHS: See the *National Committee on Vital and Health Statistics*.

NDC: See *National Drug Code*.

NHII: See *National Health Information Infrastructure*.

NOC: Not Otherwise Classified or Nursing Outcomes Classification.

NOI: See *Notice of Intent*.

Non-Clinical or Non-Medical Code Sets: See *Administrative Code Sets*.

North Carolina Healthcare Information and Communications Alliance (NCHICA): An organization that promotes the advancement and integration of information technology into the health care industry.

Notice of Intent (NOI): A document that describes a subject area for which the Federal Government is considering developing regulations. It may describe the presumably relevant considerations and invite *comments* from interested parties. These *comments* can then be used in developing an *NPRM* or a final regulation.

Notice of Proposed Rulemaking (NPRM): A document that describes and explains regulations that the Federal Government proposes to adopt at some future date, and invites interested parties to submit comments related to them. These *comments* can then be used in developing a final regulation.

NPF: See *National Provider File.*

NPI: See *National Provider ID.*

NPRM: See *Notice of Proposed Rulemaking.*

NPS: See *National Provider System.*

NSF: See *National Standard Format.*

NUBC: See the *National Uniform Billing Committee.*

NUBC EDI TAG: The NUBC EDI Technical Advisory Group, which coordinates issues affecting both the *NUBC* and the *X12 standards.*

NUCC: See the *National Uniform Claim Committee.*

OCR: See the *Office for Civil Rights.*

Office for Civil Rights: The HHS entity responsible for enforcing the HIPAA privacy rules.

Office of Management & Budget (OMB): A Federal Government agency that has a major role in reviewing proposed Federal regulations.

OIG: Office of the Inspector General.

OMB: See the *Office of Management & Budget.*

Open System Interconnection (OSI): A multi-layer *ISO* data communications standard. Level Seven of this standard is industry-specific, and *HL7* is responsible for specifying the level seven OSI standards for the health industry.

Organized Health Care Arrangement: See Part II, 45 CFR 164.501.

OSI: See *Open System Interconnection.*

PAG: See *Policy Advisory Group.*

Payer: In health care, an entity that assumes the risk of paying for medical treatments. This can be an uninsured patient, a self-insured employer, a *health plan,* or an *HMO.*

PAYERID: HCFA's term for their pre-HIPAA *National Payer ID* initiative.

Payment: See Part II, 45 CFR 164.501.

PCS: See *ICD.*

PHB: Pharmacy Benefits Manager.

PHI: See *Protected Health Information.*

PHS: Public Health Service.

PL or P. L.: Public Law, as in PL 104-191 (HIPAA).

Plan Administration Functions: See Part II, 45 CFR 164.504.

Plan ID: See *National Payer ID.*

Plan Sponsor: An entity that sponsors a *health plan.* This can be an employer, a union, or some other entity. Also see Part II, 45 CFR 164.501.

Policy Advisory Group (PAG): A generic name for many work groups at WEDI and elsewhere.

POS: Place of Service or Point of Service.

PPO: Preferred Provider Organization

PPS: Prospective Payment System.

PRA: The Paperwork Reduction Act.

PRG: Procedure-Related Group.

Pricer or Repricer: A person, an organization, or a software package that reviews procedures, diagnoses, fee schedules, and other data and determines the eligible amount for a given health care service or supply. Additional criteria can then be applied to determine the actual allowance, or payment, amount.

PRO: Professional Review Organization or Peer Review Organization.

Protected Health Information (PHI): See Part II, 45 CFR 164.501.

Provider Taxonomy Codes: An *administrative code set* for identifying the provider type and area of specialization for all health care providers. A given provider can have several *Provider Taxonomy Codes.* This *code set* is used in the *X12 278* Referral Certification and Authorization and the *X12 837* Claim transactions, and is maintained by the *NUCC.*

Psychotherapy Notes: See Part II, 45 CFR 164.501.

Public Health Authority: See Part II, 45 CFR 164.501.

RA: Remittance Advice.

Regenstrief Institute: A research foundation for improving health care by optimizing the capture, analysis, content, and delivery of health care information. *Regenstrief* maintains the *LOINC* coding system that is being considered for use as part of the HIPAA claim attachments *standard*.

Relates to the Privacy of Individually Identifiable Health Information: See Part II, 45 CFR 160.202.

Required by Law: See Part II, 45 CFR 164.501.

Research: See Part II, 45 CFR 164.501.

RFA: The Regulatory Flexibility Act.

RVS: Relative Value Scale.

SC: Subcommittee.

SCHIP: The State Children's Health Insurance Program.

SDO: Standards Development Organization.

Secretary: Under HIPAA, this refers to the *Secretary* of *HHS* or his/her designated representatives. Also see Part II, 45 CFR 160.103.

Segment: Under HIPAA, this is a group of related *data elements* in a transaction. Also see Part II, 45 CFR 162.103.

Self-Insured: An individual or organization that assumes the financial risk of paying for health care.

Small Health Plan: Under HIPAA, this is a *health plan* with annual receipts of $5 million or less. Also see Part II, 45 CFR 160.103.

SNF: Skilled Nursing Facility.

SNOMED: Systematized Nomenclature of Medicine.

SNIP: See *Strategic National Implementation Process*.

Sponsor: See *Plan Sponsor*.

SOW: See *Statement of Work*.

SSN: Social Security Number.

SSO: See *Standard-Setting Organization*.

Standard: See Part II, 45 CFR 160.103.

Standard-Setting Organization (SSO): See Part II, 45 CFR 160.103.

Standard Transaction: Under HIPAA, this is a transaction that complies with the applicable HIPAA *standard*. Also see Part II, 45 CFR 162.103.

Standard Transaction Format Compliance System (STFCS): An EHNAC-sponsored WPC-hosted HIPAA compliance certification service.

State: See Part II, 45 CFR 160.103.

State Law: A constitution, statue, regulation, rule, common law, or any other State action having the force and effect of law. Also see Part II, 45 CFR 160.202.

State Uniform Billing Committee (SUBC): A state-specific affiliate of the *NUBC*.

Statement of Work (SOW): A document describing the specific tasks and methodologies that will be followed to satisfy the requirements of an associated contract or *MOU*.

STFCS: See the *Standard Transaction Format Compliance System*.

Strategic National Implementation Process (SNIP): A WEDI program for helping the health care industry identify and resolve HIPAA implementation issues.

Structured Data: See *Data-Related Concepts*.

SUBC: See *State Uniform Billing Committee*.

Summary Health Information: See Part II, 45 CFR 164.504.

SWG: Subworkgroup.

Syntax: The rules and conventions that one needs to know or follow in order to validly record information, or interpret previously recorded information, for a specific purpose. Thus, a syntax is a grammar. Such rules and conventions may be either explicit or implicit. In X12 transactions, the data-element separators, the sub-element separators, the segment terminators, the segment identifiers, the loops, the loop identifiers (when present), the repetition factors, etc., are all aspects of the X12 syntax. When explicit, such syntactical elements tend to be the structural, or format-related, *data elements* that are not required when a *direct data entry* architecture is used. Ultimately, though, there is not a perfectly clear division between the syntactical elements and the business data content.

TAG: Technical Advisory Group.

TG: Task Group.

Third Party Administrator (TPA): An entity that processes health care claims and performs related business functions for a *health plan*.

TPA: See *Third Party Administrator* or *Trading Partner Agreement*.

Trading Partner Agreement (TPA): See Part II, 45 CFR 160.103.

Transaction: Under HIPAA, this is the exchange of information between two parties to carry out financial or administrative activities related to health care. Also see Part II, 45 CFR 160.103.

Transaction Change Request System: A system established under HIPAA for accepting and tracking change requests for any of the HIPAA mandated transactions standards via a single web site. See www.hipaa-dsmo.org.

Translator: See *EDI Translator*.

Treatment: See Part II, 45 CFR 164.501.

UB: Uniform Bill, as in *UB-82* or *UB-92*.

UB-82: A uniform institutional claim form developed by the *NUBC* that was in general use from 1983 - 1993.

UB-92: A uniform institutional claim form developed by the *NUBC* that has been in general use since 1993.

UCF: Uniform Claim Form, as in UCF-1500.

UCTF: See the *Uniform Claim Task Force*.

UHIN: See the *Utah Health Information Network*.

UN/CEFACT: See the *United Nations Centre for Facilitation of Procedures and Practices for Administration, Commerce, and Transport*.

UN/EDIFACT: See the *United Nations Rules for Electronic Data Interchange for Administration, Commerce, and Transport*.

Uniform Claim Task Force (UCTF): An organization that developed the initial *HCFA-1500* Professional Claim Form. The maintenance responsibilities were later assumed by the *NUCC*.

United Nations Centre for Facilitation of Procedures and Practices for Administration, Commerce, and Transport (UN/CEFACT): An international organization dedicated to the elimination or simplification of procedural barriers to international commerce.

United Nations Rules for Electronic Data Interchange for Administration, Commerce, and Transport (UN/EDIFACT): An international EDI format. Interactive X12 transactions use the *EDIFACT* message syntax.

UNSM: United Nations Standard Messages.

Unstructured Data: See *Data-Related Concepts*.

UPIN: Unique Physician Identification Number.

UR: Utilization Review.

USC or U.S.C: United States Code.

Use: See Part II, 45 CFR 164.501.

Utah Health Information Network (UHIN): A public-private coalition for reducing health care administrative costs through the standardization and electronic exchange of health care data.

Value-Added Network (VAN): A vendor of EDI data communications and translation services.

VAN: See *Value-Added Network*.

Virtual Private Network (VPN): A technical strategy for creating secure connections, or tunnels, over the internet.

VPN: See *Virtual Private Network*.

Washington Publishing Company (WPC): The company that publishes the X12N HIPAA *Implementation guides* and the X12N HIPAA Data Dictionary, that also developed the X12 Data Dictionary, and that hosts the EHNAC STFCS testing program.

WEDI: See the *Workgroup for Electronic Data Interchange*.

WG: Work Group.

WHO: See the *World Health Organization*.

Workforce: Under HIPAA, this means employees, volunteers, trainees, and other persons under the direct control of a *covered entity*, whether or not they are paid by the *covered entity*. Also see Part II, 45 CFR 160.103.

Workgroup for Electronic Data Interchange (WEDI): A health care industry group that lobbied for HIPAA A/S, and that has a formal consultative role under the HIPAA legislation. *WEDI* also sponsors *SNIP*.

World Health Organization (WHO): An organization that maintains the *International Classification of Diseases* (ICD) *medical code set*.

WPC: See the *Washington Publishing Company*.

X12: An ANSI-accredited group that defines EDI standards for many American industries, including health care insurance. Most of the electronic transaction standards mandated or proposed under HIPAA are *X12 standards*.

X12 148: The X12 First Report of Injury, Illness, or Incident transaction. This *standard* could eventually be included in the HIPAA mandate.

X12 270: The X12 Health Care Eligibility & Benefit Inquiry transaction. Version 4010 of this transaction has been included in the HIPAA mandates.

X12 271: The X12 Health Care Eligibility & Benefit Response transaction. Version 4010 of this transaction has been included in the HIPAA mandates.

X12 274: The X12 Provider Information transaction.

X12 275: The X12 Patient Information transaction. This transaction is expected to be part of the HIPAA claim attachments *standard*.

X12 276: The X12 Health Care Claims Status Inquiry transaction. Version 4010 of this transaction has been included in the HIPAA mandates.

X12 277: The X12 Health Care Claim Status Response transaction. Version 4010 of this transaction has been included in the HIPAA mandates. This transaction is also expected to be part of the HIPAA claim attachments *standard*.

X12 278: The X12 Referral Certification and Authorization transaction. Version 4010 of this transaction has been included in the HIPAA mandates.

X12 811: The X12 Consolidated Service Invoice & Statement transaction.

X12 820: The X12 Payment Order & Remittance Advice transaction. Version 4010 of this transaction has been included in the HIPAA mandates.

X12 831: The X12 Application Control Totals transaction.

X12 834: The X12 Benefit Enrollment & Maintenance transaction. Version 4010 of this transaction has been included in the HIPAA mandates.

X12 835: The X12 Health Care Claim Payment & Remittance Advice transaction. Version 4010 of this transaction has been included in the HIPAA mandates.

X12 837: The X12 Health Care Claim or Encounter transaction. This transaction can be used for institutional, professional, dental, or drug claims. Version 4010 of this transaction has been included in the HIPAA mandates.

X12 997: The X12 Functional Acknowledgement transaction.

X12F: A subcommittee of *X12* that defines EDI standards for the financial industry. This group maintains the *X12 811* [generic] Invoice and the *X12 820* [generic] Payment & Remittance Advice transactions, although *X12N* maintains the associated HIPAA *Implementation guides*.

X12 IHCEBI & IHCEBR: The X12 Interactive Healthcare Eligibility & Benefits Inquiry (IHCEBI) and Response (IHCEBR) transactions. These are being combined and converted to *UN/EDIFACT* Version 5 syntax.

X12 IHCLME: The X12 Interactive Healthcare Claim transaction.

X12J: A subcommittee of *X12* that reviews X12 work products for compliance with the X12 design rules.

X12N: A subcommittee of *X12* that defines EDI standards for the insurance industry, including health care insurance.

X12N/SPTG4: The HIPAA Liaison Special Task Group of the Insurance Subcommittee (N) of *X12*. This group's responsibilities have been assumed by *X12N/TG3/WG3*.

X12N/TG1: The Property & Casualty Task Group (TG1) of the Insurance Subcommittee (N) of *X12*.

X12N/TG2: The Health Care Task Group (TG2) of the Insurance Subcommittee (N) of *X12*.

X12N/TG2/WG1: The Health Care Eligibility Work Group (WG1) of the Health Care Task Group (TG2) of the Insurance Subcommittee (N) of *X12*. This group maintains the *X12 270* Health Care Eligibility & Benefit Inquiry and the *X12 271* Health Care Eligibility & Benefit Response transactions, and is also responsible for maintaining the IHCEBI and IHCEBR transactions.

X12N/TG2/WG2: The Health Care Claims Work Group (WG2) of the Health Care Task Group (TG2) of the Insurance Subcommittee (N) of *X12*. This group maintains the *X12 837* Health Care Claim or Encounter transaction.

X12N/TG2/WG3: The Health Care Claim Payments Work Group (WG3) of the Health Care Task Group (TG2) of the Insurance Subcommittee (N) of *X12*. This group maintains the *X12 835* Health Care Claim Payment & Remittance Advice transaction.

X12N/TG2/WG4: The Health Care Enrollments Work Group (WG4) of the Health Care Task Group (TG2) of the Insurance Subcommittee (N) of *X12*. This group maintains the *X12 834* Benefit Enrollment & Maintenance transaction.

X12N/TG2/WG5: The Health Care Claims Status Work Group (WG5) of the Health Care Task Group (TG2) of the Insurance Subcommittee (N) of *X12*. This group maintains the *X12 276* Health Care Claims Status Inquiry and the *X12 277* Health Care Claim Status Response transactions.

X12N/TG2/WG9: The Health Care Patient Information Work Group (WG9) of the Health Care Task Group (TG2) of the Insurance Subcommittee (N) of *X12*. This group maintains the *X12 275* Patient Information transaction.

X12N/TG2/WG10: The Health Care Services Review Work Group (WG10) of the Health Care Task Group (TG2) of the Insurance Subcommittee (N) of *X12*. This group maintains the *X12 278* Referral Certification and Authorization transaction.

X12N/TG2/WG12: The Interactive Health Care Claims Work Group (WG12) of the Health Care Task Group (TG2) of the Insurance Subcommittee (N) of *X12*. This group maintains the IHCLME Interactive Claims transaction.

X12N/TG2/WG15: The Health Care Provider Information Work Group (WG15) of the Health Care Task Group (TG2) of the Insurance Subcommittee (N) of *X12*. This group maintains the *X12 274* Provider Information transaction.

X12N/TG2/WG19: The Health Care Implementation Coordination Work Group (WG19) of the Health Care Task Group (TG2) of the Insurance Subcommittee (N) of *X12*. This is now *X12N/TG3/WG3*.

X12N/TG3: The Business Transaction Coordination and Modeling Task Group (TG3) of the Insurance Subcommittee (N) of *X12*. TG3 maintains the X12N Business and Data Models and the HIPAA Data Dictionary. This was formerly *X12N/TG2/WG11*.

X12N/TG3/WG1: The Property & Casualty Work Group (WG1) of the Business Transaction Coordination and Modeling Task Group (TG3) of the Insurance Subcommittee (N) of *X12*.

X12N/TG3/WG2: The Healthcare Business & Information Modeling Work Group (WG2) of the Business Transaction Coordination and Modeling Task Group (TG3) of the Insurance Subcommittee (N) of *X12*.

X12N/TG3/WG3: The HIPAA Implementation Coordination Work Group (WG3) of the Business Transaction Coordination and Modeling Task Group (TG3) of the Insurance Subcommittee (N) of *X12*. This was formerly *X12N/TG2/WG19* and *X12N/SPTG4*.

X12N/TG3/WG4: The Object-Oriented Modeling and XML Liaison Work Group (WG4) of the Business Transaction Coordination and Modeling Task Group (TG3) of the Insurance Subcommittee (N) of *X12*.

X12N/TG4: The Implementation Guide Task Group (TG4) of the Insurance Subcommittee (N) of *X12*. This group supports the development and maintenance of X12 Implementation Guides, including the HIPAA X12 IGs.

X12N/TG8: The Architecture Task Group (TG8) of the Insurance Subcommittee (N) of *X12*.

X12/PRB: The X12 Procedures Review Board.

X12 Standard: The term currently used for any *X12 standard* that has been approved since the most recent release of X12 *American National Standards*. Since a full set of X12 *American National Standards* is only released about once every five years, it is the *X12 standard*s that are most likely to be in active use. These standards were previously called *Draft Standards for Trial Use*.

XML: Extensible Markup Language.

Part II: Consolidated HIPAA Administrative Simplification Final Rule Definitions

45 CFR 160.103 Definitions
[from the 12/28/2000 Final Privacy Rule]

Except as otherwise provided, the following definitions apply to this subchapter:

Act means the Social Security Act.

ANSI stands for the American National Standards Institute.

Business associate: (1) Except as provided in paragraph (2) of this definition, *business associate* means, with respect to a covered entity, a person who:
(i) On behalf of such covered entity or of an organized health care arrangement (as defined in § 164.501 of this subchapter) in which the covered entity participates, but other than in the capacity of a member of the workforce of such covered entity or arrangement, performs, or assists in the performance of:
(A) A function or activity involving the use or disclosure of individually identifiable health information, including claims processing or administration, data analysis, processing or administration, utilization review, quality assurance, billing, benefit management, practice management, and repricing; or
(B) Any other function or activity regulated by this subchapter; or
(ii) Provides, other than in the capacity of a member of the workforce of such covered entity, legal, actuarial, accounting, consulting, data aggregation (as defined in § 164.501 of this subchapter), management, administrative, accreditation, or financial services to or for such covered entity, or to or for an organized health care arrangement in which the covered entity participates, where the provision of the service involves the disclosure of individually identifiable health information from such covered entity or arrangement, or from another business associate of such covered entity or arrangement, to the person.
(2) A covered entity participating in an organized health care arrangement that performs a function or activity as described by paragraph (1)(i) of this definition for or on behalf of such organized health care arrangement, or that provides a service as described in paragraph (1)(ii) of this definition to or for such organized health care arrangement, does not, simply through the performance of such function or activity or the provision of such service, become a business associate of other covered entities participating in such organized health care arrangement.
(3) A covered entity may be a business associate of another covered entity.

Compliance date means the date by which a covered entity must comply with a standard, *implementation specification*, requirement, or *modification* adopted under this subchapter.

Covered entity means:
(1) A health plan.
(2) A health care clearinghouse.
(3) A health care provider who transmits any health information in electronic form in connection with a transaction covered by this subchapter.

Group health plan (also see definition of *health plan* in this section) means an employee welfare benefit plan (as defined in section 3(1) of the Employee Retirement Income and Security Act of 1974 (ERISA), 29 U.S.C. 1002(1)), including insured and self-insured plans, to the extent that the plan provides medical care (as defined in section 2791(a)(2) of the Public Health Service Act (PHS Act), 42 U.S.C. 300gg-91(a)(2)), including items and services paid for as medical care, to employees or their dependents directly or through insurance, reimbursement, or otherwise, that:
(1) Has 50 or more participants (as defined in section 3(7) of ERISA, 29 U.S.C. 1002(7)); or
(2) Is administered by an entity other than the employer that established and maintains the plan.

HCFA stands for Health Care Financing Administration within the Department of Health and Human Services.

HHS stands for the Department of Health and Human Services.

Health care means care, services, or supplies related to the health of an individual. *Health care* includes, but is not limited to, the following:
(1) Preventive, diagnostic, therapeutic, rehabilitative, maintenance, or palliative care, and counseling, service, assessment, or procedure with respect to the physical or mental condition, or functional status, of an individual or that affects the structure or function of the body; and
(2) Sale or dispensing of a drug, device, equipment, or other item in accordance with a prescription.

Health care clearinghouse means a public or private entity, including a billing service, repricing company, community health management information system or community health information system, and "value-added" networks and switches, that does either of the following functions:
(1) Processes or facilitates the processing of health information received from another entity in a nonstandard format or containing nonstandard data content into standard *data elements* or a standard transaction.
(2) Receives a standard transaction from another entity and processes or facilitates the processing of health information into nonstandard format or nonstandard data content for the receiving entity.

Health care provider means a provider of services (as defined in section 1861(u) of the Act, 42 U.S.C. 1395x(u)), a provider of medical or health services (as defined in section 1861(s) of the Act, 42 U.S.C. 1395x(s)), and any other person or organization who furnishes, bills, or is paid for health care in the normal course of business.

Health information means any information, whether oral or recorded in any form or medium, that:
(1) Is created or received by a health care provider, health plan, public health authority, employer, life insurer, school or university, or health care clearinghouse; and
(2) Relates to the past, present, or future physical or mental health or condition of an individual; the provision of health care to an individual; or the past, present, or future payment for the provision of health care to an individual.

Health insurance issuer (as defined in section 2791(b)(2) of the PHS Act, 42 U.S.C. 300gg-91(b)(2) and used in the definition of *health plan* in this section) means an insurance company, insurance service, or insurance organization (including an HMO) that is licensed to engage in the business of insurance in a State and is subject to State law that regulates insurance. Such term does not include a group health plan.

Health maintenance organization (HMO) (as defined in section 2791(b)(3) of the PHS Act, 42 U.S.C. 300gg-91(b)(3) and used in the definition of *health plan* in this section) means a federally qualified HMO, an organization recognized as an HMO under State law, or a similar organization regulated for solvency under State law in the same manner and to the same extent as such an HMO.

Health plan means an individual or group plan that provides, or pays the cost of, medical care (as defined in section 2791(a)(2) of the PHS Act, 42 U.S.C. 300gg-91(a)(2)).
(1) *Health plan* includes the following, singly or in combination:
(i) A group health plan, as defined in this section.
(ii) A health insurance issuer, as defined in this section.
(iii) An HMO, as defined in this section.
(iv) Part A or Part B of the Medicare program under title XVIII of the Act.
(v) The Medicaid program under title XIX of the Act, 42 U.S.C. 1396, et seq.
(vi) An issuer of a Medicare supplemental policy (as defined in section 1882(g)(1) of the Act, 42 U.S.C. 1395ss(g)(1)).
(vii) An issuer of a long-term care policy, excluding a nursing home fixed-indemnity policy.
(viii) An employee welfare benefit plan or any other arrangement that is established or maintained for the purpose of offering or providing health benefits to the employees of two or more employers.
(ix) The health care program for active military personnel under title 10 of the United States Code.
(x) The veterans health care program under 38 U.S.C. chapter 17.
(xi) The Civilian Health and Medical Program of the Uniformed Services (CHAMPUS) (as defined in 10 U.S.C. 1072(4)).

(xii) The Indian Health Service program under the Indian Health Care Improvement Act, 25 U.S.C. 1601, et seq.
(xiii) The Federal Employees Health Benefits Program under 5 U.S.C. 8902, et seq.
(xiv) An approved State child health plan under title XXI of the Act, providing benefits for child health assistance that meet the requirements of section 2103 of the Act, 42 U.S.C. 1397, et seq.
(xv) The Medicare+Choice program under Part C of title XVIII of the Act, 42 U.S.C. 1395w-21 through 1395w-28.
(xvi) A high risk pool that is a mechanism established under State law to provide health insurance coverage or comparable coverage to eligible individuals.
(xvii) Any other individual or group plan, or combination of individual or group plans, that provides or pays for the cost of medical care (as defined in section 2791(a)(2) of the PHS Act, 42 U.S.C. 300gg-91(a)(2)).
(2) *Health plan* excludes:
(i) Any policy, plan, or program to the extent that it provides, or pays for the cost of, excepted benefits that are listed in section 2791(c)(1) of the PHS Act, 42 U.S.C. 300gg-91(c)(1); and
(ii) A government-funded program (other than one listed in paragraph (1)(i)-(xvi)of this definition):
(A) Whose principal purpose is other than providing, or paying the cost of, health care; or
(B) Whose principal activity is:
(*1*) The direct provision of health care to persons; or
(*2*) The making of grants to fund the direct provision of health care to persons.

Implementation specification means specific requirements or instructions for implementing a standard.

Modify or *modification* refers to a change adopted by the Secretary, through regulation, to a standard or an implementation specification.

Secretary means the Secretary of Health and Human Services or any other officer or employee of HHS to whom the authority involved has been delegated.

Small health plan means a health plan with annual receipts of $5 million or less.

Standard means a rule, condition, or requirement:
(1) Describing the following information for products, systems, services or practices:
(i) Classification of components.
(ii) Specification of materials, performance, or operations; or
(iii) Delineation of procedures; or
(2) With respect to the privacy of individually identifiable health information.

Standard setting organization (SSO) means an organization accredited by the American National Standards Institute that develops and maintains standards for information transactions or data elements, or any other standard that is necessary for, or will facilitate the implementation of, this part.

State refers to one of the following:
(1) For a health plan established or regulated by Federal law, *State* has the meaning set forth in the applicable section of the United States Code for such health plan.
(2) For all other purposes, *State* means any of the several States, the District of Columbia, the Commonwealth of Puerto Rico, the Virgin Islands, and Guam.

Trading partner agreement means an agreement related to the exchange of information in electronic transactions, whether the agreement is distinct or part of a larger agreement, between each party to the agreement. (For example, a trading partner agreement may specify, among other things, the duties and responsibilities of each party to the agreement in conducting a standard transaction.)

Transaction means the transmission of information between two parties to carry out financial or administrative activities related to health care. It includes the following types of information transmissions:
(1) Health care claims or equivalent encounter information.
(2) Health care payment and remittance advice.
(3) Coordination of benefits.
(4) Health care claim status.
(5) Enrollment and disenrollment in a health plan.
(6) Eligibility for a health plan.
(7) Health plan premium payments.
(8) Referral certification and authorization.
(9) First report of injury.
(10) Health claims attachments.
(11) Other transactions that the Secretary may prescribe by regulation.

Workforce means employees, volunteers, trainees, and other persons whose conduct, in the performance of work for a covered entity, is under the direct control of such entity, whether or not they are paid by the covered entity.

45 CFR 160.202 Definitions
[from the 12/28/2000 Final Privacy Rule]

For purposes of this subpart, the following terms have the following meanings:

Contrary, when used to compare a provision of State law to a standard, requirement, or implementation specification adopted under this subchapter, means:
(1) A covered entity would find it impossible to comply with both the State and federal requirements; or
(2) The provision of State law stands as an obstacle to the accomplishment and execution of the full purposes and objectives of part C of title XI of the Act or section 264 of Pub. L. 104-191, as applicable.

More stringent means, in the context of a comparison of a provision of State law and a standard, requirement, or implementation specification adopted under subpart E of part 164 of this subchapter, a State law that meets one or more of the following criteria:
(1) With respect to a use or disclosure, the law prohibits or restricts a use or disclosure in circumstances under which such use or disclosure otherwise would be permitted under this subchapter, except if the disclosure is:
(i) Required by the Secretary in connection with determining whether a covered entity is in compliance with this subchapter; or
(ii) To the individual who is the subject of the individually identifiable health information.
(2) With respect to the rights of an individual who is the subject of the individually identifiable health information of access to or amendment of individually identifiable health information, permits greater rights of access or amendment, as applicable; provided that, nothing in this subchapter may be construed to preempt any State law to the extent that it authorizes or prohibits disclosure of protected health information about a minor to a parent, guardian, or person acting *in loco parentis* of such minor.
(3) With respect to information to be provided to an individual who is the subject of the individually identifiable health information about a use, a disclosure, rights, and remedies, provides the greater amount of information.
(4) With respect to the form or substance of an authorization or consent for use or disclosure of individually identifiable health information, provides requirements that narrow the scope or duration, increase the privacy protections afforded (such as by expanding the criteria for), or reduce the coercive effect of the circumstances surrounding the authorization or consent, as applicable.
(5) With respect to recordkeeping or requirements relating to accounting of disclosures, provides for the retention or reporting of more detailed information or for a longer duration.
(6) With respect to any other matter, provides greater privacy protection for the individual who is the subject of the individually identifiable health information.

Relates to the privacy of individually identifiable health information means, with respect to a State law, that the State law has the specific purpose of protecting the privacy of health information or affects the privacy of health information in a direct, clear, and substantial way.

State law means a constitution, statute, regulation, rule, common law, or other State action having the force and effect of law.

45 CFR 162.103 Definitions
[from the 08/17/2000 Final Transactions
& Code Sets Rule]

For purposes of this part, the following definitions apply:

Code set means any set of codes used to encode data elements, such as tables of terms, medical concepts, medical diagnostic codes, or medical procedure codes. A *code set* includes the codes and the descriptors of the codes.

Code set maintaining organization means an organization that creates and maintains the code sets adopted by the Secretary for use in the transactions for which standards are adopted in this part.

Data condition means the rule that describes the circumstances under which a covered entity must use a particular data element or segment.

Data content means all the data elements and code sets inherent to a transaction, and not related to the format of the transaction. Data elements that are related to the format are not data content.

Data element means the smallest named unit of information in a transaction.

Data set means a semantically meaningful unit of information exchanged between two parties to a transaction.

Descriptor means the text defining a code.

Designated standard maintenance organization (DSMO) means an organization designated by the Secretary under Sec. 162.910(a).

Direct data entry means the direct entry of data (for example, using dumb terminals or web browsers) that is immediately transmitted into a health plan's computer.

Electronic media means the mode of electronic transmission. It includes the Internet (wide-open), Extranet (using Internet technology to link a business with information only accessible to collaborating parties), leased lines, dial-up lines, private networks, and those transmissions that are physically moved from one location to another using magnetic tape, disk, or compact disk media.

Format refers to those data elements that provide or control the enveloping or hierarchical structure, or assist in identifying data content of, a transaction.

HCPCS stands for the Health [Care Financing Administration] Common Procedure Coding System.

Maintain or maintenance refers to activities necessary to support the use of a standard adopted by the Secretary, including technical corrections to an implementation specification, and enhancements or expansion of a code set. This term excludes the activities related to the adoption of a new standard or implementation specification, or modification to an adopted standard or implementation specification.

Maximum defined data set means all of the required data elements for a particular standard based on a specific implementation specification.

Segment means a group of related data elements in a transaction.

Standard transaction means a transaction that complies with the applicable standard adopted under this part.

45 CFR 164.501 Definitions
[from the 12/28/2000 Final Privacy Rule]

As used in this subpart, the following terms have the following meanings:

Correctional institution means any penal or correctional facility, jail, reformatory, detention center, work farm, halfway house, or residential community program center operated by, or under contract to, the United States, a State, a territory, a political subdivision of a State or territory, or an Indian tribe, for the confinement or rehabilitation of persons charged with or convicted of a criminal offense or other persons held in lawful custody. *Other persons held in lawful custody* includes juvenile offenders adjudicated delinquent, aliens detained awaiting deportation, persons committed to mental institutions through the criminal justice system, witnesses, or others awaiting charges or trial.

Covered functions means those functions of a covered entity the performance of which makes the entity a health plan, health care provider, or health care clearinghouse.

Data aggregation means, with respect to protected health information created or received by a business associate in its capacity as the business associate of a covered entity, the combining of such protected health information by the business associate with the protected health information received by the business associate in its capacity as a business associate of another covered entity, to permit data analyses that relate to the health care operations of the respective covered entities.

Designated record set means:
(1) A group of records maintained by or for a covered entity that is:
(i) The medical records and billing records about individuals maintained by or for a covered health care provider;

(ii) The enrollment, payment, claims adjudication, and case or medical management record systems maintained by or for a health plan; or

(iii) Used, in whole or in part, by or for the covered entity to make decisions about individuals.

(2) For purposes of this paragraph, the term *record* means any item, collection, or grouping of information that includes protected health information and is maintained, collected, used, or disseminated by or for a covered entity.

Direct treatment relationship means a treatment relationship between an individual and a health care provider that is not an indirect treatment relationship.

Disclosure means the release, transfer, provision of access to, or divulging in any other manner of information outside the entity holding the information.

Health care operations means any of the following activities of the covered entity to the extent that the activities are related to covered functions, and any of the following activities of an organized health care arrangement in which the covered entity participates:

(1) Conducting quality assessment and improvement activities, including outcomes evaluation and development of clinical guidelines, provided that the obtaining of generalizable knowledge is not the primary purpose of any studies resulting from such activities; population-based activities relating to improving health or reducing health care costs, protocol development, case management and care coordination, contacting of health care providers and patients with information about treatment alternatives; and related functions that do not include treatment;

(2) Reviewing the competence or qualifications of health care professionals, evaluating practitioner and provider performance, health plan performance, conducting training programs in which students, trainees, or practitioners in areas of health care learn under supervision to practice or improve their skills as health care providers, training of non-health care professionals, accreditation, certification, licensing, or credentialing activities;

(3) Underwriting, premium rating, and other activities relating to the creation, renewal or replacement of a contract of health insurance or health benefits, and ceding, securing, or placing a contract for reinsurance of risk relating to claims for health care (including stop-loss insurance and excess of loss insurance), provided that the requirements of § 164.514(g) are met, if applicable;

(4) Conducting or arranging for medical review, legal services, and auditing functions, including fraud and abuse detection and compliance programs;

(5) Business planning and development, such as conducting cost-management and planning-related analyses related to managing and operating the entity, including formulary development and administration, development or improvement of methods of payment or coverage policies; and

(6) Business management and general administrative activities of the entity, including, but not limited to:

(i) Management activities relating to implementation of and compliance with the requirements of this subchapter;

(ii) Customer service, including the provision of data analyses for policy holders, plan sponsors, or other customers, provided that protected health information is not disclosed to such policy holder, plan sponsor, or customer.

(iii) Resolution of internal grievances;

(iv) Due diligence in connection with the sale or transfer of assets to a potential successor in interest, if the potential successor in interest is a covered entity or, following completion of the sale or transfer, will become a covered entity; and

(v) Consistent with the applicable requirements of § 164.514, creating de-identified health information, fundraising for the benefit of the covered entity, and marketing for which an individual authorization is not required as described in § 164.514(e)(2).

Health oversight agency means an agency or authority of the United States, a State, a territory, a political subdivision of a State or territory, or an Indian tribe, or a person or entity acting under a grant of authority from or contract with such public agency, including the employees or agents of such public agency or its contractors or persons or entities to whom it has granted authority, that is authorized by law to oversee the health care system (whether public or private) or government programs in which health information is necessary to determine eligibility or compliance, or to enforce civil rights laws for which health information is relevant.

Indirect treatment relationship means a relationship between an individual and a health care provider in which:

(1) The health care provider delivers health care to the individual based on the orders of another health care provider; and

(2) The health care provider typically provides services or products, or reports the diagnosis or results associated with the health care, directly to another health care provider, who provides the services or products or reports to the individual.

Individual means the person who is the subject of protected health information.

Individually identifiable health information is information that is a subset of health information, including demographic information collected from an individual, and:

(1) Is created or received by a health care provider, health plan, employer, or health care clearinghouse; and

(2) Relates to the past, present, or future physical or mental health or condition of an individual; the provision of health care to an individual; or the past, present, or future payment for the provision of health care to an individual; and

(i) That identifies the individual; or

(ii) With respect to which there is a reasonable basis to believe the information can be used to identify the individual.

Inmate means a person incarcerated in or otherwise confined to a correctional institution.

Law enforcement official means an officer or employee of any agency or authority of the United States, a State, a territory, a political subdivision of a State or territory, or an Indian tribe, who is empowered by law to:

(1) Investigate or conduct an official inquiry into a potential violation of law; or

(2) Prosecute or otherwise conduct a criminal, civil, or administrative proceeding arising from an alleged violation of law.

Marketing means to make a communication about a product or service a purpose of which is to encourage recipients of the communication to purchase or use the product or service.

(1) *Marketing* does not include communications that meet the requirements of paragraph (2) of this definition and that are made by a covered entity:

(i) For the purpose of describing the entities participating in a health care provider network or health plan network, or for the purpose of describing if and the extent to which a product or service (or payment for such product or service) is provided by a covered entity or included in a plan of benefits; or

(ii) That are tailored to the circumstances of a particular individual and the communications are:

(A) Made by a health care provider to an individual as part of the treatment of the individual, and for the purpose of furthering the treatment of that individual; or

(B) Made by a health care provider or health plan to an individual in the course of managing the treatment of that individual, or for the purpose of directing or recommending to that individual alternative treatments, therapies, health care providers, or settings of care.

(2) A communication described in paragraph (1) of this definition is not included in marketing if:

(i) The communication is made orally; or

(ii) The communication is in writing and the covered entity does not receive direct or indirect remuneration from a third party for making the communication.

Organized health care arrangement means:

(1) A clinically integrated care setting in which individuals typically receive health care from more than one health care provider;

(2) An organized system of health care in which more than one covered entity participates, and in which the participating covered entities:

(i) Hold themselves out to the public as participating in a joint arrangement; and

(ii) Participate in joint activities that include at least one of the following:

(A) Utilization review, in which health care decisions by participating covered entities are reviewed by other participating covered entities or by a third party on their behalf;

(B) Quality assessment and improvement activities, in which treatment provided by participating covered entities is assessed by other participating covered entities or by a third party on their behalf; or

(C) Payment activities, if the financial risk for delivering health care is shared, in part or in whole, by participating covered entities through the joint arrangement and if protected health information created or received by a covered entity is reviewed by other participating covered entities or by a third party on their behalf for the purpose of administering the sharing of financial risk.

(3) A group health plan and a health insurance issuer or HMO with respect to such group health plan, but only with respect to protected health information created or received by such health insurance issuer or HMO that relates to individuals who are or who have been participants or beneficiaries in such group health plan;

(4) A group health plan and one or more other group *health plans* each of which are maintained by the same plan sponsor; or

(5) The group health plans described in paragraph (4) of this definition and health insurance issuers or HMOs with respect to such group health plans, but only with respect to protected health information created or received by such health insurance issuers or HMOs that relates to individuals who are or have been participants or beneficiaries in any of such group health plans.

Payment means:

(1) The activities undertaken by:

(i) A health plan to obtain premiums or to determine or fulfill its responsibility for coverage and provision of benefits under the health plan; or

(ii) A covered health care provider or health plan to obtain or provide reimbursement for the provision of health care; and

(2) The activities in paragraph (1) of this definition relate to the individual to whom health care is provided and include, but are not limited to:

(i) Determinations of eligibility or coverage (including coordination of benefits or the determination of cost sharing amounts), and adjudication or subrogation of health benefit claims;

(ii) Risk adjusting amounts due based on enrollee health status and demographic characteristics;

(iii) Billing, claims management, collection activities, obtaining payment under a contract for reinsurance (including stop-loss insurance and excess of loss insurance), and related health care data processing;

(iv) Review of health care services with respect to medical necessity, coverage under a health plan, appropriateness of care, or justification of charges;

(v) Utilization review activities, including precertification and preauthorization of services, concurrent and retrospective review of services; and

(vi) Disclosure to consumer reporting agencies of any of the following protected health information relating to collection of premiums or reimbursement:
(A) Name and address;
(B) Date of birth;
(C) Social security number;
(D) Payment history;
(E) Account number; and
(F) Name and address of the health care provider and/or health plan.

Plan sponsor is defined as defined at section 3(16)(B) of ERISA, 29 U.S.C. 1002(16)(B). [Note: Section 3(16)(B) of ERISA defines *plan sponsor* as "(i) the employer in the case of an employee benefit plan established or maintained by a single employer, (ii) the employee organization in the case of a plan established or maintained by an employee organization, or (iii) in the case of a plan established or maintained by two or more employers or jointly by one or more employers and one or more employee organizations, the association, committee, joint board of trustees, or other similar group of representatives of the parties who establish or maintain the plan.".]

Protected health information means individually identifiable health information:
(1) Except as provided in paragraph (2) of this definition, that is:
(i) Transmitted by electronic media;
(ii) Maintained in any medium described in the definition of *electronic media* at § 162.103 of this subchapter; or
(iii) Transmitted or maintained in any other form or medium.
(2) *Protected health information* excludes individually identifiable health information in:
(i) Education records covered by the Family Educational Right and Privacy Act, as amended, 20 U.S.C. 1232g; and
(ii) Records described at 20 U.S.C. 1232g(a)(4)(B)(iv).

Psychotherapy notes means notes recorded (in any medium) by a health care provider who is a mental health professional documenting or analyzing the contents of conversation during a private counseling session or a group, joint, or family counseling session and that are separated from the rest of the individual's medical record. *Psychotherapy notes* excludes medication prescription and monitoring, counseling session start and stop times, the modalities and frequencies of treatment furnished, results of clinical tests, and any summary of the following items: diagnosis, functional status, the treatment plan, symptoms, prognosis, and progress to date.

Public health authority means an agency or authority of the United States, a State, a territory, a political subdivision of a State or territory, or an Indian tribe, or a person or entity acting under a grant of authority from or contract with such public agency, including the employees or agents of such public agency or its contractors or persons or entities to whom it has granted authority, that is

responsible for public health matters as part of its official mandate.

Required by law means a mandate contained in law that compels a covered entity to make a use or disclosure of protected health information and that is enforceable in a court of law. *Required by law* includes, but is not limited to, court orders and court-ordered warrants; subpoenas or summons issued by a court, grand jury, a governmental or tribal inspector general, or an administrative body authorized to require the production of information; a civil or an authorized investigative demand; Medicare conditions of participation with respect to health care providers participating in the program; and statutes or regulations that require the production of information, including statutes or regulations that require such information if payment is sought under a government program providing public benefits.

Research means a systematic investigation, including research development, testing, and evaluation, designed to develop or contribute to generalizable knowledge.

Treatment means the provision, coordination, or management of health care and related services by one or more health care providers, including the coordination or management of health care by a health care provider with a third party; consultation between health care providers relating to a patient; or the referral of a patient for health care from one health care provider to another.

Use means, with respect to individually identifiable health information, the sharing, employment, application, utilization, examination, or analysis of such information within an entity that maintains such information.

45 CFR 164.504 Uses and Disclosures: Organizational Requirements
[from the 12/28/2000 Final Privacy Rule]

(a) <u>Definitions.</u> As used in this section:

Common control exists if an entity has the power, directly or indirectly, significantly to influence or direct the actions or policies of another entity.

Common ownership exists if an entity or entities possess an ownership or equity interest of 5 percent or more in another entity.

Health care component has the following meaning:
(1) Components of a covered entity that perform covered functions are part of the health care component.
(2) Another component of the covered entity is part of the entity's health care component to the extent that:
(i) It performs, with respect to a component that performs covered functions, activities that would make such other component a business associate of the component that

performs covered functions if the two components were separate legal entities; and

(ii) The activities involve the use or disclosure of protected health information that such other component creates or receives from or on behalf of the component that performs covered functions.

Hybrid entity means a single legal entity that is a covered entity and whose covered functions are not its primary functions.

Plan administration functions means administration functions performed by the plan sponsor of a group health plan on behalf of the group health plan and excludes functions performed by the plan sponsor in connection with any other benefit or benefit plan of the plan sponsor.

Summary health information means information, that may be individually identifiable health information, and:

(1) That summarizes the claims history, claims expenses, or type of claims experienced by individuals for whom a plan sponsor has provided health benefits under a group health plan; and

(2) From which the information described at § 164.514(b)(2)(i) has been deleted, except that the geographic information described in § 164.514(b)(2)(i)(B) need only be aggregated to the level of a five digit zip code.

Part III: Purpose & Maintenance

Purpose

Part I provides a general glossary of terms and acronyms likely to be encountered by anyone dealing with the Administrative Simplification portions of HIPAA, or with any of the organizations, standards, and processes involved in developing, maintaining, and using HIPAA-related standards.

It evolved from a glossary developed in the Summer of 1998 to support the development of the *MOU* covering the *DSMO* process within *X12N/TG3/WG3*. That *MOU* explains how the *ADA*, *HHS*, *HL7*, the *NCPDP*, the *NUBC*, the *NUCC*, and *X12N* will coordinate their efforts to develop and maintain the HIPAA-related standards and implementation guides. In such a setting it is possible to talk for several days without using a word of English, and this document was an attempt to compensate for that.

Part II provides a single source for all definitions included in the body of the final HIPAA Administrative Simplification rules, and should reflect the cumulative effects of all related rules and correction notices. Including the complete text of those definitions in this part keeps the Part I entries comparatively short and informal. Related definitions in Part I reference the associated Part II definitions.

Part III explains the purposes of Parts I & II, and provides you with a way to complain whenever you feel that your favorite organization or subject has been abused or neglected in those parts.

Maintenance

The contents are necessarily limited by the maintainers' knowledge of and experience with the subjects and organizations included, and by the need to keep it finite. We have avoided including technical security-related terms beyond those needed to understand the rules themselves because there are so many of them, and because they are already fairly well documented by various industry and professional groups. When identifying organizations, we have tried to note when they have special responsibilities under HIPAA, such as the maintenance of a *transaction standard* or *code set*, or via the sponsorship of special educational programs.

Please send any suggestions or questions to zon4@earthlink.net.

Appendix C

HIPAA Resources

Government Sites

Centers for Medicare and Medicaid Services (CMS)
http://www.cms.hhs.gov/default.asp?

Department of Health and Human Services (DHHS): Administrative Simplification
http://aspe.os.dhhs.gov/admnsimp/index.shtml

DHHS: Health Insurance Portability and Accountability Act of 1996
http://www.cms.hhs.gov/default.asp?

National Committee on Vital and Health Statistics (NCVHS)
http://www.ncvhs.dhhs.gov

Office for Civil Rights (OCR)
http://www.hhs.gov/ocr/hipaa/

U.S. Government Printing Office
http://www.gpoaccess.gov/index.html

Professional Associations and Standards Organizations

American Association for Medical Transcription (AAMT)
http://www.aamt.org/

American Dental Association (ADA)
http://www.ada.org/

American Health Information Management Association (AHIMA)
http://www.ahima.org

American Medical Informatics Association (AMIA)
http://www.amia.org/

American National Standards Institute (ANSI)
http://www.ansi.org/

American Society for Testing and Materials (ASTM)
http://www.ansi.org/

Association for the Advancement of Medical Instrumentation (AAMI)
http://www.aami.org/

Association for Electronic Health Care Transactions (AFEHCT)
http://www.afehct.org/

College of Healthcare Information Management Executives
http://www.cio-chime.org/general/index.asp

Data Interchange Standards Association
http://www.disa.org/

Electronic Healthcare Network Accreditation Commission
http://www.ehnac.org/

Healthcare Information and Management Systems Society
http://www.himss.org/ASP/index.asp

Joint Healthcare Information Technology Alliance (JHITA)
http://www.jhita.org/

Medical Records Institute
http://www.medrecinst.com/

National Council for Prescription Drug Programs
http://www.ncpdp.org/main_frame.htm

National Uniform Billing Committee
http://www.nubc.org/

National Uniform Claims Committee
http://www.nucc.org/

Other Resources

Health Privacy Project
http://www.healthprivacy.org/

HealthLink
http://www.healthlink.com/

HIPAA Advisory
http://www.hipaadvisory.com/

HIPAA Comply
http://www.hipaacomply.com/

Privacy Rights Clearinghouse
http://www.privacyrights.org/

RX2000 Institute
http://www.rx2000.org/

Washington Publishing Company: HIPAA Implementation Guides
http://www.wpc-edi.com/About_40.asp/

Index

(continued on next page)

(continued on next page)

AHIMA Certification:
Your Valuable Career Asset

AHIMA offers a variety of credentials whether you're just starting out in the health information management (HIM) field, are an advanced coding professional, or play an important privacy or security role at your facility. Employers are looking for your commitment to the field and a certain competency level. AHIMA credentials help you stand out from the crowd of resumés.

- ✔ Registered Health Information Administrator (RHIA)/Registered Health Information Technician (RHIT)
- ✔ Certified Coding Associate (CCA), entry-level
- ✔ Certified Coding Specialist (CCS), advanced
- ✔ Certified Coding Specialist—Physician-based (CCS-P), advanced
- ✔ Certified in Healthcare Privacy (CHP)
- ✔ Certified in Healthcare Security (CHS), offered by HIMSS through AHIMA
- ✔ Certified in Healthcare Privacy and Security (CHPS), AHIMA in conjunction with HIMSS

In recent AHIMA-sponsored research groups, healthcare executives and recruiters cited three reasons for preferring credentialed personnel:

1. Assurance of current knowledge through continued education
2. Possession of field-tested experience
3. Verification of base level competency

AHIMA is a premier organization for HIM professionals, with more than 46,000 members nationwide. AHIMA certification carries a strong reputation for quality—the requirements for our certification are rigorous.

AHIMA exams are computer-based and available throughout the year.

Make the right move…pair your degree and experience with AHIMA certification to maximize your career possibilities.

For more information on AHIMA credentials and how to sit for the exams, you can either visit our Web site at www.ahima.org/certification, send an e-mail to **certdept@ahima.org,** or call **(800) 335-5535.**

Kick Your Future into High Gear Today by Joining AHIMA!

The American Health Information Management Association (AHIMA), the name you can trust in quality healthcare education, has represented the interests of HIM professionals since 1928.

We have been at the forefront of change in healthcare, anticipating trends, preparing for the future, and advancing careers. AHIMA membership affords you a vast array of resources including:

- **HIM Body of Knowledge**
- **Leadership Opportunities**
- **Latest Industry Information**
- **New Certifications**
- **Continuing Education**
- **An Award-Winning Journal**
- **Advocacy**

This list just touches on the benefits of AHIMA membership. To learn more about the benefits of membership or how to renew you membership, just visit **www.ahima.org/membership**, or call **(800) 335-5535**.

There is no better time to join than today

Fill out an online application at **www.ahima.org/membership**, or call **(800) 335-5535** for more information.

AHIMA
American Health Information
Management Association®